Chinese Philosophy and Philosophers

T0347832

ALSO AVAILABLE FROM BLOOMSBURY

A Practical Guide to World Philosophies, by Monika Kirloskar-Steinbach and
Leah Kalmanson
An Introduction to Indian Philosophy, by Christopher Bartley
Confucianism, by Ronnie L. Littlejohn
Daoism, by Ronnie L. Littlejohn
Fiction and Philosophy in the Zhuangzi, by Romain Graziani
Philosophy of the Bhagavad Gita, by Keya Maitra
Understanding Asian Philosophy, by Alexus McLeod

Chinese Philosophy and Philosophers

An Introduction

Second Edition

哲学

Ronnie L. Littlejohn

BLOOMSBURY ACADEMIC
LONDON • NEW YORK • OXFORD • NEW DELHI • SYDNEY

BLOOMSBURY ACADEMIC
Bloomsbury Publishing Plc
50 Bedford Square, London, WC1B 3DP, UK
1385 Broadway, New York, NY 10018, USA
29 Earlsfort Terrace, Dublin 2, Ireland

BLOOMSBURY, BLOOMSBURY ACADEMIC and the Diana logo are trademarks
of Bloomsbury Publishing Plc

First published in Great Britain 2015 by I.B. Tauris
This edition published 2022

Copyright © Ronnie L. Littlejohn, 2022

Ronnie L. Littlejohn has asserted his right under the Copyright, Designs and Patents Act,
1988, to be identified as Author of this work.

For legal purposes the Acknowledgments on p. xxi constitute an extension
of this copyright page.

Cover design by Louise Dugdale

All rights reserved. No part of this publication may be reproduced or transmitted
in any form or by any means, electronic or mechanical, including photocopying,
recording, or any information storage or retrieval system, without prior permission
in writing from the publishers.

Bloomsbury Publishing Plc does not have any control over, or responsibility for,
any third-party websites referred to or in this book. All internet addresses given in this
book were correct at the time of going to press. The author and publisher regret any
inconvenience caused if addresses have changed or sites have ceased to exist,
but can accept no responsibility for any such changes.

A catalogue record for this book is available from the British Library.

Library of Congress Cataloging-in-Publication Data
Names: Littlejohn, Ronnie L., 1949– author.
Title: Chinese philosophy and philosophers: an introduction / Ronnie L. Littlejohn.
Description: Second edition. | London, UK; New York, NY, USA: Bloomsbury
Academic, 2022. | Includes bibliographical references and index.
Identifiers: LCCN 2021029906 (print) | LCCN 2021029907 (ebook) |
ISBN 9781350177406 (pb) | ISBN 9781350177413 (hb) | ISBN 9781350177420 (epdf)
| ISBN 9781350177437 (ebook)
Subjects: LCSH: Philosophy, Chinese.
Classification: LCC B126.L5585 2022 (print) |
LCC B126 (ebook) | DDC 181/.115–dc23
LC record available at https://lccn.loc.gov/2021029906
LC ebook record available at https://lccn.loc.gov/2021029907

ISBN: HB: 978-1-3501-7741-3
PB: 978-1-3501-7740-6
ePDF: 978-1-3501-7742-0
eBook: 978-1-3501-7743-7

Typeset by Newgen KnowledgeWorks Pvt. Ltd., Chennai, India

To find out more about our authors and books visit www.bloomsbury.com
and sign up for our newsletters.

To all my students during these last forty years, with inexpressible gratitude for the joy and fulfillment that has accompanied our learning together.

Contents

2 Epistemology—Questions about the Nature and Scope of Knowledge 65

3 Moral Theory—Questions about the Nature and Application of Morality 125

4   Political Philosophy—Questions about the Nature and Purpose of Government 203

Focus Windows

哲学

Preface

This introduction to the study of philosophy by means of Chinese thinkers and texts provides a substantive overview to a vast and far-reaching tradition. If we do indeed mark the beginning of Chinese philosophy at 1500 years BCE and bring it to the present day, it represents the longest continuous heritage of philosophical reflection among human beings. Trying to mention each philosopher in this enduring tradition is an impossible task in an introduction such as this. In fact, even covering every *significant* thinker is not possible. So, by necessity, I have been selective, choosing those philosophers who, by virtue of the extent to which their thought has been discussed, are most representative of the key contributions Chinese philosophy can make to the emergence of a new type of philosopher whom I call a constructivist. This sort of philosopher engages the fundamental questions of philosophy no matter the culture of origin.

I should also say that I have engaged several thinkers who are often not included in a work on Chinese philosophy. I have no doubt that a first impression in looking at the table of contents of this work will lead those who know the field of Chinese philosophy rather well to conclude that I have allocated too much space to some thinkers and texts, and not enough to others. I have not tried to equalize the number of words given to each philosopher treated in this introduction. Neither have I tried to choose a thinker to represent every historical period of Chinese philosophy. In fact, I propose no periodization of philosophical reflection in China, since this work is an introduction to how Chinese thinkers have dealt with classic fundamental questions of philosophy, not a history of Chinese philosophical inquiry. Standard periodizations used in Western philosophy (i.e., Ancient, Medieval, Modern, Contemporary, Post-Modern) simply do not map with any accuracy onto Chinese philosophy. Sometimes, this means I have selected several thinkers who lived in roughly the same period, while some historical eras have no representative on a particular question. Likewise, another point to be made is that some philosophers make significant contributions in their responses to particular questions but contribute almost no real advance in the philosophical conversation on others. For example, while Confucius may be said to have added interesting and worthwhile approaches to the understanding of moral and political philosophy, he does not further the conversation on ontology or epistemology in any novel ways.

I am well aware that the magnitude of Confucius's influence on Chinese cultural and intellectual history, and indeed over much of East Asia in general, can hardly be exaggerated. Even today, there is an active and vital reappraisal of Confucianism going on in China and East Asia. Some readers may insist that all Chinese philosophy is but commentary on Confucius! Alfred North Whitehead once observed of Western thought that the safest general characterization of the European philosophical tradition is that it consists of a series of footnotes on Plato. However, what often goes unnoticed is that Whitehead amplified this comment in the following way:

> I do not mean the systematic scheme of thought which scholars have doubtfully extracted from his (Plato's) writings. I allude to the wealth of general ideas scattered through them. His personal endowments, his wide opportunities for experience at a great period of civilization, his inheritance of an intellectual tradition not yet stiffened by excessive systematization, have made his writing an inexhaustible mine of suggestion. (Whitehead 1979: 39)

One could make an argument on the basis of Whitehead's amplification of his point that all Chinese philosophy is indeed a series of footnotes on Confucius, but actually I am rather skeptical of such a view. It does not account for the often-found uniqueness and contrariness of various Chinese thinkers regarding views on questions not addressed at all by Confucius.

Since the first half of the twentieth century, English-speaking philosophers have been dependent largely on the 1953 work of Fung Yulan (1895–1990) for an overall introduction to Chinese thought. What often goes overlooked, though, is that virtually the entirety of Fung's work can be classified as a history of Chinese philosophy, not a true introduction providing an account of how philosophers in Chinese culture generated and handled the fundamental questions human beings find the need to address repeatedly.

Fung's works were complemented and supplemented by those of Wing-tsit Chan (1901–1994), including his very significant work of primary materials, *A Sourcebook in Chinese Philosophy* (1963b). In fact, Chan was unquestionably the leading translator of Chinese philosophical texts into English in the first half of the twentieth century. Together, both Fung and Chan contributed insights and interpretations to their expositions of Chinese philosophy and their contributions were many, varied, and indispensable. Nonetheless, neither of these pioneering scholars tried to provide an overview of Chinese philosophy as it might be understood to address fundamental philosophical questions in a systematic way. This task is the principal objective of this book.

In the years since the publications of Fung and Chan, ongoing dialogue, discovery of new texts, greater appreciation for comparative philosophy, and the emergence of new scholars conversant with Chinese philosophy have become factors requiring the need for the introduction to Chinese philosophical thought as a part of constructive philosophical reflection (Littlejohn 2005). This evolving situation has not escaped the notice of scholars. In 1985, Donald Bishop edited a volume of expository and critical essays entitled *Chinese Thought: An Introduction*. This work follows the periodization conventionally employed when approaching Western philosophy and divides Chinese philosophy into Ancient, Medieval, and Modern periods, even though, in my view, such a demarcation is inappropriate for Chinese philosophy. In the essays included in Bishop's work, scholars wrote on key figures from each period. Bishop's volume has the virtues of making an effort to provide a comprehensive snapshot of the most important Chinese philosophers and often offering suggestive and significant critical observations. However, it too is mostly on the model of a history of Chinese philosophy.

Chung-ying Cheng and Nicholas Bunnin edited a set of essays focused on *Contemporary Chinese Philosophy* (2002). This work is a very fine collection, and it serves as a solid introduction to modern Chinese thinkers, rightly noting that what was known about Chinese thought by most Western academics, even so recently as 2002, was almost invariably confined to the "Classical" period (i.e., more specifically that of Confucius and early Daoism). Cheng and Bunnin divided the contemporary period into four stages designed by them to cover "all the major philosophical developments and philosophical positions of Chinese philosophy in the twentieth century" (2002: xiv).

In 2006, Jeeloo Liu published an *Introduction to Chinese Philosophy: From Ancient Philosophy to Chinese Buddhism*. Liu severely restricted the scope of her introduction by considering only philosophers through roughly the ninth century. Accordingly, her introduction can give the impression that nothing of significance has been done philosophically in China since the Classical period, or certainly since the Tang dynasty, although, of course, Liu does not believe this. For many, there is a concern even more significant than the limited historical scope of Liu's book. A characteristic feature of this work is that it introduces thinkers on a historical frame, rather than by the philosophical topics and questions which most occupied them. Additionally, Liu approaches each thinker by means of Western analytic philosophical tradition. This kind of methodology tends to understand philosophical inquiry as limited to argument, conceptual distinction, and preference for the empirically verifiable as a determinative truth criterion. Often analytic thinkers do not consider "philosophical" any form of discourse that cannot be put into an argument form, with premises and conclusions. Consequently, in an effort to demonstrate to Western readers that Chinese philosophy is "real philosophy" as defined in this way, Liu recasts passages from Chinese philosophical texts into arguments of the sort consistent with what analytic thinkers expect and value.

I firmly believe Liu is right that many Chinese philosophers did make arguments, although I would claim they did so very rarely in the form that analytic philosophers would regard as normative for philosophical inquiry. Chinese philosophers often prefer analogy, as well as an appeal to historical allusions and metaphor in their way of doing philosophy. To so consistently force Chinese philosophy into the analytic model as Liu does may overlook the philosophical merits that emerge only if the method of the Chinese thinker is retained. Of course, this is not to say that Liu is not a skillful and well-informed interpreter of Chinese philosophy. She certainly is. Likewise, there are merits to sometimes exposing the argument of a Chinese thinker in such an explicit way. However, in this present work, I have endeavored to bring forward the argument structure employed as it is clearly used and intended by the Chinese philosopher, so I have also tried not to force a philosopher to make an argument of a certain form when he does not. Moreover, I have ambitiously taken on the project of considering philosophers up to the present in our overview, rather than so dramatically limiting the material historically as Liu did.

In 2008, two books of significance to an introduction of Chinese philosophy appeared. One of these was Karyn Lai's *An Introduction to Chinese Philosophy*. Lai, just as Liu had done, limited her introduction to cover only the period from the origins of Chinese philosophy to the emergence of Chan Buddhism (*c.* 700–800). Lai writes a strong introduction to the period she chooses; however, she makes no effort to talk about the contemporary philosophic scene in China and more attention to the concepts, themes, or aspects Western philosophy and Chinese philosophy both engage could have been included. When she does reference Western scholars, she is almost always concerned with their readings of a Chinese philosopher or text and not with a direct comparison between a claim or approach to a problem made in the West and one put forward in China meant to address the same or similar fundamental questions.

The second work of importance to our project that came out in English in 2008 was Bo Mou's *A History of Chinese Philosophy*. This work is in the Routledge History of World Philosophies series and is not a monograph. Mou devotes the book's chapters to various movements or periods and assigns them to individual contributors. While having many merits, this work really cannot serve readership in the English-speaking world as an introduction to Chinese philosophy principally because the philosophical issues that each contributor has picked out of a Chinese school of thought to become the focus of the chapter depend on the general philosophical perspective, knowledge, scope, intellectual interests, and academic tastes of that author. This means that the component essays, while generally carefully researched and critically valuable, lack the flow and continuity needed for an actual introduction to the span of Chinese philosophy. Also, it is noteworthy that individual contributors generally do not engage other essays in the collection and the general editor does not provide a coherent narrative to connect the contributions into a unified story. Of course, I realize this is not the purpose of the work. I also readily acknowledge that as a sourcebook for an author writing an introduction such as this present work, Mou's book is of great value.

Now, having provided a brief survey of the range of works published in English in roughly the past thirty years and intended to be introductions of sorts and not anthologies of primary texts and the like, one thing is clear. Even though a number of these works present themselves as introductions to Chinese philosophy, they are all characteristically histories. But I suggest that for the person wishing to bring Chinese sources and philosophers into a coherent conversation about humanity's fundamental questions, these works typically spend too much time on the nature and structure of Chinese texts, historical events, and internecine debates among Sinologists and specialists in Chinese philosophy to provide a thoroughly usable and ready-at-hand look at how the most dominant minds in China formulated approaches and answers to life's most basic philosophical questions.

The purpose of this work is to introduce how Chinese thinkers and texts address some of the most fundamental philosophical questions of human experience in order to put the resources of this extraordinary philosophical tradition into the quiver of tools available for a new generation of philosophers, the sort of philosopher I call a "constructivist." The stark truth is that the study of non-Western philosophical traditions has been understood within the West under what I call *the exclusionist paradigm*. This paradigmatic set of assumptions and filters originated from the initial encounters of European and British scholars with non-Western philosophies beginning in the late sixteenth century, but it has continued to exert influence until the dawn of the twenty-first century. The paradigm consists principally in the belief that there is no "real" or "true" philosophy outside of the West, especially not in China. For example, the Western thinker G. W. F. Leibniz claimed, "Among the Chinese, I believe, neither history nor criticism nor philosophy are sufficiently developed" (Leibniz 1994: 71). Immanuel Kant (1724–1804) lectured frequently on Chinese moral philosophy in his annual physical geography course, but in an unpublished version of these lectures, he stated:

> Philosophy is not to be met with in the entire orient. ... Their teacher Confucius lectures in his writings on nothing but moral precepts for princes. (Von Glasenapp 1954: 103–4)

Such exclusionism marginalized non-Western philosophical reflection from China specifically.

There are two overarching explanations for the strength and endurance of the exclusionist paradigm. First, a great deal of what is known in the West as the early Modern and Enlightenment periods was both built on a rigorous empiricism and correspondence theory of truth that relegated classical Chinese thinking to mysticism or religious nonsense and locked traditions such as Confucianism into its place as a social etiquette. Second, Western philosophers until the beginning of the twentieth century quite simply lacked any reasonable familiarity with the vast history and range of issues addressed in Chinese philosophical texts. While there were Latin, French, and eventually English versions of the Confucian classics and the Daoist work called *Daodejing* from the late eighteenth century, vast segments of China's philosophical thinking were unknown. So, what we may call "the exclusionist canon of Chinese philosophical texts" that came into the hands of Western thinkers was severely limited. In fact, consider that the first complete English translation of the hugely important *Mozi* was not done until Ian Johnston's 2010 work. One wonders whether such a thorough exclusion of Chinese philosophy from "philosophy proper" would have been sustainable had the *Mozi*'s analytical sections been available to Western thinkers beginning in the eighteenth century.

Two essays that shine light on the deleterious effects of this paradigm were written by Bryan Van Norden: "An Open Letter to the APA" (1996a) and "What Should Western Philosophy Learn from Chinese Philosophy?" (1996b). Perhaps unsurprisingly, since paradigms are often quite difficult to dislodge, not much changed, despite Van Norden's protests. So, the exclusionist paradigm has been recently criticized again. "[We] ask those who sincerely believe that it does make sense to organize our discipline entirely around European and American figures and texts to pursue this agenda with honesty and openness. We therefore suggest that any department that regularly offers courses only on Western philosophy should rename itself 'Department of European and American Philosophy'" (Garfield and Van Norden 2016).

While this tenacious exclusivist understanding of Chinese philosophy continued to manifest itself, another paradigm for studying Chinese philosophy emerged known as *comparative philosophy*. Studies that introduce comparative philosophy and its methods include those of Tim Connolly (2015) and Ronnie Littlejohn and Qingjun Li (2019). Also extremely helpful to an understanding of the work of comparative philosophers we should include Sor-hoon Tan's *The Bloomsbury Research Handbook of Chinese Philosophy Methodologies* (2016) and Van Norden's *Taking Back Philosophy: A Multicultural Manifesto* (2017). Some uses of this present volume can also aid the comparative philosopher. The inclusion of "Focus Windows" is meant to suggest comparison, but these are limited by the fact that they are almost exclusively drawn from Western philosophy. A richer comparative philosophy would set many traditions in conversation, with each tradition like a vast categorical area of some giant Venn diagram expressing points of overlap, similarity, and uniqueness in the traditions of global philosophy. For many comparative philosophers the ultimate goal is to locate and work within the "sweet spot" of what Connolly calls "comparative universalism" created by the actual dialogue of traditions and not some "view from nowhere" standing above them with some privileged view of truth (Connolly 2015: 150–3).

But in this introductory book, I want to contribute to a third paradigm shift that has been emerging in the past two decades and goes beyond comparative philosophy to create not a new methodology for philosophy, but *a new type of philosopher*. I call this new philosopher a *constructivist*. These new philosophers seek out what is framed differently in other cultures, analyzed in novel ways, and so on. They integrate, synthesize, and create. Constructionist philosophers are seeking something more and other than a consensus or middle ground between philosophical traditions of different cultures that emerge from comparative philosophy. They are reflecting, inventing, and making over philosophical understandings of fundamental human questions by appropriating insights and approaches from across cultures and traditions.

While similar introductions to Japanese, South Asian, African, and other traditions can also contribute to the constructivist project, in the present work my purpose is to help the reader develop as a constructivist philosopher by exposure to Chinese texts and traditions. In doing so, I fully acknowledge my debt to all those persons whose works I have mentioned above and to my teachers and colleagues who have labored to help me become a better philosopher.

Acknowledgments

I want to acknowledge the support and encouragement I have received in developing this second edition of *Chinese Philosophy: An Introduction* from Ms. Colleen Coalter, Senior Commissioning Editor for Philosophy at Bloomsbury Publishing. Very soon after Bloomsbury's acquisition of my work from I.B. Tauris, Ms. Coalter contacted me and began working with me on how we might enhance my works in later editions. She sent this volume to three reviewers and all of them were quite kind in their remarks about the strengths of the work, while also making extremely helpful suggestions for its improvement in a second edition. I am grateful to them and to Ms. Coalter for taking the initiative to get approval for the production of this new edition and for her guidance along the way.

Note on Translations

The interpretation and understanding of a substantial number of important Chinese philosophical concepts and terms may be affected by the translation used. For those texts cited recurringly throughout this work, I have made use of the translations below. Unless otherwise specifically noted or cited, the reader may consult the translations given below as the standard ones used throughout for the texts mentioned. When I have added interpolations or comments in clarification of the translation, I have put the content in brackets. When I offer my own translations, rather than relying on the texts below, I cite the location in the original text and note "my translation." When I alter only part of a translated passage from one of the volumes below, I cite the location in the original text and note "my changes" in the in-text citation. When I provide the Romanized *pinyin* and/or Chinese character for the reader, I put this in parentheses.

Translations Used for Recurring Texts

Ames, Roger, and Henry Rosemont, trans. (1998), *The Analects of Confucius: A Philosophical Translation*, New York: Ballantine Books.

Hutton, Eric, trans. and ed. (2014), *Xunzi: The Complete Text*, Princeton, NJ: Princeton University Press.

Ivanhoe, Philip J., trans. (2002), *The Daodejing of Laozi*, New York: Seven Bridges.

Johnston, Ian, trans. (2010), *The Mozi: A Complete Translation*, New York: Columbia University Press.

Lau, D. C., trans. (2003), *Mencius*, New York: Penguin Books.

Major, John, Sarah Queen, Andrew Set Meyer, and Harold Roth, trans. (2010), *The Huainanzi: A Guide to the Theory and Practice of Government in Early Han China*, New York: Columbia University Press.

Watson, Burton, trans. (1968), *The Complete Works of Chuang-Tzu*, New York: Columbia University Press.

哲学
Introduction

Philosophy is sometimes thought of exclusively in terms of a specific intellectual movement or method of approaching fundamental questions associated with a prominent philosopher. For example, we can speak of Platonism, Aristotelianism, Confucianism, Mohism, Epicureanism, Cartesianism, Kantianism, and Hegelianism. At other times, the method used to approach fundamental questions, and even for regarding which questions are fundamental, becomes identified with philosophy itself. This happens when we speak of methodologies *as though* they exhausted the nature of philosophy such as Empiricism, Rationalism, Idealism, Positivism, Existentialism, Phenomenology, or Pragmatism.

Sometimes we can learn about an intellectual discipline just by looking at its name. We need not puzzle about the primary content of Literature, French, Mathematics, or Accounting. Unfortunately, this is somewhat less true about Philosophy. The word *philosophy* comes from the Greek *philosophia* (φιλοσοφία), literally meaning "love of wisdom." This is certainly a project in which Chinese thinkers have been as seriously engaged. Still, at first sight this does not tell us much definitively about philosophy's subject matter.

I do not find any of these approaches particularly helpful as ways to help us grasp what sort of activity philosophy is. Actually, the best way to expose how philosophers love wisdom is to look at the kind of questions that concern them. If I ask a student, "What do you want to do when you graduate?" she may certainly answer in a completely nonphilosophical way. There is nothing about this question that requires a philosophical sort of answer. She may simply say, "Be a doctor." I may go on to inquire, "How do you get to be a doctor?" Again, a reply may be given that is not philosophical.

But suppose I ask, "Will it make you happy to be a doctor?" This sounds more like a philosophical question, although it might also be a psychological one. But if I inquire, "What is happiness, anyway?" then I have moved to the level of a philosophical question.

What is it that makes the last question a philosophical one? It is a fundamental question about human life, and it cannot be resolved by empirical means alone. Indeed, philosophers sometimes understand their work to include the task of distinguishing those claims that are decidable by empirical evidence alone and those that are not. Such a task arises from the fundamental question, "Is all knowledge gained by the same means?" or simply "What is it 'to know' something?" We shall see that philosophers such as Mozi, Wang Chong, and Zhang Dongsun are all concerned with such questions about knowledge. Fundamental questions may be grouped into a number of categories, such as those having to do with epistemology (questions about the nature and scope of knowledge), ontology (questions about the nature of reality and its processes), morality (questions about the value appraisals of human conduct and how value judgments are made), logic, personal identity, meaning of life (including questions about religion), and a host of topics known as "philosophy of" (e.g., philosophy of politics [political philosophy], philosophy of language or philosophy of psychology).

It is important to remind ourselves that fundamental questions are of concern in the work of Chinese thinkers and they are not exclusively in the purview of Westerners. Accordingly, it is not cultural ethnocentrism or intellectual imperialism to recognize that questions quite similar or even identical to those in Western tradition also show up in Chinese philosophers' writings. In choosing to move fundamental questions to the forefront of the organization of our study, I have not placed a Western grid down on Chinese philosophy. The easiest way to see that fundamental questions are both implicit and explicit in Chinese philosophy is to let the texts speak for themselves. So, I have made use of quite a number of primary texts in our introduction because these disclose not only that Chinese philosophers are dealing with fundamental questions but also how they approach and answer them. For example, some Chinese thinkers are as occupied with questions of epistemology (how we know something is true and the scope and range of our knowledge) as are some Western philosophers. Of course, this no more means that every Chinese philosopher considers epistemology to be the most important or exclusive concern of philosophy, any more than it does that all Western philosophers believe in such a narrow understanding of their field.

Moreover, Chinese philosophers often approach questions of epistemology differently and provide answers to them that very much set them apart from those offered by Western thinkers. These factors explain some reasons why Chinese Philosophy should be introduced into the development of the type of constructivist philosopher I mention in the Preface.

Bertrand Russell, a significant Western philosopher of the twentieth century who visited China, held that the value of philosophy is, in fact, to be sought largely in the very uncertainty of its answers to fundamental questions (Russell 1912: 237–50). He argued that the person who has no tincture of philosophy goes through life imprisoned in the prejudices derived from common sense, or from the habitual beliefs and convictions that have grown up in the mind without the cooperation or consent of deliberate reason and reflection. To such a person the world tends to appear obvious; common objects rouse no questions. However, as soon as one begins to philosophize, on the contrary, one finds that even the most everyday things give rise to questions of wonder and puzzlement.

Philosophy, though unable to tell us with certainty the "true" answer to all the questions it raises, is able to suggest many possibilities that enlarge our thoughts and free them from the tyranny of mere custom. Thus, while diminishing our feeling of certainty as to what things are, philosophy greatly increases our knowledge as to what they may be; it removes the somewhat arrogant dogmatism of those who have never traveled into the region of liberating doubt, and it keeps alive our sense of wonder by showing familiar things in an unfamiliar aspect (ibid.: 242–3). We will see that studying how Chinese philosophers have engaged these questions provides vibrant intellectual stimulation and sometimes a different approach to those offered by Western philosophy.

Elmer Sprague once wrote that philosophy is like the measles. It must be caught from someone who is already infected. He held that to learn to philosophize, one must try his luck arguing with a real philosopher or at least with another person who is engaged in the wonder of fundamental questions as well (Sprague 1962: 3). Another way of saying this is to follow Ludwig Wittgenstein's observation that philosophy is not a specific theory or content, it is an activity. It is with this exciting activity that I hope to infect the reader in the chapters that follow by using Chinese thinkers and texts as our springboard.

Four chapters make up this book, each taking up in a broad sense the positions of Chinese philosophers on one set of fundamental questions. In arranging things in this way, I am noticing that there are "family resemblances" or recognizable similarities between the sorts of fundamental questions posed by diverse global philosophical traditions. These resemblances make it possible to use this typological model as an organizing structure for the study. Of course, while there are family resemblances in the fundamental questions asked by Chinese and other philosophical traditions, there are likewise quite fascinating divergences in efforts to answer them.

Chapter 1 deals with a set of questions in the category known as *ontology*. *Ontology* is derived from two Greek words: *ontis*, meaning "being" or "reality," "that which is"; and *logos*, meaning "the study of" or "the knowledge of." Sometimes, ontology is also called metaphysics, referring to what can be known about reality beyond that which physics or science tells us. I choose not to use this term because to speak of *meta*physics already implies there is something that is beyond what can be known through the empirical world. Some ontological questions are these:

- What is reality composed of/made of?
- Is reality of a single type of thing (monism), two types of things (e.g., minds and bodies; matter and spirit; as in dualism), or many types of things (pluralism)?
- Is reality composed of only constantly changing and transient things or are there enduring, even eternal and universal, components to it?
- Is reality actually as it appears to us or is it something different from what we think it is (the question of appearance versus reality)?
- Does reality have a meaning, is it guided by a mind or intelligence to occur as it does, or does it follow some internal pattern of its own nature, "purposing" of its own accord, or do humans attach meaning or purpose to reality that it does not have in itself?

Chapter 2 is occupied with fundamental questions that can be gathered under the concept of *epistemology*. Again, as with the term ontology, *epistemology* has its origin in the Greek language. *Epistemis* means "knowledge," and so epistemology is the study of knowledge. Some epistemological questions are these:

- What is it "to know"? Is knowing someTHING (fact) different from knowing someONE (person)?
- Can we actually *know* someTHING (fact) to be true, or do we only *believe* things to be true (the issue of skepticism)?
- Are all claims to know someTHING (fact) of the same sort or justified in the same way?

- What are the tools we use to know someTHING (e.g., reason, experience/senses, etc.)?
- Are we born knowing some things are true?
- Is there a limit to what we can know?
- Are there laws of thinking that must be followed to obtain knowledge?

Chapter 3 concerns philosophical questions of morality and value. Some fundamental questions addressed in this chapter are these:

- How should we live?
- What is the ultimate purpose of our lives (e.g., to pursue happiness or pleasure, obey moral rules, please others or higher beings, follow our own interests, or create harmony between persons)?
- What is the origin of our morality (e.g., do we invent it and agree to it, is it inborn or part of our nature, or is it given by a higher being or intelligence)?
- What really makes something good or right to do (e.g., is it the consequences of the action, doing our duties, or going by our passionate feelings)?
- Is morality universally applicable to all persons or is it relative to its culture or to the individual?
- What is most basic and important in morality: the actions we do or the sort of persons we are?

Chapter 4 undertakes to explore those fundamental questions related to the creation of society and government. Some of these are the following:

- What is the natural state of humans prior to government and law (e.g., are they free, equal and independent, or social and interdependent; are they inevitably in conflict or do they live in innocent bliss)?
- From where does government arise (e.g., a contract between persons, the recognized superiority of some persons to lead, or is it the decree of a higher power)?
- What are human laws and from where do they come (e.g., do we arrive at them by participatory exchange of views, or are they part of the nature of reality, or are they codifications of the lives of exemplary persons, or are they decrees of virtuous rulers or a divine being)?
- What is the best form of government?
- Are there checks and balances on government/rulers?
- Is revolt against the ruler or government ever justified?

- What is the proper balance between governmental authority and individual liberty of expression and thought?
- What is the role and responsibility of government to implement justice and how should it do it (in distributing goods, for example, are there rules of entitlement, fairness, or equality of opportunity)?

While I have followed the procedure of grouping philosophical questions into four chapters, it is quite obvious that how one answers a question in one category very often requires or presupposes an answer in some other. The chapter divisions of this text are not meant to imply impermeable or nonporous silos. In fact, while useful to organize our study, we must always remember that responses to fundamental questions in one category have implications for how questions in another are dealt with. For example, approaches to morality imply and even depend on positions taken on ontological questions. Consider that Chinese philosophers engage the philosophical question of the structure of reality by using the concept of Principle (*li* 理). This ontological concept helps them understand the way humans, wherever we find them, possess and use notions like time, space, and cause. The Chinese call these Principles. But some Chinese thinkers use the concept of Principles to answer questions regarding morality too. These philosophers reject the idea that morality is a human invention, but think of our moral beliefs and concepts as related to structures within nature itself or even commands put in place by Heaven (e.g., see Mozi). We could multiply instances of this process of transference and overlap between the fourfold grouping of fundamental questions used to structure our study. Throughout the text, I will call attention to many of these.

In fact, I wish to encourage further investigation of the connections between claims made in one chapter and those in another, whether these are made by the same philosopher or by different ones. To the extent that this happens, I will have been successful not only in introducing the responses and answers of Chinese philosophers to fundamental questions but also in contributing in some measure to infecting the reader with the wonder and joy of philosophical inquiry itself.

While this book cannot be considered a work in "comparative philosophy," nevertheless, I do sometimes break up the flow of the text describing a Chinese philosopher's views by inserting windows into the text that make brief comparisons usually drawn from Western philosophers and addressing similar philosophical issues. These are meant to be suggestive and provocative for the constructivist philosopher. They are not offered as anything like a comprehensive or nuanced exposition of the Western thinkers' viewpoints, or a fully developed comparative description. Hopefully, they will entice the reader to investigate further the connections between Chinese and Western thought and learn more deeply about both traditions (Littlejohn and Li 2019). If this occurs, then I do think this present study will contribute to the response called for by Van Norden's defense of the philosophical character of non-Western thought in his *Taking Back Philosophy: A Multicultural Manifesto* (2017).

A great deal of work meant to introduce Chinese philosophy, even including those volumes mentioned in the "Preface" to this book, devotes what I consider an inordinate amount of attention to the contextualization for a philosopher's positions. Basically, I feel that a good analogy for what worries me about this approach is that it would be like thinking one must always contextualize the great twentieth-century philosopher Ludwig Wittgenstein in his home culture of Vienna and the outbreak of the Second World War before addressing his philosophy. It seems clear to me that one can read Wittgenstein's works such as *Tractatus Logico-Philosohicus, Philosophical Investigations*, and *On Certainty* without referring each remark to a historical or cultural context. The merits of works such as Ray Monk's *Ludwig Wittgenstein: The Duty of Genius* (1991) or Allan Janik and Stephen Toulmin's *Wittgenstein's Vienna* (1996) are well known, but Wittgenstein's thought may still be described without them. For this reason, I acknowledge that I may not provide what every reader will regard as sufficient Sinological background for each thinker covered. Although I recognize that sometimes historical and cultural context influences a position, I address these issues when it seems germane to the approach taken by the philosopher. But I hold to my position that in a text devoted to introducing philosophy, cultural and historical context need not always be moved to the foreground.

Finally, before we begin our study, a few comments about the ways I have treated important Chinese philosophical terms are in order. Chinese, of course, is written in characters and the current alphabetical Romanization used to know how to pronounce the characters is called *pinyin*. Throughout the text, I almost exclusively use *pinyin* rather than the characters themselves in order to increase the ease of reading. However, in some cases the failure to use a Chinese character can be confusing. For example, the *pinyin* "*li*" can have several quite distinct major philosophical uses. One is to refer to propriety in relationships, rules, or even morality (*li* 禮) and the other refers to the Principles structuring reality (*li* 理). I will use the characters when I feel that the reader may be confused about which use of a term such as *li* is being intended. I adopt the same practice for *qi* (氣) as the primordial substance of which all things are made and *qi* (器) as used for individual "concrete objects." Also, when the Chinese *tian* (天) is used as a nominative for a supreme agent I use the capital "Heaven." When it is used with *di* (earth) as in *tiandi* (天地), in order to indicate everything that is, the world, or reality, I use "heaven and earth" or "heaven" in lower case (Chang 2000). When speaking of the philosophical system of interacting correlative elemental phases of *qi* (氣) that actualize into the objects of reality, I use capitals (i.e., Five Phases 五行). When speaking of the elements themselves, I use lower case. In other instances of the use of Chinese characters I do so for clarification only.

1

哲学

Ontology—Questions about the Nature of Reality

Introduction

This chapter deals with a set of philosophical questions in the category known as *ontology*. *Ontology* is not a term that derives from Chinese thought. It comes from two Greek words *ontis*, meaning "being" or "reality," "that which is," and *logos*, meaning "the study of" or "the knowledge of." Although ontology is sometimes called "metaphysics," referring to what can be known about reality beyond what physics or science can tell us, I choose not to employ this term because its use may imply already that there is something beyond what can be known through science or empirical data. *Meta*physics is often taken to deal with that which transcends or is beyond natural phenomenon. While we shall see that some Chinese philosophers do include in their ontologies aspects of reality that lie beyond the way things appear to our five senses, generally speaking, all Chinese ontologies start and finish with what they regard as natural, even if sometimes the objects and phenomena produced by natural forces are not accessible by the limited range of human sensory powers (i.e., sight, hearing, touch, etc.).

We should also make a distinction between ontology and cosmology:

- Ontology is the set of philosophical positions concerned with the addressing fundamental questions.
- Cosmology is focused more specifically on the observable movements and processes of the phenomena of the universe.

While ontology concerns itself with the general nature of the entities, qualities, and relationships that compose and constitute reality, cosmology occupies itself with making empirical assertions about existence. Having said this, we may note that the contemporary Chinese philosopher Chung-ying Cheng prefers using the term *onto-cosmology* of Chinese thought about the nature of reality because he feels it is more accurate than the division of these two approaches, as is done in the West.[1] However, for our purposes, we will continue to refer to Chinese ontology, even if as we work our way through the texts and views of Chinese philosophers, we will notice that Cheng's term does indeed capture much of the Chinese approach to questions of reality. This chapter deals with the following questions of ontology:

- What is reality composed of/made of?
- Is reality of a single type of thing (monism), two types of things (i.e., "dualism": minds and bodies; matter and spirit; nature and supernature), or many types of things (pluralism)?
- Is reality composed of only constantly changing and transient, impermanent things, or are there enduring, or even eternal and universal components in its composition?
- Is reality actually as it appears to us or is it something different in its true nature from what we are most directly aware of?
- Does reality have a meaning, is it "purposing," or is it guided by a mind or intelligence to process as it does?
- Does reality follow some internal pattern of its own nature, or is it the case that humans attach and invent meaning and impose it on reality, although it is devoid of purpose in itself?

The Basic Vocabulary of the Chinese Theory of Reality: The "Great Commentary" to the *Classic of Changes* (*Yijing*)

The ontology of early Chinese thought comes down to us through a number of philosophical texts that are not traceable to any single author. One of the most important of these texts is the "Great Commentary" (*Dazhuan*) to the *Classic of Changes* (*Yijing*). The *Classic of Changes* is the name for a complete work that includes two parts. One section is a quite ancient manual of divination known simply as the *Changes* (*Yi*) or, more correctly, as the *Zhouyi*, or the "method of studying the changes of reality developed in the Zhou Dynasty" (Cheng and Ng 2010). Important and usable translations of this text into English include Rutt (2002) and Shaughnessy (1997). It is a handbook traceable to the period and practices of the Western Zhou dynasty as is indicated, among other features, by its use of language expressions found on the bronzes of that period (*c.* 1046–771 BCE). The other section of the *Classic of Changes* is a set of seven commentaries attached to the *Zhouyi*. Three of the commentaries are composed of two parts each. Accordingly, taken as a whole, the commentary set making up this second section of the *Classic of Changes* is known as "The Ten Wings" (*Shiyi*).

One of these ten commentaries to the *Classic of Changes* (*Yijing*) is known by various titles, including the "Great Commentary" (*Dazhuan*) and "Appended Statements" (*Xici*). The "Great Commentary" is arguably the most important single text available to us for an understanding of the earliest Chinese ontology. The divination section of the *Classic of Changes* is much less valuable to us as philosophers.

The "Great Commentary" sketches out the early Chinese worldview that was basic to all of China's philosophical systems for over two millennia. Just whether it represents a period dating to *c.* 1500 BCE is still a subject of scholarly debate (Liu 2004). It also introduces the fundamental philosophical vocabulary of Chinese ontology that has been employed by Chinese thinkers up to the Modern period. In this case, we are mining out philosophical understandings from a text whose author or authors are unknown to us. However, the editor(s) of this text created what became one of the lasting "Classics" in Chinese intellectual culture.

What Western philosophy calls *reality*, the philosophers who created the "Great Commentary" generally called by the compound "heaven and earth" (*tiandi*). As for the process of reality's change, they used the term *dao* (道). While there are many uses of the term *dao* in classical Chinese, Western English-language translators have most often used "way." This text frequently employs the term *Dao* as a nominative "the Way" and portrays it as operating according to "heavenly patterns (*tian wen*)" or Principles (*li* 理).

The "Great Commentary" speaks of both change and continuity in reality. Reality is composed of one sort of fundamental indestructible substance that may be thought of as a kind of pure energy which Chinese thinkers called *qi* (氣). Here is how the "Great Commentary" uses several fundamental ontological concepts in relation to each other:

> The *Yi* [i.e., the *Classic of Changes*] being aligned with heaven and earth, can wholly set forth the *Dao* of heaven and earth. The *Yi* looks up to observe the patterns of heaven (*tianwen* 天文), and looks down to examine the Principles (*li* 理) of earth. Thus, it knows the causes of darkness and light, origin and ends; it comprehends the meaning of birth and death, it perceives how seminal *qi* forms into things. Now *yin* 陰, now *yang* 陽 move and this is *Dao*. ("Great Commentary," Part One, IV and V, Rutt 2002: 411)

In this passage, the author makes use of a robust philosophical vocabulary. Reality (heaven and earth) is *qi* substance in constant process, but its changes are not arbitrary, chaotic, or haphazard. The term used to capture this order is *Dao,* which is used for "the Way" that the changing processes of reality follow. This path reveals Principles (*li* 理) that are evident to one who reflects on the *Dao* process. The *Dao* of *qi* gives rise of itself to forces that move it: it is self-moving and auto-generative (i.e., it is its own cause), according to its internal dynamics of *yin* and *yang*.

The "Great Commentary" makes the philosophical claim that not only all reality is in process but also there are patterns to its changes. By tradition, a legendary thinker of antiquity named Fu Xi originally developed a system of eight symbols called trigrams to express these patterns. These trigrams had three lines or rows. An unbroken line was used to indicate the *yang* forces operative in change and a broken line represented *yin* forces. According to one interpretation of the trigram figure itself, the first two lines represent *yin* and *yang*, and the third represents the relation of the previous two lines standing for reality's creative advance. Taken in this way, there are eight possible figures. Thus, in Chinese, this set of eight is called the Eight Trigrams (*bagua*).

In a commentary appended to the *Classic of Changes* entitled "Discussion of the Trigrams" (*shuogua*), the trigrams are also used as explanatory devices for the emergence of prominent families, the natural seasons, diverse colors, and varieties of animals. There is no philosophical justification offered in the commentary for these explanatory associations, and we should attribute them to the practitioners who sought to provide more concrete interpretations for the use of the trigrams for the purpose of divination of the future. What is worth noting philosophically is that this elaborate system is rooted in the belief that as *qi* is in process, it moves according to patterns and not by mere randomness.

If we look in the *Zhouyi* section, that is, the actual divination or future-telling section of the text of the *Classic of Changes*, we notice not merely Eight Trigrams, but sixty-four hexagrams (Figure 1).

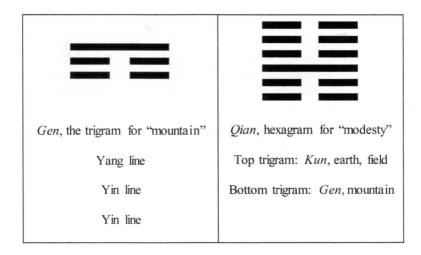

Gen, the trigram for "mountain"	*Qian*, hexagram for "modesty"
Yang line	Top trigram: *Kun*, earth, field
Yin line	Bottom trigram: *Gen*, mountain
Yin line	

Figure 1 *Classic of Changes* trigram and hexagram.

There are various traditions about how the hexagrams emerged. One is that when it came to applying the Eight Trigrams to human experiences and decisions, practitioners ran into the problem that they could not distinguish the inner and outer aspects of changing human events or what we might think of as the subjective inner feeling and the objective outer act with respect to persons' activities in history and the purpose and event in nature (Cheng 2009b: 76). In order to talk about these aspects of change, the practitioners who were the source of the *Zhouyi* stacked the Eight Trigrams, typically using the lower trigram to stand for the inner aspects of the process that is occurring and the upper to represent the outer aspects. When this procedure was followed, the total number of possible configurations of the Eight Trigrams became the sixty-four hexagrams of the current *Zhouyi* text.[2] In the *Zhouyi* divination manual, two hexagrams are of special ontological significance for expressing the patterns of reality: Qian and Kun. The "Great Commentary" offers this observation on these two hexagrams:

The *dao* of Qian [i.e., heaven] forms maleness [i.e., *yang*].
The *dao* of Kun [i.e., earth] forms femaleness [i.e., *yin*].
Qian [heaven] conceives the Great Beginning, Kun [earth] brings things to completion.
Qian [heaven] conceives with spontaneity, Kun [earth] is empowered with simplicity. ("Great Commentary," Part One, I, Rutt 2002: 409)

We might wonder just what it is that is being moved with spontaneity and simplicity. The substance that is "*daoing*" or "*pathing*" along is *qi*. *Qi* is a multiphasal phenomenon, sometimes manifesting with properties of what we might call in the West "matter" and sometimes existing in a state that Westerners would call "spirit." But *Qi* may manifest both of these features, because it sometimes may be accessible through our senses (matter) and sometimes not (spirit). But there are not two ontological realities, such as matter and spirit. *Qi* is moved by pushes and pulls of its internal opposing forces, *yin* and *yang*. These processes of reality give shape to every object whatever.[3]

> The result of its [*dao's*] process is goodness:
> It [the process of *qi* moving by *yin* and *yang*] achieves completion as the nature of something (*xing* 性) …
> Products-producing-products is [the reality] described by *yi* [i.e., the *Classic of Changes*]
> All that *yin* and *yang* do not define [into a visible object form] is called spirit.
> ("Great Commentary," Part One, V, my translation)

The general philosophical term for the process of *yin* and *yang* influence on reality that the *Classic of Changes* is describing is *correlative ontology*.

Correlation is itself the central concept of the ontological theory of early Chinese philosophy. The forces *yin* and *yang* may be mutually supportive, or one may be transforming the other, balancing it, compensating for it, enhancing it, or furthering something new in relation to the other. The relationship of *yin* and *yang* may be creative and productive, lead to harmony and stability, or deconstruct the present phenomenon and open the way to something new. Therefore, *yin* and *yang* are not equivalent to good and evil, and they possess no mentality or intentionality by which they plan or direct reality. They are regarded as natural forces.

Generally speaking, the more *yin* predominates in a process, the more the driving forces may be associated with the earth, femininity, passivity, suppleness, warmth, and darkness. The more *yang* dominates, the more we should associate the process with heaven, masculinity, aggressiveness, rigidity, coldness, and light.

Avoiding Category Mistakes in Ontology

Yin and *yang* are not kinds of things in addition to *qi*. They are not things at all, not even spiritual things. To take them in this way is to make what the Western philosopher Gilbert Ryle called a "category mistake."[4] This is an error of the sort we make if we nominalize a word like *creeps* (e.g., "He gives me the creeps.") and believe that there is some existing object named by the word *creeps* that someone has given to us in the same way that one might give us a piece of candy. Another way of saying this is that language about *yin* and *yang* is nonreferential. These terms are not names that point or correspond to objects in the way that *candy* does.

When reading about traditional Chinese medicine, which makes extensive use of the concepts of *yin* and *yang*, we must be careful to remember this fact. To say that one is sick because she has too much *yang* does not refer to some overabundance of a quantity of some substance called *yang*, even if it resembles grammatically the statement, "There is too much water in your bucket." This expression about having too much *yang* is an example of what Ryle called a "systematically misleading expression" (Ryle 1951). Even though *yin* and *yang* are nonreferential and not being used to point to some substance, they still have an important use in the ontology of early China. They are concepts in Chinese ontology used as explanatory devices for what makes *qi* take the variant forms that constitute reality.

We are now in the position to summarize the ontology of the "Great Commentary" in the following way. Reality is a process of *qi* emerging, stabilizing, passing away, renewing, and recreating itself all the time. While reality consists of one underlying substance, *qi* is not equivalent to the Western philosophical term "matter" but neither is it "spirit." The closest analogue for *qi* to be found in Western philosophy is the term *energy*.

Qi takes many forms as it is moved by the forces of *yin* and *yang*. How things appear to us is really the way they are; we are not living some dream or illusion. There are tables, chairs, cows, and so on as configurations of *qi*. And yet, there is an element of the appearance/reality distinction in Chinese philosophy, since many things appear to us to be static, fixed, and unchangeable, but they are not. Everything is in process and changing.

Western Substance Ontology

In Western ontologies, it is characteristic to think of reality as made up of objects having a unifying essence or substance that makes them what they are and separates one kind of thing from another. Western philosophers often sort things into a variety of "natural kinds" by thinking of objects as having a different nature or essence that distinguishes them from other objects. This essence is fixed in nature and remains constant, continually constituting the thing as what it is, despite superficial changes. Changes take place at the level of the features the object "accidentally" or just happens to have; they do not alter the object's essential nature or "substance." In Chinese ontology, as we notice from the "Great Commentary," the fact that all things are in process means that the important idea of a substance or essence which underwrites the Western philosophy of difference in kinds is not a prominent view. In kind, all things are *qi*, but of course, Chinese philosophers do not hold that all *qi* forms concresce in the same way, and certainly they do not think that *qi* is of multiple substantive types or kinds, as in Western philosophy. What Western philosophers consider different natural kind substances, Chinese philosophers think of as different phases of *qi* repeatedly replicating themselves, giving the impression of continuity and stability (Ames 2011: 62–4).

Even in Western philosophy, there are thinkers who criticize what is called substance or essence ontology. Among them we should include Heraclitus, David Hume, William James, Alfred North Whitehead, and Ludwig Wittgenstein. Here is an illustration from William James of how we can be misled and mystified by our language into thinking of reality as a set of fixed natural kind objects:

> *The low thermometer today, for instance, is supposed to come from something called the "climate." Climate is really only the name for a certain group of days, but it is treated as if it [were some thing that] lay behind the day, and in general we placed the name, as if it were a being, behind the facts it is the name of. But the phenomenal properties of things do not inhere in anything. They adhere, or cohere, rather, with each other, and the notion of a substance inaccessible to us, which we think accounts for such cohesion by supporting it, as cement might support pieces of a mosaic, must be abandoned. The fact of the bare cohesion itself is all the notion of the substance signifies. Beyond that fact is nothing. (James 2000: 42)*

How can we explain the beginning of the universe in terms of early Chinese ontology? The most direct answer to this question is that in Chinese thought, the formless *qi* has eternally been *dao*ing. Taken as a whole, *qi* as moved by *yin* and *yang* is the explanation for the emergence of what Western philosophy calls material objects. In Western thought, the characteristic approach is to think of material things as natural kinds that have different defining essences that make them what they are (i.e., a chair, a cat, a tree). These defining essences are called "the nature" of something. But in early Chinese ontology, there is change as well as continuity and endurance even in the so-called nature of a thing. The characteristic configuration of *qi* that something is *dao*ing (i.e., actualizing) sets it apart from other things. The distinctive correlation of *yin* and *yang* at any given time is the Chinese philosophical explanation that does the philosophical work of the Western concept of the *essence* or *substance* that makes an object what it is. Accordingly, Chinese philosophers offered an explanatory system for reality that avoided the Western philosophical problem of whether reality is one thing or many things. Early Chinese texts could explain reality as a correlation of one and many. The one being *qi*, the many being the innumerable configurations *qi* takes by the push and pulls of *yin* and *yang*.

Let us take all this one further step. In Western philosophy, thinkers habitually speak of material objects and often become involved in debates about whether material things are different from minds or souls. But in early Chinese ontology, "material" objects are not made of some substance other than *qi*; they are temporary and particularized configurations of *qi* that fall within the range of our sensory powers. When a *qi* configuration actualizes in a certain way, it may be experienced as solid, hard, rough, smooth, fluid, of a certain color, and so on. And yet, not everything that exists in reality as a configuration of *qi* is accessible by our senses.

We may wonder whether it is the case that in Chinese ontology all things are moving in the process of reality according to some purpose or overarching meaning and plan. Chinese philosophers do recognize, of course, that some phenomena move in ways for which we invent the language of purpose, interest, motivation, will, expectation, intention, and the like. In early Chinese thought, this is the explanation for our talk about mental processes, but it does not mean that some phenomena have minds (e.g., humans) and others (e.g., worms) do not. It means that the configurations of some phenomena are such that we use mental process language to talk about behaviors they exhibit (i.e., "He did that intentionally"). Again, this function of language is not to point to someone's mind and some feature of it (e.g., intentions). It is language we use to talk about the manner in which one performs an act. Enabling reality to be understood in this way was part of the genius of the creators of early Chinese ontology.

What we dare not overlook in this philosophy is that recurring patterns and order in the process of reality are not imposed from outside the process, say, by a transcendent mind. Novelty, creativity, and pattern arise from the internal processes of reality itself. The "Great Commentary" gives us a world of possibility and change, but also of order and pattern. It is a reality full of forces expressed as *yin* and *yang*, but also alterable by human effort and, indeed, by the actions of other sentient beings as well.

Daoist Ontology: Lao-Zhuang Tradition (c. 350–139 BCE)

To speak collectively of "Lao-Zhuang" tradition is to identify a set of philosophical sentiments and positions in common between the two classical works of emergent Daoism in Chinese intellectual history in about 300 BCE: the *Daodejing* (*DDJ*) and the *Zhuangzi*. Both the *DDJ*, attributed to a shadowy figure named Laozi, and the *Zhuangzi*, ascribed to Zhuang Zhou (*c.* 369–289 BCE), are composite works not actually written by a single author. Throughout the Classical period in China, there were many lineages of teachers and their disciples, as well as multiple oral and written materials, that culminated in these two works which came to represent philosophical views associated with what came to be called Daoism (*Daojia*). There were multiple versions of these collections in circulation as we know quite well now, based on archaeological discoveries made at the sites of Mawangdui (from 1972 to 1974) and Guodian (in 1993) (Cook 2013 and Holloway 2009). Accordingly, while interpreters generally agree now that there was no unified, coherent school called Daoism in the Classical period, the term Lao-Zhuang can be used to capture the resemblances between philosophical lineages and their transmitted teachings during this period (Hardy 1998). In what follows, I have isolated some of these teachings on the fundamental questions of ontology.

We have already noticed in our survey of the earliest Chinese ontologies that reality (i.e., "heaven and earth") is in constant process, but the changes are not arbitrary, chaotic, haphazard, or by mere chance. The Chinese term used to capture the course of reality is *dao*, which literally means the "way" or "path" of the flow changing processes of reality follow. In this process, there are patterns and Principles (*li* 理) that are evident to one who reflects on the *dao*. The *dao* of *qi* (the energy that composes all things) gives rise of itself to forces that move it. So, it is self-moving, according to its dynamic energies of *yin* and *yang*.

The term *dao* is one of the most important concepts in the *DDJ*.[5] Sometimes it is used as a noun (i.e., "the *Dao*") and other times as a verb (i.e., "*daoing*"). We can see a sample of the way it changes meanings in the opening lines of Chapter 1:

> The *Dao* that can be expressed in words is not the eternal *Dao*.
> The name that can be named is not the eternal name. (*DDJ* 1, my translation)

Many passages in the *DDJ* take the position that the nature of the *Dao* cannot be put into words and that *Dao* is misrepresented if we try to give it a name (e.g., God, Nature, etc.). In talking about the inability to explain *Dao* and the inherent inaccuracy of putting a name to it, the masters whose teachings are embodied in the *DDJ* were pointing both to the numinosity and ineffability of the *Dao* itself and to the limitations of human language for describing it. But the *DDJ* continues to recognize some need to talk about *Dao* and its role in an understanding of reality.

> There is a thing chaotic yet perfect, which arose before heaven and earth.
> Silent and indistinct, it stands alone and unchanging,
> Moving it is tireless,
> We can take it as the mother of heaven and earth.
> I do not know its name.
> I have styled it "the Way" (*Dao*). (*DDJ* 25, my translation)

According to the *DDJ*, the *Dao* has a sort of power in itself from which all things have come:

> *Dao* produces the One;
> The One gives birth to two;
> Two produces three.
> Three produces all things (*wanwu* 萬物).
> All things shoulder *yin* and hold on to *yang*, and by blending these *qi* they
> attain harmony. (*DDJ* 42, my translation)

In this brief statement of creation in the *DDJ*, the text puts *Dao* prior to the first thing as a formless blank that produces instantiated things by a process of the movement of *yin* and *yang*, eventuating in the emergence of all the objects that populate and furnish reality. Moreover, there is a stated confidence expressed in the *DDJ* that the process of reality is at a minimum benign and even that it is good.

> *Dao* is like an empty vessel; No one could ever fill it up,
> > Vast and deep!
> It seems to be the ancestor of all things (*wanwu*).
> It blunts their sharp edges;
> Untangles their knots;
> Softens their glare;
> Merges with their dust,
> > Deep and clear!
> It seems to be there.
> I do not know whose child it is;
> It is the image of what was before the Supreme Spirit (*di* 帝)!⁶ (*DDJ* 4, my translation)

Chapter thirty-seven of the text says, "*Dao* moves by *wu-wei* 無為 yet nothing is left undone."

Wu-wei means effortless, spontaneous, non-intentional, nondeliberative movement. In other words, *Dao* is not working by a design through some intelligence; nor is it following a rational plan for reality. It is moving unintentionally and spontaneously. Yet, on the other hand, it is not leaving loose ends or causing problems, disorder, or confusion. Roger Ames calls this an "aesthetic cosmology" (Ames 1986: 317). In fact, it is untangling knots that humans create, and blunting the sharp edges caused by those that are resisting or moving contrary to *Dao*. In a very close association of *Dao* with Heaven (*tian*), the text says,

> Who knows why Heaven dislikes what it does?
> Even sages regard this as a difficult question.
> The Way (*Dao*) does not contend, but it is good at victory;
> It does not speak but is good at responding;
> It does not call but things come of their own accord;
> It is not anxious but is good at laying plans.
> Heaven's net is vast;
> Its mesh is loose, but it misses nothing. (*DDJ* 73)
> The Way (*Dao*) of Heaven plays no favorites;
> It is always on the side of the good. (*DDJ* 79)
> The *dao* of Heaven is to benefit and not harm. (*DDJ* 81, ibid.: 84)

When we look closely at the *DDJ*'s remarks about Heaven, they make it clear that an important move is made in Chinese ontology by thinkers in this tradition. Heaven's movements (i.e., its *dao*) are life furthering and full of benefit, but they occur without deliberation or any intentional predetermination by Heaven.

In the following passages of the other major classical Daoist text known as the *Zhuangzi*, these matters of ontology are expressed in a more literary way:

"May I ask about the piping of Heaven?" Ziqi said, "Blowing on [all the things that exist, *wanwu*] in a different way, so that each can be itself, all take what they want for themselves, but who [actually] makes the sound?" ... This comes close to the matter. Although I do not know what makes them the way they are. It would seem as though they have some True Master (*zhen di* 真宰), and yet I find no trace of him. He can act—that is certain. Yet I cannot see his form. He has identity but no form. (*Zhuangzi*, Ch. 2)

Chapter six in the *Zhuangzi* shows a clear affinity with the philosophical positions advocated in the *DDJ* with respect to *Dao*:

Dao has reality and shows signs but moves by *wu-wei* and has no form. ...
It is its own source, its own root. Before heaven and earth existed it was there, firm from ancient times.
It gave spirit to the numinal beings and to God (*shen gui shen di* 神鬼神帝).
It gave birth to heaven and earth.
It exists beyond the highest point,
        and yet you cannot call it lofty.
It exists beneath the limit of the six directions,
        and yet you cannot call it deep.
It was born before heaven and earth,
        and yet you cannot say how long it has been there.
It is earlier than the earliest time, and yet you cannot call it ancient.
(*Zhuangzi*, Ch. 6, my translation)

The Limits of Language about Ontology

A philosophical point made in the *DDJ* and the *Zhuangzi* is that the *Dao* is beyond our language. One reason why this is true is because language inevitably uses categories such as space and time. The text claims that we cannot say *Dao* occupies any space or that it has any temporal description (i.e., that it began at some point in time). As such, *Dao* functions as what philosophers call a "limiting concept." The concept itself marks the point at which human reason and language are exhausted. We cannot ask when *Dao* began, because time does not apply to it. Nor can we speculate about where it exists. Daoists recognized that when reason tries to cognize the ultimate nature of reality, it is always tripped up by its own categories (e.g., space, time, and causality).

The thinkers in the earliest Lao-Zhuang tradition were committed to the view that not only were change and process the most fundamental ontological principles of reality, but this also meant that transformation is at the root of ongoing life. Consider this passage from the *Zhuangzi*:

Master Si, Master Yu, Master Li and Master Lai were all four talking together … There was no disagreement in their hearts and so the four of them became friends … Suddenly Master Lai grew ill. Gasping and wheezing, he lay at the point of death. His wife and children gathered round in a circle and began to cry. Master Li, who had come to ask how he was, said, "Shoo! Get back! Don't disturb the process of change!" Then he leaned against the doorway and talked to Master Lai. "How marvelous the Creator (*zaohua* 造化) is! What is he going to make of you next? Where is he going to send you? Will he make you into a rat's liver? Will he make you into a bug's arm?" Master Lai said, "A child, obeying his father and mother, goes wherever he is told, east or west, south or north. And the *yin* and *yang*—how much more are they to a man than father or mother! Now that they have brought me to the verge of death, if I should refuse to obey them, how perverse I would be! What fault is it of theirs? The Great Clod burdens me with form, labours me with life, eases me in old age and rests me in death. So if I think well of my life, for the same reason I must think well of my death. When a skilled smith is casting metal, if the metal should leap up and say, "I insist upon being made into a Mo-ye [i.e., the greatest of all swords]!" he would surely regard it as very inauspicious metal indeed. Now, having had the audacity to take on human form once, if I should say, "I don't want to be anything but a man! Nothing but a man!" the Creator would surely regard me as a most inauspicious sort of person. So now I think of heaven and earth as a great forge, and the Creator as a skilled smith. Where could he send me that would not be all right? I will go off to sleep peacefully, and then with a start I will wake up." (*Zhuangzi*, Ch. 6)

The Daoist master who was the source of this passage spoke of *Dao* as a creator who controls the process of the transformation of things as does a great smith tending a giant forge. Later, though, the *Zhuangzi*, chapter fourteen, which likely had a different source than the above passage from chapter six, begins with a series of questions that seem to express some doubt about whether *Dao* may be itself thought of as a creator:

> Does heaven turn? Does the earth sit still? Do sun and moon compete for a place to shine? Who masterminds all this? Who pulls the strings? Who, resting inactive himself, gives the push that makes it go this way? I wonder if there is some mechanism that works it and won't let it stop? I wonder if it just rolls and turns and can't bring itself to a halt? Do the clouds make the rain, or does the rain make the clouds? Who puffs them up, who showers them down like this? Who, resting inactive himself, stirs up all this lascivious joy? The winds rise in the north, blowing now west, now east, whirling up to wander on high. Whose breaths and exhalations are they? Who, resting inactive himself, huffs and puffs them about like this? (*Zhuangzi*, Ch. 14, ibid.: 154)

The *DDJ* suggests in a number of places that some direct awareness of the presence of *Dao* is possible. The *DDJ* speaks of this awareness of presence by using the Chinese characters *huang hu* (恍惚), sometimes translated as "shadowy and indistinct" or "vague and elusive." We might associate this experience with the term "mystical," although there is no such term in the text itself.

> The form of profound virtue (*kongde*) comes from the *Dao* alone.
> As for *Dao's* nature, it is *huang hu*.
> *Hu*! *Huang*!
> There is an image within it.
> *Huang*! *Hu*!
> There is something within it.
> Deep! Mysterious!
> Within [*Dao*] is numinal energy (*jing* 精).
> This numinal energy is undeniably real,
> Within [this experience of *Dao*] lies its own proof. (*DDJ* 21, my translation)

From this passage, we get the clear sense that the person who is its source had some awareness of a presence he associates with *Dao*. Yet, there is no attempt to prove that such a thing is possible by means of the sort of reasoned argument we value in philosophy. Instead, there is an appeal only to the immediacy of the experience itself. In fact, in other places, the text insists, "Those who know do not talk about it; those who talk about it do not know" (*DDJ* 56). When the *DDJ* speaks of an "image" within *Dao* in the passage above, it actually does not mean that we have some "picture" of a being or thing in our minds that corresponds to the *Dao*. In chapter fourteen, the text says very directly that *Dao* is the "formless form," "the image of no thing." In that same chapter, *Dao* is associated with the adjectives invisible, rarefied, and subtle. Nevertheless, the text recognizes a kind of numinosity in the presence of the *Dao* by comparing it to the "inner sanctum" (*ao* 奥)[7] of reality (*wanwu*) (*DDJ* 62).

Just what puts one into a position in which one may have this experience of *Dao* is not explained in any comprehensive way in either the *DDJ* or the *Zhuangzi*. However, in the portion of the *Zhuangzi* anthology traceable to Zhuang Zhou's disciples, we find this passage:

> Confucius went to call on Lao Dan [i.e., Laozi]. Lao Dan had just finished washing his hair and had spread it over his shoulders to dry. Utterly motionless, he did not even seem to be human. Confucius, hidden from sight, stood waiting, and then after some time presented himself and exclaimed, "Did my eyes play tricks on me, or was that really true? A moment ago, Sir, your form and body seemed stiff as an old dead tree, as though you had forgotten things, taken leave of men, and were standing in solitude itself!" Lao Dan said, "I was letting my mind wander to the Beginning of things." … Confucius said, "I would like to hear by what means this may be accomplished." [Lao Dan replied] "… In this world, all the living things come together in One, and if you can find that One and become identical with it, then your four limbs and hundred joints will become dust and sweepings; life and death, beginning and end will be mere day and night, and nothing whatever can confound you." (*Zhuangzi*, 21)

A Synthesis of Classical Chinese Ontologies: *Masters of Huainan (Huainanzi)* (c. 139 BCE)

According to his biography in the *Book of the Early Han* (*Hanshu*, 44.2145) Liu An, the king of Huainan (in modern Anhui province) and uncle of Emperor Wu of the Han dynasty, was a man of wide-ranging interests, from natural philosophy to rhetoric and poetry. He gathered a large number of philosophers, scholars, and practitioners of esoteric techniques to Huainan in the period 160–140 BCE. They were supported in the creation of written works which would synthesize their views into a comprehensive worldview reaching from natural to political philosophy. The book *Masters of Huainan* (i.e., *Huainanzi*) was one product of this interchange of ideas. Gao You tells us the work was written collectively by a group of thinkers known simply as the "Eight Gentlemen (*bagong*)" of Huainan, and that Liu An was its General Editor.[8] But the *Masters of Huainan* is far more than a text simply gathering this and that point of view. It is an attempt to present and offer a harmonious truth about reality, the human being, and moral and political order.

For the compilers of the *Masters of Huainan* everything in heaven and earth (reality) is unified. There is no dualism such as between the natural and the supernatural, or objects and the patterned structures that give them coherence. Neither did the editors believe that seeing reality as meaningful is a subjective imposition of humans on the flow of *Dao*. Instead, identifying the presence of purpose and meaning in the course of reality is equivalent to recognizing the Principles (*li* 理) that reality has in and of itself and by which it moves. These Principles are presented as the philosophical basis for the conclusion that all real things adhere and function in harmony. In fact, it is only because of these Principles that the things which exist can serve as objects of human knowledge in the natural and even the social order.

However, in the *Masters of Huainan*, reality is not guided by a Being with a mind and intention. Reality "*daoes*," or courses along, spontaneously but, in doing so, displays patterns and purposes. In this text, if humans also act spontaneously (i.e., in *wu-wei*), rather than by their own concepts and beliefs, they will be one with "the *dao* of heaven and earth" and live in harmony, with an efficacy that fulfills their lives. When humans fall away from this normative natural process, and engage their own reason and passions to displace spontaneity, then disruption and destruction follow, both individually and socially.

We can recognize immediately from this summary the similarities between this account of the *Masters of Huainan*'s ontology and the Lao-Zhuang views. This is no mistake. In fact, the *Masters of Huainan* is often understood as giving priority to a specific stream of sentiments and beliefs called "Laozi-Yellow Emperor" teachings. Textual studies have shown that these ideas are already embedded in the *Zhuangzi* (Chapters 11–16, 18, 19).[9] A succinct statement of the text's sentiments which are closely aligned with those of Lao-Zhuang through the Yellow Emperor tradition is seen in this passage:

> As for the Way (*Dao*):
> It covers heaven and upholds earth.
> It extends the four directions and divides the eight end points (i.e. eight spatial relations).
> So high, it cannot be reached.
> So deep, it cannot be fathomed.
> It embraces and enfolds heaven and earth.
> It endows and bestows the formless.
> ...
> It is dark but able to brighten.
> It is supple but able to strengthen.
> It is pliant but able to become firm.
> It stretches out the four binding cords[10] and restrains *yin* and *yang*.
> ...
> Mountains are high because of it.
> Abysses are deep because of it.
> Beasts can run because of it.
> Birds can fly because of it.
> The sun and moon are bright because of it.
> The stars and timekeepers move because of it. (*Huainanzi* 1.1)

> Of old, in the time before there was heaven and earth:
> there were only images and no forms.
> All was obscure and dark, vague and unclear, shapeless and formless, and no one knows its gateway.
> There were two spirits, born in murkiness, one that established heaven and the other that constructed earth. (*Huainanzi* 7.1, ibid.: 240)

Here the *Masters of Huainan* is telling us that in the beginning of all beginnings, there was only shapeless, formless darkness and where that came from (what its "gateway" is), no one knows. It birthed two forces, one established heaven (i.e., it was *yang*) and the other earth (i.e., it was *yin*).

The *Masters of Huainan* makes a shift in explanation about just how things were made, and it is a distinction in the nature of *qi*. Representing an anthology of many divergent streams of thought, the work brings into its characterizations of *qi* the concepts of "heavy" and "light" as well as "clear," "bright," "turbid," or "muddy" *qi*:

When heaven and earth were yet unformed, all was ascending and flying, diving and delving.
Thus it was called the Grand Inception (*taishi* 太始).
The Grand Inception produced the Nebulous Void.
The Nebulous Void produced space-time [i.e., the cosmic process, *yu zhou* 宇宙];
Space-time produced the original *qi*.
A boundary divided the original *qi*.
That which was pure and bright spread out to form heaven;
That which was heavy and turbid congealed to form earth.
It is easy for that which is pure and subtle to converge but difficult for the heavy and turbid to congeal.
Therefore,
Heaven was completed first;
Earth was fixed afterward.
The conjoined [propensities] of heaven and earth produced *yin* and *yang*.
The scattered [propensities] of the four seasons created the myriad things.
(*Huainanzi* 3.1, ibid.: 114–15)

It is just one more step in this ontology to extrapolations made about the connection between the fundamental components of reality and the lives of human persons:

Joy and anger are aberrations from the Way (*Dao*); worry and grief are losses of Potency (*de* 德).
Likes and dislikes are excesses of the mind; lusts and desires are hindrances to nature.
Violent anger ruins the *yin*; Extreme joy collapses the *yang*.
The suppression of vital energy (*qi*) brings on dumbness; fear and terror bring on madness. (*Huainanzi* 1.14, ibid.: 66)
…
Sadness and enjoyment are aberrations of Potency (*de*),
Pleasure and anger are excesses of the Way (*Dao*);
Fondness and resentment are the fetters of the mind.
Therefore, it is said [that sages]
"In their lives, act in accord with Heaven; and their death, transform with other things.
In tranquility, [they] share the Potency (*de*) of the *yin*;
In activity, [they] share the surge of the *yang*."
Being calm and limitless, their quintessential spirit (*jingshen* 精神) is not dissipated amid external things, and the world naturally submits to them.
(*Huainanzi* 7.6, ibid.: 246–7)

In these passages, the *Masters of Huainan* is transmitting an ontology based on the correlational relationship between *qi* and human emotions and even moral dispositions. The emotional states of worry and sadness are caused by deficiencies of the *Dao's* potency (*de*).

If we draw out the implications of these teachings, we can conclude that the compilers of this text held that one way of living an emotionally and morally healthy life was to enhance *qi* energy, rather than to strengthen something called the will, as we find recommended by Western philosophers. This means that in this understanding of Chinese ontology there is an inexorable relationship between health and morality, a philosophical connection rather foreign to Western thinking.

> When the chest and belly are replete and lusts and desires are eliminated, then the ears and eyes are clear, and hearing and vision are acute.
> When fluctuating attention is done away with and the circulation is not awry, then the quintessential spirit (*jingshen* 精神) is abundant, and the vital energy (*qi*) is not dispersed.
> When the quintessential spirit is abundant and the vital energy is not dispersed, then you are functioning according to the underlying patterns (*li* 理) [of reality].
> When you function according to underlying patterns, you attain [calm stillness].
> When you attain [calm stillness], you develop penetrating awareness.
> When you develop penetrating awareness, you become spirit-like (*shen* 神).
> (*Huainanzi* 7.3, ibid.: 243)

The ontology of the *Masters of Huainan* expresses the interconnectedness of all phenomena in reality. One chapter is entitled "Heavenly Patterns" (*Tianwen*, 天文). The primary argument of this chapter is that human life and natural events make a unified whole when one acts according to Heaven's regularities. In the *Masters of Huainan*, everything in the universe is situated in a dynamic cycle of the relations of the Five Phases (*wuxing*) of *qi* that are constantly changing in their configurations, producing and reconfiguring all phenomena and events.

The "Great Plan" and the Five Phase Ontology

The "Great Plan" (*Hong Fan*) is a section of the ancient Chinese *Classic of History* (*Shujing*) constructed in the style of a dialogue between King

Wu of the Zhou dynasty and Prince Jizi, the last surviving member of the royal house of the Shang dynasty. This dialogue within the *Classic of History* probably dates to the Han dynasty about 200 bce, perhaps just before or at the time of the *Masters of Huainan*. The subject of the conversation is the "Way of Heaven" (*Tiandao*). In this dialogue, Wu states that human relationships and government must follow the organizing Principles (*li* 理) of Heaven, but he wonders how humans may come to understand these patterns fully. The sage tells him that he must understand the workings of the Five Phases (*wuxing*) of *qi* because when they are in disorder, the constant Principles (*li*) of Heaven will disappear and chaos will follow.

The Five Phase ontology refers to a conceptual scheme that is found in traditional Chinese thought. The Five Phases are wood (*mu*), fire (*huo*), earth (*tu*), metal (*jin*), and water (*shui*). They are regarded as dynamic, interdependent modes of *qi* expressing itself in the universe's ongoing existence and actualization. In Chinese ontology, all objects of reality are some combination and interdependent correlation of these Five Phases of *qi*. Although this fivefold scheme resembles ancient Greek discourse about everything being made from the four elements (earth, air, fire, and water), these Chinese phases are ever-changing *qi* substance, while the Greek elements typically are regarded as unchanging and fixed kinds of differing substances. In speaking of the nine divisions of the "Great Plan" by which Heaven orders reality, the text says,

> The first is called "using the Five Phases (*wuxing*)"; the second, "giving serious attention to the five (personal) matters/relationships (*wushi*)"; the third, "employing conscientious devotion to the eight (objects of) government (*ba zheng*)"; the fourth, "making harmonious use of the five [aspects of] time (*wuji*)"; the fifth, "establishing and using royal perfection (*huang ji*)"; the sixth, "being discriminating in the use of the three virtues (*san de*)"; the seventh, "the intelligent examination of doubts (*jiyi*)"; the eighth, "the thoughtful use of the various evidence (*shuzheng*)"; the ninth, "the guiding use of the five happinesses,[11] and authority over the six sufferings."[12] ("Great Plan," 2, Sturgeon 2019, my translation)

In what follows, the *Classic of History* breaks down each of these nine divisions of Heaven's "Great Plan." With respect to the first of Heaven's ways of ordering all things, it gives this explanation:

> *First of the Five Phases (wuxing) [of qi] is water; the second is fire; the third, wood; the fourth, metal; and the fifth, earth. [The propensity of] water is to soak and descend; of fire, to blaze up; of wood, to be capable of bending and straightening; of metal, to melt and reform; while that of earth is seen in seed-sowing and in-gathering. That which soaks and descends becomes salt; that which blazes and ascends becomes bitter; that which is crooked and straight becomes sour; that which yields and changes becomes acrid; and from seed-sowing and in-gathering comes sweetness. (ibid.: 3, my translation)*
>
> The "Great Plan" does not spell out how the correlations of the Five Phases work; it only asserts that they exist. It is made clear, though, that if humans do not behave in the proper manner, they throw the phases out of harmonious operation, illness and weakness arise in the body, and disorder shows up in nature and the human world of history. Employment of the Five Phase explanatory system is representative of early Chinese ontology as a naturalistic system that does not appeal to a transcendent or external source for the origin or process of reality.

In the Five Phase system, planets are related to colors, which are tied to political dynasties, which are connected to persons' actions (*Huainanzi* 8.9, 10). Consider how the text speaks of the legendary Five Thearchs and the Three Kings (Yao, Shun, and Yu):

> Looking downward, they observed earth's patterns in order to devise standards and measures. They investigated the suitability of mountains and plains, rivers and water meadows, rich and poor land, and high and low areas … Thereupon they clarified and outlined the [respective] natures of metal, wood, water, fire and earth in order to establish the affection [that should prevail] between fathers and sons to protect the family. They distinguished the high and low sounds of the five tones and the numerology of the mutual production of the six double pitch-pipe notes in order to establish the rightness [that should prevail] between rulers and ministers so as to perfect the state. They studied the successive order of the four seasons in order to establish the propriety [that should prevail] between elders and the young so as to perfect bureaucratic rank." (*Huainanzi* 20.11, ibid.: 805)

Han thinkers used the Five Phase system to account for an ordered sequence or cycle of change in reality's process. In this way, the patterns of replicating process in nature bear some similarities to what Western philosophers call "the laws of nature." For example, in the "mutual production" (*xiangsheng*) series of the Five Phases, wood produces fire, fire produces earth, earth produces metal, metal produces water, and water produces wood. In the "mutual conquest" (*xiangke*) series, wood conquers earth, metal conquers wood, fire conquers metal, water conquers fire, and earth conquers water.

The Five Phase ontology of change is, of course, nonfalsifiable. Trying to use empirical data to prove or disprove it, even on the very broad definition of empiricism that the ontology allows in itself, is philosophically futile. One cannot really specify the results that will follow from adhering to this worldview with any precision.[13] Attempts to account for why anticipated results using the Five Phase ontology in nature, medicine, personal life, or politics do not occur may be explained as traceable to an error in applying the components of the system or interpreted into an ever more complex physics of the phases. Either one of these approaches may be followed whenever the truthfulness of the system is challenged. This is the nonfalsifiablity of the Five Phase system.

As a heuristic, the Five Phase system may call forth many different responses. One obvious reaction is to choose to accept the entire model and commit oneself to master its processes and even manipulate them to one's own advantage. This was the approach taken by what were called the "masters of techniques" (*fangshi*). We know that a great many of such persons were assembled in Huainan at the time of the formation of the *Masters of Huainan* text. Some of their approaches undoubtedly found their way into the text. But another response to the Five Phase ontology also found its way into the work:

> I live within the world, yet I am also a thing in it. I do not know whether the things of the world are complete because of me or whether only without me are things not incomplete. However, I am also a thing and things relate to things. A thing is related to other things [by this underlying unity], so why must we be things to [i.e., objectify] one another? Even though this may be so, what gain is there in its [*Dao's*] giving me life; what loss is there in its taking my life away? Because what fashions and transforms us treats me as an unfired brick, I have no way to defy it. How do I know that to practice acupuncture and moxibustion and to desire life is not a delusion and to seek death by strangulation is not a blessing? Perhaps life is just servitude, and death is a respite from this toil. The world is vast: who understands it? It gives me life, but not because I intentionally seek it. It takes my life away, but not because I intentionally seek an end. Desire life, but do not strive for it. Detest death, but do not refuse it. (*Huainanzi* 27.5, ibid.: 245)

Buddhist Ontologies

Introducing Buddhism

The founder of Buddhism was Siddhartha Gautama, who is believed to have lived in the sixth century BCE in India. Although the time of his birth and death are uncertain, most modern scholars still date his lifetime between 563 and 483 BCE. Buddha is not Siddhartha's personal name. It is a title coming from the Sanskrit *budh*, meaning "to wake up," and it honors his experience as one who has awakened to the true nature of reality and his own being. He is also known as Shakyamuni, meaning "monk of the Shakya clan." His teachings, and those transmitted by his students, cluster around a set of basic philosophical ideas that intertwine ontological, epistemological, and moral concepts. Central among these are the Four Noble Truths, the impermanence of all things, the interdependency of causes, the karmic effects and consequences of deeds, and the cessation of the ego as nirvana. These concepts tend to reoccur and even define Buddhism wherever it may be found in all its diverse forms.[14]

The Four Noble Truths

The First Noble Truth states that "Life is *Dukkha.*" *Dukkha* is most often translated as "suffering," and it is by this "truth" that Buddhism teaches that the basic human problem is suffering. But *dukkha* may be more broadly understood than what is typically taken as suffering. More directly, *dukkha* means life is full of "cares and troubles" (Rahula 1974: 99–106). Try as we may, we cannot make people turn out right, do right, and so on. We encounter problems, things, and people who are unpleasant, and when life seems to be going well, it does not last, or it is not pleasant in the way we thought it would be. So, there is always some trouble, lack, or discontent that mars even our successes and accomplishments.

The Second Noble Truth represents the Buddhist explanation for the cause of *dukkha*. Why is it that our lives are unsatisfactory? The Buddhist answer is that the problem is within us, not out in the world or even in something that someone else does. Reality itself is not problematic or flawed. Reality simply is what it is. Our lives are unsatisfactory because of *Tanha. Tanha* is usually translated as "desire," and its root meaning is traceable to "thirst." Our desires pull us along and cause our suffering and discontent. If we are to be serene, our desires must be extinguished. It is important to notice that it is not merely our "evil" desires that must be eradicated, but even desires for things we might call "good." Such desires are still desires and they can cause us to suffer (ibid.: 95–7). It is desire itself, rather than only desire for evil, that is the cause of our cares and troubles.

The Third Noble Truth claims that cessation of desire occurs when our attachments to things and others are cut off. The key concept used to describe this cessation of desire is "nirvana." Nirvana can be understood to mean "blowing out a flame." So, by extinguishing the fire of *tanha* (desire), *dukkha* will cease. Our desires are eliminated (as one would blow out a flame) when our attachments to things and persons used to try to satisfy our desires evaporate. When this occurs, there is no more unsatisfactoriness (*dukkha*) in life, only the stillness of contentment remains. This means that nirvana is not a place such as Heaven, but a serenity that arises from the extinguishing of our desires, following on the breaking of our attachments. In many Buddhist schools, the last attachment to be severed is the most difficult of all, because it is connected to our most fundamental desire. It is the attachment to the self. Our clinging to the idea that we *are* or that we *have* a self that endures through time, and the desire to exist even beyond death must be abandoned if we are to be free from suffering (*dukkha*).

The Fourth Noble Truth names the ways or methods leading to nirvana as the Eightfold Path. The Eightfold Path is Right View, Right Intention, Right Speech, Right Action, Right Livelihood, Right Effort, Right Mindfulness, and Right Concentration. Although the path to nirvana is characterized as eightfold, Buddhist thinkers describe its width as like the edge of a razor. Moreover, the eight "Rights" of the path are pursued more or less simultaneously and not in a hierarchy and, taken together, the eight "Rights" mutually support each other. Nevertheless, the eight "Rights" may not be of equal weight in the realization of nirvana for every person. What most helps one individual may be of lesser value to another person. This means that the Eightfold Path is a symbolic concept for talking about the diverse ways in which individuals achieve enlightenment. The actual number of "eight" possible paths is not meant to exhaust the methods by which persons might achieve nirvana.

As an ideology, Buddhism did not arrive in China until about the first century CE. China also did not escape the diversity of Buddhist philosophical schools, although Leon Hurvitz (1999) and David Kalupahana (1976) have shown convincingly that for quite some time Chinese thinkers did not realize that the Buddhist texts coming from India represented different schools of thought and so they tried quite unsuccessfully to harmonize them into a coherent and single philosophical system. Gradually, Chinese thinkers also created some distinctively Chinese Buddhist approaches to the Four Noble Truths and even began some schools that were indigenous to China, several of which made significant contributions to ontological reflections in the history of Chinese philosophy. In what follows, we consider two schools of Buddhism that offer importantly divergent ontologies, one distinctly Chinese and the other an Indian tradition modified by its encounter with Chinese thinkers.

Reality Is One but Variously Experienced: *Tiantai* Buddhism and Zhiyi (538–597)

Unlike earlier schools of Chinese Buddhism the patriarchs of which could trace their lineages back to Indian teachers, the *Tiantai* School (*Tiantai zong*) was a new iteration of Buddhism that was entirely of Chinese origin. *Tiantai* flourished as a Buddhist school under its fourth patriarch, Zhiyi (538–597), who asserted that the *Lotus Sutra* (i.e., *The Sutra of the Lotus Blossom of the Subtle Dharma, Miaofa Lianhua Jing*) contained the supreme teaching of Buddhism. The school derives its name from the Tiantai Mountain that served as its most important monastic community and the one at which Zhiyi studied.

The most distinctive ontological claim of *Tiantai* is that there is only one reality, which is both the phenomenal existence of our everyday experience and nirvana itself. There is no transcendent dimension or place that exists apart from the reality we can and do experience in the here and now. There is no place known as "Heaven" or "Nirvana" which is different from our present reality.

Accordingly, *Tiantai* Buddhism was a significant divergence from early Buddhist teachings in India that drew a sharp demarcation between the phenomenal world of experience and the popular Buddhist thought of some supernatural location beyond this world and its suffering. In *Tiantai* the one reality which we experience and live is ultimately empty both of meaning and of lasting substance. The concept of emptiness is one which may seem rather unfamiliar and requires some explanation. The reason all things are considered empty in *Tiantai* thought is that everything is being produced and exists as it is only through an indefinite number of interdependent causes supporting it. Nothing has a nature or essence that underlies or enables it to exist apart from the interplay of all the interdependent causes which create it. If we take away these supports and relations, then there is no abiding essence to anything that exists. This is true not only of human beings, but of literally everything that exists. All things have only fleeting existence; everything is impermanent (Hurvitz 1999: 444).

Nevertheless, although all things are ultimately empty of any permanent essence or substance, humans and other beings are able to report conscious experiences of phenomenal reality as various forms of pain and suffering, happiness and contentment. In fact, *Tiantai* writings describe ten ways in which humans may exist in reality. In doing so, it is significant to notice that the descriptions of the ten ways of existing do not reflect any use of the kinds of extrapolations offered in other Chinese ontologies. That is, they do not make use of concepts such as *qi*, *dao*, *yin*, and *yang*, or the elaborate Five Phase system.

The first four of the ten ways of existing shown in the box are characterized by suffering and at least three of them are associated with pain and disorder brought on by evil, immoral living. The other ways of existing in reality are also related closely to moral life, including our attachments to others and to the objects of reality. For example, *Tiantai* teachers used the category of Voice-Hearers to describe those who have achieved nirvana (i.e., enlightenment) and are freed from their attachments and thus no longer suffer in their lives. Dwelling in nirvana, these persons do not occupy some other place in the universe. The Voice-Hearers exist here and now just as do all other things, but they live in a different state of

The Ten Ways of Existing in Reality according to *Tiantai* Buddhism

1. Hell Beings
2. Hungry Ghosts
3. Beasts (i.e., beings of animal nature)
4. Asuras (demons)
5. Human Beings

6. Gods or celestial creatures
7. Voice-Hearers (Skravakas)
8. Self-enlightened Ones (Pratyekabuddhas)
9. Bodhisattvas
10. Buddhas

consciousness gained by hearing and following the teachings of other enlightened ones. They experience reality in a different way than do the unenlightened. The Self-enlightened Ones gain the state of enlightened consciousness on their own, not by following the teachings of others, and they exist in a state of detachment from others and phenomenal things. But the Bodhisattvas grasp nirvana as release from attachments and the suffering they bring, and yet they continue to engage in this life out of compassion for others, in order to help them find nirvana as well. Finally, Buddhas move in this life in a way that can only be characterized as existing in nirvana itself and in a form of isolation from others. They are not focused on the condition of others, nor do they desire to help them reach enlightenment.

In *Tiantai* ontology, the reality that the hell beings inhabit is the same as that in which the Buddhas live. There is no supernatural boundary between these ways of existing or transcendent place to which some go (e.g., Heaven), while others dwell elsewhere (Hell). Living and working next to us may be one who is a hell being, or a Bodhisattva, or even a Buddha. The goal is not to depart this world and go into some other reality which transcends it. The goal is to move through life in a state of consciousness that is free from suffering, cares, and troubles. An individual who is experiencing pain or punishment for his misdeeds or desires need not wait for death to go to hell; he is a hell being right now. Getting clear on this teaching helps us correctly understand the meaning of Zhiyi's statement, "One thought contains three thousand worlds." Our thoughts may propel us to exist in reality in many ways, but this is not the same as saying that our thought is the *substance* of the world (Liu 2006: 283). A single thought can make our experience that of a hell being or that of a Buddha, but thought (idea) is not all that exists in reality.

On the way of living as a Buddha, the *Lotus Sutra* text, which was regarded as the chief philosophical source of the *Tiantai* School, reports the following:

After Buddha had finished bringing great benefit to living beings, he passed into extinction. After his correct law and counterfeit law had ended, another Buddha appeared in the same land. … This process continued until twenty thousand million Buddhas had appeared one after the other, all being the same name. (Watson 2002: 110)

Here we see the basis for *Tiantai*'s view that everyone has the capacity to live in reality as a Buddha and when this one's life is over, the person passes into oblivion just as all the other Buddhas before have done. A Buddha is not a supernatural being. The Buddha-realm is not some other place in reality or a different reality. *It is existing in a particular way within the one reality that is all there is.* Zhiyi wrote,

> To keep away from the mundane dharmas [concrete things] and yet seek the ultimate Truth [elsewhere] is similar to avoiding this Emptiness and seeking Emptiness elsewhere. The mundane dharmas [ordinary things] are themselves the ultimate Dharma [i.e., Ultimate Reality]. There is no need to forsake the mundane and adhere to the sacred. (Ng 1993: 166)

Tiantai does not deny that there is a physical reality. It is no Idealism. It is a form of *ontological realism*, a philosophical view that is confident that there exist manifold numbers of concrete things. But we cannot overlook the fact that for *Tiantai* philosophers, these concrete things are utterly interdependent on each other and each is in constant process, empty of any fixed or enduring substance. Likewise, Zhiyi insists, "We do not say that the mind exists first and the dharmas [bodies, objects] come to be later; nor do we say that dharmas exist first while the mind comes to be later" (Liu 2006: 285).

The ontology of *Tiantai* is a reflection of its understanding that Buddhism is not primarily a way to salvation, and neither was the Buddha a savior. The Buddha was a healer, offering a diagnosis, prognosis, and treatment enabling one to pass from being a hell being to find the serenity and peace of Buddhahood (Batchelor 1997: 6). The Buddhist dharma (teaching) is not something to belief in, but something to do. In detaching from others and things one extinguishes the fire of desire and suffering vanishes, a person may exist as a Buddha, and not as a demon or hell being (ibid.: 17).

Buddhist Idealism: *Wei-shi (Consciousness-Only)* Buddhism and Xuanzang (c. 596–664)

Xuanzang was a Buddhist monk, scholar, traveler, and translator in the early Tang dynasty who was largely responsible for the Chinese version of ontology known as Consciousness-only Buddhism. He spent more than ten years traveling and studying in India. When he returned to Chang'an (Xi'an) in China, he brought back 657 Buddhist texts and devoted the remainder of his life to a translation school he established in that city. Xuanzang's creation in China of the Consciousness-only School of Buddhism (*Weishi zong*) was greatly influenced by the writings of the Indian Yogacara master, Vasubandhu (fl. fourth to fifth century, Chinese name, Shi Qin). Xuanzang wrote an extensive commentary in ten volumes on Vasubandhu's text *Thirty Stanzas of Consciousness-Only*. Xuanzang entitled his work *A Treatise on the Establishment of Consciousness-Only* (*Cheng Wei-shi Lun*), and he used it to set out his own views of this tradition of Buddhist teaching (Wei 1973).

The central ontological tenet of Consciousness-only Buddhism is that nothing exists but consciousness. Of course, this is in direct conflict with early Chinese *qi* ontology, since, as we have noted, *qi* is an energy that may produce consciousness but is not itself a form of consciousness. Through the Five Phases of *qi* the myriad existing things of reality come into being. However, according to Consciousness-only philosophy, we experience a flow of ideas that we call perceptions. But these ideas or perceptions are not caused by concrete things external to us and which continue to exist whether we are conscious of them or not.

In philosophical language, the ontology of Consciousness-only is called *Idealism*. According to this philosophy, the objects of our mental experience occur in particular sequences, at particular times, ways, and places, giving us the idea of an ordered reality (Fung 1953: II, 321–3). Yet, there are no objects external to our minds which produce our ideas. Accordingly, all objects of our experience are empty, because they have no substance other than as objects of our consciousness.

When we are born, that is to say, when we come into awareness, our experience is not funded by an encounter with objects in a world external to us, but by something Xuanzang called the "storehouse consciousness." The storehouse consciousness is a bank of mental ideas gathered through all time. Every ideation that has ever occurred has entered into this storehouse. Likewise, every experienced ideation depends on other ideas for its appearance. No dharma (i.e., experienced idea) exists on its own and any alteration in the way other ideas cause it to exist makes it something different. This is called "dependent co-arising" in Consciousness-only philosophy.

Not all consciousnesses experience the same level of development. Some forms of consciousness are higher than others. The ideas experienced by some consciousnesses "perfume" the highest level of consciousness into being. JeeLoo Liu clarifies just what is meant by this claim:

> The notion of "perfume" is unique to the Buddhist theory of causality. Being in a room with bouquets, one's hair will slowly take on the fragrance; walking in the mist, one's clothes will gradually become damp. Analogously, anything that takes place will slowly but surely have a perfuming effect on its agent or later events. (Liu 2006: 215)

So, the awareness of certain ideas and their relation to each other can perfume into existence as human consciousness itself, and possibly ever higher life forms as well.

In its original context in India, the Consciousness-only teachings on ontology were direct contradictions to the prevailing Indian physics of reality, according to which all things of concrete reality (*dharmas*) were believed to be constructed from the atoms of earth, water, fire, and air. This meant that the traditional Indian explanation for what reality is like was a *materialist* one. Under this description there is nothing that cannot be reduced to physical matter in some combination or another. However, a classical version of the Consciousness-only argument against this Indian atomistic materialism has been stated by Liu quite well:

1 If a single atom is to be combined with other atoms to form objects, then it must have surfaces of contact with other atoms.
2 There are six sides of contacts: up, down, left, right, front, back.
3 Therefore, every basic unit is already a unit of six parts.
4 Therefore, there cannot be a single unit that is not further divisible (that has no parts).
5 Therefore, the very concept of an *atom* is unintelligible. (ibid.: 234)[15]

Regardless of how we might judge the cogency of this argument against the ontology of atomistic materialism, in China the basic theory of reality was built around the element of *qi*, and its energetic forces *yin* and *yang*, which were said to give rise to the Five Phases from which all things are made. There was no concept of material substance in its Western or Indian philosophical meaning in early Chinese ontology. The Five Phases are not made of matter; they are phases of *qi* which are experienced in a certain way (i.e., accessible through what we call our senses). Yet, in Chinese ontology, while not being matter, *qi* was thought of as a substance external to us that is more than, and other than, an idea in our minds. Thus the Five Phase physics prevented Chinese ontology from collapsing into Idealism. This significant difference in ontology partially explains why Consciousness-only philosophy did not gain much traction in China. The Chinese already had an ontology that seemed functional and it was left relatively unassailed by the main arguments against materialism made by Consciousness-only thinkers as summarized by Liu above.

There are philosophical difficulties with the Consciousness-only ontology of Idealism. Some of these can be revealed in the following questions:

- If reality is coextensive with my consciousness, why cannot I imagine a world to exist in whatever way I desire?
- Is the "storehouse consciousness" notion adequate to explain why an individual cannot generate ideas of whatever reality he wishes?
- Alternately, if reality is only the ideas of my consciousness, why cannot I simply dispense with a number of ideas that actually do not have the function I think they do (e.g., food relieving hunger, knives causing wounds, clothing keeping me warm)?
- If reality is my experienced consciousness, on what grounds can I know that there are other minds or other consciousnesses? Am I the only mind that exists (this is called *solipsism*)?

Because of its importance, we can consider how it was that Xuanzang handled what is known as "the Other Minds Problem." Xuanzang was concerned to make it clear that in speaking of "other" minds, he meant to refer to minds that are different than his own:

> If there were only one individual consciousness, how is it that there is a variety of ordinary people, saints, the honored ones and lowly ones, and causes and effects in the ten cardinal directions? Who would then expound teachings to whom? What dharmas could there be? And what goal is there to seek? (Chan 1963b: 391–2)

Unfortunately, Xuanzang seems to simply beg the question by assuming the case that he is trying to prove. If I held that there is only my own consciousness, I could continue to hold a perfectly coherent position by saying that the ordinary people, saints, honored ones, and the like are only ideas in *my* consciousness. To assume that they exist independent of me and must be explained is to presume what I have not yet proven. Given Consciousness-only ontology, ideas of these people are no more caused by actual other consciousnesses than is my idea of a pen or desk caused by some object external to me.

A Western View of Idealism

British philosopher George Berkeley (1685–1783) expressed his Idealist philosophy principally in his 1710 work, *A Treatise Concerning the Principles of Human Knowledge* (Winkler 1988), and the 1715 text, *Three Dialogues between Hylas and Philonous* (Berkeley 1979). In these works, Berkeley sets out the dictum that "to exist is to be perceived." Following this principle, he developed a philosophy of Idealism or Immaterialism according to which the only things that exist are the ideas that we perceive. These are not caused by anything made of matter. Berkeley thought some are caused by our own minds but the great majority of them, what we call nature or reality, are given to us by God. God gives these ideas in sequences and order, and we call this natural law. But natural laws are simply the patterns of the order in which God gives us our ideas. The hypothesis that there should be something made of a substance called "matter" that causes us to have the ideas we do, is therefore unnecessary and, in fact, incoherent. It is incoherent because we talk about matter, but we do not observe it. We observe blossoms, trees, and mountains, but not *matter*. Blossoms, trees, and mountains are ideas or images before our minds. Thus, we have an ontology of immaterialism or idealism.

Xuanzang's appeal to a theory of the storehouse consciousness will not enable him to avoid either solipsism or the problem of other minds. It will not do so because if there are no other consciousnesses and there are no other sentient things or objects, the entire notion of a storehouse consciousness is erased also. How would such a consciousness ever come to exist if mine was the only mind?

A further difficulty with Consciousness-only philosophy arises if we grant that there *are* other consciousnesses. The problem to which I refer is the quandary over just how it is that I could *know* that some other consciousness has the same experience that I do. Xuanzang seems to aggravate this problem with the following remark:

The consciousness is merely like a mirror, in which what seems to be an external sphere appears. It is in this sense that it is called the mind that discriminates another. But it cannot discriminate [another mind] immediately and directly. What it discriminates immediately and directly are its own transformations. (ibid.: 391)

This remark may be interpreted to mean that I never really know another consciousness at all, only those transformations in my own consciousness that appear and recede. If this is true, upon what basis can we believe in other consciousnesses at all? Xuanzang's use of the mirror analogy is also troubling. Mirrors reflect objects, but if reality is only the ideas of my own consciousness, there are not objects to be mirrored. So, the only source of my ideas in consciousness is my own mind.

The Study of Principles: Understanding the Content and Structure of Reality

The Supreme Ultimate as Reality's Principles: Zhu Xi (1130–1200)

In the early eleventh century, a group of interdependent Chinese philosophers began to reconstruct Chinese philosophy by using a new language. They sought to merge Confucian thought with Daoist and even Buddhist concepts.[16] While they surely thought of themselves as still Confucian, it is clear that these philosophers were doing something different and novel with their appropriation of classical Confucian ideas. Accordingly, they are grouped together and called Neo-Confucians.

The term Neo-Confucianism was first used by Western scholars for the twelfth-century adaptation of Confucian thought that displayed itself specifically in the Chinese philosophy of Zhu Xi (1130–1200), whose writings were extensive (J. Chen 2000). The Chinese term for this set of thinkers was *Daoxue* (i.e., Study of *Dao*). While there is still an ongoing debate about the usefulness of the term Neo-Confucianism; nevertheless, philosophers traditionally assigned to this movement do, in fact, use a similar philosophical vocabulary in their ontologies and interact with each other on their various answers to a similar set of questions about the nature of reality.[17]

Without doubt, Zhu Xi is the most influential of these thinkers. Indeed, he set the parameters of philosophical conversation on ontology throughout East Asia for over four hundred years.[18] Master Zhu's oral teachings to students are preserved in *Conversations of Master Zhu, Arranged Topically*

(*Zhuzi yulei*, hereafter *Conversations*) (Gardner 1990). Zhu Xi's extensive philosophical work rests on the foundation of his theory of reality. The place to begin in understanding his ontology may be quite succinctly stated in this way: Everything that has shape and form is "concrete existence *qi*" (器). That which constitutes the Principles (*li* 理) of "concrete existence" is the Way (*Dao*) (Rosker 2010).

We may wonder whether the Chinese term (*li* 理) we are translating as Principles is singular or plural. Actually, Principles is sometimes used as a singular and sometimes as a plural in Zhu Xi's writing. So, I will sometimes translate it as singular and sometimes as plural, depending on my understanding of Zhu's meaning. Those thinkers who react to his ideas and who are discussed below (Wang Yangming and Dai Zhen) also make multiple uses of this concept. So, to speak of "the" meaning of Principles in Zhu Xi or Neo-Confucianism as whole is to start out on the wrong foot. We must let the philosophical text speak for itself in each case, resisting the urge to reduce all uses of the concept of Principles to a singular one.[19]

We may also be puzzled about just what to include as Principles when Zhu Xi uses this as an ontological concept. Does Principles refer to something like the logical scaffolding of reality (i.e., figure/shape, causal efficacy, logical relationality, or pattern)? Could Principles mean something like the natural laws discoverable by chemistry, physics, and the like? Maybe Principles refers to what the Western philosopher Immanuel Kant called the "categories of the mind" (i.e., causality, space, time, etc.), which are neither objects themselves nor in objects themselves, but are our mind's own means of ordering and structuring things in order to create a world or a reality.

In Zhu Xi, the Principles are the Supreme Ultimate (*Taiji tu*) of reality. He expresses this claim in the following way:

> The Ultimateless! And yet also the Supreme Ultimate! [These words] do not mean that the Supreme Ultimate is a concrete thing glittering in a glorious manner somewhere. They only mean that in the beginning, when no single concrete object yet existed, there was then nothing but Principles (*li*) ... and because these Principles are multiple, therefore concrete objects [in the existing universe] are also multiple. (*Conversations* 94, 21–2, Fung 1953: II, 535)

If we are to pin down Principles, neither existence (*yu*) nor nonexistence (*wu*) may be attributed to them, because Zhu Xi holds that before heaven and earth existed, Principles already were there (Blakeley 2004: 239, f. 30).

Another way of saying this is that since "existence" *is* itself one of the Principles, we cannot speak of Principles as existing or not existing.

In his reply to a question from Qiang Yuanqin, Zhu Xi says, "the Principles (*li*) of the myriad things, brought into one whole, constitute the Supreme Ultimate (*Taiji*). The Supreme Ultimate did not originally have this name. It is simply an appellation applied [to the set of Principles]" (ibid.: 227). As Zhu Xi says above, the Supreme Ultimate is not an object, or "concrete something glittering in a glorious manner somewhere."

We may speak of the Supreme Ultimate as all Principles governing the Five Phases and the forces of *yin* and *yang*. When a concrete thing comes into being, it has its own distinct expression of the Principles. Thinking retrospectively, the Principles for anything that exists were already present in the Supreme Ultimate of the universe before there was any concrete object. Looking from the point of view of Principles, "although a certain object may not yet exist, the Principles for that object are already there. Thus there are already Principles even when objects do not yet actually exist" (*Collected Writings* 46.26, in Fung 1953: II, 536).

Fung Yulan interprets Zhu Xi in the following way: "In other words, what we call the invention of a boat or cart is nothing more than the discovery by man of the Principle that pertains to boats or carts, and the conforming to this Principle in order to create an actual boat or cart" (ibid.). In reading Zhu in this way, Fung takes him to mean that there are Principles for specific objects such as boats and carts of which humans become aware, enabling us to create them as concrete objects. He supports his reading by citing Zhu's comments that the bricks of a porch have within them the Principle that pertains to bricks and the bamboo chair contains the Principle of bamboo chairs (ibid.).

This reading brings Zhu Xi very close to a theory of archetypes or the much older Western philosophical ontology of Plato's view of the Forms. In Plato, the Forms are the ideal patterns for all things in reality according to which humans "make" chairs, but do so by conforming to the ideal form of chairness. The chairs we make imitate the "Form" of a chair, which the craftsman is remembering from a preexistent state prior to coming into this material world. A specific chair *participates* in the Form of *chairness*, which makes it a chair and not some other object, even if it does not look identical to all other objects we call chairs. In fact, Fung Yulan thinks that Zhu Xi's concept of the Supreme Ultimate consists of nothing more than the Principles of all things brought together in a single whole, and is very much like the Form of the Good that Plato understood as gathering all the Forms into itself. In his *A Short History of Chinese Philosophy*, Fung actually titles the chapter on Zhu Xi "The School of Platonic Ideas," pointing to similarities between Zhu's conception of Principles and the doctrine of Forms in the dialogues of Plato (Fung 1948: 294–306).

Plato's Characteristics of the Forms

1. Transcendent—The forms are not located in time and space.
2. Pure—The forms exemplify one property only.
3. Archetype—The forms are the perfect examples of the property they represent.
4. Ultimately Real—Only the forms are truly real, material objects are not.
5. Original Cause—The forms underwrite why anything is the way it is and they are the source of any given thing being what it is.
6. Interconnected—The forms are arranged from the more general to the particular, the objective to the more subjective, from the Good to the lesser values.

But Zhu Xi can be read in another way that I suggest is more accurate and which avoids Fung Yulan's overzealous use of the Western philosopher Plato to interpret a Chinese thinker. In my view, Fung's interpretation has created a misunderstanding of Zhu's position. Instead of thinking of Principles as Forms or archetypes for objects, with each thing having its own single Principle (e.g., chairness), we should not neglect Zhu Xi's comment in *Conversations* 4, where he makes it clear that "each individual thing possesses the entire Supreme Ultimate" or set of Principles (*Conversations* 4.10, Fung 1953: II, 552).

For Zhu Xi, Principles are something like categories of order or structures that underlie all that is. There is no actual specific Form for each different existing kind of thing as Plato and Fung think. When Zhu Xi says that the bricks have within them the Principles pertaining to bricks, he does not mean some archetypal "Form of brick." He means that bricks are bricks because they have the underlying ontological Principles that structure reality and in their particular Five Phase configuration they "brick" (as a verb). Zhu means that the Five Phase configuration that comes together as a brick does so by universal Principles. Accordingly, Fung's translation of *Collected Writings*

46.26 above should be revised to say, "Although a certain object may not yet exist, the Principles for the form in which it *can exist* are already there."

Regardless of whether I have this right or Fung is correct, we cannot deny that for Zhu Xi Principles *do not come from* concrete things and are not merely ways in which our minds structure reality. Rather, they *enable and structure* the existence of specific concrete configurations (i.e., of the Five Phases) to yield the myriad things that furnish reality:

> The Supreme Ultimate is thus made up of the Principles governing the Five Phases (*wuxing*) and the *yin* and *yang*, and so is not something "empty." If it were "empty" it would resemble the "nature" (*xing*) of things as termed by the Buddhists ... but Buddhists see only the external shell and do not see the many Principles that lie within. (*Conversations* 94.2, ibid.: 537–8, my modifications)

More to the point, Zhu Xi responds to questions in the following ways:

> Within the universe there are Principles (*li*) and *qi* (氣). Principles are the *Dao* that has no shape; they are the sources from which things are produced. *Qi* (氣) is what constitutes concrete existence (*qi* 器); it [*qi* (氣)] is what things are made of. Hence men or things, at the moment of their existence, must receive Principles to have a nature (*xing*); they must receive *qi* (氣) to have a concrete form. (*Collected Writings* 58.5, ibid.: 542, my modifications)
> Question: "In what way are Principles displayed through *qi* (氣)?

> Answer: When *yin* and *yang* and the Five Phases (*wuxing*) intermingle, but do not lose their proper order and succession, this is due to Principles. But if *qi* (氣) was not there to form objects, Principles would have no expression. (*Conversations* 94.10, ibid.: 543, my modifications)

> The transformations of *yang* and the congealings of *yin* thus produce water, fire, wood, metal, and earth. The *yin* and *yang*, which are *qi* (氣), produce the Five Phases, which are corporeal matter (*zhi* 質). Among the emergent things of heaven and earth, the Five Phases come first. The earth is composed of the element earth, with which there is also incorporated some elements of metal and wood. There is nothing in heaven and earth that does not combine the Five Phases. These seven, the Five Phases and *yin* and *yang* boil forth and combine with one another to form tangible objects (*zhi*). (*Conversations* 94.3, ibid.: 547)

Thus we see that according to Zhu Xi, the Five Phases produced by *qi* and Principles taken together yield the objects of reality.

In *Conversations* 94.3 above, Fung Yulan translates *zhi* as "corporeal matter." But this also creates philosophical confusion. To do this may well suggest to the Western reader that *qi* is something spiritual, whereas the Five Phases and other objects are material, creating a kind of *ontological dualism* that Zhu Xi does not intend at all. *Zhi* is not "matter" as though it were some other substance in addition to *qi*. Rather it is *the Five Phase configuration of* qi *that is in our sensory range*. That is it: full stop. In Chinese philosophy prior to the eighteenth century, there is no concept of "matter" as a substance that resembles the Western notion of something shaped so as to produce in us certain perceptions and ideas. Certainly we do have experiences of objects, but these are not made of some ontological stuff called matter; they are configurations of the Five Phases, which are themselves *qi*. So, the Chinese term *zhi* should be rendered "tangible objects." To misunderstand this ontological point is to hopelessly confuse any interpretation of Chinese ontology prior to the Modern period.

We must also consider Zhu Xi's ontology to be a form of *naturalism* rather than *dualism* or *idealism*. The Supreme Ultimate (i.e., the sum total of all Principles) is neither like the Form of the Good in Plato, nor God in the Western sense. However, neither is it reducible to, or the product of, the other cosmological operators that Zhu inherited from the earlier formations of Chinese ontology (i.e., *qi, yin, yang,* the Five Phases). Donald Blakeley has called the role and function of the Supreme Ultimate "transcendent" and has argued that it is required and integral to Zhu's ontology (Blakeley 2004: 223).

Blakeley might be right. For example, there is an important distinction between Zhu Xi's approach and that of the Western philosopher Immanuel Kant (1724–1804). Zhu does not say that the Principles that are the Supreme Ultimate are empty, as Kant says of the categories of the mind, by which he believes our mind organizes the flow of manifold things into a world of rational and empirical order, creating reality as we *must* think of it.

While Zhu does say that without *qi* Principles would have no expression and cannot be spoken of as either existing or not existing, where Blakeley seems right is in noticing that *Zhu Xi thinks of Principles as part of the fabric of reality and not merely how our mind must function to order our experience.* This is what Blakeley means by stressing the "transcendence" of the Principles.[20] They order and structure concrete things but do not depend on things, or derive from them, and they are not merely the structuring power of our minds. They have ontological standing as part of reality themselves. The world and its objects are made into what they are because these Principles are themselves actual features of reality. And yet, language about the Supreme Ultimate is not pointing to some special place, or object, or mind. It is Zhu Xi's way of talking about the fundamentally authentic genuineness of the Principles as features of reality.

Reality Is Given Its Structure by the Mind: Wang Yangming (1472–1529)

In *Instructions for Practical Living*, Wang Yangming wrote, "The fact is that in my own heart I cannot bear to contradict Master Zhu Xi but I cannot help contradicting him because the Way (*Dao*) is the way it is and the Way will not be fully evident if I do not correct him" (Chan 1963a: 164). Wang Yangming's stormy career was in large measure due to his opposition to the philosophy of Zhu Xi. In fact, in the Ming dynasty, Wang Yangming became the most deliberative of Zhu Xi's critics.[21]

Wang disagreed with the way Zhu Xi distinguished Principles (*li*) from the concrete things of reality, but still he did not place the Principles of reality within the concrete things themselves. He sought to bring Principles into the fabric of the nature and workings *of the human mind*, rather than as a feature of the objects themselves or as transcending the actualized Five Phase configurations we call objects, as Zhu Xi thought. Wang wrote,

> For the Principles of things are not external to the mind. If one seeks Principles of things outside the mind, there will not be any to be found. And if one neglects the Principles of things and only seeks his mind, what sort of thing would the mind be? The substance of the mind is its nature, and its nature is identical with Principles. (*Instructions*, ibid.: 94)

Wang is often wrongly characterized as an Idealist because of his emphasis on the role of the mind in ontology. As we have seen in our discussion of Consciousness-only Buddhism, Idealism is a philosophical worldview according to which reality consists only of immaterial ideas that we may think have some concrete or material existence as reality, but which do not. With specific reference to Chinese thought, Idealism is an ontology that denies the existence of concrete things made of the Five Phase combinations of *qi*.

Liu Shu-Shien examines the claim that Wang was an Idealist (Liu 2009b: 409–11). He calls attention to the two most important passages from *Instructions for Practical Living* that are often interpreted to mean that Wang thought nothing existed except the ideas of the mind:

The teacher [i.e., Wang Yangming] was roaming in Nanzhen. A friend pointed to flowering trees on a cliff and said: "[You say] there is nothing under Heaven and external to the mind. These flowering trees on the high mountain blossom and drop their blossoms of themselves. What have they to do with my mind?" The teacher said, "Before you look at these flowers, they and your mind are in the state of *silent vacancy*. As you come to look at them, their colors at once show up clearly. From this you can know that these flowers are not external to your mind." (*Instructions*, Chan 1963a: 222)

The other passage Liu considers is also taken from *Instructions for Practical Living*:

I said, "The human mind and things form the same body. In the case of one's body, blood and the vital force (*qi* 氣) in fact circulate through it and therefore we can say that they form the same body. In the case of other men, their bodies are different, and in those of animals and plants are even more so. How can they be said to form the same body?"

The teacher [i.e., Wang Yangming] replied, "Just look at matters from the point of view of the subtle incipient activating force of their mutual influence and response. Not only animals and plants, but heaven and earth also form the same body as me. Spiritual beings also form the same body as me."

I asked the teacher kindly to explain.

The teacher said, "Among the things under heaven and on earth which do you consider to [epitomize] the mind of heaven and earth?"

"I have heard that 'Man is the mind of heaven and earth.'"

"How does man become mind?"

"Pure knowledge (*liangzhi*) and pure knowledge only. We know, then, all that fills heaven and earth is this pure knowledge. It is only because of their physical forms and bodies that men are separated. My pure knowledge is the master of heaven and earth and spiritual beings. If heaven is deprived of my pure knowledge, who is going to look into its height? If earth is deprived of my pure knowledge, who is going to look into its depth? If spiritual beings are deprived of my pure knowledge, who is going to distinguish their good and evil fortune or the calamities and blessings that they will bring? Separated from my pure knowledge, there will be no heaven, earth, spiritual beings, or myriad things, and separated from those, there would not be my pure knowledge. Thus all is permeated with one force (*qi*). How can they be separated?" (*Instructions*, ibid.: 257)

Considering these two passages together, we can see why an interpreter might think that Wang Yangming was saying something similar to Idealism, that our minds have perceptions or ideas in front of them and that these ideas constitute the sole content of reality. For example, we may interpret the first passage as saying that reality consists of our ideas of a blossom, tree, and mountain. Taken in this way, Wang would be saying that our experience is of ideas and not of concrete things, a position similar to the Idealism of Consciousness-only Buddhism.

We may ask, though, whether this is really what Wang Yangming was trying to say. If we look carefully at the first passage, the student reminds Wang that he has taught that nothing exists outside of his mind. The student took this as an Idealistic remark, but finds such a view objectionable. He insisted that blossoms and trees operate without requiring any direction or action of our minds, so they must exist outside of our minds. But, then, we see Wang's point emerge in his reply and if we pay close attention, we will notice that *Wang was not an Idealist at all*. Unlike Idealism, Wang did not begin to talk about the cause of our ideas (i.e., perceptions) and whether it is our mind or consciousness. Instead, he made his position clear.

His point is that before we look at the flowers, they just are what they are in their raw being, they exist as they do in what gets translated as "silent vacuity." We may surmise that this is the state in which the concrete objects of reality exist simply in their brute facticity. *But, when we direct our attention (i.e., our minds) to the objects, they will be organized and named. They will become "flowers" and "mountains."* That is, they are made a part of a structured and coherent "reality" *by our minds*. Why is this? It is because our minds are inevitably, inherently, innately patterning or Principling everything experienced. Our minds Principle (*li*) (here used as a verb). It is this Principling or ordering that makes the brute flow of things (i.e., the "silent vacuity") into a "Universe" or a "Reality." Otherwise, while there are still concrete objects moving around, there is really no "World." To order things into a "world" or "reality" is the patterning activity of the mind. Wang was not denying the existence of concrete things as an Idealist would, but he was insisting that none of these things are "blossoms," "trees," and "mountains" without the ordering activity the mind brings to experience.

If we look at the second passage, Wang said that our bodies are of the same substance as that of animals and spiritual beings. What he meant was that all of these are made from the Five Phases of *qi* that compose all things. However, again he stressed that what distinguishes human beings is located in the activity of the mind. Our minds give order and pattern to heaven and earth (i.e., to all that exists). Our minds impose structure on the "silent vacuity." That structuring activity includes Principles such as causality, shape, time, pattern, and order. We might think of an ordinary analogy. Taking just a nondescript roll of cookie dough, it lacks shape and order. With the impression of a cookie cutter, figures, shapes, and even meanings occur. This is what the Principles of the mind do to the raw bruteness of existing concrete things. Meaning and order emerge by the mind's application of the Principles.

Immanuel Kant's Categories of the Mind

Immanuel Kant (1724–1804) was one of the most important philosophers in what is known as the Enlightenment period of Western Philosophy. He made many notable contributions to philosophy and his analysis of the way in which we experience and understand the world is presented most completely in the *Critique of Pure Reason* (1781/7) (Smith 1965).

Kant held that we have no direct experience with "the things-in-themselves" that furniture reality. In fact, he called the "things-in-themselves" the *noumenal* world. The world we actually experience, or the *phenomenal* world, is a result of the structuring that our mind does of the content it receives through the senses. This structuring activity is done through the categories of the mind, but this activity is not a conscious or deliberate process. In terms of our *sense experience*, the two categories of **space** and **time** structure all our perceptions, but we do not consciously decide to apply space and time to our sense experience. In terms of *understanding*, the mind has twelve organizing categories which manifest themselves in four modes: **Quantity:** unity, plurality, totality; **Quality:** reality, negation, limitation; **Relation:** substance-accident, cause-effect, reciprocity; **Modality:** possibility-impossibility, existence-nonexistence, necessity-contingency. In terms of *judgments* we make, again there are four modes: **Quantity:** universal, particular, singular; **Quality:** affirmative, negative, infinite; **Relation:** categorical, hypothetical, disjunctive; **Modality:** problematic, assertoric, absolutely certain.

Kant argued that the mind takes content from the empirical world and structures it according to the categories to make a *synthetic unity*. It is this synthetic unity that is our phenomenal experience. But what the world is like in-itself, without the structuring of the mind, we do not and cannot know.

There is some room for fruitful comparisons between the philosophy of Wang Yangming and that of Kant on how the mind structures data to create "experience" and "reality."

The Principles of which Zhu Xi wrote and which are applied by the mind according to Wang Yangming are what Wang calls "pure knowledge" (*liangzhi*). Wang used this term primarily in order to distinguish what the mind does in this process from what it does when consciously deliberating about or analyzing a problem. It likewise distinguishes the mind's work in Principling from what the senses do when they gather information coming from the external objects themselves through hearing, seeing, tasting, smelling, and touching. This means that the Principles are not known through the mediation of data from our five senses, by the authority of any book or philosophical teacher, or even by our own deliberation and choice to create and apply them. They are the mind's pure knowledge.

The Principles that are this knowledge are themselves empty. For example, "Cause" has no content in itself; it is a Principle brought to bear on the concrete things that are experienced. We cannot say what "cause" is in itself. We have no direct experience of anything like "cause." The same may be said for "space" or "time." We may say that "The book is on the desk." But we do not actually experience "on." The reason is that "on" is a spatial Principle employed by the mind; it is not an object in the world. Likewise, recall Wang's example, when these pure Principles are applied by the mind to experience, then things become such objects as blossoms and trees.

So, in both of these passages, although Wang held that our mind is the instrument of world-making and reality construction, he was not denying the existence of concrete things (*qi* 器) made from the Five Phases, as an Idealist would. Even so, there is a fundamental difference in Wang's position and that of Zhu Xi. Remember that we began this section with the quote from Wang that he did not want to contradict Master Zhu Xi, but he felt he must do so. Wang's difference from Master Zhu is that Wang *gives Principles no existence apart from the human mind.* Put quite simply, if there were no human minds, there would be no "World" and no "blossoms" either. Of course, objects as configurations of the Five Phases of *qi* would not vanish; but their brute existence would not constitute a "blossom," "World," or "Universe." Accordingly, Wang said:

> What is called your mind is that which makes seeing, listening, speaking, and moving possible. It is the nature (*xing*) of man; it is the Principles of Heaven (*tianli* 天理) … In its capacity as a master of the body, it is called the mind. Basically the original substance of the mind is none other than the Principles of Heaven. (*Instructions for Practical Living* 122, Chan 1963a: 80)

If we ask *how* it is that the mind Principles (here used as a verb) to make a world and if we can know whether the world actually exists as we Principle it to be through our minds, Wang's answer was that this cannot be resolved through reason and there is no sense experience of Principles to verify their reality. Instead, he said directly that the *how* of this Principling activity is what is meant by "pure knowledge" (*liangzhi*). It is direct, immediate, and experienced as cognitive certainty. We cannot step outside of the mind's "pure knowledge" to know anything about how the world is apart from our Principling activity. The most Wang would say is that Principling has its source in Heaven (*Instructions for Practical Living* 134, ibid.: 96). Indeed, "pure knowledge" is "the mind of the universe (heaven and earth)" (*Instructions for Practical Living* 179, ibid.: 166). It is "the Principle of Nature where the natural clear consciousness reveals itself" (*Instructions for Practical Living* 189, ibid.: 176).

Ontological Realism: Dai Zhen (1723–1777)

Chung-ying Cheng says that Dai Zhen was responsible for a significant shift toward naturalism and realism in Chinese thinking on ontology (Cheng 2009a: 460). Even so, Dai was still making use of the same vocabulary of philosophical concepts that Zhu Xi employed and was still trying to answer the same ontological questions: How do we account for the differences between appearance and reality? What is the source and basis for the objects, order, and structure we find in reality? Yet, there is a difference in the answers Dai offered, and there are important and worthwhile philosophical distinctions and clarifications he provides in his comprehensive works (Dai 1980).

As a conversational partner with the Neo-Confucians, Dai, like Wang Yangming, was seeking to correct and amplify Zhu Xi's ontology. Dai completely removed the transcendent aspect from Principles (*li*) that was present in Zhu's understanding of the Supreme Ultimate. Making this philosophical move certainly represented something like the shift from Zhu's understanding Chung-ying Cheng points to. In fact, in his *Prolegomena* (*Xuyan*) Dai says bluntly that he can find no evidence for separating Principles and *qi*, but traces this division back no further than to Zhu Xi (Lee 2006: 152). Wang Yangming had also departed from Zhu's understanding of Principles as transcendent by identifying them with the workings of the human mind. It was just at this point precisely that Dai differed from Wang Yangming. So, although both Wang and Dai departed from Zhu Xi's ontology, they took different paths in doing so.

Unlike Wang, Dai did not consider Principles to be independent of objects and imposed on experience by the mind. He did not argue, as Wang had done, that the human mind is the ordering and structuring mechanism for realty. Instead, Dai argued that language about Principles was a way of talking about the actual and real order (*tiao*) and differentiation (*fenli*) of the objects that furniture reality. Principles are the *internal textures of things*, the arrangements and *order of the way the object itself is constituted*. In making this move, Dai completely naturalized Principles in a way that Wang did not, locating them in the concrete existing things of our experience and not as patterning structures coming from our minds.[22] Dai says,

> The word Principles (*li*) is the name assigned to the arrangement of the parts of anything which gives the whole its distinctive property or characteristic, and which can be observed by careful examination and analysis of the parts down to the minutest detail. This is why we speak of the principle of [differentiation between things] (*fenli*) … This is called order and arrangement. (Chin and Freeman 1990: 69)

What we have in Dai's philosophy may be called *ontological realism*, according to which objects themselves, in their Five Phase configuration, possess and display the Principles. The Principles do not exist prior to objects as in Zhu Xi, but neither are they the operations of our minds on brute objects as in Wang Yangming (Lee 2006: 158). The Principles come into being *with* the concrete objects of reality; the two are inseparable.

Some Implications of Ontological Realism

There are various ways in which ontological realism shows itself in Western philosophy and many of these have been challenged with vigor. Ontological realism is often understood as a form of *descriptivism*. What this means is that concepts often taken as subjective interpretations or perceptions belonging only to the perceiver actually are references to objectively real properties possessed by objects, persons, or behaviors. An often used example is color. It is commonly thought that color perceptions and the words we use of them are subjective. But in descriptivism color words actually point to features of the object. They are not merely products of subjective perceptions in which one person calls a piece of cloth "blue" and another insists it is "grey." Descriptivism with respect to color is built on the idea that there are real structures in objects that are objective and quite apart from any subjective feeling, cultural upbringing, or the like. These objective structure or properties of objects do, in "normally functioning humans," give rise to the color perceptions that we label with color words. The point is that color language is traceable back to the world of objects themselves (properties of objects). Disagreements over whether to use a particular color term might be traceable to such things as variances in how the context (e.g., light) is interacting with the object's structure, or disabilities in a given human's senses, or simple error. An overview of these issues relevant to the present discussion is Darwall, Gibbard, and Railton (1992).

It may be obvious now why ontological realism is both an interesting and a controversial philosophical viewpoint, but one further movement in the application of this ontology was important to both Dai Zhen and Western philosophers. David McNaughton illustrates this move in his work *Moral Vision* (1991). He builds a philosophy of moral realism on the analogy with color and makes it possible to argue that moral virtues such as kindness, courage, spite, and so forth arise from the real properties of persons. This is a place in which philosophical content on ontology and that of morality overlap. Descriptivism in ethics is a view, according to which moral language refers (or, is intended to point to) to the world and not one's subjective interpretation of it (Horgan and Timmons 2000: 124). Accordingly, Nicholas Sturgeon (1986) and others have investigated the question whether moral statements may be considered true or false, strictly as descriptions of the world. One prominent recent Chinese philosopher who insists that moral statements refer to realities independent of human opinions and ideas was Tang Junyi (1909–1978). Tang held that the apprehension of moral properties of persons and conduct could occur independent of one's culture and worldview as an immediate perception where one is trained to observe reality clearly. (Frohlich 2017: 138–9)

According to Dai, even an understanding of the teleology of the universe (i.e., the order, purpose, and design of reality) is not imposed on the course of *Dao* from the outside by interpretations made by human beings (minds). Neither is the teleology of reality derived from a transcendent realm that is wholly other than the natural process itself (i.e., in God, an objectified

Dao, or even the Supreme Ultimate). Instead, it is a part of the very nature of concrete existing things-in-themselves. Reality's order and design is *displayed* and not imputed. So, it can be counted on, not because it is created by a supreme intelligence or a transcendent mind, but simply because the process of reality (*Dao*) is self-ordering and self-purposing and it shows its order and purpose for humans to discover and observe, and then to put into language; just as Principles may be observed by humans.

Design and Order in Reality: The Blind Watchmaker

In Western philosophy a famous argument used by such philosophers as St. Thomas Aquinas (1225–1274) and William Paley (1743–1805) as a proof for the existence of God is called "the Design Argument." Paley's version of the argument compares the operations of nature and the universe to the intricacies of a watch. Just as we would not conclude upon finding a watch in the field that it simply came to exist without a maker or designer because of the symmetry of its parts and sophistication of operation; likewise, the objects of the universe display an intricacy that is not explainable without an appeal to a maker or creator.

In contrast, Dai Zhen's view that the process of reality (*Dao*) contains its own order and structure may be compared to Western evolutionary science since the publication of Charles Darwin's *Origin of Species* (1859). One well-known work describing evolutionary theory to those who are not scientists is Richard Dawkins's *The Blind Watchmaker: Why the Evidence of Evolution Reveals a Universe without Design* (1986).

In brief, Dawkins's argument in this book is that the *appearance* of design may be explained as a result of cumulative natural selection. We might consider as an example an observation often taken to support the claim that the universe is the product of an intelligent mind, creating things according to a design and purpose. For example, all the planets in our solar system are at just the right distance, possess just the right mass, and move at just the right speed to remain in orbit around our sun. Even very minute changes in distance, mass, or speed could result in a radical alteration of what our solar system looks like or even its destruction. Those accepting the design argument for God's existence understand these facts as evidence of an intelligent creator. But is this really proof of intelligent design?

Dawkins explains that this state of affairs is the result of "cumulative natural selection." What he means is that over time, all the other objects that could not remain in orbit around the sun because of their distance, speed, and mass have already long ago vanished, leaving only the "survivors." All the current planets exhibit "just the right" traits necessary to stay in orbit, because if they did not, they would have long ago vanished as well.

Imagine that the end-product of one generation of selection is the starting point for the next generation of selection and so on for many generations. In this case, without considering the cumulative effect of the natural processes at work which leave the "survivors," we instead conclude that the arrangement of the solar system (the "survivors") must have been the result of a design. Interpreters who support the claim that the solar system is designed often misunderstand this feature of evolutionary science and think only in terms of "single-step selection."

Single-step selection means that instead of thinking of the current reality as the result of a long process of selections affecting each other, there was a one-time placing of the planets as they now are and this could not have occurred except by the decisions and guidance of an intelligent mind. But Dawkins holds that this order has come strictly from the operation of natural processes over many cumulative selections. When Dawkins's interpretations are applied to genetics, they can be used to account for the development of species, rationality, and other results normally thought to be inexplicable without an intelligent creator and designer.

Of course, Dai Zhen did not have the scientific sophistication of Dawkins or contemporary evolutionary scientists, but he does offer another approach to order and design that also is a naturalistic one, making no appeal to a supreme intelligence or creator.

Dai's position may be explained by means of a rather distinctive Chinese example. A method used to determine the authenticity of a piece of jade in China is to hold it up to the light and observe whether veins can be seen in its translucence. If so, the jade is authentic. If not, it is an imitation, a fake. By analogy, we may think of Dai as arguing that concrete objects themselves have such striations within and these are Principles (*li*) that exemplify order, purpose, and meaning. Dai uses the technical term *xingerxia* ("below or within form") to say that Principles arrive with the object's appearance and give it coherence. In this case, Dai's approach may be contrasted with that of Richard Dawkins, because Dai believes that objects actually contain in themselves ordering Principles that enable them to express the process of reality (*Dao*) as they do. Objects have an order (*tiao*) in their internal arrangements that also structures the way the object is constituted and fits with the other objects that furniture reality. Dawkins's way of accounting for the appearance of order through cumulative selection does not focus on any internal Principles in objects, but only in their external interactions with other objects.

Holding his position that concrete objects contain in themselves the Principles of order and structure required Dai Zhen to explain just how it is that *qi* can possess Principle (*li*), since *qi* is the actual stuff from which all concrete things in reality are made. In order to do this, he approached the concept of *qi* very analytically. He said that for any given object, such as the human being, *qi* takes a certain tangible form (*pinwu* 品物). This tangible form distinguishes one thing from another. Dai held that *qi* and *li* (Principles) account for the objects that furniture reality and no explanation other than the natural workings of these forces was needed.

Shifting Paradigms in Chinese Theories of Reality

Arrival of Western Philosophies

With the arrival of Western Christian missionaries in the late sixteenth century, China came into sustained contact with Europe and America, and Chinese intellectuals began to believe that the West had overtaken China in various scientific and technological fields. Accordingly, to facilitate their relations with Chinese officials and literati, the Western Christian missionaries translated works of Western science and technology as well as Christian texts into Chinese. Between 1582 and 1773, more than seventy missionaries of various nationalities undertook this kind of work.[23] The missionaries were assisted by Chinese collaborators. For example, Xu Guangqi assisted Matteo Ricci when he translated Euclid's *Elements* in 1607. Ricci and Li Zhizao (1565–1630) introduced the Chinese to classical Western logic via a Portuguese university-level textbook brought to China in 1625.[24] In collaboration with the Chinese scholar Li Zhizao, Portuguese missionary Fu Fanji (Francisco Furtado, 1587–1653) translated two Western works into Chinese. They were *Huan you quan* (*On Heaven and Earth*), a translation with scholarly commentaries of Aristotle's *De Coelo et Mundo* (*On the Heavens*), and *Ming li tan* (*Inquiries into the Principles of Names*), a partial free translation of Aristotelian logic. The most general effect of these early translations was that China opened to Western knowledge in science. Among all these currents of thought, the most dramatic impact was the effect on Chinese ontologies caused by the infusion of Darwinian evolutionary science that greatly influenced Chinese intellectuals.

Tianyanlun, the Theory of Evolution: Yan Fu (1853–1921)

After the first Sino-Japanese War of 1894–5, Yan Fu, who studied in England from 1877 to 1879, became the most influential translator of Western works in China. Although Darwinian evolutionism had been introduced into China prior to Yan Fu's translation of T. H. Huxley's *Evolution and Ethics* in 1898 (known in Chinese as *Tianyanlun*, *Theory of Evolution*), Yan's translation dramatically shifted the axis in Chinese ontology toward Western science and a revision of the historic grammar and explanatory language with which Chinese had operated for over 2,000 years.

This new scientific Western ontology made no use of the traditional Chinese operators, such as *qi*, *yin* and *yang*, and the Five Phases. Moreover, in contrast to China's correlative physics that valorized harmony and mutual interdependence of natural forces, the new Western ontology was a conceptual framework employing the mechanisms of "survival of the fittest," "struggle for adaptation," and "natural selection."

One might think that the infusion of Western scientific evolutionary theory that included empirical observation of competition and theories of the transmission of dominant characteristics of cognitive and biological developments required the complete abandonment of traditional Chinese ontologies, and that Yan Fu's translation represented the herald of such change. However, the actual situation was much different. Vincent Shen has done an extensive analysis of Yan Fu's version of Huxley's work, and he argues that Yan did much more than translate *Evolution and Ethics* in some literal way. According to Shen, Yan Fu transformed Huxley's work by infusing into his translation the Chinese ontological concepts and sentiments in which he was steeped. Yan had the sense that Chinese ontology, going all the way back to the *Yijing*, always made room for process, creativity, novelty, and productivity. Even Daoist ontologies of transformation (*hua* 化) could be interpreted as evolutionary in force. Moreover, the Darwinian notion of environmental adaptation as an explanation for evolution was not totally absent from classical Chinese ontology either. In Neo-Confucian thought, as we have seen, the Great Ultimate was understood to have launched a dynamic process of interaction between movement and tranquility, first in the forces of *yin* and *yang*, then in the Five Phases, the combinations of which gave rise to the myriad of real things (Shen 2015: 55–7).

While Yan Fu made a remarkable contribution to Chinese philosophy in his translation, he was still quite attached to previous Chinese ontological language and conceptualization. His most important contribution was not the translation itself, but what Shen calls "the reconstruction of Huxley's discourse to adapt it to the current needs of the Chinese people" (Shen 2015). Shen argues that it was left to Ma Junwu (1881–1940), who translated Darwin's *The Origin of Species* into Chinese (1920), to offer a rendering of the paleontological, geographical, botanic, and zoological technical terms into good Chinese (ibid.: 16).

The New Scientific Credo about Reality: Hu Shi (1891–1962)

It was Hu Shi who completed the shift toward Western ontology begun by Yan Fu. The development of Hu Shi's ontology began while he was studying in Shanghai and with his own reading of Huxley's *Evolution and Ethics*, Darwin's *The Origin of Species*, and other works of Western science that Yan and Ma Junwu had translated. He told of the profound influence these works had on him:

> It was these essays which first violently shocked me out of the comfortable dream that our ancient civilization was self-sufficient and had nothing to learn from the militant and materialistic West except in the weapons of war and vehicles of commerce. They opened to me, as to hundreds of others, an entirely new vision of the world. (Chou 1995: I, 91)

Like many other Chinese intellectuals, Hu Shi looked to the development of science and its methods as the most important contribution Western civilization could make to China (Hsu 1995). He stayed engaged with Western learning throughout his career (Hu 1921). While still a young student in Shanghai, he summarized the changes in his conception of reality and the universe in what he entitled "New Credo." Although it was published in 1923, he continued to hold its views until the end of his life (Hu 2002). This text reads as follows:

1 On the basis of our knowledge of astronomy and physics, we should recognize that the world of space is infinitely large.

2 On the basis of our geological and paleontological knowledge, we should recognize that the universe extends over infinite time.

3 On the basis of all our verifiable scientific knowledge, we should recognize that the universe and everything in it follow natural laws of movements in change. So, what is "natural" in the Chinese sense of "being so of its self" requires no need for the concept of a supernatural Ruler or Creator.

4 On the basis of the biological sciences, we should recognize the terrific wastefulness and brutality in the struggle for existence in the biological world, and consequently the untenability of the hypothesis of a humane Ruler.

5 On the basis of the biological, physiological, and psychological sciences, we should recognize that man is only one species in the animal kingdom and differs from the other species only in degree, but not in kind.

6 On the basis of the knowledge derived from anthropology, sociology, and the biological sciences, we should understand the history and causes of the evolution of living organisms and of human society.

7 On the basis of the biological and psychological sciences, we should recognize that all psychological phenomena could be explained through the law of causality.

8 On the basis of biological and historical knowledge, we should recognize that morality and religion are subject to change, and that the causes of such change can be scientifically studied.

9 On the basis of our newer knowledge of physics and chemistry, we should recognize that matter is full of motion and not static.

10 On the basis of biological, sociological and historical knowledge, we should recognize that the individual self is subject to death and decay. But the sum total of individual achievement, for better or for worse, lives on in the immortality of the Larger Self.

11 That to live for the sake of the species and posterity is religion of the highest kind; and that those religions that seek a future life either in Heaven or in the Pure Land, are selfish religions. (Hu 1931: 260–3)

What we see in Hu Shi is a different sort of naturalism than that of Dai Zhen. Hu's commitment was to the experimental sciences, and he represented a turn away from traditional Chinese ontology and its vocabulary. He observed,

> In this naturalistic universe, in this universe of infinite space and time, man, the two-handed animal whose average height is about five feet and a half and whose age rarely exceeds a hundred years, is indeed a mere infinitesimal microbe. In this naturalistic universe, where every motion in the heavens has its regular course and every change follows laws of nature, where causality governs man's life and the struggle for existence spurs his activities—in such a universe man has very little freedom indeed. (Chou 1995: I, 99)

Hu Shi's ontology set aside the Chinese grammar of *qi, yin, yang, li, dao*, and the Five Phases. He turned toward a new scientific vocabulary. Hu thought reality is potentially entirely understandable by science. It does not possess some transcendent mystery or meaning. But the wonder of the universe is the human being in both its fragility and its activity.

Chapter Reflections

We are now in a position to make some remarks reflecting on the various approaches to ontology evident in our survey of Chinese thinkers and texts. One thing we can notice in the beginning is that Chinese philosophers up to the period of Hu Shi all defended the position that reality was composed of *qi*, an energy phenomenon, moved by forces called *yin* and *yang* to create five phasal manifestations that make up the objects of reality. The ontology we have covered has a larger view of the nature of reality because not everything that is real is accessible through our five senses. More things are real than our senses recognize. For Chinese ontology, this meant that there was no need to distinguish the natural and the supernatural as we find it in Western philosophy. There is only natural reality, but some existing things are in a phasal configuration that our senses do not recognize. Just because they are not identified by our senses, this does not mean such phenomena are unreal. This means also that Chinese ontology does not fit well into the categories employed when describing Western philosophy: monism, dualism, pluralism. Everything is *qi*, but it configures into the many objects of reality.

While *qi* is in constant process and change, nevertheless there is enough continuity to identify objects and even for some existing things to develop consciousness. Still, objects do not have any fixed substance underlying their appearance. There is no pure *qi* without expression as some combination of the Five Phases. The process of concrescence of objects evidences certain patterns (i.e., "Heavenly patterns, *tianli*) or Principles (*li*) which are often characterized as "natural laws" (including cause–effect, space, time, etc.) in Western philosophy. Chinese thinkers differ on whether these Principles are attached to and inhere in the objects themselves (Dai Zhen), originate from the human mind and structure the brute facticity of objects (Wang Yangming), express only ideas before our minds (*Wei-shi* or Consciousness-only Buddhism), or have a real and transcendent existence (Zhu Xi).

We find some ambivalence or, more precisely, two different approaches to the question of whether reality has a creator or "mastermind" and both show up in the *Zhuangzi*. Nevertheless, in that text as in the other philosophers discussed in this chapter, although we might be inclined to think there is a mind guiding reality, "he" cannot be found (e.g., *Zhuangzi*, chs. 2 and 14). In Chinese ontologies, reality is its own cause and is self-moving, exhibiting nevertheless patterns of action, although these are not intentional or expressions of any deliberate purpose or will.

Chinese philosophers, especially Daoists and Buddhists, take reality just as it is to be without flaw or evil. It is human reaction to the process of reality that causes suffering (Buddhism) and ties our lives in knots and tangles (Daoism). In Daoism this takes the form of the distinctions that we invent such as success, failure, beauty, ugly, evil, and the good. The *Dao* knows, in itself, none of these. When one empties herself of these distinctions, *Dao* shows itself for what it is and life is made free and easy. In Buddhism, if we attach ourselves to things and others, we will experience desire and then we will suffer. Only by extinguishing these attachments to ideas and other persons can we become like still water, not turbulent but serene.

Additional Readings and Resources

Ames, R. (1986), "Taoism and the Nature of Nature," *Environmental Ethics*, 8 (4): 317–50.

Arjo, D. (2011), "*Ren Xing* and What It Is to Be Truly Human," *Journal of Chinese Philosophy*, 38 (3): 455–73.

Batchelor, S. (1997), *Buddhism without Beliefs*, New York: Riverhead Books.

Blakeley, D. (2004), "The Lure of the Transcendent in Zhu Xi," *History of Philosophy Quarterly*, 21 (3): 223–40.

Chan, W. (1964), "The Evolution of the Neo-Confucian Concept Li 理 as Principle," *Tsing Hua Journal of Chinese Studies*, New Series 4 (2): 121–48.

Chang, R. (2000), "Understanding *Di* and *Tian*: Deity and Heaven from Shang to Tang," *Sino-Platonic Papers*, 108: 1–54.

Cheng, C. (2009b), "The *Yi-jing* and Yin-Yang Way of Thinking," in B. Mou (ed.), *History of Chinese Philosophy*, 71–106, New York: Routledge.

Dawkins, R. (1986), *The Blind Watchmaker: Why the Evidence of Evolution Reveals a Universe without Design*, New York: W. W. Norton.

Flanagan, O. (2011), *The Bodhisattva's Brain: Buddhism Naturalized*, Cambridge, MA: MIT Press.

Fraser, C. (2014), "The Mohist Conception of Reality," http://cjfraser. net/2013/02/21/chinese-metaphysics-conference/. Accessed February 21, 2020.

Fung, Y. (1953), *A History of Chinese Philosophy*, 2 vols., Princeton, NJ: Princeton University Press.

Gardner, D. (1995), "Ghosts and Spirits in the Sung Neo-Confucian World: Chu Hsi on Kuei-shen," *Journal of the American Oriental Society*, 115 (4): 598–611.

Hu, S. (1931), "My Credo and Its Evolution," in H. G. Leach (ed.), *Living Philosophies: A Series of Intimate Credos*, 235–63, New York: Simon and Schuster.

Hu, X. (2002), "Hu Shi's Enlightenment Philosophy," in C. Cheng and N. Bunnin (eds.), *Contemporary Chinese Philosophy*, 82–102, Oxford: Blackwell Publishing.

Liu, J. (2006), *An Introduction to Chinese Philosophy: From Ancient Philosophy to Chinese Buddhism*, Oxford: Blackwell.

Mou, B., ed. (2008), *History of Chinese Philosophy*, New York: Routledge.

Nivison, D. (1996), "Two Kinds of 'Naturalism': Dai Zhen and Zhang Xuecheng," in B. Van Norden (ed.), *The Ways of Confucianism: Investigations in Chinese Philosophy*, 261–82, Chicago: Open Court.

Pinker, S. (2003), *The Blank Slate: The Modern Denial of Human Nature*, New York: Penguin.

Shaughnessy, E., trans. (1997), *The I Ching: The Classic of Changes*, New York: Ballatine Books.

Shun, K. (2006), "Dai Zhen on Nature (*Xing*) and Pattern (*Li*)," *Journal of Chinese Philosophy*, 41 (1–2): 5–17.

Sturgeon, D., ed. (2019), "Great Plan," in *Classic of History, The Chinese Text Project*, http://ctext.org/shang-shu/great-plan. Accessed February 3, 2020.

Wang, R. (2012), *Yinyang: The Way of Heaven and Earth in Chinese Thought and Culture*, Cambridge: Cambridge University Press.

2

哲学

Epistemology—Questions about the Nature and Scope of Knowledge

Introduction

This chapter is occupied with fundamental questions that can be gathered under the concept of *epistemology*. As with *ontology*, the term *epistemology* is derived from the Greek language. *Epistemis* means "to know." When combined with *logos*, "the science or study of," we have epistemology, "the study of knowledge." These are some of the fundamental questions having to do with the study of knowing that this chapter will address:

- What is it "to know?"
- Can we *know* something to be true, or do we only *believe* things to be true?
- Are all claims to know something of the same sort or justified in the same way? Is knowing 2 + 2 = 4 the same type of knowledge as "I know the car won't start because the battery is dead?"
- What are the tools we use to know something (e.g., reason/logic/ argument, experience/senses, or direct intuition, etc.)?
- Are we born knowing some things are true?

- Is there a limit to what we can know?
- Are there laws of thinking that must be followed to obtain any kind of knowledge whatever?

When we take up these questions with respect to Chinese philosophy, a serious obstacle greets us in the very beginning. Chad Hansen expresses this barrier clearly:

> Classical Chinese philosophers had no concept of truth at all. Of course, for Chinese (philosophers and laymen) the truth of a doctrine did make a difference, and, in general, Chinese did reject false propositions and adopt true ones. However, they did not "use a concept of truth" in philosophizing about what they were doing. (Hansen 1985: 491)

Of course, not all interpreters agree with Hansen and I certainly do not. Even a cursory study of the epistemological comments made by the great philosopher Mozi alone will reveal that he considered that the way to justify a claim was to establish factors that we would associate with truth conditions. Chris Fraser has devoted several studies to Chinese epistemology in the Classical period and they also demonstrate the objective of establishing a belief's credibility sufficiently to call it "true" (2011, 2013).

Nonetheless, in traditional Chinese philosophy, epistemology was not an explicitly developed autonomous discipline, even if Chinese philosophers since ancient times were interested in problems related to human knowledge and developed some strategies for how we know that a claim is acceptable. While there was no classical Chinese term equivalent to the word *epistemology* in Western philosophy, still Chinese philosophers distinguished different types of knowledge and engaged in a discussion of standards of evidence and relative probabilities. They identified various sources of knowledge and even distinguished belief from knowledge. In all of this, Alexus McLeod thinks Chinese philosophers operated to suggest that they considered truth not to be reducible to a single method or approach, but actually plural in its realization, as shown in the multiple terms they employed for it [e.g., correct/right, *ran* (然); is/yes/affirmative, *shi* (是); is/exists, *you* (有); and definitely/really, *shi* (實)] (2011: 39). All of this will become clearer as we explore a number of different approaches to questions we may properly call epistemological in Chinese philosophy.

A Classical Chinese Model for Justifying Beliefs and Knowledge Claims: Mozi (c. 470–391 BCE)

Mo Di (aka Master Mo or Mozi, *c.* 470–391 BCE) explored the claim that Heaven orders reality and that this process can and does sometimes override human will and decision. This belief was known as *ming* (命), typically translated into English as "fate."[1] In his examination of the commonly held belief in *ming*, Mozi was asked by his students to set out the philosophical criteria for judging between views on whether there is such a thing as *ming*, and if so, what is its scope and function. In general, Mozi's responses to this question serve as a reasonable outline for his theory of how to establish a claim's truthfulness and provide a window into his epistemology (Loy 2010). When asked how to distinguish between theories, Mozi answered as follows:

> You must establish standards ... [for the choice between theories]. These must have three criteria. What are the three criteria? There is the foundation; there is the source; there is the application. In what is the foundation? The foundation is in the actions of the ancient sage-kings. In what is the source? The source is in the truth of the evidence of the eyes and ears of the common people below. In what is the application? It emanates from government policy and is seen in the benefit to the ordinary people of the state. (*Mozi* 35.5)

These three criteria require some explanation.

If we take his three criteria as a fair model of Mozi's epistemology, then the first test for judging between knowledge claims is what we may call an examination of the received belief about the claim. In Mozi's context, this was understood as a study of what the historical records reported. It was commonly believed by thinkers of the Classical period that the record of the Chinese past, known as the *Classic of History* (*Shujing*), was a literal and accurate record of the thoughts and deeds of the sage-kings of Chinese history. Moreover, Mozi clearly believed that what was recorded in this work should be regarded as the standard for truth by which to judge claims and proposals made in later eras. He did not propose a critical analysis of these sources; neither did he give evidence of any serious doubt about the records. He took them for granted as authoritative and reliable.

A second test for judging between claims is what Mozi called "the evidence of the eyes and ears of the common people." By this, he meant that one should consider whether there was experiential testimony to the reliability of a claim. Mozi offered no further direct amplification of this criterion, but his procedure in applying it shows that he paid attention to both *how widespread the testimony was* for the truth of a claim and *who was providing the experiential evidence*. Mozi did not say that the sheer number of people who believe something to be true is a sufficient criterion for regarding it as correct. This would involve him in the error of "truth by majority" and lead him down such epistemological dead ends as "the earth must be flat because most people believe it is." Likewise, Mozi did not regard a claim to be reliable simply because someone, regardless of learning or status, reported having had an experience of a certain sort. The way in which he operated demonstrates that Mozi understood the difference between belief and knowledge quite clearly, especially when a direct appeal to one's experience was the evidence being offered, even if the appeal was traceable to vast numbers of persons and/or important or well-educated individuals.

The third criterion Mozi offered for regarding a belief as correct was what Western philosophers would call a pragmatic test. He suggested that one criterion for knowledge rests upon a claim's usefulness in furthering the tasks of life or society, or the benefit to the ordinary people of the community of *acting as though* the claim were true.

We may find it both interesting and puzzling that based upon the way he worked with these three criteria, Mozi argued that several beliefs may be regarded as correct and trustworthy which we would quite likely find difficult to accept; for example, that ghosts and spirits exist, and that Heaven acts in a way that exhibits volition and will by rewarding and punishing persons through its actions.

Mozi recommended that those who wanted to determine the trustworthiness of the claim that ghosts and spirits exist should follow his three criteria. Accordingly, *Mozi* 31's examination of this claim offers a detailed study in his method (Sterckx 2013: 95–142). In approaching this belief epistemologically, Mozi first considered what is at stake in whether we act as though this belief is correct:

Nowadays, those who hold that there are no ghosts say: "Ghosts and spirits certainly do not exist." From morning to evening they teach and instruct the world's people, sowing doubt among its multitudes and causing them to be suspicious and doubtful on the question of whether ghosts and spirits exist or not. This causes disorder in the world. (*Mozi* 31.2)

In this passage, Mozi made it clear that he believed a denial of the existence of ghosts and spirits is destructive to the harmony of community and state. He thought his community had abandoned acting as though this belief were true, and some very undesirable outcomes resulted:

> The people give themselves to debauchery, cruelty, robbery, disorder, theft and plunder, using weapons, poisons, water and fire to stop innocent travelers on the roads and foot paths, seizing their carts, horses, clothes and furs to further their own benefit. And these things have increased since they began, causing disorder in the world. Why have things come to this? It is because everyone is doubtful and suspicious about the question of whether ghosts and spirits exist or not, and do not clearly understand that ghosts and spirits are able to reward the worthy and punish the wicked. Now if all the people of the world could be brought to believe that ghosts and spirits are able to reward the worthy and punish the wicked, then how could the world be in disorder? (*Mozi* 31.1, ibid.: 279)

Setting about to work epistemologically, Mozi challenged the way skeptics examined reported experiences of those who claim to have witnessed ghosts. In his approach, he began by utilizing as evidence the "ears and eyes" of commoners and villagers. He wrote, "from ancient times to the present, since people came into existence, there have been those who have seen ghosts or spirits, or have heard ghost or spirit sounds" (*Mozi* 31.3, ibid.: 281). Trusting the testimony of ordinary observers was, then, an important consideration for Mozi. He also cited notable and respected figures who reported having witnessed ghosts and spirits (*Mozi* 31.4, 31.5, 31.6, 31.7, 31.8). This appeal to testimony emphasized the large number of persons who had had certain types of experiences, but it did not focus on any expert or well-placed observer who might be positioned to offer alternative explanations for the experiences reported.

Epistemological Problems of Testimony

Western philosophers have considered a number of issues related to accepting the testimony of eyewitnesses as evidence for the truth of what they report. These discussions are limited, of course, to those cases in which a witness's report is understood to be an expansion of our knowledge about the world, rather than something stated playfully, figuratively, or fictionally. Actually, even in very rudimentary knowledge exchanges, testimony is often regarded as the weakest form of transmission of knowledge. For example, I may report to you that Ivy is in New York, but if you receive a post card from her from New York, then the card radically diminishes your dependence on my testimony as essential evidence for her whereabouts. In a related way, group reporting of experience that is mutually supporting is preferable to single-person testimony. In the case of a single witness, one with "expert knowledge" about the subject is more highly regarded than one who lacks such expertise. Still, truthfulness of witness testimony is the presupposition of the routine exchange of information in ordinary situations. If I ask directions of a known resident of the city, I expect that he will answer truthfully and based on his testimony I will establish my route to the destination. This is perhaps the case because we all often depend on such testimony. Moreover, lying and deceiving others about one's experiences is risky and may create strains in relationships unnecessarily. Finally, we should note that one who objects to direct eyewitness testimony is expected to have some grounds for doing so. Although situational grounds for rejecting personal testimony vary with the context, generally speaking we note that testimony of a witness must meet some minimal filter of *prior plausibility*. For example, saying, "I was in the Sahara last year when it flooded" will surely be challenged and the truth of the testimony will almost certainly be doubted on the grounds of prior experience with the climate of the Sahara (Adler 2012).

Mozi also appealed to the historical records which he understood to be the embodiment of long-standing support for the belief that ghosts and spirits exist:

In ancient times, the sage kings certainly took ghosts and spirits to exist and their service to ghosts and spirits was profound. But they also feared that their descendants of later generations would not be able to know this, so they wrote [the knowledge] on bamboo and silk to transmit it and hand it down to them. But they all feared that [these writings] would decay and be worm-eaten, and be lost and destroyed, so their descendants of later generations would have no record. Therefore, they carved it on ceremonial basins, plates and engraved it on metal and stone to be especially sure. (*Mozi* 31.11, ibid.: 291)

We might think that Mozi did not seem to notice that such records are based ultimately on the testimony of the ancients and thus are subject to the same criticisms or concerns as other applicable reports of experiences made by those living in his own day. However, the historical records to which Mozi appealed do often make references to "experts" known as *fangshi* or "masters of esoteric methods," who report contact with and manipulation of ghosts and spirits. We might consider these the equivalent of well-placed observers; however, there is a long history of criticism of these figures, their reliability, and motives. In fact, two of the figures discussed later in this chapter, Xunzi and Wang Chong, were among the most strident critics of the historical records of *fangshi* activities.

Finally, Mozi offered a pragmatic defense of the importance of continuing to accept as correct that ghosts and spirits exist:

> It is right to think that ghosts and spirits are able to reward the worthy and punish the wicked. If [acting on this belief] could be established at the outset in the state and among the ten thousand people, it would truly be the way to bring order to the state and benefit to the ten thousand people. If the officials of government departments are not pure and incorruptible, and if the proper separation between men and women is not maintained, ghosts and spirits see it. If people are depraved and cruel, giving themselves to plunder, disorder, robbery and theft, and use weapons, poisons, water and fire to waylay innocent travelers on the roads, … there are ghosts and spirits who see them … Therefore, the awareness of ghosts and spirits is such that it is not possible to do something in the darkest places … without the awareness of ghosts and spirits certainly knowing it. The punishments of the ghosts and spirits are such that it is not possible [to avoid them]. (*Mozi* 31.16, 17, ibid.: 297–301)

Mozi's point in applying his third criterion for testing the correctness of a claim is that we *ought to act as though it is true* that there are ghosts and spirits who pay attention to the actions of noble and commoner alike, because in continuing to affirm this belief, we are much more likely to ensure that all persons will do what is right for fear that the ghosts and spirits might find out about any of their wrongdoing and punish them. That is, acting as if this belief is correct will yield desirable outcomes in the community and this is, in itself, a basis for regarding it as trustworthy. Mozi's approach has led some to characterize his epistemology as a pragmatic one (Chin 2010). However, we may wonder whether saying that we ought to act *as though something is true* is really an epistemological criterion for determining truth. It may represent a duty we have to preserve social order, but it is certainly possible that order can and has been preserved by persons acting on beliefs later shown to be false.

A Snapshot of Pragmatist Epistemology

The philosophical approach to truth known as Pragmatism is an indigenous American philosophical movement. Its three "founding thinkers" were all American philosophers: Charles Sanders Pierce (1839–1914), William James (1842–1910), and John Dewey (1859–1952). There are many nuances of difference between the epistemological views of these thinkers. However, some significant common claims of Pragmatist thinkers nevertheless suggest a view of truth-seeking that seems compatible on the surface with the approach taken by Mozi. In his work "How to Make Our Ideas Clear," Pierce took the following position on the relationship between truth and reality: "The opinion which is fated to be ultimately agreed to by all who investigate, is what we mean by the truth, and the object represented in this opinion is the real. That is the way I would explain reality" (Peirce 1992, I: 139).

An even stronger connection between Mozi's appeal to the outcomes of holding certain beliefs as reasons for regarding a belief as true may be seen in William James's *Pragmatism: A New Name for Some Old Ways of Thinking*. James wrote, "Ideas ... become true just in so far as they help us to get into satisfactory relation with other parts of our experience" (James 1907: 34). Continuing, he took this position: "Any idea upon which we can ride ...; any idea that will carry us prosperously from any one part of our experience to any other part, linking things satisfactorily, working securely, saving labor; is true for just so much, true in so far forth, *true instrumentally*" (ibid.).

Early Chinese Rhetoricians (*Bianshi*) and Logicians

Mozi's interest in how we know something was further developed in the years following his death by his students and their students. In *Records of the Grand Historian*, Sima Qian (d. 86 BCE) identified in Chinese philosophical history a group of thinkers he called the *mingjia* (School of Names). These thinkers have been variously classified as debaters, rhetoricians, dialecticians, logicians and skeptics. Sima Qian chose the term *mingjia* because one of the main foci of this group was the connection between names and their corresponding realities (i.e., "cup" refers to/points to "this object on the table"). In Western philosophical terminology, this means they were concerned with what is known in philosophy as questions of reference. Actually, though, in the Warring States period (*c.* 475–221 BCE) the name used more broadly for thinkers occupied with questions of language and its connection to reality was *bianshi* (辯士, often rendered as "disputers" or "rhetoricians"). The *bianshi* were philosophers well known for their skill in argumentation, making finely grained distinctions between concepts and exposing the flaws in received beliefs and defenses of traditional knowledge claims. Accordingly, Karyn Lai seems on target when she writes,

> Their [the *bianshi*] ideals and philosophical methods fill an often perceived gap in Chinese intellectual thought. The debates of the pre-Qin period [before 221 BCE] are represented predominantly—some would say *overrepresented*— by Confucian and Daoist views on ethics and government, while the arguments and analyses of the *bianshi* are neglected. (Lai 2008: 113)

The approaches and arguments of the *bianshi* can be associated with the work of the so-called *Later Mohist philosophers*. The reason this group of thinkers is known in this way is that we know their views largely through the final six chapters of the *Mozi* text (chs. 40–5). These sections of the work form an entirely different unit than the earlier chapters, but they are nonetheless considered to stand within the general epistemological tradition first expressed by Mozi himself.[2]

The Chinese term *bian* (辯) is sometimes used for "argument" in the sense of "competition" (i.e., to win one's case), but it can also mean "to debate in order to clarify and articulate what is known." This second use predominates in the Later Mohist chapters of the *Mozi* (Graham 1978). The *bianshi* stressed the epistemological importance of distinctions as these:

- What can be affirmed as possible (*ke*) and what cannot be possible (*buke*)?
- How items are the same (*tong*) or different (*yi*)?
- What are the differences between true (*shi*) or false (*fei*), exists (*ran*) and does not exist (*buran*)?

All this explains the confusing fact that the *bianshi*, known for their activity in disputation, typically characterized their own work with the homophone *bian* (辨), which means "to discriminate" (i.e., discriminate between concepts, positions, etc.).[3]

In general, the task of identifying the Later Mohist apparatus for approaching problems of epistemology is complicated by the fact that the target chapters in the *Mozi* text are badly mutilated in the surviving manuscripts, and moreover, they employ a number of unique Chinese characters that are not used elsewhere.[4] Some of these chapters are concerned with the philosophical discriminations (*bian*) between moral concepts [e.g., humaneness (*ren* 仁; ch. 40, A7), appropriateness (*yi* 義; ch. 40, A8), propriety (*li* 禮; ch. 40, A9), and filiality (*xiao* 孝; ch. 40, A13)]. Other analytical distinctions made by the *bianshi* are concerned with what may be considered the meaning of scientific operators such as force (ch. 40, A21), time/duration (ch. 40, A40), space/extension (ch. 40, A41), limit (ch. 40, A42), and movement (ch. 40, A50). Chris Fraser has worked through several complicated issues related to Later Mohist distinctions and categories necessary to knowledge (Fraser 2013).

Here are a few examples of Later Mohist understandings of epistemological concepts from the Ian Johnston translation of *Mozi*. The text first offers what it calls "a canon" or the knowledge claim, and then the "explanation" of it follows:

C: A cause is that which obtains before something comes about.

E: Cause: Where there is a minor cause, the result is not necessarily so; when no minor cause is present, something is necessarily not so ... When there is a major cause, the result is necessarily so. (*Mozi*, 40 and 42, A1)

C: Consciousness is a capacity, an awareness.

E: Consciousness: With regard to the capacity of consciousness, it refers to conscious certainty. It is like seeing something. (*Mozi*, 40 and 42, A3, ibid.: 377, my change)

C: Deliberating is seeking.

E: Deliberating: With regard to deliberating, it is seeking knowledge, but not necessarily finding it. It is like peering. (*Mozi*, 40 and 42, A4, ibid.: 377, my change)

C: Knowing is by hearing, explaining, personally experiencing. It is about names, object, correlation and actions.

E: Knowing: Receiving knowledge by second hand is hearing, removing obstructions to knowing is explaining, knowing by observing something oneself is personally experiencing. What something is called by is its name. What is named is the object. The pairing of name and object is the correlation. (*Mozi*, 40 and 42, A81, ibid.: 445, my change)

C: Assent does not have just one use.

E: Assent: When both agree, both reject, knowing directly prior to experience, both assert the same claim, both allow the same possibility. These are the five uses of "assent." (*Mozi*, 40 and 42, A94, ibid.: 459, my change)

C: Difference: Different categorical classes are not comparable.

E: Difference: Of wood and night, which is longer? Of knowledge and grain, which is the greater? Of the four things [rank, family, good conduct and price], which is the most valuable? Of the tailed deer and the crane, which is the higher? Of the cicada and the zither, which is the more mournful? (*Mozi*, 41 and 43, B6, ibid.: 475, my changes)

In these examples, some significant insights into *bianshi* epistemology as expressed in the Later Mohist texts are evident.

A1's canon defining cause seems much too broad, but the explanation is an improvement on the canon. In the explanation, distinctions are made among a *contributing cause* (a minor cause that does not necessarily lead to a result, but does contribute to its occurrence), a *sufficient cause* (a minor cause in the absence of which the result will not occur, but by itself, it will not bring about the result), and a *major cause* as something that necessarily produces the result or is required in order for the result to occur.[5] All this notwithstanding, with respect to the hugely important notion of "cause," the *Mozi* does not offer any epistemological guidelines for *determining* cause such as those given by John Stuart Mill in Western philosophy.

John Stuart Mill's Methods for Determining Cause

John Stuart Mill (1806–1873) was an English philosopher who wrote on a wide range of topics, from language and science to political philosophy. In his *System of Logic*, he meant to expand our epistemological capacities in science by identifying five reliable means for the determination of the cause of an event or occurrence (Mill 1882: I, 454–70). These are as follows:

The Method of Agreement. Suppose a family went out together for a buffet dinner. Upon returning home, all of them started feeling sick and experienced stomach aches. How do you determine the cause of the illness? Mill's rule of agreement says that if, in all cases where an effect occurs, there is a single prior factor that the cases have in common, that factor (of agreement) is likely the cause of the effect. So, one should make a list of what everyone ate and determine what was eaten by everyone who is ill (e.g., let us say they ate oysters) and see if all the sick persons ate the same dish.

The Method of Difference. Suppose you are the only one in your family who did not fall ill. The only difference between you and the others is that you did not eat oysters. Oysters are probably the cause of the others' illnesses, because you are not sick and you did not eat oysters (i.e., the case *not* having the result differs also in not having the cause).

The Joint Method of Agreement and Difference. By identifying the one item that you did not eat (difference) and then determining that all those who are sick did eat the oysters (agreement), the cause is confirmed.

Method of Concomitant Variation. If across a range of situations that lead to a certain effect, we find a certain property of the effect varying in common to those situations, we can infer that that factor is the cause. If you felt somewhat sick having eaten one oyster, whereas your sister felt not well at all having eaten a few, and your father became critically ill having eating ten, since the variation in the number of oysters corresponds to variation in the severity of the illness, it would be rational to infer that the illnesses were caused by the oysters.

The Method of Residues. If we have a range of factors as possible causes for an effect and the contributing role of all factors except one can be identified, the remaining factor is the cause of the effect not yet explained. For example, when an airplane crashes, investigators look at the crash site to determine the cause of the crash. Part of the damage to the aircraft could be attributed to its impact with the ground. Another part can be attributed to the wind shear the plane experienced as it fell from the sky. However, some of the damage cannot be accounted for by either of these factors. Investigators examine the remaining results not yet explained and hypothesize that explosives are the cause of them.

A3's canon on consciousness is interesting, not because it specifies self-consciousness, as this distinguishes persons from other conscious entities, but because it defines consciousness as possessing awareness, being able to experience phenomena, having pain or pleasure, and the like. Consciousness is regarded as something direct and immediate. That is, if we close our eyes, then open them, the perceptions of our sight are directly impressed on us; it is not in our control not to see once we open our eyes, neither do we need any other instrumentation or mediation by which to see. Of course, we may be mistaken about *what* we see (e.g., is it a sheet in the wind or a ghost), but *that* we see is not something about which we can be mistaken or which we can choose not to do. This is one difference between consciousness as awareness and consciousness as deliberating and knowing in Later Mohist epistemology.

A4 and A81 deal with deliberation and knowledge. The Later Mohists considered deliberation to be a process, and we know it was one they practiced well. Deliberation is considering options, investigating, exploring, and debating. This is the enterprise in which philosophy and science are typically engaged. Often a conclusion is not reached, it is only sought after. In such cases, the explanation in the *Mozi* compares deliberating to *indirect seeing*. That is, we are not quite sure what the conclusion is, just as we may be unsure of what we see. We must investigate further, check it out, improve our point of view, rule out possibilities and the like. Is it a sheet blowing in the wind that we see, or is it a ghost? We must inspect, go and look, and eliminate competing options.

When deliberation moves to knowledge, Later Mohists thought it followed one of several paths. Knowledge came

- by indirect experience through the testimony of others who knew by their direct experience (e.g., hearing);
- through explanations that removed the obstacles and uncertainties to knowing what is the case (e.g., by argument); and
- by direct personal acquaintance with an event, object or person.

Later Mohists realized that part of the epistemological process required distinguishing categories and classes, as the passage from B6 above indicates. If these are confused, one may be misled. In classical Western philosophy, Aristotle (384–322 BCE) considered the problem of reasoning about classes or categories in his development of categorical logic in the syllogism in his *Prior Analytics*. In the contemporary period of Western philosophy, Gilbert Ryle demonstrated just how important it is to distinguish categories in his book *The Concept of Mind* (1951).

In B6, Later Mohists stressed other significant epistemological skills such as how we might be misled if we do not recognize differences in application of a concept, such as that we are using the term "longer" differently when applying it to a piece of wood (i.e., how many centimeters is it compared to another) and to the night (i.e., the night seems interminable because I cannot sleep). This is a point in the logic of language, but it has a great deal to do with epistemology as well. What counts as "longer" with respect to pieces of wood, what evidence I require to resolve the question about which is "longer," is different than the evidence I expect to receive and credit with respect to the length of the night and knowing whether it was true that it was a "long" night.[6] The *bianshi* philosophers of ancient China certainly recognized the importance to epistemology of making such logical categorical distinctions.

Some *bianshi* affiliated with the Jixia Academy between 340 and 284 BCE and became so adept at challenging various worldviews and arguments that they were often criticized, probably because of their skill at exposing weak arguments and superstitious beliefs. The great Confucian philosopher Xunzi wrote the following about them:

> They investigate things with extreme acuteness but without any beneficent intent, and they debate matters but provide no useful results. They meddle in many affairs but have few accomplishments, and they cannot be the binding thread of good order. Nevertheless, they can cite evidence for maintaining their views, and they achieve a reasoned order in their explanations, so that it is enough to deceive and confuse the foolish masses. Just such men are Hui Shi and Deng Xi. (*Xunzi* 6. 43–50)

The ideas of two of the *bianshi* are known to us through sources about which we have some degree of confidence. They are Hui Shi (307?–210? BCE) and Gongsun Longzi (b. 380? BCE).[7] Most of what we know about Hui Shi, who was likely affiliated with the Jixia Academy, is found in the Daoist text known as the *Zhuangzi*. Hui Shi shows up in nine chapters of the *Zhuangzi*, and he is typically presented as a friendly but misguided interlocutor of Master Zhuang himself. One passage says that Master Zhuang was accompanying a funeral when he passed by the grave of Hui Shi. Turning to his attendants, he said,

> There was once a plasterer who, if he got a speck of mud on the tip of his nose no thicker than a fly's wing, would get his friend Carpenter Shi to slice it off for him. Carpenter Shi, whirling his hatchet with a noise like the wind, would accept the assignment and proceed to slice, removing every bit of mud without injury to the nose, while the plasterer just stood there completely unperturbed. Lord Yuan of Song, hearing of this feat, summoned Carpenter Shi and said, "Could you try performing it for me?" But Carpenter Shi replied, "It's true that I was once able to slice like that but the material I worked on has been dead these many years." [Thus, Zhuangzi said] since you died, Master Hui, I have had no material to work on. There's no one I can talk to any more. (*Zhuangzi* 24)

In the final chapter (ch. 33) of the *Zhuangzi* an overview of various schools of Chinese philosophical thought is given. The appraisal offered of Hui Shi is direct and devastating:

Whatever contradicted other men's views he declared to be the truth, hoping to win a reputation for outwitting others. This was why he never got along with ordinary people. Weak in inner virtue, strong in his concern for external things, he walked a road that was crooked indeed! If we examine Hui Shi's accomplishments from the point of view of the way of heaven and earth, they seem like the exertions of a mosquito or a gnat; of what use are they to other things? True, he still deserves to be regarded as the founder of one school, though I say, if he had only shown greater respect for the Way, he would have come nearer being right. (*Zhuangzi* 33, ibid.: 376)

The Inadequacy of Reason for the Discovery of Truth: The Lao-Zhuang Tradition (c. 350–139 BCE)

We return now to a look at the Lao-Zhuang tradition first introduced in Chapter 1's discussion of ontology. In this chapter we consider some of the most prominent passages and positions on questions related to epistemology within this tradition.

There is much that seems to suggest anti-intellectualism in the classic foundational text of Daoism known as the *Daodejing* (hereafter *DDJ*). For example, the text says that sages make sure the people are without knowledge (*DDJ*, 3). Those who pursue the *Dao* are cautioned to abandon learning (*DDJ*, 20). States are difficult to rule because the people "know too much" (*DDJ*, 65). The knowledgeable are considered deficient in understanding compared to the enlightened Daoist adept (*DDJ*, 33).

However, if we take a more comprehensive view of the entire project of Daoism, we realize that the *DDJ* is not actually saying in a literal sense that being ignorant or unlearned is better than having knowledge of the world in which one lives. The text is making a point by exaggeration. It is saying that persons may come to rely so much on human knowledge, and its reduction of truth to what reason and sense experience allow as evidence, that they may miss the kind of knowledge that is most important and life furthering.

Daoists were not suggesting that the normal pursuit of knowledge and learning were to be set aside and that all people should return to some primitive stage of simple ignorance, not knowing facts of science, technology, or history. Actually, interpreted in their context within Daoism, the statements that seem to suggest anti-intellectualism are part of the

Lao-Zhuang insistence that the distinctions and concepts by which human reason works in its pursuit of knowledge are of human design and may *mislead* people about the nature of reality or tangle them in problems they create for themselves based on human concepts and distinctions. Karen Carr and Philip J. Ivanhoe argue that the Lao-Zhuang tradition takes a position they call "antirationalism." In antirationalism, the employment of the powers of reason to gain knowledge of reality and understanding about how to live in it is seen as useful but not ultimate. Excessive reliance on reason, for the antirationalist, can "interfere with proper perception, thought, evaluation, and action" (Carr and Ivanhoe 2000: 46). The *DDJ* says,

> In the pursuit of human learning, one does more each day;
> In the pursuit of the *Dao*, one does less each day;
> In fact, one does less and less until one acts effortlessly (*wu-wei* 無為).
> (*DDJ*, 48, my changes)

The *Zhuangzi*, too, sounds a similar opposition to critical inquiry and the reliance on reason and logic as the sole means to truth. Throughout the text, Daoist sage heroes, whether Laozi (aka Lao Dan) or Zhuangzi himself, often engage with those committed to disputation and argument (the *bianshi*), repeatedly showing the flaws in such an approach as the method for achieving oneness with *Dao* and its moral excellence (*de* 德) to live in spontaneous, effortless efficacy (*wu-wei*). In the *Zhuangzi*, the *zhenren* (真人 perfected person) even does not love life and hate death; he forgets these distinctions entirely and delights in the transformations of life, even if it sounds contrary to reason to not consider one's death (*Zhuangzi* 6).

In the *Zhuangzi*, there are numerous and sustained attacks upon reliance on reason and discursive argument as methods for arriving at fundamental truth. The people are cautioned not to wear out their brains with distinctions (*Zhuangzi* 2, ibid.: 41). The text uses many examples to show that what a person thinks he knows is always relative to context and never absolute truth (*Zhuangzi* 2, ibid.: 45; *Zhuangzi* 17, ibid.: 179–83):

> Let me ask you some questions. If a man sleeps in a damp place, his back aches and he ends up half paralyzed, but is this true of a loach? If the man lives in a tree, he is terrified and shakes with fright, but is this true of a monkey? Of these three creatures, then, which one *knows* the proper place to live? … Men claim that Mao Qiang and Li Ji were beautiful, but if fish saw them they would dive to the bottom of the stream, if birds saw them they would fly away, and if deer saw them they would break into a run. Of these

four, which *knows* how to fix the [true] standard of beauty for the world? The way I see it, the [true] rules of humaneness [*ren* 仁] and [true] appropriate conduct [*yi* 義] and the paths of right and wrong are all hopelessly snarled and jumbled. How could I know anything by using such discriminations? (*Zhuangzi* 2, ibid.: 46)

This appreciation for the various uses of what it means "to know" and whether all knowledge is obtained in the same way may actually have been one of the most basic agreements between Master Zhuang and Hui Shi. But Zhuangzi warns that skillfulness in argument culminating in winning a point is not equivalent to arriving at truth either, a point seemingly directed at Hui Shi and the *bianshi* dialecticians in general:

Suppose you and I argue (*bian*). If you have beaten me instead of my beating you, then are you necessarily right and am I necessarily wrong? If I have beaten you instead of you beating me, then am I necessarily right and are you necessarily wrong? Is one of us [surely] right and the other wrong? Are both of us right or are both of us wrong? If you and I don't know the answer, then other people are bound to be even more in the dark. Whom shall we get to decide what is right? Shall we get someone who agrees with you to decide? But if he already agrees with you, how can he decide fairly? Shall we get someone who agrees with me? But if he already agrees with me, how can he decide? Shall we get someone who disagrees with both of us? But if he already disagrees with both of us, how can he decide? Shall we get someone who agrees with both of us? But if he already agrees with both of us, how can he decide? Obviously, then, neither you, nor I, nor anyone else can decide for each other. Shall we wait for still another person? (*Zhuangzi* 2, ibid.: 48)

In this passage, Zhuangzi is calling our attention to the fact that there is not a "view from nowhere" from which one may stand and judge the truth of a disputation with complete objectivity and without any bias, and this is one reason why he concludes that reason is insufficient for truth.

The View from Nowhere

The View from Nowhere is the title of a book published by the Western philosopher Thomas Nagel (1986). In this work, Nagel considers the ways human beings have an ability to view the world in a detached way. Humans can consider the world and questions of knowledge in ways that transcend their own experience or interest. To think of questions of knowledge in this way is to consider a question from "nowhere in particular." Nagel recognizes, though, that each of us is a particular person, in a particular place, each with one's own view of the world. Nagel, like Zhuangzi, is interested in how we might reconcile this tension intellectually and practically, but he has quite a different solution than the one proposed by Zhuangzi. As he says, "This book is about a single problem: how to combine the perspective of a particular person inside the world with an objective view of that same world, the person and his viewpoint included" (Nagel 1986: 3). For Nagel, the solution is not to inhibit the requirement of objectivity. But objectivity is a method itself. "To require a more objective understanding of some aspect of life or the world, we step back from our initial view of it and form a new conception which has that view and its relation to the world as its object. In other words, we place ourselves in the world that is to be understood" (ibid.: 4).

Nagel's position is to hold at least some version of the belief that humans are capable of knowing the world in all of its quandaries, or at least all of those relevant and substantial ones. But his position has by no means been universally accepted, and Zhuangzi's concerns seem as relevant now as ever. Indeed, some philosophers argue that much can be gained in retaining one's subjectivities, whether those are rooted in gender, race, political ideology, or other factors (Stitzlein 2004: 12–14).

Noting Master Zhuang's epistemological move questioning absolute objectivity also explains why rhetoricians and logicians are compared in the *Zhuangzi* to nimble monkeys and rat-catching dogs (*Zhuangzi* 12, ibid.: 132). Like monkeys and dogs that provide entertainment by demonstrating their tricks, the *Zhuangzi* portrays the debaters as proficient at rational gymnastics such as winning arguments, but poor at realization of truth. Consider this comment in the *Zhuangzi*, Chapter 13:

Those who spoke of the Great Way (*dadao*) in ancient times could count to five in sequence and pick out "forms and names," or count to nine and discuss "rewards and punishments." But to jump right in and talk about "forms and names" is to lack an understanding of the source; to jump right in and talk about "rewards and punishments" is to lack an understanding of the beginning. Those who stand the Way (*Dao*) on its head before describing it, who turn it backwards before expounding it, may be brought to order by others, but how could they be capable of bringing others to order? Those who jump right in and talk about "forms and names," "rewards and punishments," have an understanding of the tools for bringing order, but no understanding of the way to bring order. They may work for the world, but they are not worthy to make the world work for them. They are rhetoricians (*bianshi* 辯士), scholars cramped in one corner of knowledge. (*Zhuangzi* 13, ibid.: 147–8)

The references to "forms and names" in this teaching represent the concepts and argumentative strategies associated with the ordinary pursuit of knowledge. These comments should be understood as a criticism of the *bianshi*, the disputers and rhetoricians who work in the style and methods of the Later Mohists.

So, for all the affection and friendship between them, Zhuangzi did not approve of the *bianshi* Hui Shi's work as a philosopher. While he thought Hui Shi's argumentative skills were close to perfection, he believed that Hui was far away from possessing the knowledge necessary to be a perfected person (*zhenren* 真人) and live a life of free and easy contentment. Hui was always trying to make truth apparent, but Zhuangzi held that truth could not be made clear through rational arguments using language and its concepts. The attempt to arrive at truth through the means of language had led Hui "into the foolishness of the minute quibbling over the meaning of 'hard' and 'white'" (*Zhuangzi* 2, ibid.: 42). This is, of course, a reference to the *bianshi* reputation of making logical distinctions about categories and attributes and using them to impress and confound their opponents.

One recorded disputation between Hui Shi and Zhuangzi demonstrates well how Hui tried to employ the techniques of the *bianshi*, whereas Zhuangzi was making a philosophical claim that was not really approachable by such means:

Huizi said to Zhuangzi,	"Can a man really be without feelings?"
Zhuangzi:	"Yes."
Huizi:	"But a man who has no feelings—how can you call him a man?"
Zhuangzi:	"The Way (*Dao*) gave him a face; Heaven gave him a form—why can't you call him a man?"
Huizi:	"But if you have already called him a man, how can he be without feelings?"
Zhuangzi:	"That is not what I mean by feelings. When I talk about having no feelings, I mean that a man does not allow likes or dislikes to get in and do him harm. He just lets things be the way they are and does not try to help life along."

Huizi:	"If he does not try to help life along, then how can he keep himself alive?"
Zhuangzi:	"The Way gave him a face; Heaven gave him a form. He does not let likes or dislikes get in and do him harm. You (Hui Shi), now—you treat your spirit like an outsider. You wear out your energy, leaning on a tree and moaning, slumping at your desk and dozing—Heaven picked out a body for you and you use it to gibber about "hard" and "white." (*Zhuangzi* 5, ibid.: 75–6)

In another debate between Zhuangzi and Huizi, Zhuangzi challenged him by saying that there are five schools of thought: the Confucians, Mohists, Yangists, Ping (i.e., Gongsun Long), and Hui Shi himself. Zhuangzi asked which is right. Hui Shi replied that although all the others engaged him in debate, none had ever proven his views wrong. But Zhuangzi's reply was that such argument did little except create grudges and ill will between persons (*Zhuangzi* 24, ibid.: 267–8). When challenged by Hui Shi that his words were "useless," Zhuangzi replied in the following way:

"A man has to understand the useless before you can talk to him about the useful. The earth is certainly vast and broad, though a man uses no more of it than the area he puts his feet on. If, however, you were to dig away all the earth from around his feet until you reached the Yellow Springs, then would the man still be able to make use of it?" "No, it would be useless," said Huizi. "It is obvious, then," said Zhuangzi, "that the useless has its use." (*Zhuangzi* 26, ibid.: 299)

In the Lao-Zhuang philosophical tradition, the function of these exchanges between Zhuangzi and Huizi is to display the limitations of human reason when trying to approach the Way (*Dao*) itself. Accordingly, while there is always an air of some affection toward Hui Shi in the *Zhuangzi*, its final conclusion leaves little doubt about the tradition's evaluation of his method for pursuing knowledge, and indeed of that characteristic of the debaters/rhetoricians (*bianshi*) in general:

Hui Shi, however, could not seem to find any tranquility for himself in such an approach. Instead he went on tirelessly separating and analyzing the ten thousand things, and in the end was known only for his skill in exposition. What a pity that Hui Shi abused and dissipated his talents without ever really achieving anything! Chasing after the ten thousand things, never turning back, he was like one who tries to shout an echo into silence or to prove that form can outrun shadow. How sad! (*Zhuangzi* 33, ibid.: 377)

Whereas the friendship and disputation between Zhuangzi and Huizi form the background for a rejection of the use of argument and debate in some passages in the *Zhuangzi*, a series of narratives in Chapters 12–14 are directed toward the same end by being very critical of Confucius.

These sections of the *Zhuangzi* usually portray Laozi (aka Lao Dan), the putative founder of Daoism, as Confucius's teacher and master, but in doing so they demonstrate a criticism of reliance on reason and human knowledge in pursuit of the *Dao*.[8] The following is one such dialogue with Confucius (called by his personal name, Qiu), in which Laozi's dialogue offers his view of the rhetoricians:

> Confucius said to Lao Dan, "Here's a man who works to master the Way (*Dao*) as though he were trying to talk down an opponent making the unacceptable acceptable, the not so, so. As the rhetoricians (*bianshi*) say, he can separate 'hard' from 'white' as clearly as though they were dangling from the eaves there. Can a man like this be called a sage?" Lao Dan said, "A man like this is a drudging slave, a craftsman bound to his calling, wearing out his body, grieving his mind. Because the dog can catch rats, he ends up on a leash. Because of his nimbleness, the monkey is dragged down from the mountain forest. Qiu (i.e., Confucius), I'm going to tell you something—something you could never hear for yourself and something you would never know how to speak of … Forget things, forget Heaven, and be called a forgetter of self. The man who has forgotten self may be said to have entered Heaven." (*Zhuangzi* 12, ibid.: 132)

In the *Zhuangzi*, the power to master life is not an achievement of reason or human knowledge.

In what are called the Yellow Emperor-Laozi passages found in Chapters 11–22 of the *Zhuangzi* text, the legendary hero and founder of Chinese civilization, the Yellow Emperor, is held up as a possessor of truth that is portrayed as a "Dark Pearl." When the Yellow Emperor lost this "Dark Pearl" he sent Knowledge to look for it. When Knowledge was unsuccessful at finding it, the Yellow Emperor next sent the scientist Li Chu, and finally he sent Wrangling Debate, but none could find it. Not until he employed Shapeless was it found (*Zhuangzi* 12, ibid.: 129). To be "shapeless" is to have forgotten the distinctions of human language, rules of argument, and human standards of knowledge. It is to stand devoid of these and be one with *Dao*.

This distinction between truth and knowledge shows up again when contrasting what Daoists call the "perfected person" (*zhenren*真人) with ordinary persons. The perfected person in the Lao-Zhuang tradition is in possession of "the wordless teachings" that are realized when acting in oneness with *Dao*. In the Lao-Zhuang tradition, whenever "perfected persons" "get the *Dao*," they become like the figurative numinal powers of the universe: the Big Dipper (*beidou*), the Yellow Emperor (*Huangdi*), and the Queen Mother of the West (*Xiwangmu*). They can enter Kunlun (i.e., the Daoist paradise), but none of this transformation comes by the employment of human knowledge or rational proof (*Zhuangzi* 6, ibid.: 82, 87).

Knowledge by Analogical Inference: Mencius (c. 372–289 BCE)

The *Records of the Grand Historian* (*Shiji*) provides information about the biography of Mencius (aka Meng Ke, or Master Meng, Mengzi), whose influence was so significant that he became recognized as the most authoritative interpreter of Confucius's teachings in all of Chinese history and was known as "Mengzi, the Second Sage" (*Yasheng Mengzi*). Mencius was a defender of Confucianism during the period of the One Hundred Schools (*baijia*) and was quite possibly one of the major teachers at the Jixia Academy (*c.* 340–284 BCE). Participation in this community created a rich environment of engagement with a diverse group of thinkers, many of whom stood in the tradition of the Later Mohist debaters. The work editing Mencius's remarks is known simply as the *Mengzi*. It is composed of seven books, with each book divided into two parts (i.e., A and B), and each part containing a number of long or short passages (i.e., 1, 2, 3, etc.). Mencius's thoughts are all illustrated in separate passages, which are arranged neither in a chronological order nor in a sequential order (Yan and Xiong 2019: 542). Mencius wrote:

> I am not fond of disputation, … [but] I have no alternative … If the way of Yang [Yangzi, *c.* 440–360 BCE] and Mo [Mozi] does not subside and the way of Confucius does not shine forth, the people will be deceived by heresies and the path of morality will be blocked. … Therefore, I am apprehensive. I wish to safeguard the way of the former sages against the onslaught of Yang and Mo and to banish excessive views. Then advocates of heresies will not be able to arise. (*Mengzi* 3B9)

Although it is often said that classical Chinese philosophers did not place an emphasis on argumentation as a way to achieve knowledge, we have already seen through a study of Mozi and the debaters (*bianshi*) that this view is certainly false. While finely grained skills of distinctions and technicalities of argument characterized the *bianshi* and also represented the points at which they were most criticized, other classical Chinese philosophers pursued rational appeals designed to persuade persons to adopt certain points of view and change their way of living. Mencius was worried that people in his day would be overcome by the intricacies of argument and dispute associated with the debaters who were heirs to Mozi's philosophy. In fact, Mencius's own epistemology may be reconstructed from the criticisms he makes of other thinkers.

Mencius principally, although not exclusively, made use of analogical reasoning in his epistemological method and his employment of this way of doing philosophy has been evaluated throughout the history of Chinese philosophy (Liu 2017). The use of this kind of philosophical strategy to validate knowledge claims in classical Chinese philosophy has been carefully studied by Xie Yun (2019). Mencius's use of such an approach was meant to expand knowledge by including both the use of one thing to throw light on another and the use of one proposition known to be true to throw light on another of similar form. Two advantages of this form of argument in the Classical period have been identified. One is that an analogy is often as valuable epistemologically when it breaks down as when it works, because in this case it shows what may not be the case. The second advantage is that analogy is often the only tool available to reason to explore a subject that is obscure or elusive of direct experience.

Actually, both Mencius and his interlocutors carried on their debates reported in the *Mengzi* largely through the method of analogy. Indeed, it was the leading type of reasoning in Chinese argumentation during the Classical period (Xie 2019: 326). Mencius, like Confucius, was a confidant and counselor to many rulers during his life. He made frequent use of analogical argument to provoke these kings and ministers to evaluate their governing strategies. Mencius was often quite bold in his attempts to provoke kings to be self-reflective about the effectiveness of their ruling:

> Mencius said to King Xuan of Qi, "Suppose a subject of Your Majesty's having entrusted his wife and children to the care of a friend, were to go on a trip to Chu, only to find upon his return, that his friend had allowed his wife and children to suffer cold and hunger, then what should he do about it?"

"Break with his friend."
"If the Marshal of the Guards was unable to keep his guards in order, then what should be done about it?"
"Remove him from office."
"If the whole realm within the four borders was ill-governed, then what should be done about it?"
The King turned to his attendants and changed the subject. (*Mengzi* 1B6)

The King had to avoid this topic because Mencius's analogies made it easy for him to conclude that his own throne should be abolished if his people were hungry, cold, or poor (Xiong and Yan 2019: 376). Mencius even once led King Hui of Liang to conclude that there was no difference between destroying his people's lives by poor rule and being himself a murderer:

King Hui of Liang said, "I am ready to listen to what you have to say."
"Is there any difference," said Mencius, "between killing a man with a staff and killing him with a knife?"
"There is no difference."
"Is there any difference between killing him with a knife and killing him with misrule?"
"There is no difference." (*Mengzi* 1A4)

Easily the best-known examples of how Mencius used argument by analogy to arrive at truth are his famous exchanges with a thinker named Gaozi over the question of whether human nature is intrinsically good or bad. Arguably the best discussion of the analogical arguments used by these two thinkers on this subject was done by D. C. Lau (2003: 200–29). One of the most important points that Lau made in setting the stage of his analysis of the use of analogy in the *Mengzi* was that only the bare bones of the arguments actually got included in the text. The cultural and philosophical backgrounds necessary to understand the subtleties and mechanisms of the analogies were assumed to be familiar to the original readers of the *Mengzi* but are actually unfamiliar to the modern reader (ibid.: 200). This caution applies to the use of analogical arguments, whether cross-culturally or across historical periods.

In order to better understand how this strategy works epistemologically, we begin with Gaozi's opening analogy designed to argue that human nature is not intrinsically moral, whether good or evil. Human nature is inherently amoral or indifferent to morality, and bending the human to think of life under moral terms must be a social or political action of shaping one's nature in a certain way:

Gaozi said, "Human nature is like the willow. Appropriate behavior (*yi* 義) is like the cups and bowls. To make benevolence (*ren* 仁) and appropriate behavior out of human nature is like making cups and bowls out of the willow." (*Mengzi* 6A1, my changes)

Gaozi was saying that it is not the nature of a willow to make cups and bowls. The willow is the raw material from which cups may be made. By analogy, then, making humans moral is like the process of making cups and bowls from a willow. It is not in human nature to seek morality. A human being does not by nature interpret its way of being morally, as a spider weaves webs. It is actually against human nature to turn toward moral development and self-cultivation. Morality is a veneer placed on human nature, which is, in itself, amoral. Mencius disagreed with Gaozi's position by showing that if Gaozi is correct, then this would have disastrous consequences for the institution of morality that brings order and structure to social existence:

"Can you," said Mencius, "make cups and bowls by leaving the willow untouched? Or must you mutilate the willow before you can make it into cups and bowls? If you have to mutilate the willow to make it into cups and bowls, then, on your analogy you must also mutilate a man to make him moral. Surely these words of yours would cause all men to consider benevolence (*ren*) and appropriate behavior (*yi*) to be calamities." (ibid.)

In his argument, Mencius went straight to the heart of the disanalogy in Gaozi's strategy as he understood it. He wanted Gaozi to conclude with him that the downfall of morality would result if there could be no appeal to the inner nature of a person. If each person's nature had to be radically changed and reshaped (mutilated) in order to act morally, then the educational and policy implications of such a belief, although not completely stated, were still immediately obvious as calamities.

Evaluating Analogical Arguments

- One must first think of the similarities that exist between the two items being compared. How many similarities are there and what is their relevance?
- Next, one must consider what are the differences or dissimilarities between the two things being compared.
- How many dissimilarities are there and what is their relevance?

- It is possible that a single, highly relevant dissimilarity may render an analogy epistemologically valueless in demonstrating one's claim or make it what logicians call a "false analogy."

Trudy Govier (1985) has an informative overview of techniques for analyzing arguments from analogy. With respect to Chinese and Aristotelian uses of analogy, Xie (2019: 333–5) has a sustained discussion of judging false analogies.

In his reply to Gaozi, Mencius pointed to a significant dissimilarity between how morality is to be fashioned in a person and the method by which cups and bowls must be made from a willow tree. Mencius insisted that if this analogy is taken seriously, then just as the wood must be mutilated to make the cup, so also must human nature be mutilated for one to become moral. The methods which would be used to do such a thing would result in various kinds of undesirable policies and treatment of persons.

Gaozi offered another analogy which was meant to criticize Mencius's view that human nature has an inborn tendency to seek goodness and the following exchange resulted:

Gaozi said, "Human nature is like whirling water. Give it an outlet in the east and it will flow east; give it an outlet in the west and it will flow west. Human nature does not show any preference for either good or bad, just as water does not show any preference for either east or west."

"It certainly is the case," said Mencius, "that water does not show any preference for either east or west, but does it show the same indifference to high and low? Human nature is good just as water seeks low ground. There is no man who lacks the tendency to seek the good; there is no water that does not flow downwards. Now by striking water and causing it to splash up, you may make it go over your forehead, and, by damming it up you may force it up a hill—but are such movements according to the nature of water? It is the force applied which causes water to act in this manner. When men are made to do what is not good, their nature is dealt with in this way." (*Mengzi* 6A2, my changes)

Mencius's point was that in comparing the natural flow of water to morality, Gaozi had mistakenly assumed that his belief that human nature can become either good or bad meant that human nature shows no preference for becoming good. This hidden assumption reveals a flaw present in many analogical arguments. "Whether the analogy with the indifference water shows to flowing east or west is acceptable or not depends on whether one accepts or rejects the view of human nature it is meant to illustrate" (ibid.: 204).

Mencius may have been able to avoid this error of assuming what one wants to prove. For him, to say that humans can be made either good or bad does not imply that both are equally natural inclinations. However, Mencius also thought that Gaozi overlooked a strategic analogical similarity between the two that actually proves the opposite of Gaozi's claim. He begins at the same starting point as Gaozi, saying human nature is like water. But he held that just as water naturally flows downhill, so human nature naturally moves toward the good. Mencius insisted that water does have a natural preference for how it flows; it has a tendency to flow downward. Indeed, water can be made to flow upward only by forcing it. Accordingly, to do good is not contrary to human nature; it is doing evil that is inconsistent with it. Just how and why human nature has this natural tendency to the good is explained by another analogy in the *Mengzi*: that human nature's sentiments and tendencies to be good are like a field with seeds planted within it. For further development of Mencius's argument on this subject see the chapter on Moral Theory.

What we see in these exchanges is that Mencius had rather strong confidence in the powers of human reason to arrive at knowledge and truth, even when these ends had to be pursued indirectly by analogy, rather than by direct experience or logic.

Reasoning without Prejudgment: Xunzi (c. 310–220 BCE)

In most cases, the problem for people is that they become fixated on one twist and are deluded about the greater order of things. If they are brought under control, then they will return to the right standards. If they are of two minds, then they will be hesitant and confused. (*Xunzi* 23)

The Confucian master simply called Xunzi (Master Xun) was named Xun Kuang (aka Xun Qing), and he seems to have come from a different lineage of descent from Confucius than did Mencius. Xunzi was interested in obtaining a clear enlightened state of mind, and arguably, he can be seen as the greatest theorist of epistemology in classical Chinese philosophy since the time of Mozi. As one of the last great leaders at the Jixia Academy, Xunzi developed his epistemological thinking as an intellectual. He emphasized a person's cognitive ability to discern knowledge by means of "disputation" (*bian*), and his views on debate and argument are largely consistent with those of the Later Mohist debaters known as the *bianshi* (Fraser 2016: 291). He insisted on one major revision in the method of these rhetoricians. Xunzi held that gaining knowledge by use of reason is achievable if one's mind is clear and unprejudiced. Unless this step of removing one's partialities is taken, then one may simply cultivate arguments that prove only one's prejudices or inherited beliefs, and even superstitions.

Xunzi focused on the importance of the sources of knowledge. He made no appeal to any source of knowledge or power to obtain it beyond human experience and rationality. He emphasized the importance of the senses in contributing to our knowledge and in resolving disputes. Speaking of the use of general terms in language, he wrote,

> What does one follow and use to distinguish the same and the different? I say, one follows one's Heaven-given faculties [i.e., the senses]. For all creatures belonging to the same category [i.e., species] and having the same dispositions, their Heaven-given faculties cognize things in the same way. Thus, one compares similarities with another party and thereby has communication. This is the means by which one shares agreed-upon names so as to align people with one another. (*Xunzi* 22)

Xunzi's reliance on the senses is a move toward direct experience as a source for knowledge and away from subjective presuppositions which may be rooted only in prejudice or blind adherence to traditional beliefs or one's cultural upbringing.

In addition to the senses, Xunzi also recognized the epistemological role of the heart-mind (*xin*) as a source of knowledge. Xunzi followed the pattern of all Chinese thought in the Classical period by associating the heart and mind together. Another way to put this is that for Xunzi the mind is never reducible to calculating reason or logical analysis devoid of feeling or sentiment. In fact, he believed that as a source of knowledge, rationality and feeling work simultaneously and complementarily in order to yield truth. Feeling and emotion are not enemies of rationality, so long as they are not allowed to run amok or overwhelm what reason understands and the senses disclose. On the one hand, emotions must not prevent the heart-mind from considering all aspects of a knowledge claim. On the other hand, discursive rationality will not be able to resolve epistemological quandaries if it excludes feeling and emotion. To modernize Xunzi's point about the role of the human heart-mind by which knowledge is gained we could say that he did not think of the pursuit of knowledge on the analogy of a computer or calculator. Just as the senses provide perceptual content, the mind works by reason and logic, and the heart-mind processes this information into concepts and yields understanding whenever it operates properly.

Xunzi held that to judge between competing views one has to put one's heart-mind in a clear state (*da qingming*). This state is attained by emptying one's mind of preconditions and presuppositions, and quietening the emotions and passions often associated with them. Xunzi insisted that knowledge comes only when we examine a problem by setting aside our assumptions. Some Western philosophers call this *bracketing* our presuppositions in order to allow experience/evidence to be described without prejudging it.[9] Xunzi provided many accounts of persons who allowed their emotions to cloud their reason and the following is only one of them:

In the south of Xiashou there was a man named Juan Shuliang. His character was such that he was foolish and readily fearful. While walking under a bright moon at night, he looked down, saw his own shadow, and mistook it for a ghost lying in wait. He looked up, saw his own hair, and mistook it for a monster standing over him. He turned about and ran, but as he was about to reach home, he had completely dissipated his *qi* and died. Is this not sad! Whenever people have experience of ghosts, it is sure to be something they have on occasions when they are confused and unclear. These are the occasions when people believe something there is not there, or believe something not there to be there, and Juan Shuliang had already used this experience to determine things. And so, if one has become ill from dampness and beats drums [and sacrifices a pig], then one is sure to have the expenses of wearing out the drums and losing the pig but not yet have the good fortune to recover. (*Xunzi* 21, ibid.: 233)

According to Xunzi, in the process of knowing and arguing for truth, one must, negatively, discard all obscuring factors, presuppositions and overwrought emotions and, positively, be alert to other, easily neglected aspects of an issue in dispute. The function of the heart-mind in epistemology is not to perceive; that is the role of the senses. However, the heart-mind is the organ of understanding. "How do people know the Way (*Dao*)? I say: it is through emptiness, single-mindedness, and stillness" (*Xunzi* 21, ibid.: 228). Xunzi provided some instruction for how to go about putting the heart-mind into the state in which knowledge can be confidently obtained:

The human heart can be compared to a pan of water. If you set it straight and do not move it, the muddy and turbid parts will settle to the bottom, and the clear and bright parts will be on top, and then one can see one's whiskers and inspect the lines on one's face. But if a slight breeze passes over it, the muddy and turbid parts will be stirred up from the bottom, and the clear and bright parts will be disturbed on top, and then one cannot get a correct view of even large contours. The heart is just like this. Thus, if one guides it with good order, nourishes it with clarity, nothing can make it deviate, then it will be capable of determining right and wrong and deciding what is doubtful. If it is drawn aside by even a little thing, then on the outside one's correctness will be altered, and on the inside one's heart will deviate, and then will be incapable of discerning the multifarious patterns of things. (*Xunzi* 21, ibid.: 231)

In Books 6 and 21 of the work that bears his name, Xunzi offered lists of his opponents and diagnoses of their errors. In all these cases he charged that his opponents had placed too much emphasis on some part of the understanding process and thus created misunderstanding:

Mozi was fixated on the useful [i.e., pragmatic utilitarian considerations] and did not understand the value of [well-formed rules] ... Huizi [i.e., Hui Shi] was fixated on [language[and did not understand the value of [the substantial truth behind words]. Zhuangzi was fixated on [thoughts of Heaven] and did not understand the value of the human. Thus, if one speaks of it in terms of usefulness, then the Way [*Dao*] will consist completely in seeking what is profitable ... If one speaks of it in terms of (language), then the Way will consist completely in discoursing on matters. If one speaks of it in terms of [thoughts of the Heaven], then the Way will consist completely in following along with things [in their courses]. These various approaches are all merely one corner of the Way ... No one corner is sufficient to exhibit it fully. (*Xunzi* 21, ibid.: 226–7)

To prevent such confusions in understanding, Xunzi turned to the concept of *fa*, meaning "criterion" or "standard." He held that reasoning, whether analytically making distinctions or synthesizing diverse positions, operates by rules that approximate the way in which a geometer might judge a circle by using a compass. To know something is to be guided by *fa* (standards) to a conclusion. In chapter twenty-two of the *Xunzi*, he said the heart-mind draws distinctions among reasons, explanations, motions, and desires, in much the same way the eye draws distinctions among colors (Robins 2007).

Xunzi illustrated his views on epistemological standards by focusing on language. Language is one way of expressing our knowledge about reality by means of names (*ming* 名) and statements (*yan* 言). In the *Xunzi*, "names" means nouns, whether in singular or in general terms. "Statements" means any utterance that conveys a thought, including commands and imperatives.

Xunzi relied on his structure of the epistemological process and understanding of language to dispel superstitious ideas, correcting beliefs about the facts and calming emotional reactions to the world:

> If stars fall or trees groan, the people of the state are filled with fear and say, "What is this?" I say: it is nothing. These are simply rarely occurring things among the changes in heaven and earth and the transformations of *yin* and *yang*. To marvel at them is permissible, but to fear them is wrong. Eclipses of sun and moon, unseasonable winds and rain, unexpected appearances of strange stars—there is no age in which such things do not occur. (*Xunzi* 17, ibid.: 178)

Xunzi's ultimate goal was not to use reason to turn everyone into religious skeptics or unbelievers.[10] His point was that instead of fearing natural occurrences that happen according to the processes he considered "scientific" (*yin* and *yang*), it is human irresponsibility that should really be feared. When villagers fail to make provision for dikes to withstand floods, homes and persons are lost. When farmers fail to weed their crops, the harvest is slight. These are the real enemies of humankind according to Xunzi. To use a belief in Heaven's expression of pleasure or displeasure as an explanation for natural phenomena is to create fear about strange things and to live by superstition. Weather, eclipses, and the like are examples of natural actions describable as the permutations of the *yin* and *yang* and do not require any appeal to the activity of Heaven in order to explain them. Heaven and earth exist according to organizational and repeatable patterns. This means crops must be planted in certain seasons and locations, suitable clothing must be worn according to the weather, and villages must be built near adequate water supplies. If ill-fortune results for failing to follow these known patterns, it is not because of Heaven's punishment, but the inattention to necessary work by humans themselves:

> One performs the rain sacrifice and its rains. Why? I say: there is no special reason why. It is the same as when one does not perform the rain sacrifice and it rains anyway. When the sun and moon suffer eclipse, one tries to save them. When Heaven sends drought, one performs the rain sacrifice. One

performs divination and only then decides on important affairs. But this is not to be regarded as bringing one what one seeks, but rather is done to give things proper [cultural] form (*li*). Thus the [exemplary person] regards this as proper [cultural] form, but the common people regard it as connecting with spirits. (*Xunzi* 17, ibid.: 179)

Xunzi's most distinctive epistemological ideas are in Chapter 21 of the *Xunzi*. In this chapter he was not occupied primarily with how we know facts about the world, but how one can come to know the Way (*Dao*). While Master Xun said the heart-mind knows the Way by becoming empty, unified, and still (i.e., by removing presuppositions and calming its passions), he took a very different view than that of the Lao-Zhuang tradition. Instead of calling for us to rid ourselves of all distinctions and abandon discursive reasoning, Xunzi did not regard prior learning and obtained knowledge as something that prejudices our ability to know the truth. He understood prior learning as essential to our "storehouse of knowledge," and he recommended that we never cease learning and investigating. Such cumulative knowledge can save us from obsessions and superstitions and lead us to focus on activities that will create a more humane world (Robins 2007).

Differentiating Belief from Knowledge: Wang Chong (c. 27–100)

Wang Chong was a critic of the views on ontology, morality, religion, and politics he received from earlier thinkers. He was well informed about not only the beliefs of the past but also the ways in which these were supported epistemologically. His writings on these subjects were compiled into a work entitled *Critical Essays* (*Lunheng*). The work has eighty-five chapters. In these essays, Wang shows that he is a thinker with a skeptical disposition, a critical intellect, and a flair for originality in approaching philosophical problems. If we try to reduce Wang's epistemology to one sentence, it would be that he held that a claim or belief must be supported by evidence.[11] Speaking of his own work, Wang said, "The *Lunheng* with its minute discussions and thorough arguments, (is) intended to explain the common errors and elucidate the right and wrong principles so that future generations can clearly see the difference between truth and falsehood" (Forke 1907: 88).

Wang was keenly aware of the tensions between empirical direct experience and rational pursuit of truth. He insisted both must play a role in the advance of knowledge. No person can depend only on sense experience because it can be deceptive. Intellectuality (*xinyi*) must be involved. In this sense, he took a position on epistemology very much like that of Xunzi. He said bluntly that the Mohists did not use their intellectuality to verify things, but merely accepted what they heard as so-called eyewitness testimony and thus fell into deception.

On the other hand, Wang Chong certainly did not accept the Daoist doubts about rational argument, nor that tradition's call for empting the mind of concepts in order to know the truth. Against the Daoists, he argued that history never affords any instances of persons knowing what is true spontaneously without study or of persons being enlightened without inquiry and reasoning. For Wang, even the Daoist "perfected person" is not apt to bring about anything without study or to know anything in default of analysis.[12]

In his actual practice of testing differing positions and claims, Wang often uses the method known in Chinese as *arguing from a lodging place*. This is similar to the strategy known in Western epistemology as "assuming an opponent's position for the sake of argument." Most often when he does this, Wang is examining a particular kind of belief for which he uses the Chinese term *xu* (虛), and he practices what is called a *reductio ad absurdum* technique. That is, he shows that an untenable or absurd result follows if we assume (for the sake of argument) that the belief is true. Here is an example of his approach:

When the minister of Chu, Sun Shu Ao was a boy, he saw a two-headed snake, which he killed and buried. He then went home, and cried before his mother. She asked him, what was the matter? He replied, "I have heard say that he who sees a two-headed snake must die. Now, when I went out, I saw a two-headed snake. I am afraid that I must leave you and die, hence my tears." Upon his mother inquiring, where the snake was now, he answered, "For fear that others should see it later, I have killed it outright and buried it." The mother said, "I have heard that Heaven will recompense hidden virtue. You are certainly not going to die, for Heaven must reward you." And, in fact, Sun Shu Ao did not die, but went on to become prime minister of Zhou. For interring one snake he received two favours. Does this make it clear that Heaven rewards good actions? No, this is idle talk. That he who sees a two-headed snake must die is a common superstition; and that Heaven gives happiness as a reward for hidden virtue is also a common prejudice. Sun Shu Ao, convinced of the superstition, buried the snake, and his mother, addicted to the prejudice, firmly relied on the Heavenly recompense. This would amount to nothing else than that life and death do not depend on fate, but on the death of a snake. (ibid.: 160–1)

In the last lines of this passage, Wang put himself, for the sake of argument, in the place of one who believes this story. This enabled him to show the absurdity of thinking that everything that Sun Shu Ao did in life up to and including becoming a prime minister had nothing to do with his talents and learning, but only with the death of a snake.

Wang Chong was devoted to the development of a strategy for obtaining truth (*shi* 实) because of the failure of the common people to recognize the truth and their tendency to give themselves over to superstitions. He wrote, "If the multitude in their works had not gone astray from truth and some discussions had not gone bad and become disordered, then Huan Tan[13] would not have written his works" (ibid.: 84).

According to Alexus McLeod's study of Wang's epistemology, Wang's use of the concept of truth (*shi*) is specifically opposed to a certain kind of belief captured by the Chinese concept of *xu*, often translated as "falsity" as well as "emptiness" (2011: 39). McLeod holds that Wang clearly does not believe that all questions can be resolved, because he insists that one cannot find the truth on the basis of partial evidence alone and many beliefs are supported by only fragmentary proof. It is just at this point that Wang Chong's approach brings into light the distinction between belief and knowledge, and noticing the difference between these two is one of Wang's important contributions to Chinese epistemology. Basically, we have to note that many more things can be believed than can be known but merely believing something is not knowing it.

The sense of *xu* that Wang was interested in refers to a belief that is supported by "*merely apparent or insufficient* evidence." Wang recognized that claims that have been shown conclusively to be false do not attract us, but *xu* beliefs have two important characteristics that distinguish them from claims that are known to be false. First, they are attractive to us, believing them makes us feel better about ourselves or life events, and thus they are difficult to give up. Second, conclusive evidence for either their truth or their undeniable falsehood is not available.

Wang was working on an important feature of epistemology. He demonstrated that we tend not to abandon a belief if two things obtain: (1) the belief has some evidence in its favor, even if it is not determinative, and (2) the belief is important emotionally or personally to our understanding of life's meaning. In this way, Wang focused on a category of beliefs not previously studied in Chinese philosophy and likewise unaddressed in Western thought of this period.

This way of understanding *xu* beliefs helps us to make sense of passages in which Wang talked as if such beliefs possess an allure that entices the undisciplined mind. He recognized that no one knowingly believes a proven falsehood. However, persons may believe (but not know) *xu*-type claims. These beliefs have an appeal or promise to them that is attractive. Wang extended his analysis by observing that it is the nature of common people to enjoy strange stories and sayings, and to delight in empty and absurd writings because truth (*shi*) is not easily or quickly substantiated, but dramatic stories astound the hearers and excite their minds. He argued that this lure of the fantastic and compelling is why even scholars with talent add to and exaggerate beliefs about the world (Forke 1907: 85).

Wang's epistemology is often characterized as *the method of the four doubts*, and it is so named because he expressed doubts about several types of *xu* beliefs. He was concerned with the *xu* beliefs associated with *hanwen* ("heat and cold"), *qiangao* ("reprimands"), *biandong* ("phenomenal changes"), and *zhaozhi* ("results of moral behavior"). In his objections to *hanwen*, Wang undercut beliefs such as that the ruler's joyful or angry *qi* could directly affect the weather, altering the temperature or producing storms. He held that changes in weather are traceable to the "natural" causes of *yin* and *yang*. So, the conduct of human affairs has no influence on these processes in his view. In his doubt about *qiangao* beliefs, he questioned the belief that Heaven interferes with the course of things through visitations, prodigies, or portents, thereby providing reprimands of immoral conduct. His procedure was to reveal the assumption behind the belief. Such a belief assumes that Heaven has a consciousness and a will by which it may act; otherwise, how could it warn humankind or punish us? However, Wang argued that this assumption is an unshared one and that there is no way to prove or falsify it, since anything that happens could be made to conform to it, or be consistent with it. This was a rather sophisticated mode of argument. Wang contended that the belief in Heaven's guidance of reality is a nonfalsifiable one. As a result, it is much like a prejudice in that for one who holds it, no amount of evidence can dissuade one from believing it.

Wang doubted *biandong* beliefs because he thought natural explanations can account for the occurrence of phenomena and events that *biandong* beliefs are meant to explain, and moreover, that following natural explanations does not require that one believe in beings, powers, or objects that are beyond what is already known to be true. Understood from one point of view, this means that Wang was already working with what in Western philosophy came to be called *the law of parsimony* or *Occam's razor*: namely, the simplest explanation for an event or phenomenon is to be preferred.

Finally, Wang objected to such *zhaozhi* beliefs as that the ruler's actions (and, by extension, possibly those of all people) can influence Heaven to grant prosperity or longevity. He said that based on our observations, we can recognize that humans are weak and inferior compared to Heaven, so it is impossible for the human being to move or change Heaven's operations, since these are so much more superior to ours.

The question of whether life and the course of history are controlled by fate/destiny (*ming*) was one that preoccupied many philosophers, and we recall that Mozi was one of them. While Mozi argued that reality is not fated or predetermined, he did hold that life's results are subject to Heaven's intentional action shown in the rewards and punishments meted out by ghosts and spirits based on our actions. Wang took a much different view. He argued that most, if not all, aspects of human existence *are* determined (*ming*) at birth. A person's gender, strength, and physical being are fixed at birth without regard for one's choice or effort. Likewise, Wang held that the individual's aptitude for learning, moral goodness, longevity, and likelihood of success are also set by forces not in one's control. Lacking control over such factors is what Wang understood as fate (*ming*) (Nylan 2003: 745). Large sections of several of his essays are devoted to this topic (Chs. 1–7, 9–12, 42–3, and 53–5). In one of these, Wang wrote:

> King Cheng's ability did not equal that of the Duke of Zhou. Duke Huan's intelligence fell short of that of Guan Chung. Nevertheless, Cheng and Huan were endowed with the most glorious fate, whereas the Duke of Zhou and Guan Chung received inferior appointments. ... That shows that rank depends upon destiny, and not on intelligence, and that wealth is good fortune, and has nothing to do with mental faculties. (Forke 1907: 146)

What is particularly interesting about Wang's arguments for the fated (*ming*) character of a person's life and achievements is that they relied on the science of his day. That is, they made use of the *qi* theory of reality of early Chinese ontology. Here is a summary of how his argument goes in Chapter 4 of *Critical Essays*. The reason that so many things about a person or natural object are destined (*ming*) is because of the original endowment of *qi*, its quantity and quality, and the specific blend of *qi* which is constitutive of the person or thing. For example, a person's *qi* actually determines what events and other persons he will encounter in life (external factors), as well as how he will react to them (internal factors) (Nylan 2003: 745).

Accordingly, just as he depended on this "natural" explanation to support his argument that human life is fated, Wang also rejected the idea that Heaven can establish the destiny of all things according to some purpose it wishes to achieve. Instead, Wang thought of Heaven's operations as spontaneous, nondeliberative, and non-intentional (i.e., *wu-wei*). But Wang understood this effortless action of Heaven in a way much different from how *wu-wei* was understood in Daoism:

> The Way of Heaven (*tiandao*) is one of effortless action (*wu-wei*). Therefore in spring it [Heaven] does not act to germinate, in summer to cause growth, in autumn to give maturity, and in winter to store up. But the *yang qi* comes forth of itself (in spring and summer), and things of themselves germinate and grow; the *yin qi* arises of itself (in autumn and winter), and things of themselves reach maturity and are stored up. (*Critical Essays*, Ch. 19, my translation)

Wang was extremely critical of the popular belief in ghosts and therefore of Mozi's position that Heaven gives out rewards and punishments through the actions of ghosts and spirits. His intention in rejecting this belief was actually twofold. First, he wanted to counter the belief that ghosts and spirits arrange for one's actions to correlate with one's success, benefit, or longevity. For Wang, the natural endowment we have at birth gives shape to the destiny that will be realized in our lives. Second, he meant to deny the existence of ghosts and spirits completely. They simply do not exist. Belief in ghosts is not merely a *xu* belief as Wang understood it; he thought it was demonstrably false. His argument against belief in ghosts and spirits is as follows: A person is brought into existence by means of *qi* and at death *qi* is dissipated. The dissipation of *qi* is shown in the decay of the physical frame. Accordingly, the person returns to the state prior to birth. Before birth a person has no individuation but is part of the primal *qi*, and upon death the person reverts to this *qi*. Before birth, man is devoid of consciousness, and after death he reverts to this original condition of unconsciousness. So, the dissipation of *qi* means that human death is just like "extinguishing a fire" (Forke 1907: 194–5).

In pursuing this claim further, Wang offered several points. He rhetorically wondered why, if it is true that there are ghosts, there are not ghosts of creatures other than humans (since all creatures are made from *qi*). He also held that if there were ghosts, they should surely outnumber living persons, since there are many more people who have died than who are currently living.

If we focus specifically on Wang's method, we notice that he did not hold that knowledge was limited to the information coming through our sense experience. Testimony about experience may be a source of knowledge, but both our senses and the reports given by other persons based on what they saw or heard must be checked by the use of the intellect (i.e., critical and careful reason and argument).

Wang made a significant contribution to the development of Chinese epistemology by distinguishing three philosophical categories: justified belief (i.e., knowledge), demonstrated falsehoods, and *xu* beliefs (i.e., beliefs lacking sufficient evidence to be considered true, but which are emotionally seductive and continue to be embraced because of our sentimental attachment to them).

Knowledge as Justified True Belief in Plato

According to Plato (*c.* 428–348 BCE), in order to say we know something, we must have a "justified true belief." Like Wang Chong, Plato made a distinction between knowledge and belief. Belief is very much like opinion and is not necessarily grounded in any facts or supported by reasoned argument. A person could believe that the earth revolves around the moon, or that the tooth fairy does indeed leave quarters under a child's pillow in exchange for a tooth. The person could even believe that these are facts and alter his action accordingly, and even devote himself to these beliefs with great passion and enthusiasm. One might even die for a belief. Yet without justifying such a belief through evidence and reason, it will remain only a belief and not something one knows.

At the same time, if one knows that the moon orbits the earth, it makes no sense to say of him that he does not believe it. Within Plato's construction of these epistemological distinctions, knowledge implies belief. But it is not enough to constitute knowledge that one merely believes something, even if one believes it with all one's heart. To have knowledge, it is also a requirement that it be a true belief.

Moreover, one cannot *know* something false. We can know *that* something is false, but we do not know a falsehood. The final component of knowledge, according to Plato, is justification. Without justification, all we have is simply an opinion. Even if the opinion happens to be true, we cannot be said to know it if it lacks justification. Although his epistemology shows some parallels to that developed by Plato, Wang's parsing of the relationship between knowledge, truth, falsity, and belief is somewhat different from Plato's and Mozi's. For Wang, there are justified true beliefs (knowledge), false beliefs, and *xu* beliefs. Neither Plato nor Mozi offered a developed philosophical discussion of what Wang called *xu* beliefs.

Buddhist-Influenced Epistemologies

Truth Is Threefold: *Tiantai* Buddhism and Zhiyi (538–597)

As we saw in the Chapter 1 discussion of *Tiantai* Buddhist ontology, there is only one reality, not a twofold structure of the phenomenal world of objects and a spiritual world of minds or spirits. But the defining thesis of *Tiantai* is actually an epistemological one. It is the teaching of Threefold Truth (*san di*) put forward by the *Tiantai* philosopher Zhiyi.

Zhiyi held that the philosophy of Threefold Truth was not unique to *Tiantai* but was actually the teaching of all Buddhist schools. In taking this approach, Zhiyi argued that not all truth is of the same type. He thought that Twofold Truth was readily obvious, but a third dimension of truth was often overlooked. Threefold Truth may be described best by expressing what we can make true statements about:

1 We can make true statements about the world of concrete things. These truths are about things that exist and their interactions in a network of interdependent causes. These are the truths of history, science, etc. They are concerned with what *Tiantai* philosophers call provisional existence (*jia di*). The truth of such statements is verified by testing them over against the world of experience and the use of reason. This is the first type of truth.

2 It is also true to make the statement that all things are empty (*kong di*) and have no permanence, or enduring defining substantive essence that continues through time. There is no permanence to anything in our world of experience. Of course, in *Tiantai*'s form of Buddhism it is realization of this truth that liberates one from suffering because it

breaks one's attachment to things and persons who are the objects of our desires, including one's own self. Suffering comes from the desires tied to these attachments. If our attachments are extinguished by the truth that all things are empty, then our desires will cease, and we will no longer suffer. This is the second type of truth.

3 The first and second types of truth can be found in all forms of Buddhism. But Zhiyi argued that there is also a third type of truth. It is the truth that the mundane or phenomenal world is real (as known by the first type of truth) and, at the same time, both impermanent and ultimately empty (as known in the second type of truth). Zhiyi wrote,

> Now, if one knows that the mundane is not mundane [but empty], then the extreme [truth] of the mundane is put to rest, and if one realizes the non-mundane [the empty] is the mundane then the extreme [truth] of emptiness is put to rest. This is called "cessation as an end to both extremes." (Swanson 1989: 118)

My modifications added in the brackets in the quote above are designed to make clear that in *Tiantai* all Threefold Truths are identical, and that only when one is taken as "more true" than another does one go astray epistemologically. As Paul Swanson translates from Zhiyi's *The Esoteric Meaning of the Lotus Sutra*, "emptiness is identical to [mundane] existence and the Middle Way" (ibid.: 182). To put it differently, there are not really three separate types of truths, but simply the *Threefold* Truth.

The Threefold Truth epistemology of *Tiantai* means that objects of our experience may be studied and used. We may possess knowledge about how they interact in a nexus of interdependent causes, how to make various objects from other materials, how to use them for our benefit, and the like. In this sense, we carry on just as do other persons in ordinary life. All the while, though, we know that we are using and studying things that are empty of a substantive nature in themselves. Having this knowledge is liberating and enlightening because we can use it to break the attachments we have to things that are the sources of our suffering. We may illustrate how the Threefold Truth epistemology works by applying it to the example of the life of the historical Buddha.

There was a historical Buddha named Siddhartha. We may gain knowledge about his birthplace, disciples, travels, teachings, and so forth. We may do literary and historical critical analysis of the sutras attributed to him and the narratives told about him. The statements we make about all of these things are mundane truths about the Buddha.

We may also make truth statements about his enlightened way of living, his freedom from attachment, and his overcoming of suffering. In doing so, we are not uttering "symbolic" truths, compared to the former examples, which are "literal" truths. Neither are these "spiritual" truths, while the former are "empirical" truths. Statements of this second type are as truthful as are those of the first type. But we may move on to realize the truth that the mundane Buddha and all that can be said about him is also the empty Buddha, and equally truly the enlightened Buddha. This is the realization of Threefold Truth.

Zhiyi thought that persons had different epistemological capabilities that put them on divergent lived or operational levels of truth. This means that persons must be taught differently. In *Esoteric Meaning* he said, "Teachings are basically responses to capabilities. There are distinctions and differences in the texts because the capabilities [of inquirers] are not the same" (ibid.: 165). We may take this to mean that some people are only able to grasp truth in its mundane expression. For them, truth is confined to the mundane and they are caught up in the pleasures, desires, and attachments that accompany what is known in this manner. Such persons suffer because they live only on the basis of this knowledge. Even though they may strive to resist desires through moral action, prayer, and devotion, they will not be able to extinguish their desires and will continue to suffer. This claim of Zhiyi is not as simple as saying as a Westerner might that they hold on to "material things." It is not materiality or concreteness that is the enemy of enlightenment. The obstacle to enlightenment is that we regard mundane things as substances that can be held on to in order to fulfill our desires.

In contrast to such persons, others live only with the truth of emptiness. What others know as mundane, these persons know to be impermanent. They realize that clinging to them for relief from suffering is illusory. Accordingly, they detach from things and live apart from the mundane as much as possible. Such persons are those who trust in the ascetic way and only go so far as to deny the mundane world. They are off track of what Buddhists call "the middle way."

But for those who are capable of it, truth is seen for what it is. Such persons live in the mundane, knowing it is real but also seeing its emptiness. At this stage, Threefold Truth is perfectly integrated; three in one and one in three. And yet, there is one more thing to be said about Threefold Truth. In *The Great Calming and Contemplation* Zhiyi said:

All three are empty because the path of speech and discursive thought is a dead end. All three are provisional because they are names [in language only]. (Donner and Stevenson 1993: 178)

The difference between the capabilities of persons explains epistemologically why some are able to grasp the threefold character of truth and others become fixated on either mundane truth or emptiness.

This understanding of truth has implications for teaching. In the *Lotus Sutra*, the Buddha expounds many parables. "The Burning House and the Three Carts" is one of the most famous of these. This parable is important for its epistemological significance. The Buddha used the parable to offer an explanation for teaching different people in varying ways and even for teaching what may be false on a mundane level. Ultimately, the point is that the Buddha made use in his teachings of the way of truth that was most helpful for the specific person. The Threefold Truth may be arrived at even by teaching what is false on a mundane level. In *Tiantai*, this epistemological method is called the use of *expedient means*.

In the parable of "The Burning House and the Three Carts" a rich father, upon seeing his house on fire, tried to save his children's lives. He commanded them to get out of the house, but they were occupied in playing games and would not flee. So, the old man said, "I have marvelous toy carts drawn by goats, deer and oxen waiting outside for you. You must come outside right now to get them." The children excitedly went out of the house. After the children reached safety outside, they discovered there were no toy carts as promised (*Lotus Sutra*, Watson 2002: 35–6). The point of the parable is that the children were saved by what was an undeniable mundane falsehood, which was used as an expedient means to their salvation. The parable concludes with the Buddha saying, "but the father later gave them carts filled with jewels."

Zhiyi used this parable to focus on how Buddhism may have many teachings, some of which contradict each other or some may even be untrue as statements about mundane existence. But they may still function as *expedient means* to enable people with different intelligence, education, and capacity to gain the "jewel of enlightenment." In the doctrine of expedient means, it is not what a statement *says* that makes it a truth, but what it *does*. This is what JeeLoo Liu rightly calls the "pragmatic understanding of truth" in *Tiantai* Buddhism (2006: 294). If a statement, even though false, may be used to gain enlightenment, then this use, in itself, justifies it as an expedient means.

From an epistemological point of view, *Tiantai* is teaching that what counts as knowing something is true cannot be reduced to a single method. But even given his philosophy of Threefold Truth, many interpreters still insist that Zhiyi holds that "real" truth is actually unspeakable and beyond human conceptualization. For example, Burton Watson comments on the stream of Mahayana Buddhism of which *Tiantai* is a sect in this way, "Mahayana Buddhism has always insisted that its highest truth can never in the end be expressed in words, since words immediately create the kind of distinctions that violate the unity of Emptiness" (*Lotus Sutra*, Watson 2002: xxviii). It seems correct to say that truth as the Middle Way (i.e., the Threefold Truth) is something inexpressible, since expressing it would involve making a statement that might be mistaken as a mundane truth or the truth about emptiness. So, for those who have attained enlightenment as Buddhas, truth is simply the knowledge of Threefold Truth and has no need of further expression.

Pure Knowledge: Wang Yangming (1472–1529)

In order to understand the uniqueness and originality of Wang Yangming's epistemology, consider that in Western philosophy in the twentieth century, the great Austrian philosopher Ludwig Wittgenstein showed that there are many uses for the word "know," and that the criteria for saying that one "knows" vary with these multitudinous uses. This holds true also for satisfying the conditions for saying that some knowledge claim is "true." "True," like "know," has many uses in language and the grounds for saying something is true are set by the specific use one is making of the term in a context, or what Wittgenstein calls a *language game*. On the basis of this claim, some interpreters call Wittgenstein an epistemological relativist. The reason

Wittgenstein on the Language Games of Truth

From On Certainty (1969)

6. Whether a proposition can turn out false after all depends on what I make count as determinants for that proposition.
11. We just do not see how very specialized the use of "I know" is.

105. All testing, all confirmation and disconfirmation of a hypothesis takes place already within a system [language game]. And this system is not a more or less arbitrary and doubtful point of departure for all our arguments: no, it belongs to the essence of what we call an argument. The system is not so much the point of departure, as the element in which arguments have their life.

142. It is not single axioms that strike me as obvious [i.e., indubitable], it is a system in which consequences and premises give one another mutual support.

152. I do not explicitly learn the propositions that stand fast for me. I can discover them subsequently like the axis around which a body rotates.

204. Giving grounds, however, justifying the evidence, comes to an end;—but the end is not certain propositions' striking us immediately as true, i.e. it is not a kind of seeing on our part; it is our acting, which lies at the bottom of the language-game.

205. If the true is what is grounded, then the ground is neither true, nor false [it is the ground for establishing truth and falsity].

262. I can imagine a man who had grown up in quite special circumstances and been taught that the earth came into being 50 years ago, and therefore believed this. We might instruct him: the earth has long ... etc.—We should be trying to give him our picture of the world. This would happen through a kind of persuasion.

279. It is quite sure that motor cars don't grow out of the earth. We feel that if someone could believe the contrary he could believe *everything* that we say is untrue, and could question everything that we hold to be sure. But how does this *one* belief hang together will all the rest? We should like to say that someone who could believe [that cars grow out of the earth] does not accept our whole system of verification.

611. Where two principles really do meet which cannot be reconciled with one another, then each man declares the other a fool and heretic.

612. I said I would "combat" the other man,—but wouldn't I give him reasons? Certainly; but how far do they go? At the end of reasons comes persuasion. (Think what happens when missionaries convert natives.)

616. Why, would it be unthinkable that I should stay in the saddle however much the facts bucked?

> 617. Certain events would me into a position in which I could not go
> on with the old language-game any further. In which I was torn
> away from the sureness of the game.

this view should not be classified as a form of relativism is that for each use of "true" in a language game, there is indeed a recognized set of conditions for making the judgment that a claim is true. In contrast, relativism might be taken to mean that "there is no truth; only various interpretations," or "what is true for me, may not be true for you." Wittgenstein was not advocating relativism in this sense. He was insisting that we can know what is true if we know the conditions for the truth of the claim being made in a given language game. While the conditions vary depending on the claim, there are nonetheless recognized and accepted criteria for saying one knows something, or that a claim is true within a specific game. But there is no "essence" of "true" that unites all these different uses.

On these terms, Wang Yangming's notion of "pure knowledge" (*liangzhi*) may be regarded as a particular use of the word *know* (*zhi*). In this way, Wang makes an interesting contribution to the philosophical conversation about epistemology by introducing into the "language game" about knowing the new term "pure knowledge" (*liangzhi*). His description of the use of this concept is revealing.

As we saw in our discussion of Wang's ontology, "pure knowledge" consists of the direct and immediate apprehension of the Principles (*li*) by which the mind orders and structures reality. Acting in the world requires knowing the world through these structures. For example, working with things regarded as in a causal relationship with each other, there are not two separate events, one epistemological and the other behavioral. We do not break experience down into knowing and acting. We pour coffee into cups, mount horses, cross bridges, care for the sick, etc. We could not act in any of these ways without the mind's Principling (*li*) activity giving structure to sense content. Actually, our behavior shows we do not doubt the Principles used in this activity. In this sense, we take them as "certain" or "indubitable," even if we have never proven the Principles to be true or to exist. There is unity of action and knowledge, and Wang uses the concept "pure knowing" to point this out.

Accordingly, because Wang disassociates "pure knowledge" from any single transaction such as rational deliberation, use of the senses, or application of the will, some interpreters align it with a kind of sixth sense.[14] Western philosophers sometimes speak of this kind of knowing as "intuition" in order to distinguish it from knowing sourced in reason or the senses. In fact, this is exactly how the notable translator Fung Yulan renders the Chinese term *liangzhi* (良知; Fung 1953: II, 601).

Here a point of caution is in order. One must be careful not to turn "pure knowledge" into some sort of mysterious or mystical capacity that discloses knowledge contradictory to or not yet confirmed by reason or the senses. Wang is not saying that "pure knowledge" is some intuitive insight that there is something such as life on Mars. Ascertaining whether there is life on Mars will come by use of reason and the senses, but the application of these will depend on the underlying Principles by which the mind structures reality and which are themselves called "pure knowledge."

Wang is using "pure knowledge" as an epistemological neologism. He is inventing a way of talking about something that had not been captured by Chinese philosophy prior to his work. So, he needs a new word. In fact, Wang's account of *liangzhi* makes a novel contribution to global philosophy as well. "Pure knowledge" is a type of cognitive gain that does not come by deliberation or sense data. It expands the way we can be in the lived world. It is not reducible to a thought, idea, or perception. It is not the result of study. Neither does it come at the end of an argument as an inferred conclusion. It can be considered direct (not dependent on sense data or logical reasoning) and immediate (not arrived at by use of other knowledge).

Having said this, we should pay close attention to Wang's corrections of misunderstandings about "pure knowledge" offered to his own students. For example, in his reply to a letter from Lu Yuanqing he wrote the following:

> Your letter says, "*Liangzhi* [Pure knowledge] also arises from somewhere. ..." Perhaps you did not get exactly what I said. Pure knowledge is the original substance of the mind ... The original substance of the mind neither rises nor does not rise. Even when erroneous thoughts arise, pure knowledge is present [in their structure] ... And although pure knowledge is perhaps sometimes obscured, its substance is always clear. The thing to do is to examine it. To say that pure knowledge arises from somewhere is to say that sometimes it is not present. That would not be the original substance of the mind. (*Instructions for Practical Living* 152, Chan 1963a: 132)

Wang makes it clear that "pure knowledge" which consists of the Principles is always necessary to reasoning and sense experience, even when the inferences we draw or the perceptions we report are erroneous. Even false claims require the employment of the Principles in order to be intelligible enough to be proven false. We can never step outside the Principles even if what we report or claim is in error. The content is still based on and dependent on the Principles, which are the substance of the "original heart-mind" (*xin*). The "original heart-mind" means the mind *as it is* not with reference to any specific thought, perception, or feeling, but how the heart-mind works to make all sorts of knowledge and experience possible (*Instructions for Practical Living* 169, ibid.: 150). Thinking requires the functioning of "pure knowledge." Error is rooted in the manipulation of sense data or rational ideas according to personal desires or perverse and careless employment of "pure knowledge." So, Wang wrote,

> Now, pure knowledge is one. In terms of its wonderful functioning, it is spirit; in terms of its universal operation, it is force, and in terms of its condensation and concentration, it is essence. (*Instructions for Practical Living* 169, ibid.: 152)

Pluralistic Cultural Knowledge: Zhang Dongsun (1886–1973)

While the history of Chinese epistemology is not altogether a uniform one (Rosker 2008), in the early half of the twentieth century, Zhang Dongsun was one of the most important philosophers in China, especially owing to his efforts to establish, in dialogue with Western philosophy, a unique and new philosophical epistemology never before present in Chinese tradition. His approach has been labeled *Pluralistic Cultural Epistemology* (X. Jiang 2002: 57). Zhang's epistemological theory was deeply attentive to the role culture plays in all aspects of knowing, so much so that Haridas Muzumdar characterized Zhang's work as the ground-breaking exposition of a "sociology of knowledge" (1956: 12, 14).

For Zhang, the answers to philosophy's fundamental epistemological questions—including what counts as evidence, what we seek to know, what we think it is possible to know, what we notice through our senses, how we interpret our sense perceptions, how we use language to talk about what we know, and what qualifies as a sufficient reason to say we know something—are all inevitably culturally defined and structured. Persons are not merely acculturated to observe festivals, organize themselves socially, or valorize certain heroes. They are also shaped by their cultures to operate epistemologically in different ways.

In his 1939 article "Thought, Language and Culture," Zhang put forward four guidelines for the study of epistemology:

1 A theory of knowledge and cultural history must be treated simultaneously.
2 Not only does concrete social thought have its background in cultural determinants; but also, so do the logical forms and theoretical categories which structure epistemological philosophy.
3 The differences between Western and Eastern epistemologies can be explained from this point of view.
4 From this, we may understand that Western philosophy is nothing but a particular form of epistemology characteristic of and for the use of Western culture, but that there are plural epistemologies deriving from the many diverse human cultures. (Muzumdar 1956: 12–13)

The force of these four guidelines is that knowledge cannot be reduced to any way of proceeding that does not consider the culture in which the claims and descriptions are embedded.

Comparing Philosophical Traditions: The Basic Tasks and Their Vices

The importance and challenge of the sort of pluralistic cultural epistemology that Zhang called for shows up particularly in the current discipline of comparative philosophy. Some more extended expositions of the following tasks and vices may be found in Nussbaum (1998: 113–48), Littlejohn (2017), and Connolly (2015: 28–93):

Task: Descriptive Comparison is the task of being sure we have each philosophical text and position being compared correctly stated as derived from its cultural tradition.

Vices:

Descriptive Chauvinism is the vice in which one reads the "Other" as though it is the same as one's own cultural tradition. For example, reading Confucianism as though it has a God, faith, and prayer, just like Christianity does.

Descriptive Romanticism is the vice according to which the "Other" is considered exotic and nothing like the familiar, but mysterious and not understandable. An example of this vice would be holding the view that Buddhism is too profound to be understood by a Westerner.

Task: Evaluative Comparison is the task of making relative judgments about the value or truth of different philosophical cultural traditions of practice or human well-being.

Vices:

Normative Chauvinism is the vice in which the familiar is regarded as the most preferable and true, and wherever the "Other" is unlike it, then it is inferior, futile, or false. For example, assuming without examination that Chinese "acupuncture" or traditional medicine is ineffectual or superstitious compared with Western medicine and practice.

Normative Skepticism is the vice according to which philosophers encounter other traditions and suspend judgment about competing views, accepting all of them as equally unable to establish epistemological preferability. For example, an illustration of normative skepticism would be to say of a difference in philosophical claims, "Well, that's their culture. Mine is different but neither is better than the other." Such an approach leaves one with no epistemological basis for judging the merits of practices in different historical periods such as slavery, footbinding, honor rape, and so on.

Zhang distinguished perceptual and theoretical knowledge, but he insisted that both of these types of knowing are still socially and culturally constituted, even if perceptual knowledge points toward the external world and its structure. He wrote:

It seems to me that human knowledge may be considered as having four elements, each penetrating into and mutually dependent upon the others. The first is the external "structure" [of the world available to our senses] which accounts for our immediate sensations. The external world being [known] merely as "structured," we can only know its "mathematical [i.e., structural] properties," to borrow a term from [Bertrand] Russell. As to its [the object's] qualitative nature, we know nothing. But it must be pointed out that these mathematical properties are not static and rigid, but flexible and changeable. The second element is the "sensa," to use the terminology of neo-realism. Our sensation is a curious thing. Although externally aroused, it [i.e., the actual sensation] is different from the external world in nature.

There may be said to be correspondence but not identity between the two. Sensation by its nature is something independent. The third element consists of "constructions." The ordinarily perceived tables, chairs, houses, friends and so forth, are "constructions." These constructions are often taken naively as independent self-existent things. But as a matter of fact, these things are constructed through the perceptions of the observer. The fourth element is what we have already discussed as "interpretation." These four elements are interdependent. (D. Zhang 1939: 20–1)

Zhang thought that knowledge was constructed as the intricate workings of these four elements by including content gathered through the senses, structural forms of pattern and order, and concepts derived from culture. We cannot have any direct knowledge of the external world as it is in itself (X. Jiang 2002: 63).

While much of what Zhang wrote about these four elements of epistemology is not as original as he thought, a great deal of it having been set out in British Empiricism and Kantian philosophy, there are some unique emphases that should be noted. One of these is Zhang's lingering Buddhism, mediated to him through Chinese culture from his youth when he was a devotee of that tradition. Zhang, perhaps appreciating the problems Western philosophers Bertrand Russell and Ludwig Wittgenstein were both having at the time explaining the nature of an "object" in itself without any essence,[15] took the position that the objects of sensation do not have any ontological status themselves. Zhang's Buddhist acculturation made it readily apparent to him that there is no fixed substance underlying the objects of our phenomenal experience. Of course, this is not the same as saying that there is no external world. It is only to hold that the external world is not composed of fixed objects that cause experiences in us, but which we cannot know in themselves. Instead, our experience is of objects which are the products of mutually interdependent, transient relations. Accordingly, Zhang held that the term *matter*, like *mind* or *reality*, is an empty structural notion derived from the way some (i.e., specifically Western) cultural epistemologies work. This is why Zhang believed that only some (e.g., Western) epistemologies even ask what is "real" or what is "matter."

According to Zhang, the most obvious way in which all epistemology can be shown to be cultural is that knowledge is inevitably expressed in a particular language, or better put, *knowledge is linguistic thinking* or *knowing is through/in language*. Of course, language is a cultural product. Languages not only have names for objects but also grammar and structure, and these embody a logic and the rules for reasoning. For example, Zhang argued that the structure of Western languages leads philosophers to look for the essence (substance) underlying the attributes predicated of an object. So, he held that the investigation of the nature of substance itself became one of the central problems of Western philosophy but it did not arise as an issue in Chinese philosophy, because the languages are differently constructed. Zhang wrote the following about how English language prompts its users to approach knowing in ways in which Chinese do not:

> For example, when we say, "this is yellow and hard" yellowness and hardness are the so-called "attributes" which are attributed to something, the something in this case being "this." The "something" in general is the substratum. With a substratum emerges the idea of "substance." This is the reason why in the history of Western philosophy no matter how different the arguments may be, pro and con, about the idea of substance, it is the idea of substance which itself constitutes the central problem. (D. Zhang 1939: 8)

Zhang held that Chinese language did not set up the categories of substance and attribute, so it did not create for its users the epistemological problem of how they might be related. However, for English-language users the obvious and evident distinction between substance and attribute creates many issues. One such epistemological difficulty can be expressed in this question: if you strip away all the attributes of an object, what remains and how can it be known?

The differences between the cultural epistemologies of the West and China are deep, reaching down into the very act of reasoning itself. In Western thought, the so-called "law of contradiction" or "mutual exclusiveness" is taken as a necessary truth of logic. Something must be either A or not-A. Zhang insisted that this kind of rule of reasoning was not employed in Chinese philosophy because in Chinese language and culture, relationality and inclusiveness were rooted in its correlative thinking (i.e., *yin/yang* and the Five Phases). In Chinese logic, something cannot be A at all, *unless* it is in relation to and participates in not-As. Zhang believed this explained in part why modern Chinese thinkers found the dialectical thinking of G. W. F. Hegel more compatible with their epistemologies than other Western philosophies. In the *Phenomenology of Spirit*, Hegel emphasized that new knowledge comes from a synthesis of what were previously regarded as contradictions in what he called the triadic structure: thesis, antithesis, synthesis (Miller 1977: 29).

Another example of the ways in which culture influences what is considered knowledge and truth is the concern over whether something exists or does not exist. While significant in Western epistemology the question of existence is not a prominent preoccupation in Chinese epistemology. Zhang thought this was because Western philosophers are always asking, "What is it?" The Chinese, on the other hand, confronted by the same situation, ask: "How should one react to it?" For Zhang, this meant that Western thought is characterized by the "what-priority," Chinese by the "how-priority" (D. Zhang 1939: 16). Accordingly, this stress on how one must react to an experience has led Chinese philosophers to concern themselves with human affairs and how man must react to nature and his fellow human beings (Muzumdar 1956: 16).

One epistemological problem raised by Zhang Dongsun's theory of pluralistic cultural epistemology is that of incommensurability. The term "incommensurable" means "incapable of being measured together." It is a concept used when laying different cultural practices or beliefs alongside each other but being unable to find points of contact, similarity, and overlap. Zhang even noticed incommensurability in matters typically considered universal, such as logic. "The type of logic used by Chinese philosophers is different from that of the West, while the Hindus may have a logic different from both the Chinese and the Western" (D. Zhang 1939: 3). Understanding pluralistic cultural epistemology requires bringing the problem of incommensurability to the front of philosophical discussion. Some of the more helpful analyses of the topic of incommensurability can be found in Davidson (1974), Wong (1989), and Connolly (2015: 67–104). Three types of incommensurability seem most problematic for Zhang's epistemological theory:

1. *Fundamental Worldview or Paradigm Incommensurability* lies at the level of absolute presuppositions, unexamined assumptions about the world and how it is to be seen, including what counts as evidence for knowledge claims and what is regarded as sufficient proof for them. Such fundamental beliefs and assumptions rest like the bedrock of our ways of proceeding epistemologically. They are "gulped down" by each new generation, without being first proven true anew each time. Indeed, they are instead the basis for proving truths in a culture.

One example of incommensurability at the fundamental worldview level is that it would not really make sense to ask what view Confucius held of democracy. There is nothing in the bedrock of his worldview to suggest that the people should rule or control who might be a ruler by voting and selecting the ruler. Consider the following as another example. We might wonder whether we should really be surprised that Western physicians do not use acupuncture. And would it be correct for a Westerner to say simply, "It is unscientific?" This practice is not part of the fundamental worldview of Western biology, neurology, and medicine. Still another example would be to confuse the Chinese concept of *qi* (氣) with the Western notion of matter.

Zhang called attention to the differences between Chinese and Western worldviews on the matter of religion and stressed that there were deep foundational differences between these philosophical understandings. He wrote: "But as far as Heaven and God are concerned, the Chinese have never been concerned with them primarily. When we speak of Heaven we have in mind only Providence, which is merely a manifestation of Heaven. In other words, the Chinese are concerned with the will of Heaven without being too particular about Heaven itself" (D. Zhang 1939: 15).

2. *Linguistic Incommensurability* arises from differences in terms and concepts in language and how they are used. This is a common problem in comparing plural cultural epistemologies as Zhang thought about them. For example, Zhang called attention to the multiplication of terms in Chinese related to kinship and familial relationships compared with English, and explained that this was owing to the socio-cultural significance of the family in Chinese culture. He went on to say that he was not surprised to find that "a lumping together" of many such terms may be found in English, because the family does not play as prominent a role in American culture (D. Zhang 1939: 18).

One view of language's role in incommensurability between traditions is what may be called the "linguistic relativity thesis." This thesis says that language determines thought, and persons can only have the thoughts for which they have terms and concepts (Penn 1972: 23–32). This theory that thought is determined by language was criticized and rejected by Zhang (1939: 21). It has been regarded now as substantially refuted (Pinker 1994: 57–67). Yet, it often still shows up in comparisons between philosophical cultures. For example, it was commonly thought in comparative circles throughout the twentieth century that since the Chinese language of Confucius's day had no term for "justice," then this must have meant that there was no concern for "justice" or the practice of "justice" in Chinese history of that period. Erin Cline has put this specific claim of "term determinism" to rest conclusively by showing that a sense of justice is deeply present in the Confucian *Analects* even while there is no single term for "justice" in the work itself (Cline 2013: 119–67). In so doing, she made significant strides in overcoming one understanding of linguistic incommensurability.

Nevertheless, other issues of linguistic incommensurability are still important. One of these concerns the translatability of terms. What should we do with concepts such as *qi* or *wu-wei* for which no single-word substitution in English presents itself? Should we always assume there must be a word substitute in the target language (e.g., English)? But could not this forcing of word substitution contract or expand the actual use of the term in the source language? Or, is it preferable to keep the term from the source language (Chinese) without translating it and introduce it into the target language, learning to use it appropriately. If we take this latter approach, Zhang reminded us, "Viewing human history as a whole, any new creation in language, e.g., new terminology, represents a development of thought along a new line" (D. Zhang 1939: 5).

> **3.** *Evaluative Incommensurability* is one source of the idea of cultural relativity. The reason why such a view of incommensurability is important philosophically is that relativism suggests that one tradition cannot evaluate, criticize, or be found more true or life furthering than any other. In cultural relativism, each tradition stands on its own, possessing its own values and discrete criteria of knowledge and truth that is different from and maybe even contradictory to that of another tradition in something as depicted in Figure 2.

Attempts to manage cultural relativity have taken many forms in history. One of the most divisive of these is the effort to raise one tradition over another. This has been shown by one tradition considering another as "primitive" or "uncivilized." Suppose instead of the physicist, a people consult an oracle. We might call them primitive for doing so. But if we call this "wrong," are not we using our philosophical culture as a base from which to combat theirs? In international relations the term most often used

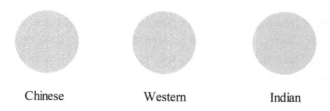

Chinese   Western   Indian

Figure 2 Illustration of discrete and autonomous cultures in relativism.

for this strategy of managing cultural relativity by elevating one culture over another is imperialism, in which one tradition imposes its standards and values rather than the other's, while also regarding the other as inferior.

It is crucial to note, though, that Zhang did not think of his theory as reducing the comparisons of philosophical cultures to relativism. He spoke instead of *pluralistic* cultural epistemology. "It [the comparison of cultural views on what is true] is not to be taken to mean that it is not possible to have universal categories applying to human thought in general, or that only ethnically and culturally determined forms of thought are possible" (D. Zhang 1939: 2). If we think of Zhang's understanding of the pluralistic relationship between traditions in terms of a Venn diagram, we will notice points of overlapping beliefs and practices, while still preserving the uniqueness and distinctiveness of each tradition (Figure 3). Zhang thought that the common overlapping beliefs and structures might serve as a ground for evaluating all traditions. Tim Connolly even calls this "comparative universalism" (2015: 150–7).

Clearly, then, although Zhang's pluralistic cultural epistemology made no room for the position that real or true knowledge transcends all cultures, neither did he mean to undermine our ability to assess the worth and truth

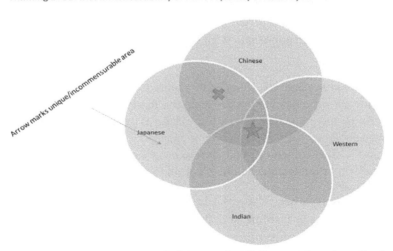

Thinking about Incommensurability of Philosophical/Cultural Systems

Arrow marks unique/incommensurable area

Chinese

Japanese

Western

Indian

Here the star marks the region of what Connolly calls "comparative universalism"

Figure 3 Illustration of overlapping practices, beliefs, and values in cultural pluralism.

of various beliefs and values found in traditions differing from our own. Knowledge is always mediated through culture. Knowledge and truth are functions of the criteria set up within a specific cultural epistemology, and there is no way to approach "reality" that can be bleached free of the cultural constraints determining what one is looking for, what questions one asks, or what is taken as sufficient evidence for a claim to know. Yet, cultures do overlap and in this space we find not only universal affirmations and values, but epistemological ways of operating that enable us to address comparatively practices and beliefs in each individual culture that differ from those held in common.

Chapter Reflections

Western philosophers historically insisted that there was little to learn from Chinese philosophy and have largely ignored it (Van Norden 2017: 19–31). In the Preface to this book, I called this the *exclusivist paradigm*. As far back as the seventeenth century, Western philosophers held that the Chinese tradition lacked a rigorous critical epistemology for determining the true of knowledge claims and was only concerned with moral and social philosophy, but our survey has shown that this was a mistaken understanding traceable to only a modest awareness of the diversity of Chinese philosophy. Gottfried Wilhelm Leibniz (1646–1716), otherwise a thinker with a deep appreciation for the value of Chinese culture and global impact, wrote,

> In profundity of knowledge and in the theoretical disciplines, we are their [the Chinese's] superiors For besides logic and metaphysics, and the knowledge of things incorporeal, which we justly claim as particularly our province, we excel by far in the understanding of concepts which are abstracted by the mind … The Chinese are thus seen to be ignorant of that great light of the mind, the art of demonstration. (Cook and Rosemont 1994: 46)

However, we have seen that even in the Classical period before 220 BCE, philosophers such as Mozi and the *bianshi* debaters, as well as Xunzi, established criteria for substantiating knowledge claims and clarifying rational concepts. These thinkers examined the epistemological value of direct experiential testimony, the place of knowledge claims handed down traditionally, and the role of the pragmatic value of acting as though a claim were true for the individual and society.

As early as the 300s BCE, critical philosophy was practiced at the Jixia Academy and thinkers such as Zhuangzi, Mencius, and Xunzi were all quite probably teachers there. The intricate arguments developed on epistemological issues in that period led the Lao-Zhuang thinkers to express a view Karen Carr and P. J. Ivanhoe have labeled "antirationalism" (2000). Lao-Zhuang philosophers noticed that on some questions of truth the evidence is inconclusive and the arguments may be equally compelling on both sides (*Zhuangzi* 2). Even Mencius's analogical way of reasoning, as indeed may be said of that mode of argument in general, did not always provide a resolution to questions of truth, as his debates with Gaozi demonstrate. Such lack of epistemological resolution created a space in which Wang Chong noticed that *xu* beliefs could and did thrive. Wang pointed out that when one cannot be said to "know" that a claim is true, one may continue to believe it because of the appeal of the claim or its use in furthering society's order or betterment. Mozi's defense of the claim that ghosts and spirits act as the instruments of Heaven to reward the good and punish the evil is a prime example of what Wang Chong would call a *xu* belief. Although Wang Chong's identification of *xu* beliefs and their function was novel, nevertheless it lacked the explicit move made by Xunzi, when he stressed that the pursuit of truth required setting aside presuppositions and prejudgments to allow reason to work with clarity. Xunzi recommended a way for controlling our emotional attachments to beliefs which might cloud our recognition of the cogency of evidence and argument that might threaten a *xu* belief.

Zhang Dongsun made an important contribution to Chinese epistemological discussion when he noticed that what is understood as appropriate and sufficient evidence for confirming a belief is established by systems within a culture, what Wittgenstein called language games. Instead of leaving the philosopher with the relativity of knowledge as an outcome of Lao-Zhuang's antirationalism, or forcing one use of "know" to dominate over all others within or between cultures, Zhang Dongsun offered a more robust approach. He held that there are significant overlapping epistemological beliefs about truth and also regarding the procedures for establishing and refuting knowledge claims among cultures. This is why he spoke of *pluralistic* cultural epistemology, rather than *relativistic* cultural epistemology. Zhang may be understood to have claimed that some generalizable or universal ways of proceeding to establish truth and knowledge may be empirically and sociologically identifiable by simply watching how persons from different cultures share similar ways of proceeding epistemologically. Some of these may, indeed, be similar to the kind of knowledge that Wang Yangming called the "pure knowledge" by which our minds structure reality and position us to ask some epistemological questions and not others.

While Lao-Zhuang thought of resolving what counts as true by putting oneself in a particular position of unity with *Dao*, it seems that the truth one knows as a result of this oneness is concerned with fundamentally enabling a new way of being-in-the-world, not a key for unlocking knowledge about facts and objects in reality. A similar judgment seems reasonable to make about Buddhism's doctrine of Threefold Truth and its use of expedient means as a way to enlightenment, even at the expense of "mundane" truth statements.

Additional Readings and Resources

Adler, J. (2012), "Epistemological Problems of Testimony," *Stanford Encyclopedia of Philosophy*, E. Zalta (ed.), https://plato.stanford.edu/archives/win2017/entries/testimony-episprob/. Accessed February 12, 2020.

Carr, K., and P. Ivanhoe (2000), *The Sense of Antirationalism: The Religious Thought of Zhuangzi and Kierkegaard*, New York: Seven Bridges Press.

Chen, Y. (2021), "The Core of Pragmatism and Its Echo in Chinese Philosophy," in R. Ames, Y. Chen, and P. Hershock (eds.), *Confucianism and Deweyan Pragmatism: Resources for a New Geopolitics of Interdependence*, 27–39, Honolulu: University of Hawaii Press.

Clark, M. (1990), *Nietzsche on Truth and Philosophy*, Cambridge: Cambridge University Press.

Cua, A. (1982), *The Unity of Knowledge and Action: A Study in Wang Yangming's Moral Psychology*, Honolulu: University of Hawaii Press.

Fraser, C. (2011), "Knowledge and Error in Early Chinese Thought," *Dao: A Journal of Comparative Philosophy*, 10 (2): 127–48.

Fraser, C. (2013), "Distinctions, Judgment, and Reasoning in Classical Chinese Thought," *History and Philosophy of Logic*, 34 (1): 1–24.

Fraser, C. (2016), "Language and Logic in the *Xunzi*," in E. Hutton (ed.), *Dao Companion to the Philosophy of Xunzi*, 291–321, Dordrecht: Springer.

Graham, A. (1989), *Disputers of the Tao: Philosophical Argument in Ancient China*, Chicago: Open Court.

Hu, S. (1928), *The Development of the Logical Method in Ancient China*, Shanghai: Oriental Book.

James, W. (1907), *Pragmatism: A New Name for Some Old Ways of Thinking*, Cambridge, MA: Harvard University Press.

Jiang, X. (2002), "Zhang Dongsun: Pluralist Epistemology and Chinese Philosophy," in C. Cheng and N. Bunnin (eds.), *Contemporary Chinese Philosophy*, 57–81, Oxford: Blackwell.

Liu, C. (2017), "On the Analogical Rhetoric in *Mencius*," *Journal of Tsinghua University (Philosophy and Social Sciences)*, 32 (1): 67–73.

McLeod, A. (2011), "Pluralism about Truth in Early Chinese Philosophy: A Reflection on Wang Chong's Approach," *Comparative Philosophy*, 2 (1): 38–60.

Muzumdar, H. (1956), "A Chinese Philosopher's Theory of Knowledge," *Midwest Sociologist*, 19 (1): 12–17.

Ryle, G. (1949), *The Concept of Mind*, London: Hutchinson.

Van Norden, B. (2017), *Taking Back Philosophy: A Multicultural Manifesto*, New York: Columbia University Press.

Wittgenstein, L. (1969), *On Certainty*, G. E. M. Anscombe and G. H. VonWright (trans. and eds.), Oxford: Basil Blackwell.

Zhang, D. (1939), "Thought, Language and Culture," *Sociological World*, 5.10, A. Li (trans.) as "A Chinese Philosopher's Theory of Knowledge," (Summer 2011): 1–23, http://www.vordenker.de/downloads/chang-tung-sun_thought-language-culture.pdf. Accessed March 4, 2020.

Moral Theory—Questions about the Nature and Application of Morality

Introduction

Ethics is the study of how humans make moral appraisals. The main branches of ethics are meta-ethics, normative ethics, and applied ethics:

- *Meta-ethics* concerns matters such as what distinguishes moral judgments from other nonmoral value appraisals; the nature of moral language such as the creation and use of moral concepts (i.e., brave, kind, spiteful, callous, etc.); whether moral norms and judgments can be true or false; whether there are absolute ethical truths that have no exceptions; whether there are moral requirements that are universal in scope for all humans; and what is the origin of morality (i.e., is morality invented by humans?).
- *Normative ethics* is concerned with issues such as how a degree of moral responsibility is assessed (i.e., are there conditions that diminish or exacerbate blame?); how do guilt and shame function as moral controls; how does one decide a course of conduct in cases of moral dilemmas; and what is the range of conduct with which morality is concerned (e.g., actions, omissions, attempts, etc.).

- *Applied ethics* goes beyond theory and steps into real-world moral practice by exploring questions such as whether or when specific actions are morally permissible and how ethical recommendations relate to societal policies and laws.

Some fundamental questions addressed by Chinese philosophers and explored in this chapter are these:

- How should we live (i.e., what is the ideal sort of person who should be created following moral values)?
- What is the ultimate purpose of our lives (i.e., to pursue happiness or pleasure? Obey moral rules? Please others or higher beings? Follow our own interests? etc.)?
- What is the origin of our morality (i.e., do humans invent it? Is it inborn or part of our nature? Is it revealed to us by a higher being or intelligence?)?
- What really makes something good or right to do (i.e., is it the consequences of the action? Performing our moral duties? Or going by our passionate feelings?)?
- Is morality universally applicable to humans wherever we find them or relative to particular cultures or even to each individual?
- What is most basic and important in morality: the actions we do or the sort of persons we are (i.e., doing or being)?

Morality as Cultural Propriety: Confucius (c. 551–479 BCE)

The first access that most people have into Chinese philosophy in general, and certainly into the thought of Confucius (*c.* 551–479 BCE), is through the text called the *Analects* (*Lunyu*). This work is an anthology of selected sayings in which Confucius is often, although not exclusively, the main teacher. Its literary structure and layers of sources have been widely studied (Brooks and Brooks 1998). In this text, Confucius advocates for his conception of the kind of project in which our human lives should be invested. This collection of his teachings contains almost nothing directly about ontology or epistemology, but is devoted rather exclusively to the philosophical viewpoints of Confucius about what it means to be a person, how to live a worthwhile and fulfilling life, and even what it takes to lead and organize a state. This text has been among the most discussed and studied works in philosophy.[1]

What distinguishes the human being from other life forms for Confucius is the particular *kind* of being we are. It is not just our rational powers, ability to create art, or the development of language that makes us unique. Instead, we represent the appearance of a certain sort of being, which we call a *person*. The person emerges when a human being (*ren* 人) self-transcends to become a humane person (*ren* 仁). Unlike other animals, the emergence of the human person is the coming of a being that requires others like itself, mutually interacting and creating each other. This relational formation of the person takes place in such a way that we should say that to become a person is a moral achievement. Being humane is inseparable from becoming a person and one who is not humane falls short of being fully a person. In holding this view, Confucius is referring to a way of being-in-the-world. The Chinese character *ren* (仁) is composed of two parts: "human (*ren* 人)" and what is usually taken simply as the number "2" (二). Herbert Fingarette understands humane (*ren* 仁) to refer to the value-laden accomplishment that exists when two *homo sapiens* are making each other into persons, transcending their mere human biological facticity (Fingarette 1972: 37). In terms of moral philosophy, we should pause and notice just how the ground on which Confucius built the ideal of humaneness as personhood may be compared to that found in Western philosophy.

Conditions of Personhood

Daniel Dennett (1976) begins his important discussion of the conditions of personhood by calling attention to the philosophical position that the concepts of "person" and "human being" are not co-extensive. "Human" is a biological category. "Person" is a philosophical one, and to satisfy this designation an entity must possess certain necessary traits. Dennett holds that these are six in number. They are interconnected and in some ways represent hierarchical stages of achievement:

— Persons are beings that display powers of rationality.
— Persons possess states of consciousness (pain, pleasure, memory, intentionality, etc.).
— Persons are the sort of beings who can evoke from others the stance of treating them as persons.

> — Persons are capable of reciprocating toward others this treatment as persons, thereby treating others as persons.
> — Persons must be capable of verbal or standardized, reliable communication.
> — Persons are distinguishable from other entities by being conscious in a special way. This is identified as self-consciousness. In terms of verbal language, this is displayed in the ability to use "I" and other personal pronoun discourse.

Confucius did not develop the sort of philosophical rubric for defining the conditions of personhood that we find in Dennett or other Western thinkers. He insisted that displaying certain cultural proprieties (*li* 禮) in one's relationships both constitutes and evidences humane personhood. In this way, for Confucius, being a person and engaging the world through a moral lens are inseparable. We might rightly insist that exercising the proprieties of conduct (*li*) Confucius was interested in requires something like the cognitive capabilities that Dennett advances, but we must remember that Confucius was invested in the position that becoming a person is primarily a moral achievement.

According to Confucius, the crucible in which this process of interactive relationality with others in the project of person-ing begins is the family (*jia* 家). In the family one learns how to treat others, and this carries over to life in the community and even the state (*Analects* 1.6, 11). By approaching matters in such a way, Confucius set aside any requirement that we think of morality as having a transcendent origin (e.g., coming from God). He naturalized the process of moral self-cultivation. He held that humans can improve and shape one another into humane persons.

The moral concept Confucius used for the familial relationality that eventuates in humaneness is filiality (*xiao* 孝). Observing filial proprieties functions as training for relating to others in the community or state, treating them *as though they were relatives*. In Confucius's thought, it was not so much the institution of the family in the abstract that was important to the emergence of persons, but how one learned to be humane in the family's context and practices (ibid., 1.6). This explains also why Confucius characteristically thought of the relationship between ruler and subject on the model of parent to child. He thought the ruler should care for all his subjects, as a father does for his children (ibid., 2.20). Subjects should give their ruler the same loyalty, obedience, and respect they give to their parents. Instead of recommending that a community should be structured by abstract moral concepts, Confucius shifted the ground to a relational concept and found humaneness to be expressed in thinking of others as family or relatives who we treat reciprocally as we wish to be treated (*shu* 恕, ibid., 15.24). In Confucian tradition, the *Five Relationships* are extensions of the birth family as laboratories in which the human person is developed and actualized. These are parent to child, spouse to spouse, older sibling to younger, ruler to subject, and friend to friend. Insofar as we do not learn and realize humaneness in these relationships, we are to that extent still not yet fully persons.

Confucius highlighted the rites of cultural propriety (*li*) in these relationships as the guidelines for the self-cultivation of humaneness and the moral achievement of personhood (ibid., 1.12). Accordingly, these proprieties do the work that moral rules and duties perform in Western moral theory. Confucius did not make finely grained distinctions between morality, etiquette, personal taste, and proprieties of good manners, although we do find such divisions in many Western moral theories. Following the broad rites of propriety (*li*) within the five relationships is the means by which one *both creates and displays* human personhood (humaneness, *ren*). The sayings collected in *Analects* 4.1–4.8 give us a good picture of Confucius's understanding of such a person. This is someone who is able

1 to endure hardship and enjoy happy circumstances (ibid., 4.2);
2 to identify without prejudice and with accuracy the individuals who are truly good and evil (ibid., 4.3);
3 to be free from the desire to do wrong (ibid., 4.4); and
4 to stand out from those who go astray (ibid., 4.7).

A humane person will assist others in cultivating themselves. That is, they will make those around them better (ibid., 6.30) and actually reciprocally improve themselves in doing so.

A humane person is someone who has improved not merely this or that trait, but their own very being itself; someone who is reaching beyond the current level of personhood to embody something higher. In this way, Confucius took the position that not just the individual but also each generation of humans faces the challenge of self-transcendence, developing with each new iteration. Confucius called persons who excel in humaneness *exemplary persons* (*junzi* 君子) and traces the development of cultural propriety (*li*) largely, although perhaps not exclusively, to them (Ivanhoe

2007). In speaking of exemplary persons, he observed that they "learn broadly of culture, discipline this learning through observing the proprieties (*li*) and moreover, in so doing, they can remain on course without straying from it" (ibid., 6.27). He made the point consistently that *li* is not merely about a superficial action (e.g., giving a gift of jade and silk or knowing when to play the bells and drums in a ceremony). It is about changing one's very being (ibid., 17.11).

Confucius realized that cultural proprieties (*li*) change over time as human need requires and yet he does not approve what is known in Western philosophy as moral relativism. He regarded as authoritative the *li* practiced during the Zhou dynasty extending back to *c*. 1000 BCE, and he insisted that its *li* simply should be emulated (ibid., 2.23, 3.9, 3.21, and 9.3). But he recognized that even Zhou's proprieties developed from previous dynasties and peoples (ibid., 3.14). We may use an analogy to help us understand how Confucius understood the emergence and function of cultural proprieties. Imagine a river flowing within its bed. Culture is like this river and its proprieties, necessary to the cultivation of humane persons, are like the sand. Confucius believed some cultural proprieties come to be fixed like the bedrock, even while some other standards for appropriateness are like the loose sand in the river, or the soft banks deposited by the river's flow. The bedrock itself does not have any source other than the sand in the flow of the river, but it does come to function as the fixed foundation for the river itself. While some proprieties appear and then move along, some settle and become part of the bedrock channel in which the human project itself flows in a given culture.

Confucius counseled rulers to prefer propriety (*li*) as a means to establish order in a state, rather than resorting to law and punishment (ibid., 2.3, 4.13). He held that an exemplary person (*junzi*) disciplines his conduct by such proprieties and does not need the threat of punishment or promise of reward (ibid., 6.27, 15.18). Confucius's favorite student Yan Hui once reported, "The Master is good at drawing me forward a step at a time; he broadens me with culture and disciplines my behavior through the observance of *li*" (ibid., 9.11). Indeed, we can best understand the importance of acting according to *li* in interpersonal relationships when we notice Confucius's response to Yan Hui's question about what is entailed in being a truly humane person. He replied, "Do not look at anything that violates the observance of *li*; do not listen to anything that violates the observance of *li*; do not speak about anything that violates the observance of *li*; do not do anything that violates the observance of *li*" (ibid., 12.1).

Confucian self-cultivation is not simply learning from books; it includes character development, enhancement of talents (e.g., archery, music, building, management, etc.), and obtaining cultural refinement (*wen*) (ibid., 5.15). In thinking of the dedication and commitment needed for cultivating oneself, Confucius called on his students to give their utmost (*zhong*, ibid., 3.19). Self-cultivation does not occur automatically or naturally; it requires sustained and vigorous effort (ibid., 5.15).

Being willing to learn from others is crucial to self-cultivation. Confucius said, "When walking with two other people, I will always find a teacher among them. I focus on those who are good and seek to emulate them, and those who are bad remind me what needs to be changed in myself" (ibid., 7.22, my translation). In Confucianism, persons must "make something out of themselves" through their relationships; there is no natural evolution to development of a humane person. However, others can help us refine ourselves and move toward the goal of being exemplary persons. If others are of exceptional character, we should stand shoulder to shoulder with them (ibid., 4.17), but if they are not, we should not imitate them, but look inwardly and examine ourselves and we should not befriend anyone who is not as good as we are (ibid., 9.25).

Being a humane person cannot be reduced to the dichotomy often found in Western moral theory that characterizes ethics as concerned with either action (doing) or character (being). Confucius recognized the synergy of both what persons *do* and the sort of person they *are*. However, Confucius did not provide the kind of extended philosophical discussion of character development as doing and being which we find in Aristotle's notion of virtue in *Nicomachean Ethics* (Irwin 1999: 18–39).[2] Still, he noted that a humane person will act in a certain way externally, but he will have the proper internal disposition as well (*Analects* 2.8). Such a humane person will become exemplary.

The ideal toward which humans are moving for Confucius is expressed in the notion of the exemplary person (*junzi*). The exemplary person in the *Analects* is a quite different moral ideal than those advocated in many Western moral philosophies. For example, the Confucian exemplary person was not portrayed as "perfect." Confucius does not hold up a concept of abstract flawlessness as the goal for persons to achieve or as the objective of morality. Neither is the exemplary person the same ideal we find in the Western notion of a saint, for whom moral duty overrides all other values, so that the saint does not rest or pursue other nonmoral values if there is yet remaining good to do for others.[3] Nevertheless, exemplary persons in the past and present are the source of the cultural proprieties essential to becoming a human person. The source of *li* is historical and traceable to the actual lives of such persons, not some transcendent being or structure.

In the *Analects*, six of Book 4's remarks specifically describe exemplary persons as those who never abandon humane personhood, but always do what is appropriate (*yi* 義) (ibid., 4.10, 16). They cherish moral excellence (*de* 德) (ibid., 4.11). They are not driven by their desires (ibid., 4.10). Exemplary persons take the high road and not the low one (ibid., 14.23), and they feel ashamed if their high-sounding words are not fully reflected in their deeds (ibid., 14.27). Exemplary persons cherish their excellence of character and self-cultivation over land or thought of gain. They take as much trouble discovering what is right as lesser men take to learn what will pay (ibid., 4.16). Confucius said,

> Wealth and rank are what people want, but if they are the consequences of deviating from the Way [*Dao*], I would have no part in them. Poverty and disgrace are what people deplore, but if they are the consequences of staying on the Way [*Dao*], I would not avoid them. Wherein do the exemplary persons who would abandon their [*ren*] warrant that name? Exemplary persons do not take leave of [*ren* 仁] even for the space of a meal. (*Analects* 4.5)

Book 15 of the *Analects* also preserves a collection of remarks on the exemplary person (*Analects* 15.19, 20, 21, 22, and 23). The positions taken seem consistent with those we find in Book 4. Exemplary persons are the sort of individuals who are distressed by their own deficiencies, not by the failure of others to praise them (ibid., 15.19). They cannot stand the thought of not distinguishing themselves in virtue and excellence (*de*) (ibid., 15.20). They make demands on themselves, whereas petty persons make demands on others (ibid., 15.21). They are self-possessed, calm, and not contentious (ibid., 15.22). When ruling, they promote others on merit, not on their mere words (ibid., 15.23).

In his instructions to his students, Confucius told Zixia to seek to be a scholar-advisor (*ru*) for an exemplary person, not a petty one (ibid., 6.13). He approved of Shiyu's estimation of Qu Boyu, noting that Qu showed himself to be an exemplary person because when the Way (*Dao*) of Heaven was being followed in a state, he gave it his service, but when it was not, he left government (ibid., 15.7). And in an exchange with Ji Kangzi, Confucius made clear why such a choice of association is possible. The ruler who is an exemplary person can affect the entire kingdom with appropriateness (*yi*) and moral excellence (*de*), like the wind that blows over the grass (ibid., 12.19).

As we have noted, Confucius held that cultural proprieties (*li*) arose from the style of life lived by exemplary persons. Of course, there is an obvious, but nonvicious circularity here. Exemplary persons establish the proprieties for relationships, but they also follow those handed down to them through their culture. Interestingly, Confucius set no upward limit for human development in this process, but he did not set abstract perfection as a goal. Instead, he offered specific examples of sages of the past, exemplary persons whose lives were the sources of the cultural *li*: Yao, Wu, Wen, and Shun. He looked back to them.

Persons such as Yao and Shun were theomorphized in Chinese culture, but not because they were nonhuman divinities; it was rather because of the way in which they lived. In fact, later followers did the same for Confucius. We find this remark in the final passages of the *Analects*: "Confucius is the sun and moon which no one can climb beyond" (ibid., 19.24). But these forms of valorization do not hold up these exemplars as perfect or flawless; neither do they necessarily mean that the most creative persons are those of the past. There is always a forward-looking vision in Confucian ethics. He lifted up the ideal that each new generation may produce its own set of exemplary persons and rewrite the *li* for future self-transcendence (Littlejohn 2008 and Rosemont 2002).

Morality as Heaven's Commands: Mozi (c. 470–391 BCE)

While a study of Mozi's moral thought is of paramount importance to an understanding of Chinese philosophy, the dependence of his views on his ontological positions, especially as these are set out in Books 8–37 and 46–9 of the work entitled *Mozi*, is sometimes underappreciated.[4] An understanding of Mozi's views on morality actually begins with what he has to say about Heaven (*tian*). In classical Chinese, the word *tian* has many uses. When in the compound "heaven and earth" (*tian di*), it is used for "reality" or "the totality of existing things." When *tian* occurs by itself, it is used sometimes as "sky," or "nature," or as a nominative for some quasi-personal reality (i.e., more or less as a numinal person) that has a will and guides the course of the universe (Chang 2000). This last use predominates in Mozi's ontology and greatly shapes his moral philosophy.

In the *Mozi*, Heaven is characteristically described as though it is an "agent" capable of intentional action (*yi* 意, and *zhi* 知) and pursuit of its desires (*yu* 慾) (e.g., Chs. 26–8). Accordingly, Heaven is praised by using the moral virtues impartial, generous, wise, and just. According to Mozi, it cares for humans and benefits the worthy by providing resources and blessings, as consequences of moral behavior that it reveals as good and right. Understood in this way, Mozi located the source of moral goodness in the will of Heaven and traced the validation of what is good to the decrees of Heaven's will. Accordingly, we may say that Mozi's moral theory is a version of what is called a *divine command morality*. Heaven commands and rewards what is good, and forbids and punishes what is evil.

Divine Command Theory in Western Philosophy

One of the earliest philosophical works in the West is concerned with the claim that what makes an action morally right and good is that it is commanded by God. In Plato's dialogue *Euthyphro*, the central dilemma explored is whether God commands something because it is good, or whether something is good for the reason that God commands it. Throughout the history of Western philosophy, this concern over the ultimate validation of fundamental moral norms and virtues shows up time and again. Divine command theorists insist that the use of mere human rationality and preference for certain actions in relational situations is insufficient to identify and validate particular moral norms, either because humans are inevitably flawed and limited beings, or because the variety of behavioral expectations among human cultures ultimately reduces morality to a matter of cultural taste and relativity. Accordingly, divine command theorists in the West insist that only a revealed morality originating from a transcendent personal source of unlimited goodness and knowledge can guarantee the correct morality. The significance of the theory of divine command morality is confirmed by noticing that it remains a subject discussed in virtually every contemporary introduction to ethics in the Western academy (e.g., Mackinnon and Fiala 2018: 20–32).

According to Mozi, Heaven orders all things in the course of reality (*dao*) according to its intentions and purposes, including the direction of nature and human history. If we use a philosophical concept from the West, we would say that Heaven is *providential*. It is purposefully directing reality.

When referring to Heaven's exercise of its will, Mozi used the term "mandate or decree" (*ming*). Heaven influences history, decreeing such things as the rise and fall of rulers and states. Mozi insisted that Heaven uses spirits, ghosts, and ancestors as its instruments to reward and punish behavior based on its own ultimate ethical standards and purposes (Graham 1989: 17, 49).

Because he held that Heaven provides commands that express what is desirable and what is not, Mozi rejected any idea that events are predestined or fated to take the form they do. His arguments gathered in the "Against Fate" chapters of his text (35–7) are an attack on the claim that reality is fated; that things must occur as they do. As shown in Chapter 2 of our study, Mozi used a pragmatic type of argument against the position that reality is fated. He said that if we accept the position that life is fated, it would mean that one's position, health, wealth, success, longevity, and the like are already determined and are not consequences of human effort or one's moral choices in life. If this were true, there would be no point in striving to be moral or working diligently to succeed in life. Mozi claimed that the world's rulers, if they genuinely wanted to promote the world's benefits and eliminate harms, must reject this line of reasoning, because such a philosophical view means that everything occurs just as it must and there is no point in trying to change it (*Mozi* 37.10).

Mozi thought a world in which the morally good suffer misfortune and the evil prosper, or rewards and punishments are dispensed for outcomes not in the control of persons, would be irredeemably unfair. Such a world could not be a meaningful one, because humans could not rely on a connection between their moral actions and what they deserve. So, Mozi was driven to take his ontological position that the nature of reality and its processes cannot be determined in advance largely because of his views on moral desert. In other words, the process of reality cannot be fated precisely because Heaven responds and must respond to the conduct of persons in the actual flow of history. It is ultimately Heaven that insures those who practice moral goodness will prosper and the evil will fail.

Mozi argued that Heaven used ghosts and spirits as its instruments to bring about ill-fortune or success depending on the moral choices of persons (ibid., 48.20). However, one could inquire why ghosts and spirits do not intervene to prevent adversities, such as sickness or crimes against persons, protecting the good person from illness or wrongdoing. Chris Fraser holds that if we analyze Mozi's positions on the activity of Heaven, we cannot find a single example of his advocacy of *preemptive intervention* to keep evil from occurring either naturally or because of the actions of humans. Fraser thinks Mozi's position is that if we follow Heaven's way (*Dao*), ghosts and spirits will help our endeavors to be a success. If we turn toward evil, Heaven will send calamities. However, in both cases, we see that Heaven *reacts* to human action, but does not proactively or preemptively intervene to prevent distress or evil caused by the operation of natural processes (i.e., *qi, yin/yang*, and the Five Phases) or by other persons as moral agents. In short, Heaven does not bring us benefits to *encourage* us to be good, but only *rewards* us for being good. Fraser writes, "Similarly, in the Mohist interpretation of history, Heaven does not intervene to prevent wicked tyrants from misgoverning their states and harming their people. Once they do so, however, it responds by punishing them and supporting challengers who depose them" (2014: 15).

Fraser seems right that Mozi did not offer any philosophical theory of preemptive intervention to control or prevent evil. But simply noting this is not enough. It seems clear that this is a serious deficiency in Mozi's understanding of Heaven's role as a purposive agent committed to moral goodness. In fact, his failure to engage this problem calls into question the very basis of his moral theory.

The Mohists used the concept of "Heaven's intention" (*tian zhi* 天知) to underwrite their moral philosophy. They conceived of Heaven as a moral agent and thought that Heaven's intentions, expressed as duties, represent an objective standard of what is morally right. In fact, Mozi held that a coherent social order can rest only on a single, universal, and objective morality applied to all persons and validated by Heaven's response to human actions. If a pluralism of moral values is allowed to exist in a culture, disorder and conflict will be the result:

> Master Mozi spoke, saying: "Ancient times, when people first came into being, were times where there were as yet no laws or government, so it was said that people had differing rules (*ze* 則). This meant that, if there was one person, there was one principle; if there were two, there were two [different] rules. ... The more people there were, the more things there were that were spoken of as rules ... The consequence of this was mutual condemnation ... This resulted in the world's desire to unify the rules of the world, so there was the selection of one who was worthy, and he was established as the Son of Heaven ... If the world is well ordered, it means that the Son of Heaven has also unified the rules of the world through exalting unity with Heaven." (*Mozi* 11.1; see also 13.3 and 13.8)

In itself, this is a crucial philosophical position, embracing moral universals and rejecting moral relativism. Mozi prized order, stability, and the transmission of a unified moral system over the diverse expression of value choices among the populous. He understood his preeminent philosophical task to be the defense of a true morality and the identification of the source from which it originates.

Clarifying Moral Distinctions

Moral Universalism is the notion that there are moral goods and evils that hold regardless of culture, time, or place. That is, slavery, for example, has always been wrong, is wrong, and always will be wrong, quite apart from what any human thinks or culture practices.

Moral Absolutism is the concept that if some action is a moral evil, there are no exceptions to it; even if there might be moral excuses for having done it and these may diminish one's blame, still the act is morally wrong.

Moral Relativism may be of two types. In *descriptive moral relativism*, one notes that simply as a matter of fact individuals and/or cultures differ on what they think or believe morally right or wrong. One could hold this descriptive view and still be a moral universalist or absolutist, because this position focuses on what persons "think" or "believe"; it does not say that true morality is *actually* variable. In *meta-ethical relativism*, the claim is that there is in reality no objectively true moral right or wrong.

While Confucians held that persons should adhere to a culturally received traditional code of appropriate behavior (*li* 禮) that was transmitted from one generation to another by exemplary persons, Mozi's view of the origin of morality was different. He criticized the Confucian position, accusing it of resting morality on nothing more than an elitist consensus about how to behave (i.e., relying on the behavior of *junzi*) (ibid., 39.1–39.13). He thought such a position is both unconvincing and flawed *because it could not distinguish mere custom of behavior from true morality.*

Mozi made a sharp distinction between custom and morality. He held that conformity to traditional proprieties associated with exemplary persons did not ensure that their conduct was actually *morally* right. It proved only that this is the way the elite live. Another way to put this is to say that simply because something is culturally accepted or embraced, this does not mean it is morally good. For Mozi, societies must be built upon actual, demonstrable moral truth that has always been true and will always be so. Only Heaven is an agent able to guarantee such truth. Mozi's point may be extended to notice the fact that although people may *think* something is morally right to do, this does not make it so. Mozi was aware of the diversity of moral norms among persons and cultures. However, he held that simply noticing the diversity in moral views does not mean that there is no universally true and correct morality. It simply means that some people are wrong or blinded by their own desires (Fraser 2011: 142):

> Now the arguments of those who adhere to elaborate funerals and prolonged mourning say: "If elaborate funerals and prolonged mourning are really not the way of the sage kings, how do you account for the fact that the *junzi* (exemplary persons) of the central kingdom practice them and do not stop them, implement them and do not abandon them?" Master Mozi said: "This is what is called '[considering] one's habits convenient and one's customs appropriate [*yi*].' Formerly, to the east of Yue, there was the country of the Kaimu. When a first son was born, they cut him up and ate him. They called this 'fitting for the younger brother.' When the paternal grandfather died, they carried the maternal grandmother away and abandoned her, saying: 'We cannot live with a ghost's wife.' If above, these things are taken to be government practice and, below, they are taken to be customs, and are carried out and not stopped, implemented and not discarded, then are they the way of true humaneness [*ren*] and appropriateness [*yi*]? This is what is called '[considering] one's habits convenient and one's customs as appropriate [*yi*].' " (ibid., 25.14, my changes)

Clearly Mozi understood the problem known in philosophy as cultural relativity and associated Confucius with a version of it. He took the view that even if a practice is a matter of custom in a culture, it is not necessarily morally right. He advocated instead for objective moral standards which he called models, or *fa* (法).

Mozi made use of the notion *fa* as a way of talking about the pattern, order, and structure Heaven gives to reality. He held that Heaven moves intentionally. As it does so, it follows laws and rules (*fa*) in a way analogous to how one who steers a ship makes use of a compass or a carpenter employs a square, plumb line, or level (ibid., 4.1; 27.10). The instructions of Heaven given to worthy persons are examples of these models for living, but the behavior of exemplary persons in a culture is not sufficient, in itself, to be identified with universal true morality. It may be nothing more than custom. For Mozi, Confucius's failure to make this distinction is what led him astray. Indeed, Confucius's valorization of the Zhou dynasty's rules of cultural propriety (*li*) was simply an elevation of one specific culture's customs over that of other communities. Mozi considered this to be a move lacking philosophical foundation and insisted morality must rest on a true, objective, and universal foundation from Heaven.

Not only did Mozi differ from Confucius on the foundation of morality in a meta-ethical sense, but he also advocated an alternative normative ethics. He departed most sharply from the Confucians on the idea that caring for others should be scaled or graded based on who the other persons are and what is their relationship to us. Mozi recommended instead a concept he called "inclusive concern" or "universal love" (*jian ai* 兼爱). We have seen that the Five Relationships play a strategic role in Confucian morality and the creation of the humane person (*ren* 仁). Confucius held that we have different moral duties and are responsible for different actions based on what relationship we have with a person. In fact, the Confucian relational ethic is rooted in the cultivation of particular attachments. When thinking about what to do, I must first consider who is the other person involved and what is my relationship to him or her.[5]

Mozi's philosophical concept of "inclusive concern or universal love" (*jian ai* 兼愛) is quite different as a conduct guide from the Confucian reliance on the Five Relationships.[6] Mozi took the position that in order to achieve social order *all people* must be concerned for each other, showing care for everyone *regardless of their relationship to the agent*. When asked what is the ultimate will of Heaven, Mozi replied, "It is to love all the people in the world universally (*jian ai*)" (ibid., 13.3, my translation). He argued that the lack of *jian ai* or mutual love (*xiang ai* 相愛) is the source of all the harm and injury in the world, while attributing the exact opposite position to the Confucians:

> If this is so, then how can we not examine from what this harm arises? Master Mozi spoke saying: "It arises through *lack* of mutual love (*xiang ai*). Nowadays, feudal lords know only to be concerned for their own states and not to be concerned with the states of others, so they have no qualms about mobilizing their own state to attack another's state. Nowadays, heads of houses know only to be concerned with their own houses and not be concerned with the houses of others, so they have no qualms about promoting their own house and usurping another's house. Nowadays, individual people know only to be concerned with their own person and not to be concerned with the persons of others, so they have no qualms about promoting their own persons and injuring the persons of others ... When the people of the world do not all show concern for each other, then the strong inevitably dominate the weak,

the many inevitably plunder the few, the rich inevitably despise the poor, the noble inevitably scorn the lowly, and the cunning inevitably deceive the foolish. Within the world, in all cases, the reason why calamity, usurpation, resentment and hatred arise is because mutual love [*xiang ai*] does not exist. (ibid., 15.2, my translation)

Mozi claimed that the ultimate will of Heaven can be expressed as *jian ai* (inclusive concern or universal love) or as *xiang ai* (mutual love) toward others, and that all *fa* (moral norms) which express such love are consistent with Heaven's will.

A point of caution is in order. When Mozi called for acting according to "universal love" or "mutual love," he did not mean that we were required to have an emotional feeling of love or attachment to all persons; neither did he mean that Heaven requires that we set aside our own interests and practice self-sacrifice. He was not advocating that all persons love each other in such a way as to make everyone into a friend or a relative. He did not hold that we should love others as ourselves (ibid., 15.4).

Mozi used *jian ai* and *xiang ai* in a way more closely resembling what Western moral philosophers call "reciprocal altruism." He suggested that when we help others, we can expect their help in return. This creates a harmonious morality of mutual benefit:

If, for a moment, we take as a basis what the former kings wrote, in the worlds of the *Da Ya* it is said: "No words are without response, no virtue is without reward. If you present me with a peach, I repay you with a plum." This, then is to say that those who are [inclusively concerned, *jian ai*] for others must themselves receive [concern], and those who hate others must themselves be hated. (ibid., 16.13)

This moral order (*fa*) of Heaven operates in such a way that our own interests include those of others, improving the entire community. Mozi thought that this process would work as follows:

Now if I am to seek to promote the world's benefit and eliminate the world's harm, I shall choose inclusive concern (*jian ai*) as being right. As a result, people will use their acute hearing and keen sight to help each other see and hear; they will use their strong and powerful limbs to help each other in action; and they will use principles to encourage mutual instruction. As a result, those who are old, without wives and children, will have the means of support and nourishment through their old age, and those who are young and weak, or who are alone without a father or mother, will have the means of help and support while they grow into adulthood. (ibid., 16.4)

We may wonder whether Confucius realized the importance of extending the particularized concerns of the Five Relationships into the community at large. The answer is, of course he did. But he seemed to believe that the spread of moral concern would arise in a different manner than Mozi's reciprocal altruism. He thought it would proceed from formed habits of action when following the culture's proprieties (*li*). In practicing concern toward those within my Five Relationships, I will habitualize my heart to carry over my actions to strangers. In being a filial son toward my father, I come to act filially toward other fathers as well. Once the root takes hold, the Way grows from it (*Analects* 1.2, 1.6). Interestingly, Mencius later defends this Confucian position by calling it the extension (*tui*) of the moral virtues we have learned from close relationships to people more generally as a kind of operative moral principle (*Mengzi* 1A7).[7]

Moral Effortlessness: Lao-Zhuang Views on Morality (c. 350–139 BCE)

The *Daodejing* (*DDJ*) sets forward the position that when we try to take actions to make something happen in the world by our own reasoning, plans, and contrivances, we inevitably make a mess of it. This includes trying to make the world a better place, to improve it (or ourselves) morally. Whereas, if we take our hands off of the course of our lives and move with *Dao*, it will untangle all life's knots, blunt its sharp edges, and soften its harsh glare (*DDJ*, 56). For the philosophical masters in the Lao-Zhuang tradition, it was only when people abandoned oneness with *Dao* that they began to make moral distinctions and employ moral virtue and vice concepts in language. When humans speak of beauty and ugliness, courage and cowardice, good and evil, we are using discriminations of our own making. These distinctions do not belong to *Dao* itself. The *DDJ* makes this point in the passage below by specifically mentioning several of the virtue distinctions made in Confucian moral and social philosophy: humane personhood (*ren*), appropriateness (*yi*), filial piety (*xiao*), and kindness (*ci*):

When the great *Dao* is abandoned, humaneness (*ren*) and appropriateness (*yi*) appear.
When wisdom and erudition emerge, great hypocrisy arises.
When the six relationships (between persons) are out of harmony, then the distinctions of filiality and kindness arise. (*DDJ*, 18, my translation)

Distinction making in morality, which includes the employment of virtue concepts (e.g., courage, honesty, kindness, etc.), is regarded as a kind of disease in Lao-Zhuang tradition. This "disease" is likewise condemned in the *Zhuangzi*, Chapters 2 and 5 (Watson 1968: 45–6, 68–9, 72, and 74). In Lao-Zhuang, it is not so much the lack of inclusive concern (*jian ai*) that is the source of all the world's moral evils, as it is in Mohism, but rather the fighting and struggling over human-made distinctions that causes suffering, strife, and injury (*DDJ*, 18, 38).

The cure for this disease, and the conflicts it causes, is not to begin the process of distinction making at all, or if one is already engaged in it, one should empty oneself of it by forgetting such distinctions and returning to unity with *Dao*. To be "empty" is a way of talking about getting rid of the moral and social distinctions that Daoist believe tie us in knots and erupt in the desires that are the source of our all-human suffering, violence, and immorality. Thieves arise from stealing. Stealing arises from the distinction that this thing is mine not yours. Once this distinction is made, greed emerges and the desire to steal and become a thief follows from it.

If we empty ourselves of such distinctions in the very beginning, the whole degenerate process dissolves and we are free to be one with *Dao* and live out of a sense of its presence and power. The result of such free and easy living is what Lao-Zhuang masters called by the concept *de* (德; *DDJ*, 10, 21, 23, 28, 38, 41, 49, 51, 54, 55, 59, 60, 63, 65, 68, and 79). Just as we have seen with respect to the term *tian*, *de* also has multiple uses. In Chinese, its uses include "excellence," "virtue," "power," and "charisma." It is not a good idea to reduce the meaning of *de* to any one of these translations exclusively. So, in what follows, the term is left untranslated and this gives the interpreter a chance to place it in context and see the actual work it is doing in a passage:

> To act with no expectation of reward;
> To lead without lording over others;
> Such is mysterious *de* (*xuande*). (*DDJ* 10, my translation)
> Cultivate *Dao* in your person, and the *de* you develop will be genuine.
> Cultivate *Dao* in your family, and the family's *de* will be more than enough.
> Cultivate *Dao* in your village, and the village's *de* will long endure.
> Cultivate *Dao* in your state, and the state's *de* will be abundant.
> Cultivate *Dao* throughout the world, and the world's *de* will be pervasive.
> (*DDJ* 54, my translation)

Since the Lao-Zhuang project advocates emptying oneself of moral distinctions, it is very important to note that the tradition is not recommending that one become amoral, and certainly not immoral. Although the person has set aside or emptied himself of human moral designations, and does not view life and relationships through the lens they represent, he is now empowered by a presence (*Dao*) that results in the expression of great virtuous power (*de*).

It may be surprising to notice that in the Lao-Zhuang materials, *de* is not shown through effort, striving, or training of the sort we find in cultivating oneself to perform cultural proprieties as in Confucianism. It is exhibited with an effortlessness for which Daoists use the concept *wu-wei* (無為; *DDJ* 2, 3, 10, 43, 47, 57, 63, and 64). "The [persons who possess] highest *de* do not strive for *de* and so they have it" (*DDJ* 38). These characters (*wu-wei*) were rendered into English by the previous generation of translators as "nonaction." Consequently, many interpreters understood *wu-wei* to mean that the *DDJ* was recommending quiescence and inactivity as the way to practice *Dao*. But the text says clearly that persons should be active:

Act, but as *wu-wei*.
Be active, but do not let your conduct be intentional and deliberative.
(*DDJ* 63, my translation)

Conduct Theory and Morality

In morality, there is a wide range of conduct for which humans are appraisable. Indeed, the sorts of conduct that is the subject of moral evaluation show up across cultures as part of what we might consider the grammar of the moral form of life in which humans engage. Conduct is distinguished broadly from "happenings" that occur in persons' lives, but are not morally appraised. There are many noteworthy works studying the types of conduct significant for moral appraisal. A few of the classical studies include Donald Davidson (2001), Carl Ginet (1990), Judith Thomson (1977), and Eric D'Arcy (1963). Typical conduct that is subject to moral evaluation includes the following:

Action. An intentionally caused event is no longer simply a happening, it is an action. One is no longer just an entity with events happening in life; one is an agent. One is the direct cause of an event; one brings it about. One not only intends it, but desires to do it. It is known to the agent, and the agent is not surprised at its occurrence. The agent has control over causing the action.

Attempt. Attempts share many of the same characteristics as actions, such as intention, effort, and desire. But they are unsuccessful efforts to cause an action and their failure may be traced to any number of factors in one's control or not. We may ask whether the attempt was a convincing one or one employing a reasonable effort to realize an action.

Omissions. One is appraised for an omission when one should act but does not. We may ask whether the omission was an intentional one, as in the case of a refusal, or if it was a result of negligence or carelessness.

The Lao-Zhuang concept of *wu-wei* is used for a type of conduct. We typically think that morality is concerned only with our actions. But upon reflection we notice it can also focus on our omissions (things we should have done but did not do) and our attempts. Action, omission, and attempt are types of conduct of moral importance. Moral appraisals may be directed toward any of these conduct types: action, omission, and attempt. *Wu-wei* is another kind of discriminator for conduct. It differs from action in being nondeliberative and nonintentional. It differs from omission in the doing of something. It differs from attempt in realizing *Dao.* It is felt as natural and spontaneous movement coming directly from the storehouse of *Dao* and displays its *de* in the person's effortless movements.

This emphasis on acting effortlessly, naturally, and spontaneously in *wu-wei* may seem somewhat problematic for a person steeped in Western moral traditions. Characteristically, Western philosophers insist that in order to act morally we must think about what we are choosing to do and weigh out the consequences. But in Lao-Zhuang, moving spontaneously and naturally along with *Dao* results in the highest moral efficacy (*de*). *Wu-wei* conduct is free from the tangles we have created for ourselves by the institutions, rules, and distinctions that clutter our minds and generate tension in our life together. As long as we apply our deliberations, pay attention to our motivations, and calculate the consequences, we will be entangled in human distinctions and unfilled and discontent. The morality of *wu-wei* conduct lies in the fact that it accords in the situation with an efficacy that can only be attributed to *Dao* and not to the result of human wisdom, planning, or contrivance. This is the meaning of the claim that the person who is moved by *Dao* exhibits profound and mysterious *de* (*DDJ* 10).

The *DDJ* does not say that this efficacy has no connection with the standard virtues we use as distinctions in moral language. This is not the point of the text's thoroughgoing criticism of human moral distinctions. The text takes the view that following the demands and rules set up by convention, as though they were ends in themselves, will lead only to frustration and misery, whereas *wu-wei* conduct rooted in an experience with *Dao* will result in "gaining the world," and things will be in harmony. Everything becomes well ordered (*DDJ* 3). Should barons and kings be able to express it (*de*), the myriad creatures would transform themselves (*DDJ* 37).

What seems clear philosophically is that the Lao-Zhuang teachers advocate a position on the origin of moral knowledge and the impetus of ethical behavior that is ultimately unassailable by reason. Any criticism we might make of the Lao-Zhuang position can be deflected simply by saying that the critic has no experience of being one with *Dao* or of having received its power of moral excellence (*de*).

This Daoist response is related to the association of emptying oneself of moral distinctions with a rhetorical analogy challenging persons to preserve "the feminine":

Know the male but preserve the female
And be a canyon for all the world.
If you are canyon for all the world,
constant *de* will never leave you. (*DDJ* 28)

In Lao-Zhuang, femininity represents receptivity, probably because in sexual relations, the female receives. To the would-be follower of *Dao,* the *DDJ* asks:

Opening and closing Heaven's gate,
Can you play the part of the female? (*DDJ* 10)

When the text speaks of opening and closing Heaven's gate, it is referring to the entry into a state of alternate awareness, one devoid of the commonplace distinctions we make habitually. If one succeeds in playing the part of the female, one will receive an awareness of *Dao* that is transformative, and the person will be enabled to move in *wu-wei* and display boundless *de*.

In the *Zhuangzi*, the essay taking up chapters 8 through 10 is devoted to an exposition of *Dao* and *de*. The essay uses the first person and employs illustrations of its points internally. The most crucial difference between this essay in the *Zhuangzi* and the *DDJ* remarks is that the essay makes no mention of the concept of *wu-wei*. Instead, the stress is placed on finding one's moral bearings by returning to naturalness and embracing one's "inborn nature" (*xingming*).[8] The writer of the essay says,

> My definition of expertness has nothing to do with humaneness (*ren* 仁) and appropriateness (*yi*); it means being expert in regard to your *de* that is all. My definition of expertness has nothing to do with humaneness or appropriateness; it means following the true form of your inborn nature that is all. (*Zhuangzi* 8, Watson 1968: 102)

The essay makes the argument that human society has been on a steady decline from the distant past when persons ceased following *Dao* and expressing its *de*, and began to set up their own moral discriminations. The author argues that holding elite Confucian values, such as humaneness and appropriateness, and the making of other moral distinctions is actually the source of confusion, unlawfulness, and disorder, and not the remedy of these evils. The writer of the essay claims that it was not until *Dao* and its *de* were cast aside that the various moral distinctions and ideals by which humans live were created, and following on the use of these came disorder and disharmony (*Zhuangzi* 8, 9, ibid., 101, 105, 106). This claim is parallel to that made in *DDJ* 18.

The author of this essay also argued that the use of rules of cultural propriety (*li*) as in Confucianism is not the proper means by which one can become moral and enjoy a fulfilling life, but naturalness and spontaneity born of unity with *Dao* resident in one's inner nature are the true means for such an achievement:

> If we must use cords and knots, glue and lacquer to make something firm, this means violating its natural virtue. So the crouchings and bendings of *li* [i.e., the cultural proprieties] and music, the smiles and beaming looks of humaneness and appropriateness, which are intended to comfort the hearts of the world, in fact destroy their naturalness. (*Zhuangzi* 8, ibid., 100)

In the *Zhuangzi*, chapter 9, the author makes the point that the domestication of horses destroys their nature, and "as far as inborn nature is concerned, the clay and the wood surely have no wish to be subjected to compass, curve, and plumb line" (*Zhuangzi* 9, ibid., 104–5). The author says

Confucians "huff and puff" after humaneness and stand on their tiptoes to reach appropriateness, but if *Dao* had not been cast aside, no one would have ever even called for these values. Everyone would have lived by "inborn nature" and expressed true *de* (*Zhuangzi* 9, ibid., 105).

Elsewhere in the *Zhuangzi* we see an interest in trying to describe what it is like for one to act in *wu-wei*. These passages may certainly be connected in sentiment and philosophical function to the remarks we have noted about *wu-wei* in the *DDJ*. The perfected person's (*zhenren* 真人) *de* comes from oneness with *Dao*, so that he flows in life spontaneously and effortlessly, without thought. *Wu-wei* conduct exhibits the efficacy of action and possesses the emotional feel that can only be associated with examples; it cannot be explained in language. Accordingly, the *Zhuangzi* offers several analogies for how moving in *wu-wei* feels. Moving in *wu-wei* is like the ferryman in the gulf of Shangshen who handles his boat with commensurate skill (*Zhuangzi* 19, ibid., 200); the amazing hunchback cicada catching man (*Zhuangzi* 19, ibid., 199); Bohun Wuren's skill in archery (*Zhuangzi* 21, ibid., 230–1); Qing, who makes bell stands that seem to be the work of the spirits (*Zhuangzi* 19, ibid., 205–6); and Chui the artist who can draw free-hand as true as a compass or T-square (*Zhuangzi* 19, ibid., 206). All of these stories are examples of persons who seem to be able to perform in highly skilled and efficacious ways without deliberation and who report feelings of naturalness, effortless, and spontaneity as they act. These examples are presented as analogues for what it is like to move in *wu-wei* and express moral excellence (*de*) apart from human distinctions.

Morality as Cultivating Our Inborn Endowments: Mencius (c. 372–289 BCE)

The *Mengzi* records Mencius's position that human persons are distinct from other sentient creatures in having four moral propensities or seeds (*siduan*) that dispose them to view reality and human persons through what can be called a moral lens. Another way of saying this is that humans "moral" (as a verb) naturally in the same ways that a kernel of corn yields corn and not tomatoes. According to Mencius, humans do not have to learn to feel compassion toward other sentient beings or be disposed to act morally. It is in our nature to do so. Of course, Mencius realized all humans must learn specific human or cultural moralities, but he argued that they are enabled and inclined to do so because of incipient predispositions in their natural endowment. A crucial passage that sets out this understanding reads as follows:

> My reason for saying that no man is devoid of a heart-mind (*xin*) sensitive to the suffering of others is this. Suppose a man were, suddenly, to see a young child on the verge of falling into a well. He would certainly be moved with compassionate apprehension, not because he wanted to get in the good graces of the parents, nor because he wished to win the praise of his fellow villagers or friends, nor even because he disliked the cry of the child. From this it can be seen that whomever's heart-mind is devoid of compassion is not human, whomever's heart-mind is devoid of shame is not human, whomever's heart-mind is devoid of courtesy and modesty is not human, and whomever's heart-mind is devoid of the ability to make moral discernment is not human. The heart-mind's compassion is the seed of humaneness; the heart-mind's shame is the seed of dutifulness; the heart-mind's courtesy and modesty is the seed of propriety; the heart-mind's moral discernment is the seed of wisdom. Humans have these four seeds (*duan*) just as they have four limbs. For a person possessing these four seeds to deny his own potentialities is for him to cripple himself; ... If a man is able to develop all of these four seeds, it will be like a fire starting up or a spring bubbling up. When these are fully developed, he can tend the whole realm within the Four Seas, but if he fails to cultivate them, he will not be able even to serve his own parents. (*Mengzi* 6A10, my translation)

In this passage, Mencius was making the difference between his position and that of Mozi very clear. Mencius held that all humans have inborn moral endowments, just as assuredly as we are born with four limbs. His point about the child on the verge of the well is that these endowments will naturally incline us toward the compassionate action of saving the child. The cultivation of these seeds enables a person to increase in humaneness just as a fire continually builds or a spring that has begun to vent will flow ever more strongly (ibid., 6A6). Mencius believed a person can, by virtue of cultivating his inborn moral endowments, find a special kind of energy that he calls "flood-like energy (*haoran zhi qi*)" that brings joy over his decisions and power to perform virtue. That is, one becomes a lover of the good and the right as a result of cultivating and exercising one's internal inborn moral dispositions.

Accordingly, Mencius took the interesting position that for a morally cultivated person, doing what is right pleases the heart-mind in the same way that succulent meat pleases the palate. He also likened the morally accomplished individual to a connoisseur of fine food or music (ibid., 6A7). The significance of this way of arguing by analogy for moral philosophy is that Mencius held the position that the moral cultivation of a person will so refine his judgment that he can rule the entire realm humanely like Yao or Shun, the sage-kings of the past, and will love doing what is morally right, good, and just. Self-centered actions such as greed, dishonesty, or corruption fall away because they no longer hold any attraction. What one desires will be directed toward the good. A morally cultivated person will experience the thought to do something evil as though he were eating rancid meat or hearing sour notes. On the other hand, if we try to interact with our world without the benefit of having cultivated our incipient moral endowments, we will wander around lost and puzzled or even become evil and wicked. Mencius said:

> For a man to give full realization to his heart-mind is for him to understand his own nature, and a man who knows his own nature will know Heaven. By retaining his heart and nurturing his nature, he is serving Heaven. (ibid., 7A1) There are cases where one person is twice, five times or countless times better than another person, but this is only because there are people who fail to make the best of their native endowment. (ibid., 7A6)

Western Philosophy and the Blank Slate (*Tabula Rasa*)

In Western philosophy since the early Modern period (*c.* eighteenth century), philosophers have taken the view that the human mind at birth is a blank slate (*tabula rasa*) and that experience furnishes it with ideas and concepts as the senses provide it with information. John Locke (1632–1704) is perhaps the philosopher most clearly associated with this position. Under this theory, the mind is born without built-in mental content or innate moral dispositions. All ideas derive from one's sense experience, acculturation, and socialization, and none are inborn (Locke 1959: I, 37–91). When extended to moral philosophy, this position leads to the view that morality is a human invention and one learns moral distinctions based on the culture in which one is raised. However, recently, philosophy and evolutionary science have moved in tandem toward a coherent assault on the blank slate theory and more toward an appreciation of certain natural and hereditable endowments that may be similar to what Mencius pointed to in the 300s BCE. For example, there is a fruitful area of comparison between Mencius's position about natural moral endowment and the position of Steven Pinker in his work *The Blank Slate: The Modern Denial of Human Nature* (2003). Likewise, a substantial amount of research into the life-world of higher primates done by Frans De Waal (1996) and others invites us to connect Mencius's position with the findings of evolutionary ethics and the hereditary transmission of a number of important moral dispositions and behaviors (e.g., cooperation, reciprocity, compassion, and others).[9]

When reading Mencius, we cannot forget what we have learned about early Chinese ontology. In Mencius, there is no object that is a self or soul, such as we find in Western philosophy. The fact that Mencius chose the process metaphors of agriculture to describe the way in which the nature of the heart-mind thinks morally (i.e., moral seeds that grow and develop an individual into a full-blown moral person) reveals that he was being consistent with the ontology of the early Chinese worldview in which he was steeped. The Chinese word for *nature* (*xing* 性) is related to a word that means "to live/grow" (*sheng*). So, to speak of the nature of a thing as Mencius did can refer to the defining characteristics of a thing as these will develop over the course of time, if given a normal, healthy environment. Mencius used the term "human nature" in this sense. Accordingly, the Chinese view of human nature with which Mencius was working may be summarized in this way: humans are in the process of "selfing," but as they do so, they make use of preloaded propensities that lie behind the complex and dynamic conduct that comes to define them as selves.

Of course, we actually have no problem accepting this idea of developmentalism with respect to the body. We realize that it is endowed with incipient messaging from the biological DNA by which it grows, changes, and takes shape through a process that is inborn. Mencius's point is that we "person" or "self" as well as "body." So here we are speaking of verbs, not exclusively of nouns. To the extent these concepts function as nouns (the body, the self), they are naming an ongoing process not a fixed, immutable object.

About these views, Dennis Arjo wrote, "Mencius presents a sophisticated and plausible moral psychology that unites our basic psychological endowment with our moral nature. Since he argues that all humans have these hearts, Mencius is able to equate their development into moral virtues with proper human development" (Arjo 2011: 457). However, even inborn moral endowments cannot develop into virtues without cultivation. Mencius lamented that he had heard some people say they were unable to actualize one or more of the virtues. He believed that such persons were "destroying themselves" (*Mengzi* 4A10). In one case, Mencius and King Xuan of Qi engaged in a dialogue about the king's having spared an oxen being led to slaughter for use in a ritual. The king said, "I cannot bear its frightened appearance." Mencius told the king that this feeling is the kind he should act upon in order to be a great monarch. The king replied that he did not understand the usefulness of his feelings until Mencius explained it to him. Mencius had, in effect, helped the king reflect on and appreciate the function of his innate moral sensibility of compassion (Van Norden 2011: 93). As the dialogue progresses, Mencius tried to help the king understand that while the king felt it was right to show compassion to the ox, he was not showing the same compassion to his people, who were suffering from high taxes and wars (*Mengzi* 1A7).

One way of accessing Mencius's ideas on morality is to notice how they are embedded in his responses to Mozi, who is a principal target of several philosophical assaults in the *Mengzi*. For example, Mozi advocated "inclusive concern," calling for persons to treat all others alike morally without any partiality. Mozi thought impartial concern is a realistic moral norm because it has nothing to do with emotional, kinship, or other attachments to others. It consisted of treating everyone without favoritism in order to produce the best consequences for all concerned. In his response, Mencius was not so much bothered by the universality of Mozi's ethical norm, as by Mozi's aligning morality with the beneficial consequences or profit of an action and his association of such utility with the establishment of the norms (*fa*) of inclusive concern.

Mencius argued that validating what is moral to do based on the concept of beneficial consequences means losing sight of the nature of morality itself. He held that doing what is the morally right thing may actually not benefit us or be profitable to the greatest number, but it might be still be acting according to our natural, inborn moral endowments. Sometimes doing what is right will even cost one's life. Mencius observed:

Life is something I want; appropriate moral propriety is also something I want. If I cannot have both, I will forsake life and select appropriate moral propriety. On the one hand, although I want to live, there is something I want more than life. That is why I do not just hang on to life at all costs. Death is something I hate, but there is something I hate more than death. That is why there are troubles I do not avoid. If there is nothing a person wants more than life, then why should one have scruples about undertaking any action so long as it will keep him alive? (*Mencius* 6A10, my translation)

The moral self in Mencius's philosophy is described by means of an agricultural analogy, as we have seen. The four internal moral dispositions Mencius described are characterized as "seeds." There is much about a seed that grows naturally but its health and development can be enhanced by cultivation and care. Mencius held that humans grow morally in a similar fashion and just as growth of a crop is gradual, development of a person into a humane being is likewise so.[10]

It is very important that we understand Mencius's position. His claim about inborn moral dispositions cannot be falsified by the simple fact of human wrongdoing. He did not mean that humans are innately programmed to be morally exemplary; or that they will automatically grow into morally good beings. Here the comparison between Mencius's position and the irresistibility of a kernel producing corn breaks down. He meant that human nature is predisposed or inclined by means of inborn tendencies to see and feel the world through a moral lens, but not that moral goodness or virtue of character is inevitable. Mencius insisted not only on the gradual nature of self-cultivation and the effort required to achieve it but also on the importance of a certain kind of environment as necessary to produce the morally mature person. Circumstances can affect us, just as our natural endowments may do so. Evil and violent times can retard the youth, just as drought can harm the crops (*Mengzi* 6A7; 6A9).

Mencius used another analogy to talk about how one's moral life, even after being cultivated, may yet be destroyed. Persons looking at such an individual might think that he had no inherent moral sensibilities, but this is the wrong conclusion to draw. Mencius employed the analogy of Ox Mountain to make his point:

There was a time when the trees were luxuriant on Ox Mountain, but since it is on the outskirts of a great city, the trees were constantly being cut down. Is it any wonder that they are no longer luxuriant? People seeing only its current baldness think that the mountain never had any trees. A person's letting go of his true heart-mind (i.e., its sensibilities) is like the case of the trees and the axes ... if this happens repeatedly, then he will no longer be able to preserve what was originally in him, and when that happens, the man is not far removed from an animal. Seeing his resemblance to an animal, persons will be led to think that he never had any native endowment (of the sensibilities). (*Mengzi* 6A8, my translation)

The environment in which one lives, the persons whom one befriends, or the net result of habitual activity may destroy the evidences of the natural moral endowment all possess.

Still, Mencius said that water naturally flows downhill, if dikes and dams do not restrict it. By analogy, human beings tend toward the good, just as water flows downhill (*Mengzi* 6A2). So, against Mozi, Mencius argued that moral self-development is not rooted in our assessment of the consequences of behavior, but in human nature itself and the sensibilities that, if heeded, lead us to the virtues.

Morality as Carving and Polishing the Person: Xunzi (310–220 BCE)

By the time Xunzi (i.e., Master Xun or Xun Kuang) matured into the position of leader of the Jixia Academy in about the fourth century BCE, the situation in China was grave indeed, much worse than in Mencius's day. The chaos, violence, and political corruption of Xunzi's time influenced his thinking and interpretation of Confucius's teachings. In short, the context made him feel that it was obvious that Mencius was wrong about the inherent moral structure of human nature. Unlike Mencius, Xunzi believed that human nature is disposed to self-interest and that, left alone without moral guidance and the restrictions of law, self-interest will degenerate into selfishness and breed disorder and chaos. While Xunzi specifically attacked Mencius in chapter 23 of the *Xunzi*, his objections to the goodness of human nature and acting according to our inner nature apply as well to the Lao-Zhuang tradition, which valorizes acting naturally.

Xunzi argued that goodness will not grow from within like corn stalks from kernels, because human inclinations are not the four propensities Mencius identified, but desires for beautiful sights and sounds, comfort, and power. Unless controlled, these and other self-interested desires propel one to use of violence, willful violation of others, and destruction of social order. Xunzi said,

> People's nature is bad. Their goodness is a matter of deliberate effort. Now people's nature is such that they are born with a fondness for profit. If they follow along with this, then struggle and contention will arise, and yielding and deference will perish therein. They are born with feelings of hate and dislike in them. If they follow along with these, then cruelty and villainy will arise, and loyalty and trustworthiness will perish therein. They are born with desires of the eyes and ears, a fondness for beautiful sights and sounds. If they follow along with these, then lasciviousness and chaos will arise, and ritual [i.e., proprieties of conduct *li*] and *yi* [appropriateness], proper form and good order, will perish therein. Thus, if people follow along with their inborn dispositions and obey their nature, they are sure to come to struggle and contention, turn to disrupting social divisions and order, and end up becoming violent. (*Xunzi* 23, Hutton 2014: 248)

Given his position on human nature, we can understand why Xunzi held that persons must be transformed by following the guidance of moral proprieties of human conduct (*li*) handed down to each generation. Individuals require substantial external control to become fully moral and humane (*ren* 仁).

In the development of his moral philosophy, Xunzi turned away from the agricultural analogies employed by Mencius and made use of craft analogies: woodworking, jade carving, and filing of metal. He described the original human nature of persons as crooked wood that requires the steaming and straightening of a frame in order to be good. He also compared human nature to blunt metal that requires honing and grinding in order to become sharp, as well as to raw jade that requires cutting and polishing in order to become something of worth:

> Thus, crooked wood must await steaming and straightening on the shaping frame, and only then does it become straight. Blunt metal must await honing and grinding, and only then does it become sharp. Now since people's nature is bad, they must await teachers and proper models, and only then do they become correct. They must obtain *li* [i.e., cultural proprieties] and *yi*, and only then do they become well ordered. Now without teachers or proper models for people, they will be deviant, chaotic, and not well ordered. In ancient times, the sage kings saw that because people's nature is bad, they were deviant, dangerous, and not correct, unruly, chaotic, and not well ordered. Therefore for their sake they set up *li* and *yi*, and established proper models and measures. ... Among people of today, those who are transformed by teachers and proper models, who accumulate culture and learning, and who make *li* and *yi* their path, become [*junzi*, exemplary persons]. Those who give rein to their nature and inborn dispositions, who take comfort in

being utterly unrestrained, and who violate *li*, become petty men. (*Xunzi* 23, ibid., 248–9)

Given the importance of the cultural proprieties (*li*) established by the sages of old to the task of the crafting of a humane person, Xunzi offered an explanation of the origin of the *li*:

From where did *li* [proprieties of conduct] arise? I say: Humans are born having desires. When they have desires but do not get the objects of their desires, then they cannot but seek some means of satisfaction. If there is no measure or limit to their seeking, then they cannot help but struggle with each other. If they struggle with each other then there will be chaos, and if there is chaos then they will be impoverished. The former kings hated such chaos, and so they established *li* and *yi* [appropriateness] in order to divide things among people, to nurture their desires, and to satisfy their seeking. They caused desires never to exhaust material goods, and material goods never to be depleted by desires, so that the two support each other and prosper. This is how *li* arose. (*Xunzi* 19, ibid., 201)

Xunzi held that if persons conform their temperament, will, and understanding according to the proprieties of conduct (*li*), they will be disciplined and successful in the community; if not, they will be perverse and violent or slovenly and rude. Accordingly, a person who disregards *li* cannot find a place of fulfillment in the culture, and a state without *li* cannot attain peace.

Thomas Hobbes and the Veneer Theory of Morality

While there are many contemporary theories of what is called the original state of nature of humans prior to the emergence of morality and social order, most are modifications in one way or another of the theories of Thomas Hobbes (1588–1679).

Hobbes's understanding of human nature and the establishment of morality as a rule structure to bring order and create society as expressed in his work *The Leviathan* (1651) bears some striking similarities to Xunzi's positions. In the state of nature without morality and law, Hobbes thought each person decided for himself how to act, and was judge, jury, and executioner in any dispute with other persons. He thought that human nature was selfish (not merely self-interested) and brutish. Each individual pursued his own interests and desires and thus this condition of existence became a state of war, all against all (Hobbes 2018: 113–14). Life was filled with fear and existence was made short, brutish, and nasty (ibid.: 115).

Hobbes believed, though, that humans in the state of nature nevertheless had the power of reason and they determined that war of all on all was ultimately destructive for everyone. So, humans created morality as a kind of veneer or cultural overlay of their selfish nature as a way to control conduct and create order and peace. Hobbes called the principles of morality and law the "laws of nature," but they should be understood as the rules for prudent coexistence. Hobbes argued that in order to enforce these rules, the people handed authority over to a sovereign power (government or the Leviathan). While similar in some ways to Xunzi's position on morality, Hobbes's view did not explicitly trace the establishment of proprieties in morality and law to the actions and wisdom of sages of old as did Xunzi.

Xunzi argued that if Mencius were correct and human nature were such as to move persons toward the good like water flowing downhill, there would have been no necessity for the emergence of proprieties of conduct (*li*). There seems to be a crucial difference between Xunzi and Mencius to be noted here. For Mencius, the seeds of morality are inborn. While we have to cultivate them, nevertheless, they are embedded in human nature and provide the inclination to do good in the same way that water seeks the downhill path. But for Xunzi, the proprieties of conduct (*li*) are created by humans. They have their source outside of human nature in the ordinary exigencies of survival of the individual, the community, and the state. We might have had different proprieties of conduct from those we now live by if actual history had been different. Moreover, the moral distinctions we have at present might also change over time.

Even so, while the differences between these two philosophers seem dramatic, actually they may not be as deep or far-reaching as we think at first. Much of what Mencius said does not necessarily contradict Xunzi's view of the proprieties (*li*). If pushed far enough philosophically, it seems Mencius would be forced to maintain that there is a limit to the extent to which morality can change because it is established by the inherent moral "seeds" in all persons. But all this depends on what view we take of Mencius's position on the question, "From where the seeds of human nature come?" Are they endowments of Heaven as some have interpreted him to have believed or perhaps they became part of human nature only after a long history of action and decision in the development of the human species much as a contemporary evolutionary ethicist might claim? Under an evolutionary interpretation of the origin of the Mencian seeds of morality, his position may be compatible with that of Xunzi. That is, cultural proprieties (*li*) may be said to have originated from the style of living exhibited by exemplary persons, but over time, dispositions to act as they did might have become heritable inclinations. Such an approach takes Xunzi's position that the *li* was invented by humans based on the actual lives of the sages and harmonizes it with Mencius's inborn seeds of morality by explaining them as heritable tendencies based along the generations. Of course, neither Mencius nor Xunzi made such an argument.

Xunzi certainly did not believe that Heaven gave us a nature that is disposed to goodness and compassion, or even impartial care (Mozi's *jian ai*). He claimed that Heaven does not care about human behavior at all or how the course of things affects humans. Heaven cannot be appeased or persuaded to bring humans good fortune. Xunzi thought that if there is good fortune for humans, they make it happen through responsible government and a well-ordered society. Likewise, Heaven does not make people poor or bring calamities. Xunzi held that Heaven has no will and no mind, and thus does not act to bring judgment or reward, quite to the contrary of what Mozi had said:

> If you strengthen [agriculture and textile production] and moderate expenditures, then Heaven cannot make you poor. If your means of nurture are prepared and your actions are timely, then Heaven cannot make you ill. If you cultivate the Way [*Dao*] and do not deviate from it, then Heaven cannot ruin you. … If [agriculture and textile production] are neglected and expenditures are extravagant, then Heaven cannot make you wealthy. If your means of nurture are sparse and your actions are infrequent, then Heaven cannot make you sound in body. If you turn your back on the Way and act recklessly, then Heaven cannot make you fortunate. (*Xunzi* 17, ibid., 175, my modifications)

Xunzi employed philosophical argument to move us to cease fearing a Heaven that cannot act and lacks a mind and will. He warned that it is human irresponsibility that should really be feared. The enemies of humankind are villagers who fail to make provision for dikes to withstand floods, resulting in homes and persons being lost; or farmers who fail to weed their crops, making the harvest slight; or a corrupt government that takes more than is appropriate. Humans have only themselves to blame for such hardships. These hardships are not sent by a transcendent being or force such as Heaven. Xunzi held that the proprieties of conduct (e.g., moral discriminations of right and wrong, etc.) were established by the sage-kings to prevent such calamities.

Xunzi was a humanist and believed that human beings invented morality; they did not discover it within or have it disclosed to them by Heaven (Goldin 2005: 126). If the sage-kings had not created the *li*, there would have been no civilization and no order. Accordingly, Xunzi's view was that the sage-kings were moral experts of a sort. In fact, we should adopt the moral practice and advice that they offer even when, perhaps especially when, we cannot appreciate for ourselves the considerations supporting it (Tiwald 2012: 275).

Several fundamental moral issues arise for anyone taking such a view. One of the most significant is the moral difference that exists when one does something based on following another's authority and when one does it for oneself or based on one's own rationally chosen decision. In terms of its implications for one's character, it is fair to ask philosophically whether we should make the same appraisal of one who acts rightly because he follows the example or instruction of an authority, as we do of one who acts rightly as a result of his own judgment or desire.

Justin Tiwald (2012) argues that Xunzi distinguishes the moral expert as model (*you fa*) from the expert as teacher (*you shi*). Tiwald claims that Xunzi thought we need a moral teacher because the teacher instructs us in the particular acts that are appropriate instantiations of the proprieties (*li*). The moral expert is one who acts according to *li* without the aid of a teacher. In his chapter "Cultivating the Self," Xunzi put the matter in the following way:

> *Li* [proprieties of conduct] is that by which you correct your person. The teacher is that by which to correct your practice of the proprieties of conduct. If you are without *li*, then how will you correct your person? If you are without a teacher, how will you know that your practice of *li* is correct? … If you do not concur with your teacher and the proper model but instead like to use your own judgement, then this is like relying on a blind person to distinguish colors, or like relying on a deaf person to distinguish sounds. You will accomplish nothing but chaos and recklessness. (*Xunzi* 2, ibid., 14, my modifications)

For Xunzi, moral experts consistently do the correct thing on the basis of their own aptitude and volition. Moral experts are exceedingly rare; nevertheless, almost all humans spend their entire lifetimes dependent on experts and teachers. In Xunzi's philosophy, such experts are the sages (*shengren*), moral teachers (*shi*), and selected rulers. *The sages are recognized as experts through the sheer force of the life they lead.* They have, in word and deed, established morality and the proprieties of conduct (*li*) are derived from their examples. Teachers are those who serve society after thorough study and intensive education. They are relatively few in number because no society can afford to provide all citizens with such extensive training. Some rulers are moral experts based on their education and training. This is the basis for Xunzi's claim that the citizenry should typically regard their leaders as moral experts and obey them even if it is not clear why or how the direction of the ruler is the correct one. In Xunzi's view, no ruler who betrays his people or does not provide for their needs and for social harmony is displaying moral expertise.

Buddhist Thinking about Morality in the Chinese Context

The Way of Precepts

In Chinese Buddhism, the moral life is understood in a way similar to the notion of Threefold Truth in its epistemology. There are multiple levels of enlightenment, or stages of enlightenment. On the one, Buddhist morality looks in many ways like a conventional Western moral system containing rules and precepts to guide conduct. At this level are the ordinary lay followers of the Buddhist way. Various Buddhist schools share the basic code of ethics called the Five Precepts used for the guidance of life when a seeker is at this level. These precepts prohibit harming sentient beings, stealing, sexual misconduct, lying, and intoxication. The specific Buddhist philosophical justification of these precepts is that following them guides one away from the desires that cause suffering. In Buddhism, the central human problem is suffering, not offense against God for moral wrongdoing. While living by moral precepts will not ultimately extinguish suffering, it will certainly lessen one's own suffering and the suffering one causes others. So, while not a cure, moral goodness and benevolence is a treatment of the symptom. According to Buddhist teaching, the vast majority of people down through history have spent their entire lives at this level of enlightenment, realizing that morality may lessen suffering, but not yet achieving the detachment needed to extinguish their own suffering or their role in causing it.

Numerous Buddhist sects add to the Five Precepts. For example, the Ten Precepts (*dasa sila*) are taken as appropriate for monks and nuns, as following them typically best fits the monastic life. Here is a commonly used list of the Ten Precepts:

1 Refrain from killing sentient creatures.
2 Refrain from stealing.
3 Refrain from sexual misconduct.
4 Refrain from incorrect speech (lying but also manipulating and using hurtful words).
5 Refrain from consuming intoxicants.
6 Refrain from taking food at inappropriate times (after noon).
7 Refrain from singing, dancing, playing music, or attending entertainment programs (performances).
8 Refrain from wearing perfume, cosmetics, and decorative accessories.
9 Refrain from use of luxurious instruments (sitting on high chairs, sleeping on soft beds, etc.).
10 Refrain from accepting money.

The goal of training by means of following moral precepts is twofold: (1) to lessen the suffering one experiences and inflicts on others and (2) to enable one to extinguish one's attachments and desires (i.e., reach nirvana).

The best-known companion concept to Buddhist morality at the level of precepts is the concept of *karma*. *Karma* may be regarded in its most basic sense as the product of one's past actions. These products may be behavioral consequences, mental conditions, or physical states that result from one's acts. The psychological habits and states caused by one's actions are as much karmic results as are the physical ones. The physical ones may include the length and condition of one's life, and the social results may be the effects on one's friendships, wealth, family life, and even the community and the world at large.

At the level of ordinary knowledge, folk beliefs coming into Buddhism evolved the idea that one's *karma* is the source of constant rebirth, and that at death one pays for the *karmic* debt of the weight of one's immoral deeds in a set of eighteen hells that are judicial courts. Then, after paying one's debt, a person enters the wheel of rebirth that casts one back into the mundane world in the form of being most appropriate to what remains of one's being after paying the karmic debts owed. If one's karma is pure then one becomes a celestial being, freed from the wheel of rebirth and the phenomenal world of the mundane.

Individuals living by moral precepts may stand out among others as good and ethical. They may receive awards and recognitions. We may seek them out in our relationships. In its highest forms, this understanding of morality as precepts gives rise to the Buddhism of compassion for the world that seeks to remove evil and suffering by living a pure life and contributing to the welfare of others.

But while persons are still thinking of life and existing relationships under moral precepts, they remain "in training" for enlightenment and to that extent somewhat still in bondage to volition and names and forms of discrimination that persons use in the employment of moral concepts (courage, jealousy, spitefulness, etc.). They are still subject to mental anguish, physical attunement, and even to the desire to protect the self.

Among the many Buddhist philosophical schools, there is a great deal of controversy and mutual criticism. Much of it centers on the place of morality in the ultimate aim of Buddhism to eliminate suffering. Some sects in the Theravada School of Buddhism hold that many, perhaps most, human beings are not able to reach enlightenment and, thus, should follow the way of precept morality and pass through life with as little suffering and harm to themselves and others as possible.

Confucianism and Buddhism on Moral Precepts

1. Celibacy was already an established custom among Indian ascetics when the Buddha enjoined its practice on his monks and nuns. In China, however, not only did celibacy play no role in its indigenous cultural proprieties (*li*) but it also conflicted with the familialism at the heart of Confucian teachings. The continuation of the family line was a duty in Confucianism. The emphasis placed on producing progeny was stated by Mencius: "There are three things which are unfilial, and to have no posterity is the greatest of them" (4A26). A celibate son, renouncing his sacred duty to the family line for a life as a Buddhist monk, thus, seemed to threaten the very cohesiveness of Chinese society.

2. The monastic life itself became institutionalized in India, where it existed as an autonomous social body outside of secular authority. In China, on the other hand, the existence of a class of nonproductive monks offended the sensibilities of the Confucian

work ethic. It was also decried on purely pragmatic grounds by generations of government officials, who saw in it a loss of vital sources of tax revenue and manpower.

3. Breaking attachments to persons and things, extinguishing desires so that one will find the serene peace of nirvana in one's inner life, is a central teaching in Buddhism. In Buddhism there is a strong sense of self-denial and a feeling that having desires, possessions, and position are morally debilitating; but such views are alien to Confucianism.

4. In Buddhism, harmony comes through withdrawal and removing oneself from things to which one is attached, and which, in turn, can cause suffering and distress. The result is a kind of placidness that emerges as one has extinguished desire. If one is not attached to family, friends, career, nation, and such, one will not be affected by what happens to them. In contrast, the Confucian understanding of harmony is much different. For Confucians, harmony must play out in relationships, as one is immersed in the messiness of family and village life. Harmony is found in the Five Relationships. But in Buddhism, harmony comes in isolation and turning inward. This isolation may be physical, as in becoming a monk and moving to a monastery, or spiritual, as one remains in the world, but not of it. Persons are encouraged to make themselves like an island in Buddhism. In Confucianism, harmony is a social achievement, requiring many persons to cooperate.

5. In Buddhism, there is an important stress on self-cultivation, and this is also an emphasis in Confucianism. However, the manner of self-cultivation is very different. In Buddhism, cultivation is expressed as resistance to corruption and attachment, keeping oneself pure in mind and body. This wisdom comes through meditation, not study, art, music, or intellectual conversation, as in Confucianism. But more strikingly, of course, is that the result of self-cultivation in Buddhism is the awareness that there is no self to be enlightened or to escape suffering. Confucianism does not follow this path.

6. In contrast to the Confucian ideal of an exemplary person (*junzi*), the Buddhist holds up the ideal of the *Brahmana*. This is one who has by restraint and contemplation freed himself from passions and blame. This person is nonviolent. He is in complete control of his body. He meditates alone and finds the

path himself. He keeps aloof from others and does not frequent houses of friends. All these characterizations of the spiritual ideal of Buddhism run in different directions from the exemplary person, who is quite involved in family, state, and interpersonal relations.[11]

In Buddhism, the rules of morality are only tools or means to a higher end. They are used as training mechanisms to eliminate desires. But when moral precepts do bring about the extinguishment of desires and thus of suffering (i.e., enlightenment), then there is no longer any need for morality. All moral precepts are dispensed with. One who has climbed to the heights no longer needs the ladder. Once a person is emptied of the desires moral precepts are meant to control and erase, then there is no longer any need for morality, nor any function for it to perform. An enlightened one transcends duties and prohibitions and is set free from morality totally. Obviously, any unenlightened person who discards morality will plunge into evil and suffering. However, the enlightened one, freed from attachment and desire, lives above and apart from all moral expectation and moves through existence as one who has transcended morality. Such a person neither causes suffering nor experiences any. He is beyond good and evil.

The Bodhisattva in *Hua-yan* Buddhism

Hua-yan (Flower Garland) Buddhism valorizes the form of existence known as bodhisattva, regarding it as the supreme moral accomplishment. The *Hua-yan* worldview is based primarily on the *Avatamsaka Sutra*, known by its Chinese title, *Huayan jing* or *Flower Garland Sutra*. The name "Flower Garland" suggests the crowning glory and even the sublime fragrance of the Buddha's profound understanding of ultimate reality. The role of bodhisattva is not exclusive to *Hua-yan* Buddhism, and Leslie Kawamura (1981) provides an overview of the various schools and countries of origin for diverse understandings of this important concept in Buddhism. There is no one single description of a bodhisattva that encompasses all Buddhist sectarian groups (Williams 2005: 997). Our focus will be on the concept of the bodhisattva in the distinctively Chinese tradition of *Hua-yan* and the form given to it by Fazang (643–712), the principal founder of this tradition. At about the same time that Fazang was teaching about the bodhisattva in

China, Acharya Shantiveda, a monk from the Nalanda Buddhist monastery in India wrote what many regard as the classic study of the bodhisattva way, entitled *A Guide to the Bodhisattva's Way of Life* (*Bodhisattvacaryavatara*) (Batchelor 1979). As of this writing, no comprehensive study has been made comparing Fazang's and Shantiveda's understanding of the bodhisattva.

To be a bodhisattva is to dwell in the margins between experienced enlightenment and the karmic world of moral precepts governing the ordinary and mundane existence of cause and result. It is commonly said that a bodhisattva is enlightened but postpones nirvana in order to minister to the world in compassion. This statement, however, can be misleading.

Two interesting considerations surface here to help us avoid being misled in our thinking about what is a bodhisattva. (1) To experience enlightenment as a Buddha is to know the freedom from suffering that results from the extinguishment of desire and attachment; even the attachment to those who suffer and to the role of being their savior. The point is that bodhisattvas can be moved by the world's hurt and suffering, but Buddhas cannot. Buddhahood is beyond compassion. This is why the Jataka tales of Shakyamuni's (the historical Buddha) life so often speak of him as a bodhisattva in his salvific role and not as a Buddha (Williams 2009: 60–1). (2) To have compassion for those trapped in the illusions of this world that promise peace and satisfaction but deliver only suffering and to minister to them through moral action is the work of the bodhisattva. But what the bodhisattva does in trying to free the unenlightened is ultimately still directed toward the goal of helping them grasp the truth that the way of morality is one which must be transcended. Bodhisattvas can enter into the Buddha realm at any time. This means that they could detach themselves from the suffering of this mundane world and from any attachment to it, or anyone in it. But they take a vow to continue serving and working with the ordinary beings of the world as instruments of compassion and guides to enable others to achieve release from their desires and attachments, thereby avoiding suffering. The bodhisattva is able to combine simultaneously a direct meditative awareness of emptiness internal to himself/herself with an external compassion for others, and engagement in the project of helping them be relieved of their suffering.

Fazang puts this very simply: Buddhahood is already present at the first stage of the bodhisattva's path (ibid.: 144). Even when giving food, clothing, or aid of any sort, the bodhisattva has no attachment to the gift or the recipient, but the act is experienced by the one in need as a deed of generosity and benevolence. In this sense, the bodhisattva engages the world and others morally. Morality is the bodhisattva's skillful means, used to liberate others from their attachments and the suffering these cause, although the bodhisattva has no attachment even to the moral act itself, realizing that it is empty (Flanagan 2011: 114). Still, in his pure nonattachment to the moral act, the bodhisattva is nonetheless performing what is to the benefit of others. This kind of understanding characterizes every moral act in speech, compassion, and care for others attributable to a bodhisattva (Williams 2009: 206).

What is it that a bodhisattva does that makes such a person a distinctive moral being? The bodhisattva has already abandoned desires and the discriminations of the mundane world that are the cause of suffering. Such a one dwells in this world with a mind that transcends the causes of suffering and even has no attachment to the self, whereas those still caught in this world are attached to the self and to the discriminations of existence, and they suffer because of the desires such attachment creates. When a bodhisattva lives among such people, the difference is obvious and the other sentient beings see that the bodhisattva does not suffer. This draws them to their bodhisattva savior, who is living in enlightenment among those still trapped in attachment, desire, and suffering. Bodhisattvas are dedicated to waking others from the illusions of the world. Traditionally, the bodhisattva takes four vows, but some schools require more, and the actual wording varies with traditions. However, here is one classical statement of the Four Vows as their implications are explored by Stephen Harris (2018):

> Sentient beings are numberless; I vow to liberate them.
> Delusions are inexhaustible; I vow to transcend them.
> Dharma teachings are boundless; I vow to master them.
> The Buddha's enlightened way is unsurpassable; I vow to embody it.

The bodhisattva may be said to exemplify compassion, lovingkindness, appreciative joy, and equanimity (equal concern for all sentient beings). From one view, moral requirements of the bodhisattva far exceed those set out in the Five or Ten Precepts, but to the bodhisattva, they are empty.

The most famous of all bodhisattvas in the Hua-yan Chinese tradition is Dizang (Sanskrit: Ksitigarbhai; Japanese: Jizo; Korean Jijang). In Fazang's work *Chronicles of the Flower Adornment Scripture* (*Huayan jing zhuanji*), he related a famous tale of Dizang's miraculous work at the entrance to the hells (Shi 2007: 169):

In the first year of *wenming* 文明 [684], a metropolitan person, one Mr. Wang, whose first name is today not known, did not cultivate good acts and moreover was lacking in moral conduct. When he died of illness, two persons came to lead him to the entrance of hell, where they encountered a monk who said, "I am the Bodhisattva Dizang." [The bodhisattva] then taught Mr. Wang to recite a line of verse, which states: "If a person seeks to apprehend all the Buddhas of the three realms, he or she should contemplate thus: It is the mind that creates all *tathagatas* [i.e., Buddhas]." After delivering the scriptural line, the bodhisattva addressed him, saying, "recitation of this *gatha* [verse] can dissipate [the fate of] hell." Mr. Wang recited most earnestly, and then he was brought to meet King Yama [king of the hells], the king asked, "What merits does this person possess?" Wang replied, "Only the observance of the above *gatha* of four phrases." the king subsequently released and pardoned him. (ibid.: 170)

Dizang as a bodhisattva wished to save Mr. Wang from the fate of the hells, but the means for doing so is significant. It was not Mr. Wang's morality that saved him; neither was it the simple recitation of the verse given to him by Dizang as though it were magic. His salvation was rooted in Mr. Wang's internalization (i.e., observance) of the verse. Doing so enabled him to detach from the illusions of the hells and their punishments.

The Way of Morality in Chan Buddhism

Chan Buddhism developed in China between the sixth and eighth centuries. It is a uniquely Chinese form of Buddhism that later was transplanted into Japan, where it became prominent and known as Zen. The Chinese word *chan* is used to translate the Sanskrit *dhyana*, which means "meditation." Although regarded as Chinese in origin and tenor, the founding legend of Chan goes back to India and tells that the Buddha transmitted a private esoteric teaching about meditation, never written in any sutra, but passed only from one teacher to another. The twenty-eighth patriarch in this lineage of transmission is known as Bodhidharma (semi-legendary) and is said to have brought the teaching to China at the Shaolin monastery in the Songshan mountains. Although meditation is not the only practice employed in Chan, its central role in epistemology and morality is important to understand. The function of meditation in Chan is a different path to enlightenment from reaching intellectual conviction through study of texts or arriving at conclusions that certain beliefs are true based on disputation and argument. One way of gaining clarity on how meditation functions in morality is to contrast the approach of Chan with the Western manner of doing ethics.

In some streams of Western morality, the task is to determine the duties or moral rules that should guide conduct and then to follow them. Indeed, the prominent Western philosopher Immanuel Kant wrote more than one work dedicated to the identification of these duties and their application.[12] In Western moral philosophy, norms function in ways similar to how a pilgrim traveling in a country would use a map. In fact, this is the exact image that Robert Carter uses to contrast Chan Buddhism (Japan: Zen) with Western philosophy (Carter 2001: 11–34). In Chan, the task is not to use reason or even a calculus of consequences of actions in order to arrive at a set of duties and rules to follow as a road map by which to live. Instead, a person readies himself to act morally by putting himself in an altered state of consciousness through meditation.

In Chan, this meditative state is empty of content, lacking any recognizable known set of rules and duties. Indeed, one who practices Chan sitting meditation as a source of moral understanding does not say that he "knows" what to do or "knows" what is right. He has set aside the need to speak of the moral life as connected to the possession of some kind of specific knowledge. Neither does one who is in this state have a need to draw bearings from culture (i.e., as in the Confucian proprieties, *li*). In fact, one empties himself of any reliance on such sources for the moral life. Such a one does not check himself against them. He sets them aside and gives no deliberation or place to them. Instead, one meditates; sits in emptiness. In this state, one's original Buddha nature comes into awareness. One does not learn moral truths in this state, but it is, nevertheless, from this state that appropriate action arises.

In our original minds, we have awareness of absolutely certain truth. D. T. Suzuki says this knowledge "is not derivative but primitive; not inferential, not rationalistic, not mediational, but direct, immediate; not analytical but synthetic; not cognitive, but symbolical; not intending but merely expressive; not abstract, but concrete; not processional, not purposive, but ultimate, final and irreducible; not eternally receding, but infinitely inclusive; etc." (Barrett 1956: 34).

The Philosophical Reset Button: A Manifesto

In 2015, Michael Slote published "The Philosophical Reset Button: A Manifesto," a long overdue protest against the Western tradition's hyper-reliance on rationality as a guide for the moral life. He called for this one-sided tendency to be corrected and argued that Confucian Chinese philosophy was in the best position to implement this rebalancing. He claimed that Confucianism never went to the extremes of Western rationalism, but that it always recognized the value of emotion, sentiment, and feeling much more than has been typical in the West. The resulting effort at a reset of Western philosophy is now most often simply called "moral sentimentalism," an approach with which Slote has been identified as one of the principal architects (Slote 2015). Chan Buddhism's way of morality is not a form of sentimentalism and does not accept the suggestion that morality must be built on either reason or sentiment, or as in Slote's approach, on some combination of them. Chan, like the Lao-Zhuang tradition, instead focuses on the will of a person, not the rational or emotive sides of an individual (Littlejohn 2021). Moving in the state of altered consciousness created by sitting meditation, whether in Chan Buddhism or Daoism, results in spontaneous, effortless morally virtuous movement.

Western morality counsels a person not to act in a situation of moral import until he has weighed out the options rationally and calculated the possible outcomes and consequences for the widest range of persons involved. Only then can one know what to do. In this sense, reasoning plays a role not merely in setting out the rules and guidelines that illuminate action but also in helping one assess the actual conduct to undertake. Chan Buddhism has a contrasting approach. In Chan, the person seeks a shift away from the rational and calculating mind, but not toward the emotions or sentiments of a person, as though these were the only options for the roots of morality. Meditation, quietude, stillness, and emptiness are the way of Chan. In this there is a sort of consciousness that is recognized by one moving spontaneously without calculation or being swayed by one's emotions and desires.

A further contrast between Chan and Western morality can be drawn. An important task in Western morality is the strengthening of the will so it can resist the pull of desires to act contrary to what is right. Doing what is right in Western philosophy is portrayed as a struggle of the will, a test of strength of character to stand up against temptation, or to choose the good and right over self-interest. In Chan the result of meditation is quite different. Masao Abe explains it this way:

Through the practice of *dhyana*, meditation, one can be emancipated from it [the will] and awaken to boundless openness, *sunyata* [emptiness, nothingness]. ... In this awakening to *sunyata*, human free will is realized entirely anew in its pure form by eradicating its self-attaching and self-binding character. Instead of producing a chain of causation and transmigration, free will, which is now based on the awakening to *sunyata* freely works in this phenomenal world without attachment, delusion, or bondage. (Abe 1990:56)

Morality Books and Ledgers: *Tract of the Most Exalted on Action and Response* (c. 1164)

The moral life of persons in China was not shaped exclusively by one and only one of the so-called three teachings (*sanjiao*): Confucianism, Daoism, or Buddhism. These streams flowed into a much more synthetic and eclectic river of moral life than cannot be described by any one of these traditions alone. This is most evident in the morality books used in Chinese culture from the tenth century until the end of the Qing dynasty (1911). These works helped form a coherent system for the transmission of a unified moral culture in China. Some preliminary versions of morality books may have first appeared as early as the 300s–400s, but they began to make a dramatic impact in the Song dynasty (960–1279) and were very popular throughout China. These books served not only the lower levels of society, but all types and classes of people irrespective of social status, economic position, and religious affiliation.

The underlying philosophical idea of the morality books is that good deeds are rewarded and evil ones punished. The Chinese term for this reward/punishment dynamic is *ganying* and can be traced at least as far back as the *Masters of Huainan* text (*Huainanzi*). Besides identifying a rather comprehensive set of good deeds and their rewards, and evil deeds and their retributions, the books were frequently accompanied by moral tales and fables designed to illustrate how these processes of reward and retribution show up in "real life."

If the influence of a book is measured by the sheer number of copies printed, the morality book *Tract of the Most Exalted on Action and Response* (*Taishang Ganying Pian, c.* 1164) will rank first among all others, at least according to D. T. Suzuki and Paul Carus at the time of their edition of the work (Suzuki and Carus 1906: 3). More copies of this work have been printed than any other book in history. The *Tract* was printed in millions and millions, often from small presses all over China, and was (and is still) given in distribution for free, usually from literature tables located at popular Daoist, Buddhist, and City God temples throughout China. By the time of European missionary contacts the *Tract* had sufficient prominence to inspire French and English translations in 1816, 1828, 1830, 1835, and 1884. It was almost always included in any series of Chinese philosophical texts in the early period of translation of Chinese works into Western languages. In fact, it was included along with the *Daodejing* and *Zhuangzi* in James Legge's *Texts of Taoism* done for the massive fifty-volume set *Sacred Books of the East*, edited by Max Muller (1891). Legge included this work as a major text of Daoism because he was aware of its extensive use in China based on his decades of missionary work in the country. Actually, though, while the *Tract* is often regarded as a Daoist work, it includes moral teachings and precepts traceable to Buddhism and Confucianism, although there is no direct citation given in the *Tract* of which tradition serves as a source for a given moral instruction. The text was a popular tract and cited the source of all of its teachings as "Taishang," known in the title as "the most exalted." It is generally understood that this name is used as a title for Laozi, the putative founder of Daoism.

The morality books were used by adults and school children alike. In this sense, it was not greatly different than the moral primers teaching proper behavior to boys (*The Three Character Classic, Sanzijiing*), girls (*Classic for Girls, Nuerjing*), and women (*Analects for Women, Nu Lunyu*). While it was common for the morality books to be widely available throughout southern and southeastern China, copies were used as far north as Manchuria. Aside from religious sects and groups which distributed these books in the temples of the villages and market towns, benevolence societies, community compacts, public lectures, and even traveling village theatrical troupes also provided them to ordinary citizens. In fact, membership in some societies was linked to the number of good deeds performed by an applicant as specified in the morality books or their accompanying ledgers that quantified a person's deeds. These ledgers were used to obtain membership and places of leadership in various governmental and guild societies (Brokaw 1991: 61–109).

As we begin looking at the *Tract* philosophically, the first thing we notice is that it is built upon a highly quantifiable understanding of morality which tallies good and evil deeds. We should imagine a ledger with good deeds listed on one side and evil ones on the other. Moreover, evil deeds do not disappear from the ledger, and their effects continue. However, by performing more good deeds of merit than evil ones, the ledger can be weighted to gain more desirable results. Ledger entries of good deeds promise success and happiness, whereas those of evil deeds predict deleterious effects. Evil deeds were each reported to cause the loss of between a hundred days and twelve years of a person's lifespan, depending on their gravity. Not only may the days and years of one's life be shortened, but an evil doer will also be alienated from the community. "Not only is his term of life reduced, but poverty also strikes him. Often he meets with calamity and misery. His neighbors hate him. Punishments and curses pursue him. Good luck shuns him. Evil stars threaten him" (Suzuki and Carus 1906: 52).

A comparison between the lists of good and evil deeds given in the *Tract* yields an interesting fact. The number of evil deeds is almost exactly double that of the good deeds.

Moral Virtue as the Golden Mean

On the surface, the *Tract*'s compendium of good and evil deeds, with the evil deeds exceeding the good ones by about double, suggests that there might be a similarity to be noted with Aristotle's position that virtue lies in the golden mean between the twin evils of an act of excess and one of deficiency. For example, in Aristotle's analysis of the virtue of courage there is one way to go right and two ways to go wrong. Courage is the mean between foolhardiness (an act of excess) and cowardice (an act of deficiency). In Aristotle's view, only the golden mean will yield virtue (*Nicomachean Ethics* 2.6–9, McKeon 1973: 376–85).

Scholars have often given their attention to a comparison between Aristotle's understanding of virtue and that of Confucius (Sim 2007 and Yu 1998). But it is important to notice that there are actually at least two important differences between the approach to morality taken in the *Tract* and that of Aristotle. First, the *Tract* focuses on *actions* and Aristotle's attention is directed toward the *character traits* of virtues and vices. Second, the *Tract*'s lists of good and evil deeds do not actually map onto Aristotle's model of mean, excess, and defect. The *Tract* has no interest in making a philosophical argument for determining that an action is good or evil based on its status between

> excess and defect. This decree of the moral standing of the action is decided by Taishang. So the *Tract* does not offer such an explanation as Aristotle's discussion of the golden mean. The *Tract* simply lists good and evil actions, drawing from the wealth of moral precepts contained in the three teachings of Confucianism, Daoism, and Buddhism.

A partial list of morally good acts in the *Tract* includes the following: loyalty; filiality; friendliness; self-correction; compassion on orphans and widows; respecting authority, the elderly, and one's ancestors; not injuring any life; grieving at the misfortunes of one's neighbors and rejoicing at their good luck; not calling attention to the faults of others; humility; renouncing desires; bearing no grudges; and generosity. A representative list of the misdeeds of the evil person includes these:

- being unfilial; treating one's ruler or parents with contempt; being disrespectful of one's elders;
- rebelling against those one should serve;
- being unkind and unfaithful to one's spouse;
- lying; breaking promises; being cruel or inhumane; oppressing subordinates;
- bearing grudges and not forgiving;
- murdering; stealing; taking bribes and being unjust;
- not correcting mistakes;
- disrespect for the holy and displaying impropriety and disregard for the proper way to do things;
- not controlling desires; not being content with one's place; ambition for power;
- being shameless; having impure thoughts and motives; being deceptive; being wasteful; being envious;
- delighting in the misfortunes of others; using violence; being greedy; being full of vile talk and slander;
- being self-indulgent, rebellious, or bragging and being conceited; being frivolous; and
- deceiving the ignorant, molesting orphans, and oppressing widows; being happy about a neighbor's misfortune.

The morality book tradition continued for centuries in China. It represents not only a highly quantitative view of morality where numbers of good or evil deeds are what matters but also an appreciation for what is often called in moral philosophy *special role obligations*. By the seventeenth century a morality book was printed entitled *Meritorious Deeds at No Cost*. The significance of the book was in its careful delineation of the moral expectations of persons by their roles in life. The categories it provided were: local gentry; candidates for officialdom; peasants; craftsmen; merchants; physicians and pharmacists; subordinate office workers; women; soldiers; Buddhist and Daoist monks; household slaves and servants; and people in general (De Bary and Bloom 1999: 911–16).

Morality books like the *Tract* first circulated apart from what became known as the moral ledgers. However, gradually, the ledgering tradition in China became popular and it was not uncommon for individuals to fill out their ledgers at each day's end. The *Ledger of Merit and Demerit of the Taiwei Immortal* (1171), which appeared perhaps less than a decade after the *Tract*, was the first extant ledger that carried the logic of the *Tract* to its natural conclusion by assigning different moral merit points to specific good actions and demerits to evil deeds. By the period of the Ming dynasty in the 1600s, ledgers did such things as allocate one hundred merit points to a man who saves the life of another, but deduct one hundred from the account of a man who hoards rice, rather than distributing it to the needy in times of famine. Yuan Huang (1533–1606) explained his keeping of a moral ledger to his children in this way:

> As soon as I performed a good deed, I would record it with a brush. Your mother could not write, so each time she performed a deed, she would use a goose quill to stamp a vermillion circle on the calendar. We might give relief to the poor, or buy fish and shellfish and set them free. One day there was as many as ten-odd circles on the calendar. By the eighth month of 1583, the three thousand (meritorious deeds) had been filled in. (Brokaw 1991: 87)

Cynthia Brokaw has discussed the ways in which the morality books and ledgers served to preserve social hierarchy and stability in China. Persons even presented their ledgers to obtain positions in government or social clubs and organizations as a testament to the way others might expect them to act (ibid.: 157–228).

The philosophical concept underlying the ledgering tradition is rather straightforward. One identifies good and evil deeds, and then counts good deeds, so that they exceed evil ones by some measure to satisfy the desired goal, whether that is long life, advance in education or social position, or business and familial success. As the ledgering tradition developed a sense of the different gravity of various deeds this began to show in the ledgers.

Instead of each good deed counting one merit, some counted ten, fifty, or one hundred, and the same held for evil deeds. For example, we see in Yuan Huang's ledger that rescuing a person from death is one hundred merits, whereas urging someone to have an abortion is one hundred demerits. Helping someone dedicate himself to Buddha is thirty merits; making up slander about a person is thirty demerits. Reacting to a wrong done to oneself without anger is three merits and refusing to aid a sick person is five demerits (Brokaw 1987: 192–5).

There is another philosophical insight gained from the morality books and ledgers. These works give us a look into a view the Chinese held on punishment and reward as moral controls. The morality books and ledgers do not emphasize the notion of moral pollution and the subsequent need for cleansing, confession, and repentance that is found in some Western philosophies, especially those influenced by the Abrahamic religious traditions. Instead of seeking forgiveness for their demerits, those who kept ledgers worked the balance sheet themselves until the impact of a demerit was diminished by the doing of good deeds to such a point as to make evil deeds hardly negligible. While forgiveness which one shows to a neighbor is meritorious in the ledgers, whether one is forgiven does not matter ultimately in the determination of the ledger keeper's situation. What matters fundamentally is the way one's own ledger sheet tallies; the number and gravity of the good deeds one performs to rebalance the ledger. A person must make the ledger tally out and it is left to him to do the meritorious deeds which will counteract the evil ones. According to popular belief, failure to tally the ledger at one's death will mean punishment in the Earth Prisons (Hells) and the transference of the imbalance of evil to one's family and succeeding generations. Evil deeds themselves are never removed, deleted, erased, or absolved. They can only be trumped by a greater number of meritorious ones and/or meritorious ones of great gravity.

In one respect, this is a highly realistic system which recognizes that the moral evil which we do in some very basic ways can never be erased. Yet there is no internalization of this fact. The situation is not so much like Lady Macbeth who cannot rid herself of the stains of her malevolent deeds, as it is of the business man who has purchased a new piece of equipment. The cost of that equipment never leaves the ledger, but it can be counter-balanced.

The morality and ledger books reveal still another important philosophical position on morality. While the ledgers look like highly prescriptive behavior guides and may seem to be concerned only with conduct and not with intention and motive, these works make an important philosophical move that reveals their compilers most definitely understand the moral import of these internal factors. This move is best seen in the basic concept of the ledger itself. The ledgers place the judgment of what to enter, whether one's deed has been meritorious or not, into the hands of the ledger keeper himself/herself. Another person cannot complete the ledger for someone else. No one watches over what one is recording in the ledger. The ledger keeper performs an *act of moral self-regulation* in completing the record. No one says, "Yes, you did this" or "No, you cannot give yourself credit for that." The ledger keeper must decide.

Moral Self-regulation and Other Minds

Philosophically, the elevation of the principle of self-regulation into a fundamental role in a moral system may be a way to overcome one of the central difficulties in morality: *the other minds problem*. Consider that it is often the case that we want to know the intentions of a person in order to assess the moral value of an action. For example, providing someone incorrect or false information, if not intentional or deliberate, may very well be excusable. It is at least differently appraised than if one intentionally tells a falsehood (i.e., lies). Causing someone's death is serious in any situation, but intentionally and deliberating doing so (e.g., murder) is a more grave act than is unintentionally doing so. But how are we to get in the minds of others? How may we know their intentions and motives? This is an exact overlap between moral philosophy and the "other minds" problem. The solution of the morality book and ledgering tradition in Chinese philosophy was to turn this matter of introspection over to the ledger keeper himself/herself.

If we consider it carefully, it seems clear that something like this is exactly the move which should be made in a moral system. After all, no one knows my motives or intentions better than I do. To put this in a Chinese context, no member of the community can really say what I am able to do (financially) for my parents, or whether I am really being deferential to them in performing some action as expected in filial piety. No one else knows whether my action is merely perfunctory, or if it is genuine. As we have seen earlier in this chapter, even the Confucius of the *Analects* (2.2, 2.6, 2.7) tells us that two people could be doing very different things and both be filial, or the identical things, but one be filial and the other not. Filiality is highly contextualized into a determined time and a specific situation, and with particular people.

> The ledgers invite their users to engage in just this sort of reflection on their own filiality and other moral conduct through the discipline of self-regulation.

Yuan Huang wrote an autobiographical essay reflecting on the self-regulatory use of moral ledgers entitled *Determining Your Own Fate* (*Liming pian*). In it, he stated the following:

> When I performed righteous deeds I was still not sincere, and when I examined my conduct I found many errors … Or, although I did help other people, at heart I often doubted my motives in doing so … These faults cancelled out my merits, and days frequently passed empty of merits. (Brokaw 1991: 86)

Of course, we may ask whether such self-regulation is vulnerable to deception of self or others. However, if this is a problem for the morality books and ledgering tradition, it is one as well for all other moral systems. The morality books are built on a philosophical assumption that may minimize the impact of this problem. Since the morality books promise familial, relational, and community flourishing based on doing the good deeds they enumerate, then the idea is that if one is deceptive in completing his ledger, the only person who is hurt is the keeper of the ledger or his descendants (Suzuki and Carus 1906: 64). The community is not so easily misled and will recognize that a deceptive ledger keeper is not living in the meritorious ways he deceives himself into thinking he is.

We should not get lost in trying to think about the control of abuse of self-regulation. If we do, we will miss what is important. The point is that in this part of the Chinese practice of morality the culture was inclined to accept the possibility of abuses in order to recognize the relational and contextual nature of morality and the central truth that we are the ones who best know our moral action and character.

Actually, putting aside the morality books' tie between morality and well-being or failure, the ledgers are really all about a very important idea in Chinese moral culture we have seen before: self-cultivation. If we fault the ledger tradition for being overly quantitative in its view of the moral life, we can at least recognize the seriousness with which they take the project of becoming a good, cultivated human being. In these respects, the ledgers transmit the venerable Chinese belief that morality is above all about making yourself into a humane person and the benefits which come thereby.

In the tradition of the morality books and ledgers elementary learning is at an end and great learning begins when one assumes responsibility for one's own self-assessment and self-cultivation. In their best light, the ledgers were tools for this transition to great learning. They gave into the hands of the individual the awesome responsibility for moral self-regulation and self-evaluation.

In the preface to the *Ledger of Merit and Demerit of the Taiwei Immortal* a Daoist master living at the Yulong Wanshou Gong explains the ultimate value of moral ledgering in this way:

> Usually, when at the end of the day a man has finished recording his merits, he will feel easy; when he has finished recording his demerits, he will feel troubled. These feelings force the sensitive man to recognize the causes of transgressions and good fortune, and the sources of good and evil. If he is aware of these, then he can reduce the number of his failings by half. If he is really careful, he can avoid them altogether. (Brokaw 1991: 47)

The Ultimacy of Harmony: Zhu Xi (1130–1200)

Whereas Western philosophers often engage in a discussion of the ultimate meaning or goal of human life, frequently associating it with a life of optimal achievement of the morally good, Zhu Xi identified the fundamental goal of human life as living in harmony (*zhonghe*) in one's relationships with others and nature. He took his inspiration for this view from the classical Confucian text entitled the *Zhongyong*, which is attributed to Confucius's grandson Kong Ji (488–402 BCE, aka Zisi):

> Before the feelings of pleasure, anger, sorrow, and joy are aroused it is called equilibrium (*zhong* 中). When these feelings are aroused but each and all attain due measure and degree, it is called harmony (*he* 和) ... When equilibrium and harmony are realized to the highest degree, heaven and earth will attain their proper order and all things will flourish. (*Zhongyong* 1, Chan 1963b: 98)

For Zhu Xi, the most important task facing human beings is *self-mastery*, not merely self-realization. He believed such mastery occurs in the midst of life and its many-layered relationships with others, and not in some form of solitary meditation, as in Buddhism. Self-mastery is revealed when one is in harmony in all of one's relationships and at equilibrium internally.[13] The problem of balance in life arises at the point when one first engages the world. Stepping into relationships with others produces the arousal of feelings and desires, which Zhu called "the seven emotions" (*qi qing*): joy, anger, melancholy, worry, grief, fear, and fright. When these emotions are stirred up one's internal equilibrium is upset and harmony in one's relationships is also destroyed.[14]

Therefore, self-cultivation for Zhu Xi ultimately meant learning to discipline oneself so as to make internal equilibrium (*zhong*) manifest itself in our outer actions as harmony (Metzger 1977: 94). Self-cultivation brings the still and active phases of life into an interpenetrating harmony (Adler 2008: 65). So, internal stillness is never an end in itself. Actually, regarding stillness or a lack of turbulence in life as the ultimate goal for a person was an error Zhu believed Buddhism to have made. In his "Letter to the Gentlemen of Hunan," Zhu Xi wrote:

> So long as in one's daily life the effort at seriousness and cultivation is fully extended and there are no selfish human desires to disturb it, then before the feelings are aroused the heart-mind, [*xin*] will be as clear as a mirror and as calm as still water, and after the feelings are aroused, it will attain due measure and degree without exception. This is the essential task in everyday life. (Chan 1963b: 601)

Zhu Xi did not directly say that moral perfection is insufficient as a model for complete personal well-being toward which humans should strive. However, his descriptions reveal that there is much more to living in harmony with others than how we treat them morally. Zhu's position represents an important example of a philosophy calling upon persons to live together with others in an aesthetic consonance and balance. Cultural propriety (*li* 澧) itself is only one component of the broth that is harmonious living:

> Harmony is like broth. One uses water, fire, vinegar, sauce, salt, and plums to cook his fish and meat. It is made to boil by the firewood, and then the cook mixes the ingredients. (Ni 2010: 148)

There are nonmoral values to be considered in creating harmony between persons, just as there are many ingredients in a fine broth. Zhu Xi's notion of harmony is broad enough so that moral virtues do not crowd out the nonmoral virtues we value in those with whom we have relationships. Indeed, there are times when the single-minded pursuit of what is morally appropriate alone may create disharmony. Zhu Xi's bold step away from moral goodness as the ultimate goal of human life, and his turn toward harmony as the ideal of self-cultivation, is consistent with Confucius's approach as well.

Is Moral Perfection Desirable?

The contemporary Western philosopher Susan Wolf disavows moral perfection or flawlessness (i.e., being a moral saint) as the proper goal of human life:

> In other words, if the moral saint is devoting all his time to feeding the hungry, healing the sick, or raising money for Oxfam, then necessarily he is not reading Victorian novels, playing the oboe, or improving his backhand. Although no one of the interests or tastes in the category containing these latter activities could be claimed to be a necessary element in a life well lived, a life in which none of these possible aspects of character are developed may seem to be a life strangely barren. (Wolf 1982: 421)

Zhu Xi does not actually offer an argument for the primacy of harmony over goodness, or for the inclusion of nonmoral values in a program of self-cultivation. Nevertheless, we could surmise how such an argument might go in his philosophy. As Wolf notes, there are nonmoral characteristics that a morally perfect or flawless person cannot encourage in himself for the reason that they undermine or make impossible the achievement of optimal moral goodness. Moreover, a great many nonmoral pursuits are necessary to harmonious relationships with others and to one's balance internally. Wolf points to a number of these:

> An interest in something like gourmet cooking will be, for different reasons, difficult for a moral saint to rest easy with. For it seems to me that no plausible argument can justify the use of human resources involved in producing a pate de canard en croute against possible alternative beneficent ends to which these resources might be put. ... Presumably, an interest in high fashion or interior design will fare much the same, as will, very possibly, a cultivation of the finer arts as well. A moral saint will have to be very, very nice. It is important that he not be offensive. The worry is that, as a result, he will have to be dull-witted, humorless, or bland. (ibid.: 422)

Zhu Xi was not suggesting that we abandon a commitment to morality, but only that there are some nonmoral personal qualities and practices that we also ought to strive for, and which contribute to living in relationships harmoniously. In other words, some of the qualities that a morally perfect individual would necessarily lack are still human virtues, albeit nonmoral ones. And some of the traits that a person living in harmony with others possesses are nonmoral ones in Susan Wolf's sense (e.g., a sense of humor, love of sports, passion for outdoors, etc.).

Aside from these interests in the relationship between harmony and goodness, there is also a reason to inquire how harmony is related to happiness. This question arises as a fundamental one. Consider that even Aristotle in his *Nicomachean Ethics* explored the question, "What is the ultimate purpose of human existence?" He held that the ultimate end or *telos* of life is "that which is always desirable in itself and never for the sake of something else" (McKeon 1973: 354–5). Aristotle argued that only happiness (*eudaimonia*) satisfies this criterion. For Aristotle, happiness is not a subjective state of mind which may vary with life's exigencies, and neither is it reducible to pleasure, as when one is "having fun" with one's friends. In fact, as a final end or goal that encompasses the totality of one's life, one cannot know if one has lived a happy life until it is over.

In contrast, if we take happiness to mean harmonious living, as Zhu Xi argued, then happiness is *an activity*, not some state of being or consciousness that can only be known at the end of life. Zhu believed that the self-cultivated person *lives* happiness (happily?) through harmonious relationships. Happiness is something lived, rather than possessed. Another way of putting this is, happiness is not the reward of living harmoniously. *Living harmoniously is happiness.*

Nietzsche on the Will to Power

We can contrast Zhu Xi's valorization of harmony as life's ultimate end with a formidable challenge from the Western philosopher Friedrich Nietzsche (1844–1900). Nietzsche holds up the exercise of one's "will to power" rather than harmony as the way to achieve an optimal life. For Nietzsche, the most fulfilling life is one that transcends both external and internal efforts to restrain or rein in one's own desires for self-determination. Indeed, Nietzsche closely associated "will to power" with "revaluation of all values." The "will to power" leaves behind the mediocre and resists the pull to weaken one's self-realization by constantly adjusting one's attitudes, values, goals, desires, and actions in order to harmonize with the views of others (Reginster 2006: 103). While the "will to power" is not a desire to control and dominate others, it is likewise not a pursuit of harmonious living. It is a capacity to seek and realize one's own self-determining style of life (Clark 1990: 211–13).

The position that the exercise of one's "will to power" represents the ultimate purpose of life runs headlong into Zhu Xi's elevation of harmonious living as life's fulfillment and the understanding that harmonious living is happiness. Nietzsche was greatly influenced in the formation of his understanding of the "will to power" by Arthur Schopenhauer, who thought happiness was unattainable in life (Reginster 2006: 106, 107). In contrast to Schopenhauer, Nietzsche advocated what he called a Dionysian life. Such a life lacks satiety, disgust, passionless conformity, and weariness. It is the life of a self-creating circle of joy (Nietzsche 1968: 1067). "But all expansion, incorporation, growth is striving against something that resists; movement is essentially tied up with states of displeasure; that which is here the driving force must in any event desire something else [than happiness] if it desires displeasure in the way" (ibid.: 704). In this sense, the "will to power" is a way of talking about the manner of overcoming resistance exercised by the self-transcending person. That resistance may be internal, in which case it is overcoming drives and desires one wishes to set aside. Or, it may be external as expressed by the force of others and the restrictions of morality. In this resistance lies true self-mastery (Reginster 2006: 131–2). For Nietzsche, we may say that the Dionysian life emerges in the triumph over the various forms of resistance that assault self-definition, including those that require agreeing, compromising, adapting, and conforming ... in short, harmonizing. In *Beyond Good and Evil*, Nietzsche stated that acquiescing to these pathways makes man contemptible and ridiculous, and his destruction desirable (ibid.: 184, 186).

For Zhu Xi, embracing a philosophy such as Nietzsche's would be taken as a demonstration of how cloudy one's heart-mind has become. It would, in fact, display the imbalance or lack of equilibrium (*zhong*) that destroys the person and conceals the ultimate Principles (*li* 理) of reality behind a veil of conflicting desires. A person without internal equilibrium lacks the capacity to create harmonious relationships and would be devoid of happiness. Zhu Xi claimed:

> When the person is born, he understands Principles (*li* 理) without expending any effort. People nowadays are mired in confusion; and only when the sages have spoken to them repeatedly [through their texts] are they willing to take leave of it. But if they are already stupefied and do not even know to pursue Principles, in the end they will become mere beasts. (Gardner 1990: 104)

Zhu Xi thought the foremost problem facing human beings was the obscuring and polluting nature of our desires. In taking this position, he did not go so far as we find in Buddhism. He did not say that all desire leads to suffering. He recognized that desires for food, drink, reproduction, and so forth are shared by all human beings and cannot be eliminated. But it is the lack of regulation and control of desires that is the source of disharmony. Accordingly, Zhu often described the ideal state of the heart-mind as *gong* (i.e., operating the way in which Heaven operates), and the problematic elements that get in the way as selfish desires (*siyu*) (Shun 2005: 1). Individual and selfish desires, if not regulated, unbalance one's internal equilibrium and what follows is the unraveling of harmonious living.

Zhu Xi held that chaotic internal desires will make one numb to others. To illustrate what he meant, Zhu made use of an analogy drawn from two other Neo-Confucian thinkers, Cheng Hao (1032–1085) and Cheng Yi (1033–1107):

> In medical books, a paralyzed arm or leg is said to be [numb]. This expression is perfect for describing the situation. The humane person (*ren* 仁) regards all things in the universe as one body; there is nothing which is not a part of him. If he regards all things as parts of himself, where will his feelings not extend? But if he does not see them as parts of himself, why would he feel any concern for them? It is like the case of a paralyzed arm or leg: the life-force [*qi* 氣] does not circulate through them so they are not regarded as part of one's being. (Angle 2009: 78)

When persons do not balance their desires, they become numb to others and harmonious living becomes impossible.

Zhu Xi borrowed a Buddhist image to speak of how we might go about regulating our selfish desires, comparing this activity to polishing a mirror. The brightness of the mirror is *gong* (the way of Heaven) and selfish desires (*siyi*) are the dust particles that becloud one's heart-mind and obscure the brightness of the Way (Gardner 1990: 145, 146). A person whose heart-mind is clear will live in harmony; one whose heart-mind is crusted over by selfish desires will be unable to do so.

For Zhu Xi, learning to live harmoniously by balancing desires is like developing as an artist. That is, it is more similar to learning how to play an instrument, carve a sculpture, or paint a picture than it is to solving a problem in math. An analogy to musicality is suggestive of various ways in which Zhu thought self-cultivation is like aesthetic development. On this analogy, the self-cultivating person is learning how to move within in a community just as a musician develops the sense of what it means to play in an ensemble. In fact, an ensemble is constituted by the various musicians playing in harmony (和), and it does not exist apart from this activity of mutuality. Reality's moral Principles may be like a score, but the playing of them rests in the hands of the self-cultivated person. Indeed, the life of such a person in mutuality with others *is itself* the harmony of the Principles. This is the way Zhu Xi unites his metaphysics and his value theory. Zhu Xi's famous dictum to his students that they should investigate things (*gewu* 格物) is an admonition to study relationships, exemplars, and the arts of harmony.

This explains why only humans are interested in self-cultivation and why only humans may live in "harmony." Harmony is more than absence of conflict and more than moral purity. Living harmoniously is happiness.

Moral Willing as Moral Knowing: Wang Yangming (1472–1529)

The British thinker Gilbert Ryle wrote in some detail about the distinction between "knowing that" and "knowing how" (1949: 25–61). "Knowing that" he took to refer to knowing whether a proposition alleging to provide information about the world was true or false. Such knowing was concerned with the facts of the world; the sum total of the true statements that could be made about the objects that furnish the world and their relationships to each other. Ryle considered "knowing how" to be knowledge about the way to perform a task (how to make a table) or undertake an activity (how to swim, dance, etc.). Actually, while Ryle's analysis was quite instructive, this distinction is probably too reductionist to be complete. What knowledge is seems a good deal more complicated than even Ryle noticed. In fact, one way of approaching knowing that does not fit neatly into Ryle's categories is that developed by Wang Yangming when dealing with morality.

According to Wang's biography, while exiled in the Guizhou region of China, he began teaching what he called "the unity of knowledge and action" (*zhixing heyi*). We can see how the simultaneity of knowledge and action works epistemologically by noticing such ordinary matters as that we pour coffee, ride bikes, cross bridges, and so forth. Here there is a unity of action and knowledge. On a much more general scale, we could not do these things, except for the Principling (*li* 理) activity of the mind that Wang calls "Pure Knowledge." However, we do not first "know" the Principles by which experience is structured and then "act" upon them. There is a unity of knowledge and action in all that we do. We experience this simultaneity as a seamless process, occurring without consent of reason and with a kind of felt naturalness and certainty (Ching 1976).

Commenting on the very famous example from the writings of Mencius about how one will naturally come to the aid of a child upon seeing the child about to fall in a well (*Mengzi* 2A6), Wang wrote,

> When I see a child fall into a well [and have a feeling of commiseration], there must be the Principle of commiseration ... Is it really in the [experience of the] person of the child or does it emanate from Pure Knowledge (*liangzhi* 良知) of my mind? What is true here is true of all things and events. From this we know the mistake of dividing the mind and Principles into two. (*Instructions for Practical Living* 135, Chan 1963a: 99)

Wang said to Lu Yuanqing, "Pure Knowledge" is identical with the *Dao* (ibid.: 146).

Indeed, while he was surely quite critical of Zhu Xi's thought, nevertheless Wang was influenced by the Neo-Confucian thinkers who went before him. For example, he adopted the moral vision of Neo-Confucianism that the goal of the fully human person is to think of his activity and relationships as forming one harmonious body with all things without differentiation (Cua 2003: 762). Wang's version of this teaching is expressed in his work *Inquiry on the Great Learning*:

> The great person regards heaven, earth, and the myriad things as one body (*yiti*). He regards the world as one family and the country as one person ... Therefore, when he [the great person] sees the child about to fall into a well, he cannot help a feeling of alarm and commiseration (*Mencius* 2A.6). This shows that his humaneness forms one body with the child. Again, when he observes the pitiful cries and frightened appearance of the birds and animals about to be slaughtered, he cannot help feeling an "inability to bear" their

suffering. This shows that his humanity forms one body with birds and animals. (Chan 1963a: 272)

Wang's point here is that the great person moves by "Pure Knowledge." Seeing a child about to fall into the well, one possessed of clear Pure Knowledge moves to immediate action. Such movement is not the result of any rational process in the mind, nor anything external to the mind:

> For instance, in the matter of serving one's parents, one cannot seek for the Principle of filial piety in the parent. In serving one's ruler, one cannot seek for the Principle of loyalty in the ruler. In the intercourse with friends and in governing the people, one cannot seek for the Principles of faithfulness and humaneness in friends and the people. They [i.e., all these Principles] are all in the mind. It is the mind that manifests Principles. When the mind is free from the obscuration of selfish desires, it is the embodiment of Heavenly Principles [tianli] which requires not an iota added from the outside. (Instructions for Practical Living, ibid.,7, my modifications)

In this passage, Heavenly Principle (tianli) as a norm or standard is discovered by introspection, turning back into oneself. Knowing what is good or evil, right or wrong, belongs to a certain sort of clarity of the mind rather than to the circumstances of external situations, possible consequences of the action, or rationally derived duties. Wang wrote, "The thousand sages are all passing shadows; Pure Knowledge alone is my teacher" (Ivanhoe 2000: 68):

> The sense of right and wrong is knowledge possessed by men without deliberation and an ability possessed by them, without their having acquired it by learning. It is what we call "Pure Knowledge" (liangzhi). This knowledge is inherent in the human mind whether that of the sage or of the stupid person, for it is the same for the whole world and for all ages. If [exemplary persons, junzi] of the world merely devote their effort to extending their [Pure] Knowledge they will naturally share with all a universal sense of right and wrong, share their likes and dislikes, regard other people as their own persons, regard the people of other countries as their own family, and look upon Heaven, Earth, and all things as one body. When this is done, even if we wanted the world to be without order, it would not be possible. (Instructions for Practical Living, Chan 1963a: 166–7, my modifications)

For Wang, Pure Knowledge, if unobstructed by self-centered desires, spontaneously responds to any moral situation in a seamless process of perceiving, understanding, judging, willing, and action (Ivanhoe

2002: 99–100). In a poem entitled "Four Verses on Pure Knowing Written for My Students," Wang's third verse is revealing:

> Everyone has within an unerring compass;
> The root and source of the myriad transformations lies in the heart-mind.
> I laugh when I think that, earlier, I saw things the other way around;
> Following branches and leaves, I searched outside! (Ivanhoe 2009: 181)

According to Wang, Pure Knowledge is a form of consciousness that is best understood by means of an analogy to vision. It is a type of knowing that can be compared to seeing clearly, without any fuzziness or distortion. In this sense, it is neither a thought upon which the rational mind deliberates, nor a product of the senses. It is a direct, unmediated apprehension that is an intrinsic capacity (*benti*) of the human consciousness (*Instructions for Practical Living*, Chan 1963a: 199).

Wang spoke of "the vision of humaneness (*ren*, 仁)" and in this way, "Pure Knowledge" is like seeing the way of humaneness to be taken in a situation that another person misses, because his heart-mind is clouded by selfish desires.

Instead of thinking primarily of moral development by employing agricultural metaphors as Mencius did or analogies to carving and polishing as Xunzi did, Wang brought forward a "discovery" model of moral awareness that likens "Pure Knowledge" to visual clarity (Ivanhoe 2011: 285). He did not hesitate to talk about sudden and complete moral enlightenment, as though the clouds of desire and confusion are blown away and the sun suddenly comes bursting through.

Even though Wang studied Buddhism and Daoism for many years, he objected to both traditions. He differed with Buddhism because he felt Buddhists confined themselves to meditation, turning it into an end in itself, and using it as an excuse to remove themselves from relationships and engagement with the world (ibid.: 41, 123, 205, 265). He thought the purpose of "Pure Knowledge" was to help one know how to engage with the world, not retreat from it. At one level his concern with Daoism is similar:

> One day the business of study was discussed. The Teacher said, "In teaching people, don't insist on a particular, one-sided way. In the beginning, one's mind is like a restless monkey and his feelings are like a galloping horse. They cannot be tied down. His thoughts and deliberations mostly tend to the side of selfish human desires. At that point, teach him to sit in meditation and to stop those thoughts and deliberations. Wait a long time till his mind

becomes somewhat settled. If, however, at this time he merely remains quiet in a vacuum, like dry wood and dead ashes [i.e., a Daoist expression found in the *Zhuangzi*], it is also useless." (*Instructions for Practical Living*, Chan 1963a: 35)

While we might find Wang's position convincing with regard to ordinary movement, it may seem more difficult to agree with his view when it is applied to morality. After all, we daily come in to contact with those that have different moral views than we do. In response to the direct evidence of moral divergence, Wang held that unlike ordinary movement in the world, the obstructions of selfish desires barnacle over the clear "Pure Knowledge" of morality and therein lies the source of different moral beliefs. Wang was quite well aware that we do not live in a world where all persons follow their "Pure Knowledge" of morality. He wrote,

If one ponders and manipulates according to his personal wishes that is "the exercise of cunning and selfishness." Generally speaking, the trouble with students is either sinking into emptiness and maintaining silence or manipulating and pondering. (ibid.: 151–2)

People have used their selfishness and cunning to compete with and rival one another. Consequently each one has his own opinion, and one-sided, trivial, perverse, and narrow views as well as dishonest, crafty, underhanded, and evil tricks have become innumerable … They overcome one another with anger … They are jealous of the world and envious of the talented … No wonder the world is confused and calamity and disorder endlessly succeed each other. (ibid.: 167–8)

In his important exposition of the volitional force of "Pure Knowledge," Wang's position made a novel contribution to our thinking about the relationship between knowledge and moral action. He did not compartmentalize knowing and willing into separate activities as these are characteristically handled by Western thinkers. To greatly oversimplify the matter, we may say that in "Pure Knowledge" attraction and desire, or repulsion and hate, *accompany the moral Principle known*.

In Western philosophy, when we speak of *willing* to do something, we do so to mark acting in a way that did not come spontaneously, but rather that required effort, as though we had to overcome a desire born of a feeling drawing us toward some other act or no act at all. We may know what is required morally, but lack the attraction and desire to do it. This disconnection is not present in "Pure Knowledge" of morality:

[The Teacher] said, "[Pure] Knowledge is the original substance of the heart-mind. The heart-mind is naturally able to know. When it perceives the parents, it naturally knows that one should be filial. When it perceives the elder brother, it naturally knows that one should be respectful. And when it perceives a child fall into a well, it naturally knows that one should be commiserative. This is Pure Knowledge of good and need not be sought outside. If what emanates from Pure Knowledge is not obstructed by selfish ideas, the result will be like the saying 'If a man gives full development to his feeling of commiseration, his humanity will be more than he can ever put into practice.' However, the ordinary man is not free from the obstruction of selfish ideas. He therefore requires the effort of the extension of knowledge and the investigation of things in order to overcome selfish ideas and restore principle." (ibid., 15)

For Wang, the experience of moral enlightenment brings not only knowledge about what is right and good but also the accompanying desire and affection that pulls us toward it, so that we effortlessly act in a moral way. This was a crucial contribution to moral philosophy. Wang was not saying that we have only a cognitive gain in knowing what is right or wrong, and then we must use our will to redirect our desires and passions to act upon that knowledge. Here is how Wang expressed his view:

Pure Knowledge [*liangzhi*] is to minute details and varying circumstances as compasses and measures are to areas and lengths. Details and circumstances cannot be predetermined, just as areas and lengths are infinite in number and cannot be entirely covered. If compasses and squares are truly set, there cannot be any deception regarding areas, and the possibility of correct areas in the world cannot be exhausted. If measures are well exhibited, there cannot be any deception regarding length, and the possibility of correct lengths in the world cannot be exhausted. If Pure Knowledge is truly extended, there cannot be any deception regarding minute details and varying circumstances, and yet the possibility of minute details and varying circumstances in the world cannot be exhausted. (ibid., 109)

For Wang, moral discernment can come through reason and experience, but when it does so, the natural interpenetration and simultaneity of knowledge and action is not present, as it is in "Pure Knowledge." There is this exchange between Wang and one of his students:

I asked, "It is by nature that the sage is born with knowledge and can practice it naturally and easily. What, then, is the need of any effort?"

The Teacher said, "Knowledge and action are effort. The difference lies in whether it is thorough or shallow, and hard or easy. Pure Knowledge is by nature refined and clear. In the wish to be filial toward parents, for example, those [grasping the inborn] knowledge of filial piety can practice filial piety naturally and easily, merely follow their Pure Knowledge (*liangzhi*), and sincerely and earnestly practice filial piety to the utmost. ... As to those who learn filial piety through hard work and practice it with effort and difficulty, their obscuration and impediments are already quite great. Although they are determined to follow their Pure Knowledge and practice filial piety, they cannot do so because they are hindered by selfish desires. They must apply a hundred efforts where others can succeed by only one, and a thousand efforts where others can succeed by ten." (ibid.: 229, my changes)

Although the clarity of Pure Knowledge might be achieved by meditation, Wang did not discourage study and investigation:

I have never warned people against investigating the Principles of things to the utmost, nor urged them to live in deep seclusion, sit erect, and do nothing ... [However,] If an unenlightened student can really carefully examine the Principles of Heaven in the heart-mind in connection with things and events as they come, and extend his pure knowledge of the good, then though stupid he will surely become intelligent and though weak he will surely become strong. The great foundation will be established and the universal way [in human relations] will be in operation. (ibid.: 103)

For Wang, the most interesting and important outcome of "Pure Knowledge" is its power to enable our moral discrimination in actual conduct. Xu Ai (1487–1518), Wang's first disciple and also his brother-in-law, recorded this conversation:

I did not understand the teacher's (i.e., Wang's) doctrine of the unity of knowledge and action ... Therefore I took the matter to the teacher ... I said, "For example, there are people who know that parents should be served with filial piety and elder brothers with respect but cannot put these things into practice. This shows that knowledge and action are clearly two different things." The teacher said, "The knowledge and action you refer to are already separated by selfish desires and are no longer knowledge and action in their original substance. There have never been people who know [by Pure Knowledge] but do not act. Those who are supposed to know but do not act simply do not yet know. When sages and worthies taught people about knowledge and action, it was precisely because they wanted them to restore the original substance, and not simply to do this or that and be satisfied." (Mou 2008: 407)

Where does Wang Yangming's philosophy of the power of *liangzhi* to discriminate actions fit among models of investigation and analysis of conduct? Ultimately, Wang believed that our puzzles over what to do morally are rooted in the way in which our selfish desires obscure and cloud the natural functioning of "Pure Knowledge" (*Instructions for Practical Living*, Chan 1963a: 142–3). Absent the obstruction caused by our selfish desires, we are never confused about how to act. In the fourth of the "Four Verses Written for My Students," Wang wrote:

> Lacking sound or scent—the moment when one understands on one's own,
> This is the foundation for all within Heaven and Earth.
> Those who abandon their own limitless treasury
> Go door-to-door with alms bowl in hand—like a beggar!" (Ivanhoe 2009: 182)

Wang's position was that being able to will what is right to do is an immediate realization of knowledge of the right. No one who truly has moral Pure Knowledge will fail to practice it.[15]

Early Modern and Contemporary Reflections on Moral Philosophy

The Proper Place of Desire in Morality: Dai Zhen (1724–1777)

Dai Zhen (1724–1777) was a philosopher during the Qing dynasty and one of the most prominent scholars in what was called the "Evidential Learning" school, which often criticized the Neo-Confucian thinkers. Many Chinese philosophers shared the negative attitude of Zhu Xi and Wang Yangming toward desires possibly traceable to their study of Buddhism, but Dai was not one of them. Zhu and Wang were very suspicious of human desires, feelings, and sentiments, charging them with obscuring our clear awareness of Heaven's Principles (*tianli* 天理) and inhibiting our true moral knowledge and impulse to right activity. They argued that we cannot realize coherence with the Principles of Heaven until we successfully control our desires. For Zhu, this meant returning to our internal equilibrium, a state of balance free from the turbulence caused by desires. For Wang, our task was to empty ourselves of desires through meditation and stillness so that Pure Knowledge (*liangzhi*) could appear. However, Dai Zhen explored the concept of desire and human feelings from another point of view and insisted it was relevant to a person's self-cultivation (Tiwald 2009).[16]

Dai thought we could not be virtuous *until our moral behavior and our desires join hand in hand*. In order to be virtuous, one must not only *do the good* but also *desire to do the good*, and *feel satisfaction in doing the good*. He held that there is something philosophically at stake about our development as moral beings in the view we take toward desire, and he disagreed with those who rooted morality in a suppression or erasure of all desire and feeling. Justin Tiwald puts this well:

> If we see our work in moral self-cultivation as primarily subtractive or eliminative – as a matter of overcoming bad feelings and desires so as to let the refined parts of nature act of their own accord—then, Dai, maintains, it makes no sense to think of moral education as contributing to the growth and maturation of the moral understanding. What we learn in the process of study might be understood as having instrumental value, helping to free us from the grip of our bad dispositions and realize the dormant moral sensibilities in ourselves, but once that is accomplished the content of our knowledge would seem to play no constitutive part in moral comprehension. (Tiwald 2010a)

Tiwald's point is that Dai thought self-cultivation required more than emptying ourselves of the desires that drag us down morally. It also demands that we undertake the practices that strengthen our good desires and feelings.

Dai held that Zhu and Wang actually created a substantial difficulty for moral philosophy because they devalued the role of desire. The net effect of their attacks on desires was to leave us blind to what really matters morally. Dai claimed that morality is in large measure about the two sides of (1) how we treat others with respect to what *they desire* and (2) what are the possible detrimental effects of our actions with respect to what others do *not desire* to be done to them. By relegating all desires to the category of what must be suppressed or erased, Zhu and Xi made irrelevant the many ways in which morality should consider the role of desire in moral reciprocity.

Moreover, Dai argued that we would not even be capable of recognizing what contributes to our own well-being if we extinguish all of our desires. In their defense, Zhu and Wang may both be understood to have meant that desires are not bad *in themselves*, so long as we regulate them. Of course, Dai did not say that we should ignore the regulation of desires, but he came at the place of desire in morality from another direction. He insisted that we should actively consider both the desires of others and those of ourselves when determining what we should do. His position regards desire as a positive force in morality, and it does not seem to be addressed by Zhu or Wang. In fact, he seems to be on target in his criticism of their views. They both suggest that moral knowledge is rooted in moving to a place of stillness in our minds where Heaven's Principles are clear and evident, and that this can only be done by removing any influence of our desires.

According to Dai, since desires differ among persons and may be the source of conflict and disharmony, this is the point at which the "cognitive mind" may be a guide to determine how much weight to give to competing desires. He did not think that we could open ourselves up to some Pure Knowledge (*liangzhi*) that was only knowable apart from the action of our rational mind. Dai valorized the use of reason and evidence in all philosophical endeavors, including morality. In his *Evidential Commentary on the Meanings of Terms in Mencius*, Dai wrote:

> When I do something to others, I should examine myself and think quietly: would I accept it should someone do the same thing to me? When I demand something from others, I should examine myself thinking quietly: were this demanded of me, could I do it? When I gauge the response of others by my own, Principles (*li*, 理) will become clear. The Principles of Heaven refers to the Principles that are differentiated on the basis of what is natural. The Principles that are differentiated on the basis of what is natural means this: gauging the feelings of others by one's own so that there is fairness in every [action]. (Chin and Freeman 1990: 70)

The "cognitive mind's" application of the *method* of reciprocity (*shu* 恕) that is set out in the quote above represents a distinctive trait characteristic of the superiority of human moral actions to the behaviors we notice in the animal world.

Reciprocity has a long and venerable tradition in Chinese philosophy. It is found in Confucius, Mozi, and Mencius as a virtue associated with how one treats another. But Dai made use of the concept as a tool in moral judgment and not simply a virtue in itself (i.e., "Do unto others what you want them to do to you"; or "Do not do to others what you do not want done to you"). The actual result of Dai's emphasis on reciprocity is to highlight the role of the "cognitive mind" in moral judgment. One way in which this is seen is to identify how what one desires for oneself may be extended to others. An application of this tool yields what Dai calls "invariant norms" (*buyi zhi ze*). These norms are not mere subjective guidelines but principles that can attain a kind of universal agreement across all times and places (Tiwald 2010a).

A major difficulty with Dai's line of argument arises here. If the act of moral judgment is guided by taking my desires and extending them to others, it is at least possible that I may seriously misjudge the well-being of others who might benefit a great deal more from some action than I would. I might well treat others in deeply deficient ways simply because I lack the desires that they have.

Dai may have seen this problem. In chapter 2 of his *Evidential Commentary on the Meanings of Terms in Mencius* he asked, "If one genuinely returns to oneself and reflects on the true feelings of the weak, the feudal, the dull, the timid, the diseased, the elderly, the young, the orphaned, or the solitary, can those [true feelings] of these others really be any different from one's own (Tiwald 2010a)?" In this sense, then, Dai suggested that when the "cognitive mind" works properly in making a moral judgment or establishing a principle, it does not strictly consider only how *I* would want to be treated or what *my desires* are. My mind reflects not only on my desires but "on the true feelings of the weak, etc." When Dai asked rhetorically, "can those [true feelings] of these others be any different from one's own," I suggest that he did not mean this comment only to be a stepping stone to a universalization of feelings and desires but also to apply in a particular kind of way. He meant "can they be any different from the feelings *I would have if situated as the weak, etc.*" This requires not only that we imagine how these persons feel and what they desire but also that we simulate in ourselves such feelings and desires. Tiwald associates this with sympathetic concern (i.e., *shu* 恕, reciprocity) and calls it a "perspective-taking" emotion (2010b: 78, 79). I have no real objection to this interpretation, so long as we do not lose sight of what perspective is being employed.

The perspective to be taken is not that we simulate the feelings or desires of "everyman" or "the universal person" trying to understand what "all people desire or need" and what "universal feelings" everyone has. Neither is the perspective that of the specific person standing before me in a moral interaction. It is rather the *feelings and desires that are associated with the weakest and most disadvantaged*. So, reciprocity is given its content when we place ourselves in the position of the least advantaged and most vulnerable. It is when this perspective is adopted that desires demonstrate their moral function and it becomes clear to the cognitive mind how to proceed.

Morality and the Veil of Ignorance

Dai Zhen thought that our moral principles and indeed what specific actions we should perform could be determined by imaginatively applying the cognitive mind to the question, "What would I want (desire) done if I were weak, poor, dull, timid, diseased, aged, young, an orphan, or lonely?" He thought this was the constructive force of desire and feeling in morality. His approach is somewhat different from that taken by John Rawls in his *Theory of Justice* (1971), although the two may be more complementary than contradictory.

Like Dai, Rawls was concerned with the negative influence desires could have on morality because he believed all people are biased toward their own self-interest. Accordingly, if a person is in the position of knowing certain facts about himself such as gender, race, physical and mental well-being, wealth, age, and so forth, then the application of the principle of reciprocity as a tool of moral guidance may be skewed. The reason why this is true is that how one would want to be treated will be very different from the desire formed by a person of a different situation. So, Rawls argued that in order to allow desires to function in a fair and moral way, one imaginative exercise would be necessary. All persons should consider themselves behind a *veil of ignorance* in which they know certain basics about social order, but nothing about any of the personal facts about themselves that would allow their desires to be self-serving to the exclusion or detriment of others (Rawls 1971: 11–22). Rawls thought that a person behind the veil of ignorance, even though operating on the basis of rational self-interest, would nonetheless advocate principles of morality that would actually resemble norms of benevolence, rather than merely those of fairness or justice. His explanation for this was that persons who did not know the facts of their own standing in the world would desire to assure their self-interest. The way to do this rationally would be to set up principles behind the veil of ignorance which would protect them if they later came into the actual social world and found themselves in the most disadvantaged of positions. So, if they put into place principles that safeguard the desires of the disadvantaged, then they would be protected no matter what they later found out about themselves.

The reason why Dai's position on reciprocity and Rawls's position on the establishment of rules behind the veil of ignorance may have some resonance with each other is that in both of these constructions the way to reach moral principles and right activity is still based on desire, but these desires are framed by considering oneself in the position of weakness and vulnerability. One asks, what would I desire or want if I were in the position of the most vulnerable agent involved in it?

Dai Zhen did not believe that each new generation of persons had to renegotiate or decide anew what moral principles should guide action. He emphasized that we have the examples and teachings of the sage-kings and philosophers of the past embodied in the classics. Accordingly, the moral principles of the past can serve as instructions for all people. "The system of proprieties (*li* 澧) is the order and arrangement of heaven and earth" (Chin and Freeman 1990: 156). Nevertheless, Dai did not recommend a simple return to the authority and tradition of the past. What we learn from the classics is not merely the principles of action but also how to apply our "cognitive minds" in reciprocity, now and in the future. In this way, the classics provide evidential nourishment to our minds and a path to the moral life.

Moral Metaphysics: Mou Zongsan (1909–1995)

Mou Zongsan (1909–1995) coined the term "moral metaphysics" in the context of Chinese philosophy and understood this activity to be primarily occupied with the most basic existential inquiries of humans, such as "What should I do?" and "What makes my life meaningful?" (Cheng 2009a: 430). He argued that moral metaphysics is a two-directional movement between humanity and Heaven. One movement is upward, from the human toward Heaven and is represented in the *Analects* and the *Mencius*. The other is in a downward direction, from Heaven toward the human, represented by the Chinese texts known as the *Zhongyong* and the "Ten Wings" (i.e., the *Commentaries on the Book of Changes*; ibid.: 431–2).

Mou compared his study of Zhu Xi and other Neo-Confucians with the philosophical framework of the German philosopher Immanuel Kant (1724–1804), and he offered the Neo-Confucian approach to morality as a corrective to points where he believed Kant had misunderstood the metaphysics of morals (Tan 2009: 559). Mou understood Kant's view to be that morality in its most basic form as a set of categorical duties required of all humans is not derived from empirical experience (i.e., these duties are *a priori*). In both *The Groundwork of the Metaphysics of Morals* (1956/1785) and *The Critique of Practical Reason* (2002/1788) Kant developed a method for identifying the pure and universal moral duties humans have by subjecting any candidate duty to the test whether it could be rationally derived from what he called the Categorical Imperative: "Act always on the maxim which you can will to be universal law."[17]

According to Mou, the Neo-Confucian philosophy of the *equilibrium* (*zhong* 中) in the heart-mind of every person, where the Principles of Heaven (*tianli*) are known immediately, rather than by rational derivation, was preferable to Kant's approach using the Categorical Imperative as the source from which our moral duties and principles could be ascertained. Mou realized that his position required one to commit to a metaphysical basis for morality in a way that Kant's does not. This is one of the reasons he inverted Kant's way of speaking about "the metaphysics of morals." For Kant, the metaphysics of morals referred to the *transcendental presuppositions for morality* as we know it (i.e., what must be presupposed for us to have morality). Mou used the concept of "moral metaphysics" to focus instead on *the transcendent sources of morality* (i.e., what is the source of our moral duties beyond human reason and culture). He called his approach "the teaching of complete virtue" (*cheng de zhi jiao*). Mou thought that the Neo-Confucians, including Zhu Xi, Wang Yangming, and Dai Zhen, all had an ontological (transcendent) dimension to their moral theories that Kant lacked, thereby making their theories more complete.

Kant's Three Postulates for Morality (Freedom, Immortality, and God)

Immanuel Kant argued that morality (i.e., Practical Reason) requires three postulates that cannot be proven true but which are inseparably tied to it and should be believed. These postulates are freedom, immortality, and the existence of God. The first (freedom) comes from the necessary supposition of a faculty capable of determining the exercise of one's will independent of the laws of the sensible world; the second (immortality) derives from the practical necessary condition of a duration adequate to the complete fulfilment of the moral law, which is that virtue should produce happiness; the third

(God) proceeds from the necessary condition of the existence of a supreme independent and all-powerful morally good Being that is able to bring about the coincidence of living virtuously and being happy (Kant 2002: 2.2.60).

Kant thought that it was rational for us to believe in the truth of these three postulates because of their inseparable role as presuppositions for morality to work, even though they are not provable by human rational knowledge (Willaschek 2010: 169). Freedom is a postulate required by morality because only the agent who is independent of total determination by causal law is able to actualize being the ultimate cause of fulfilling its moral duties. Immortality must be postulated because in the normal course of life there is no fully realized coincidence of living virtuously and being happy. God must be postulated because there must be a Being that both desires bringing virtue and happiness together perfectly, and also has the power to assure the realization of this end.

Although Kant regarded freedom as the foundation of the very concept of moral duty, he did not think that a scientific or empirical description of human behavior could locate freedom or prove that it exists in the empirical world. Instead, empirical description will be directed by the concept that all events have a cause and would, therefore, always seek to provide a comprehensive causal explanation for human action and never appeal to freedom. The presupposition that humans are free, one of the basic postulates to moral life, must be, then, about a dimension of reality that is not describable by science. Kant called this the *noumenal* realm, whereas he held that science deals with the *phenomenal* world.

Mou disagreed with Kant's approach to the postulates of the moral life because his critique divided reality unsatisfactorily, both ontologically (noumenal and phenomenal worlds) and morally. He held that Neo-Confucian thinkers offered a superior philosophical exposition and grounding for moral metaphysics.

Following the Neo-Confucian thinkers, Mou held that knowledge of Heaven's moral Principles is a direct, immediate awareness of the heart-mind. These Principles are not derived from the Categorical Imperative and neither are they validated by it. Mou resisted Kant's insistence that morality must be built on three postulates that are not capable of rational substantiation. He argued that the actual lived experience of the sages in

China's past displayed both freedom of choice and the coincidence of virtue and happiness. Creative free action, according to Mou, was a manifest reality in the lives of the sages, not merely a postulate of practical (moral) reason as Kant held (Mou 1968: 10–13, 43–5). Mou also argued that the sages connected the finite (what Kant calls the phenomenal world) with the infinite (i.e., Heaven's Principles or what Kant calls the noumenal world), revealing that freedom is a fact of reality, shown in moral action, and not merely a way we think of ourselves as existing in the world. He understood his position as a completion of Kant's work by use of an explicit metaphysics.

In Kant's philosophy, the highest good is the exact coincidence of virtue and happiness; that happiness occurs in exact proportion to our virtuous living. But Kant said the confluence of optimal virtue and happiness does not and cannot occur in this world, because the natural and physical laws of empirical reality operate without regard for virtue or morality. The natural laws just do what they do without considering the moral action of an individual. Accordingly, we cannot expect any actual or historical necessary connection to exist between happiness and even the most careful realization of our moral duties.

The significance of this for Kant was that morality requires that we postulate both an immortal soul (i.e., that our lives extend beyond the years given us here and now) and a supreme power able to bring virtue and happiness together (i.e., God). Together with the postulate of freedom necessary to any moral system we must also assume immortality and God in order for the moral order of reality to be intelligible.

Mou objected to Kant's line of reasoning because he thought that appealing to God only pushed the problem of the convergence of virtue and happiness to another level. Mou held that Kant would still have to explain why such a being as God (who belongs to the noumenal and not the phenomenal world!) should be interested in bringing about the coincidence of virtue and happiness. He also wondered how we could know philosophically that a Being of supreme power would wish to bring virtue and happiness together.

In contrast to Kant's approach, Mou insisted that the sages of the past provide examples of persons who actually united Heaven's Principles in their free action and thereby realized the unity of virtue and happiness in ordinary life (Mou 1985: 323). He argued that the sages were concrete examples of virtuous well-being in Chinese history, proving that Heavenly Principles can be manifested in human practice and we need not resort to the rational postulation of an afterlife as Kant argued (Mou 1971: 257). Mou thought that an appeal to concrete lives is preferable to the bifurcated reality of Kant's phenomenal and noumenal distinction. The sage of the past attained Heaven's Principles, and through his autonomy, he brought about benefit and happiness through creative action. In this way, Mou concluded that the sage completed Kant's philosophy by uniting the kingdom of nature (phenomenal world) and the kingdom of ends (noumenal world), with no need to postulate immortality or God (Mou 1985: 323).

Chapter Reflections

Surprisingly few generalizations will hold for the broad sweep of Chinese moral philosophies. If we take a meta-ethical question such as what distinguishes moral judgments from other nonmoral value appraisals, there were some Chinese thinkers who are not very interested in this question at all. Confucius, Xunzi, and Zhu Xi all focus on cultural proprieties (*li*) and do not set up criteria for distinguishing value judgments along the lines of what Western philosophers would call morality, etiquette, and personal taste. Indeed, many proprieties that these philosophers believed to mark the advancement of the exemplary person (*junzi*) would almost certainly be considered good etiquette or manners by Western thinkers rather than moral goods. Perhaps this should not be surprising, as each of these Chinese philosophers also held that the ultimate end goal of morality is harmony (*zhonghe* 中和, or simply *he* 和) and not "the good." Accordingly, these same three thinkers did not ask whether morality or cultural propriety (*li*) is true or false, and they seem not to object to the twin ideas that these proprieties are of human derivation and that they do, from time to time, change. In the contemporary period, Mou Zongsan holds up the sages of the past as lived examples of exemplary persons, leaving no doubt that he thought that human evolution had been moved along by such representatives. These emphases on the plurality of moral proprieties and their human origination were the grounds for the significant objections Mozi had against the Confucians. Mozi's insistence that morality is rooted in divine command and, therefore, that Principles (*li*) form a unity with Heaven formed counter-arguments to what he considered to be the moral relativism of multiple sets of Principles (*li*) and the human invention of misguided morality from which they derive. We might think, too, that Mencius's view of the inborn endowments of moral sentiments offers philosophical ammunition for a criticism of the pliability of cultural proprieties, without taking the more transcendent point of view represented by Mozi. But actually, Mencius's notion of the four seeds of predisposition to morality suggested only that human persons move toward values like the good as water flows down the mountainside. Mencius did not offer us the specific moral content that is the result of these heritable propensities.

Some traditions of Chinese moral philosophy developed catalogs of moral precepts. We see this in the sectarian Buddhist groups expressed as the Five or Ten Precepts. However, what is often overlooked is that the practice of following moral precepts is not an end in itself in Buddhism. Following moral norms diminishes suffering, both for oneself and for others by rather directly focusing on and controlling one's attachments and desires. The morality book and ledger tradition greatly expanded the conceptualization of morality as a quantitative system of rights and wrongs, and folded this in with Daoist strategies for longevity and Buddhist notions of afterlife punishments in the earth prisons (aka hells). But the Lao-Zhuang and Chan traditions, as well as Wang Yangming's version of Neo-Confucianism, considered following moral precepts to be a practice that ties life in knots and actually causes anxiety and suffering, rather than relieving it. Moreover, all three of these anti-precept approaches emphasize the effortlessness of a life free of the distinctions and discriminations of morality, provided one puts oneself in a position to empty the mind of morality and its proprieties.

Additional Readings and Resources

Ames, R. (2011), *Confucian Role Ethics*, Honolulu: University of Hawaii Press.

Bloom, I. (2004), "The Moral Autonomy of the Individual in Confucian Tradition," in W. Kirby (ed.), *Realms of Freedom in Modern China*, 19–44, Stanford, CA: Stanford University Press.

Brokaw, C. (1991), *The Ledgers of Merit and Demerit: Social Change and Moral Order in Late Imperial China*, Princeton, NJ: Princeton University Press.

Carter, R. (2001), "The 'Do-Nothing' and the Pilgrim: Two Approaches to Ethics," in R. Carter and Y. Yuasa (eds.), *Encounter with Enlightenment: A Study of Japanese Ethics*, 11–34, Albany: State University of New York Press.

Chan, W., trans. (1963a), *Instructions for Practical Living and Other Neo-Confucian Writings by Wang Yang-Ming*, New York: Columbia University Press, https://archive.org/details/instructionsforp00wang. Accessed April 4, 2020.

Fan, R. (2010), *Reconstructionist Confucianism: Rethinking Morality after the West*, Heidelberg: Springer.

Harris, S. (2018), "Promising across Lives to Save Non-Existent
   Beings: Identity, Rebirth, and the Bodhisattva's Vow," *Philosophy East and
   West*, 68 (2): 386–407.
Ivanhoe, P. (2007), "Heaven as a Source for Ethical Warrant in Early
   Confucianism," *Dao: A Journal of Comparative Philosophy*, 6 (3): 211–20.
Ivanhoe, P. (2011), "McDowell, Wang Yangming, and Mengzi's Contributions
   to Moral Perception," *Dao: A Journal of Comparative Philosophy*, 10
   (3): 273–90.
Kant, I. (2002), *The Critique of Practical Reason (1788)*, T. Abbot (trans.),
   Project Gutenberg, url= http://www.gutenberg.org/files/5683/5683-
   h/5683-h.htm#link2H_4_0037. Accessed April 13, 2020
Lee, H. (2006), *Dai Zhen's Ethical Philosophy of the Human Being*, PhD diss.,
   School of Oriental and African Studies, University of London.
Li, C. (2014), *The Confucian Philosophy of Harmony*, New York: Routledge.
Littlejohn, R. (2021), "Which Button Do I Push? More Thoughts on Resetting
   Moral Philosophy in the Western Tradition," *Dao: A Journal of Comparative
   Philosophy*, 20 (1): 49–67, https://doi.org/10.1007/s11712-020-09761-w.
   Accessed January 12, 2021.
Pinker, S. (2003), *The Blank Slate: The Modern Denial of Human Nature*,
   New York: Penguin.
Shi, Z. (2007), *The Making of a Savior Bodhisattva: Dizang in Medieval China*,
   Honolulu: University of Hawaii Press.
Shun, K. (2006), "Dai Zhen on Nature (*Xing*) and Pattern (*Li*)," *Journal of
   Chinese Philosophy*, 41 (1–2): 5–17.
Sim, M. (2007), *Remastering Morals with Aristotle and Confucius*,
   Cambridge: Cambridge University Press.
Slote, M. (2015), "The Philosophical Reset Button: A Manifesto," *Dao: A
   Journal of Comparative Philosophy*, 14 (1): 1–11.
Suzuki, D., and P. Carus, trans. (1906), *Treatise of the Exalted One on Response
   and Retribution (T'ai-Shang kan-ying P'ien)*, Chicago: Open Court.
Tiwald, J. (2009), "Dai Zhen on Human Nature and Moral Cultivation," in J.
   Makeham (ed.), *The Dao Companion to Neo-Confucian Philosophy*, 399–
   422, Heidelberg: Springer.
Tiwald, J. (2012), "Xunzi on Moral Expertise," *Dao: A Journal of Comparative
   Philosophy*, 11 (3): 275–93.
Wolf, S. (1982), "Moral Saints," *Journal of Philosophy*, 79 (8): 419–39.
Yu, J. (1998), "Virtue: Confucius and Aristotle," *Philosophy East and West*, 48
   (2): 323–47.

4

哲学

Political Philosophy—
Questions about the Nature
and Purpose of Government

Introduction

Political philosophy is the normative study of government, relationships between individuals and communities, civil rights, and social and criminal justice. In this chapter we will explore some fundamental questions related to the creation of society and government as these are handled by Chinese philosophers. Some questions we will explore include the following:

- What is the natural state of humans, prior to government and law (are they free, equal, independent, or social; are they inevitably in conflict or do they live in innocent bliss)?
- From where does government arise (a contract between persons, the recognized superiority of some persons to lead, or the decree of a higher power as a divine right)?

- What are human laws and from where do they come (do we arrive at them by participatory exchange of views, do they derive from the nature of reality, are they codifications of the lives of exemplary persons, or are they decrees of government, rulers or a divine being)?
- What is the best form of government (democracy, meritocracy, monarchy, or some hybrid of these)?
- Are there checks and balances on government/rulers?
- Is revolt against the ruler or government ever justified?
- What is the proper balance between governmental authority and individual liberty of expression and thought for its citizens?
- What is the role and responsibility of government to implement social justice and how should it do it (e.g., in distributing goods, e.g., are there rules of entitlement, fairness, equality of opportunity)?[1]

The Classical Chinese Political Theory of Meritocracy

Rulership and the Function of Government: Confucius (551–479 BCE)

In the *Analects*, the ideal ruler is called a sage-king. This is no accident, because Confucius's understanding of government may be characterized as a meritocracy, or rule by the worthy. Speaking to aspiring young political rulers, Confucius said, "Do not worry over not having an official position; worry about what it takes to have one. Do not worry that no one acknowledges you; seek to do what will earn you acknowledgment" (*Analects* 1.1). Meritocracy is quite different than selecting rulers by the vote of the people (democracy), or administration by the elite (aristocracy), or even leadership of a hereditary lineage through a single king at a time (monarchy). Institutionally, a functioning meritocracy requires a system of training in order to educate and prepare rulers, followed by an apprenticeship for the one who would rule. Confucius's notion of political leadership was expressed simply as "only the worthy should rule," and following his teachings, China had to create a system of validation and confirmation of the worthiness to rule. This became known as the "Confucian Examination System" or the "Imperial Civil Service System."

Plato's *Republic* and the Models for Government

The *Republic* of Plato, a book which took shape around 375 BCE, is an extended dialogue in which Socrates is the principal interlocutor seeking to establish what justice is in itself and how a state may be just. In Book VI of this work, Socrates explains why philosophers should rule the government. He offers these reasons. Philosophers should be kings because they are better able to know the truth and thus they possess the relevant knowledge by which to rule. The philosophers' natural abilities and virtues prove that they have what is necessary to rule well because they love truth and hate falsehood (485c), exhibit moderation in conduct (485d–e), possess courage (486a–b), are quick learners (486c), have a good memory for history and its lessons (486c–d), and have a pleasant nature (486d–487a). Socrates offers a plan of education for training philosopher-kings according to which they become devoted to the Good (502–509b) and are carefully nurtured to be fit to rule (521d–540b). Plato's theory of rulership is as much of an aristocratic meritocracy as is that of Confucius.

In Book VIII of the *Republic*, Socrates provides an overview of the way in which governments may devolve from meritocratic rule into deviant forms. He describes the following.

Timocracy and oligarchy are two perversions of the just government of the meritorious philosopher-king. Timocratic governments are those in which the military generals and warriors rise to rule and seek only to stay in power and be honored and privileged (547d). Oligarchic states are those in which the ruler comes to power because of his wealth, and these rulers concentrate on protecting and enhancing their wealth and position (551c–552e). In the oligarchic state there will be division between the rich and the poor; the haves and the have-nots. Both of these systems are forms of the state in which the rulers do not control their greed and practice injustice to aggrandize themselves, and suppress the people in order to remain in power.

Socrates was also strongly critical of democracy as an attempt to prevent the rise of either timocracy and oligarchy, especially as he was familiar with it in Athens. Democratic rule empowers all equally but it does not control for the lack of knowledge of a potential ruler. Neither does it guard against the propensity for the masses to be deceived and be persuaded by the rhetoricians who, although convincing, do not pursue the truth. In a democracy, those who wish to rule are not vetted for their knowledge, but only for their abilities to convince the majority they should be in power (557e).

In the *Republic*, tyranny is the outgrowth of democracy. Ultimately, democracies devolve into states in which everyone insists on the freedom to do as they wish (562b–c). The tyrant steps up and uses any expediency that will work to gain power, telling the people that he is protecting their liberty, but actually he is enslaving them (563e–564a). The tyrant corrupts the courts, brings false charges against those who oppose him, kills or exiles his critics, and promotes only those who are absolutely loyal to him (565e–566a). He targets the educated and wealthy because he sees them as threats to his power. Since he cannot trust his military, he spends the state's funds to hire mercenaries, who answer only to him because he pays them, but he wrecks the economy of the state in doing so (567d–568e).

Another work is important to an understanding of Plato's political philosophy in the period roughly one hundred years after Confucius. The *Laws* is one of Plato's last dialogues. In it, he sketches the basic political structure and laws of an ideal city named Magnesia. There is substantial scholarly debate about the relationship between the *Republic* and the *Laws*. The prevailing interpretation most commonly advocated is that the *Laws* represents the government Plato thought was most realizable. It is a state organized and administrated under a detailed constitutional system of shared powers, rather than ruled only by the elite philosopher-kings.

Confucius's strong belief in meritocracy was formed and reformed through the history of Confucianism (Tao 2010). Originally, it directly related to his position that the ultimate purpose of government is to constantly fine tune or correct the life circumstances and situations of the people in order to establish an environment that is life furthering and proper for all the citizens (*Analects* 12.17). This broad sweep brings within the scope of government the power and responsibility to help in natural disaster, enable the free and responsible flow of trade, protect the people from internal and external enemies and destructive forces, and create the conditions that allow for the self-cultivation of the citizens (*Analects* 12:7). According to Confucius, in order to care so profoundly for the people and to orient the political functions of government to their self-improvement, the ruler must be both morally upright and administratively adept. If he is, all the people will follow. Confucius used this analogy. He said the character of the ruler is like the wind and that of the citizens is like grass. The people will bend in the direction the wind blows (*Analects* 12.19). The person who directs the state by his virtuous character is also like the pole star (i.e., North Star) which holds steady and all other stars turn toward it (*Analects* 2.1).

It is rather easy to overlook the significance of Confucius's advocacy of meritocracy or treat it as a mere platitude. It expresses quite a different point of view from one that relies on law and punishment to create order in a society. Of course, Confucius did not doubt that order might be created by strict laws and severe punishments. But in his view, order alone is not the final purpose of government. The cultivation of a humane and harmonious society in which all the people can flourish and become humane persons (*ren*) is the ultimate goal of government. Under a government of strict law and severe punishment, the people might try to avoid being caught by obeying the law or else they might strive to find technicalities that allow them to escape punishment when they violate the law. But whether they obey the law or not, there is no guarantee they are actually growing in their own self-cultivation and improving the human being itself. Emulation of an upright leader who is demonstrating life as an exemplary person (*junzi*) is a preferable way of fulfilling government's ultimate function (i.e., as the wind blows, the grass bends). So, Confucius observed,

> Lead the people with administrative injunctions and keep them orderly with penal law, and they will seek to avoid punishments but will be without a sense of shame. Lead them with moral excellence (*de* 德) and keep them orderly by observing proprieties (*li* 禮) and they will develop a sense of shame and will order their own selves. (*Analects* 2.3, my changes)[2]

Political philosophy is often taken to possess a dual emphasis. On one hand is the philosophical rationale for an ideal social order, and on the other hand is the sense that the real world requires compromises and applications that may be principled but are certainly less than the ideal. Indeed, some interpreters of Plato's political philosophy believe this stress between the ideal and the practically realizable expresses precisely the relationship between the *Republic* (i.e., the ideal) and the *Laws* (i.e., the practical).

Confucius did not address the question whether the exemplary moral character of a ruler would actually guarantee his political effectiveness. The reason he did not talk about this problem may well be that he made no distinction between political efficacy (i.e., getting things done) and doing what is right. Unfortunately, one cannot merely assume that an efficient government is also a moral one, or that a moral state will always be efficient.

Confucius did not believe that any given ruler had a "divine right" to be king. The right to rule, he held, must be earned by the evident force of the ruler's own self-cultivation and his implementation of the corrections of real or potential harms to the people, thereby winning their respect and loyalty. "If proper in their own conduct, what difficulty would they have in governing? But if not able to be proper in their own conduct, how can they demand such conduct from others?" (*Analects* 13.13, ibid.: 165). The sage ruler is no mere ideal in Confucius's teaching. He believed there were actual historical instantiations of such rulers and he named specifically the heroes of China's misty past: Yao and Shun. In the *Analects*, when Ji Kang asked how to cause the people to reverence their ruler, to be faithful to him, and to go on to serve virtue, Confucius said, "Let him be filial and kind to all; then they will be faithful to him. Let him advance the good and teach the incompetent; then they will eagerly seek to be virtuous" (*Analects* 2.20, my translation).

The objective of policies and laws in Confucian political theory is to create a harmonious society by controlling the social conditions which make it possible for persons to achieve their own self-cultivation.[3] In fact, there is a reciprocal relationship to be noted here. A harmonious society is one in which the people have cultivated themselves and yet, the people can only develop themselves fully within a harmonious society. Confucius held that the government should provide citizens with an environment in which they can cultivate themselves and live exemplary lives. This is what is meant by the statement in the *Analects* that politics means rectifying (*Analects* 12.17).

Politics is a never-ending process of monitoring the community looking for situations and practices that prevent cultivation of humane people and correcting them. Politics is a constant "tweaking" of social, economic, and moral dynamics under which the citizens live. We may extrapolate this point from Confucius to apply to present political systems. If there is poverty in the state, it must be corrected, because it stands in the way of the poor achieving self-cultivation, and keeping others in poverty may allow the rich to become corrupt. If there is prejudice and discrimination, those wronged by such practices cannot fully cultivate themselves because of these injustices, and those who inflict such injustices also ruin themselves in the process. If there are homeless people, then this reality is an example of a community failure, not merely some shortcoming or character flaw of the homeless person. For Confucius, moral and social proprieties (*li*) were an indispensable instrument in the task of self-cultivation for each person in a state (Tan 2011: 468–91).

The "Li Yun" chapter of the *Book of Rites* (*Liji*) purports to give a picture of how Confucius's image of a proper society found expression in the Warring States period (prior to 221 BCE):

Zhongni (i.e., Confucius) was one of the guests at the Ji sacrifice. When it was over, he went out and paced back and forth on the terrace over the Gate of Proclamations, looking sad and lamenting. What made him lament was the state of Lu. Yan Yan was by his side and asked him, "Master, why are you sighing?" Confucius replied, "I have never seen the practice of the Great Dao and the eminent men of the Three Dynasties, but I aspire to follow them. When the Great Dao was followed, a common spirit ruled the world. Men of talent, virtue, and ability valued mutual trust and cultivated harmony. They did not love only their own parents, nor treat only their own sons as sons. Provision was secured for the aged till their death, employment for the able-bodied, and the means of raising up the young. People showed kindness and compassion to widows, orphans, childless men, and those who were disabled by disease, so that they were all sufficiently provided for. Men had work and women had homes. Possessions were not wastefully discarded, nor were they greedily hoarded. People enjoyed laboring for others. In this way selfish scheming was discouraged and did not arise. Robbers, thieves, and rebellious traitors were unknown, and doors remained open and unlocked. This was the period called Grand Unity." (*Book of Rites*, "Li Yun"; Legge 1885: Section 1)

This portrayal of what we may take as the Confucian political ideal of a harmonious society does not suggest that such a community depends on any advanced technology or even an abundance of material resources. Neither does it assume there will be an absence of natural disasters. It emphasizes the excellence of the ruler that infects the people with a spirit of harmony, thereby creating a flourishing society that manages its resources and processes appropriately in order to establish conditions in which all the people may live a cultivated life. This is why the Grand Unity of the "Li Yun" chapter of the *Book of Rites* is contrasted with the society of the Small Tranquility in the same chapter:

Now that the Grand Dao has fallen into disuse and obscurity, hereditary families rule the kingdoms. People love only their own parents as parents, and cherish only their own sons as sons. People accumulate things and use their strength only to their own advantage. Noblemen believe in their right to hereditary power. They seek only to build strong city walls, trenches and moats for security. The proprieties of conduct (*li* 澧) and what is right are used to enforce the relationship between ruler and minister; to ensure affection between father and son, harmony between brothers, and the sentiment of concord between husband and wife; to establish institutions and measurements; to organize farms and villages; to honor the brave and the wise; with a view to their advantage. Schemes and plots multiply, and armed conflicts arise. And so it was that Emperor Yu, King Tang, King Wen, King Wu, King Cheng, and the Duke of Zhou obtained their distinction. Each of these six great men attended to the rules of propriety to manifest their appropriateness (*yi*) and demonstrate their sincerity, identify error, exemplify humaneness (*ren*), and promote courtesy, thus promoting virtue (*de*) ... Such was the Small Tranquility. (ibid.: Section 2)

Although the Small Tranquility state is not completely bankrupt, it is an incomplete realization of the Confucian ideal.[4]

The State of Nature and the Creation of Government: Mozi (c. 470–391 BCE)

Mozi is reported to have said the following:

> In ancient times, when people first came into being there were no penal codes and government, so it is said that people had different norms of moral appropriateness (*yi* 義). If there was one person, there was one rule (*ze* 則), if there were two people, there were two [different] rules, and if there were ten people, then there were ten [different] norms. The more people there were, the more different things were called appropriate. People considered their own rules right and others' wrong. The consequence was mutual condemnation ... The people of the world injured each other with water, fire, and poisons. It finally reached the point that having surplus strength, they did not use it to labor for each other; they let surplus resources rot and didn't share them with each other. The world became disordered like that among the birds and beasts. (*Mozi* 11.1, my translation)

Unlike Western philosophical descriptions of the "state of nature" prior to government, such as we have seen in chapter 3's window on Thomas Hobbes, in which self-interest leads to conflict and a condition in which the weaker seeks protection from harm done by the more powerful explains the creation of government and laws, in Mozi's version it is diverse conceptions of what is morally right that is the source of conflict leading to political structure. Mozi thought that what was missing in the state of nature before government was an upright ruler whose moral views came from Heaven and could be followed by all. In his reconstruction of the origin of government the first among these worthy rulers was called "The Son of Heaven" and was supported in his governance by the "Three Dukes" of antiquity and the feudal lords and rulers of smaller states (*Mozi* 11.2).

The sections setting forward the "Ten Doctrines of Mohism" in the *Mozi* begins with a chapter entitled "Elevating the Worthy" (*shang xian*). This doctrine is divided into three parts called a triad. The opening triad begins with a description of the state in Mozi's day, portraying it as one of disorder, poverty, and conflict. Mozi's explanation for this lamentable state of affairs was that the rulers lacked not only skills of rulership but also the commitment to two basic political principles: exalting the worthy and utilizing abilities. Because of these two failures, Mozi argued that the government of his own time had fallen back into the primal disorder that obtained when the great sage rulers of the past moved humanity from chaos into civilization. The *Mozi* says,

> If a state has many worthy and good officers, then its order will be "thick." Whereas, if worthy and good officers are few, then its order will be "thin." So the responsibility of the high officers properly lies in increasing the number of worthy men and nothing more. (*Mozi* 8.2)

In this sense, the Mohists, like the Confucians (*ru* 儒), believed government should be ruled by a meritocracy and laws ought to be established by these exemplary rulers.

At this point, a difficulty presents itself. Mozi did not explain how the worthy ruler should be selected. It appears that he thought a rising consensus to follow a specific person would emerge, because of the person's demonstrated virtue and abilities. In Mohist political theory, leadership depends on a person's competence and moral excellence without regard for the person's social status or family origin. According to the *Mozi*, in the misty past, the first worthies that created civilization taught the people how to make buildings and houses (6.1); clothing and garments (6.3); ornaments and adornments, carvings, and engravings (6.3); fine and nourishing dishes and wines (6.5); boats and carts (6.6); as well as how to write, make law, and create poetry. In his own day, Mozi called for rulers who were morally just and conscientious and also practically creative and technologically inventive.

According to the Mohist philosophical doctrine of "Exalting Unity" (*shang tong*), the purpose of government is to create a stable social and economic order by enforcing a unified conception of what lifestyles are appropriate (*yi*). Here we must not fail to notice that for the Mohists government's purpose is not to provide the greatest amount of liberty or freedom to its citizens, as we might think appropriate based on Western political theories. In fact, such liberty might lead to a fractured community, with persons pursuing their own individual desires and thereby coming into conflict. The Mohists believed that the function of government is to create an ethos in which human beings can flourish and achieve their greatest potential. To do this, there must be a unified consensus on what a good human life amounts to and how it is expressed in community with others. Mozi held that the ordinary citizen in a state can flourish in such a community by "identifying upward" and conforming to the values and conduct of the state's worthy leaders, thereby exalting a unity of values and lifestyles:

> This is why the village head was the most benevolent man of the village. It was the village head who brought administrative order to the people of the village, saying: "When you hear of good or evil, you must inform your district head. What the district head takes to be right, all must take to be right. What the district head takes to be wrong, all must take to be wrong." (*Mozi* 11.3)

So, Mozi did not hesitate to recommend giving government the power to enforce a particular moral code for social life, even if it restricted freedom of expression and liberty of lifestyle.

With respect to the relationship between morality and law, Mozi recommended a society in which what was immoral was also illegal and what was moral to do was not simply legally permitted but obligated. The *Mozi* observes,

> This is the reason Master Mo Zi said: "The ancient sage kings put into effect the five punishments, which was truly how they brought order to the people. The five punishments were like the main thread in a skein of silk, or the controlling rope of a fishing net, and were the means used to bring into line the ordinary people of the world who did not respect, and make themselves like, those above." (*Mozi* 11.5)

Morality and Law

Moral and legal	Immoral and illegal
Illegal but moral	Legal but immoral

Both morality and law seek to guide and even control human conduct in a community and culture. One way of thinking about the relationship between morality and law is by means of the table above. In Western civil libertarian societies, where the approach is to maximize one's free choice of how to live by minimizing the number of laws controlling conduct, actions falling in all four of the categories in the table can be found.

Some Western models such as that implemented by John Calvin (1509–1564) in Geneva in the early 1500s, various forms of Islamic caliphate rule. and even proponents of the government's right to enforce a moral code such as that of the more recent political theorist Lord Patrick Devlin (1905–1992) have been associated with the reduction of the relationship of law and morality to the top two categories only: moral and legal, immoral and illegal (Delvin 1965). Although we lack sufficient textual and historical material to know for sure, there is much in the *Mozi* text that suggests Mohists might also have supported such a limitation.

With respect to the tasks he believed proper for government to perform, Mozi held that providing food, clothing, shelter, preventing war, and not overtaxing the people will, in the long run, be in everyone's interest and thus these must surely be regarded as obligations from Heaven. Such actions are examples of inclusive concern (*jian ai*) and, therefore, the will of Heaven. This is true even if providing such social goods required extensive intervention of government in the lives of the people. On the other hand, actions which benefit only some at the cost of the many were condemned by Mozi as examples of moral and political wrongs.

The "Moderation in Funerals" (*Jie Zang*) sections of the *Mozi* are devoted to showing that the common understanding of the filial obligation for children to have elaborate funerals for their parents was a misplaced custom that contradicts true morality. Mozi's argument is that elaborate funerals are unprofitable not only for the persons involved but also for the village because such funerals spend resources needed for the living. Likewise, those sections in the *Mozi* that criticized aggressive war-making (17.1–19.10) stress that armaments and war represent wastes of human capital and lives; so, only temporary and limited defensive wars can be justified morally.

Mozi's political theory was designed to create stability and order. Its strength lay in its communitarian sensibilities expressed as eliminating harms and promoting benefits for the entire community. However, one difficulty with Mozi's theory is that its success depended significantly on the moral virtue of the rulers. Although theoretically only the virtuous should rule, historically in China this was not always the case. Indeed, in Mozi's own day, he protested the lack of virtue of the political leaders of his generation (e.g., 8.1, 9.1, 9.4). The Mohists recognized this potential difficulty with their theory. They held that Heaven would punish a corrupt ruler and withdraw its mandate of approval (i.e., *tianming*); this would lead to the ruler's overthrow or downfall.

Another difficulty with Mozi's political theory is that the enforcement of a single morality required a rather strong authoritarian governmental reach into the daily lives of the ordinary people, controlling many of their life choices. Historically, such governments have restricted liberty of expression, seriously undermining the individual's ability to pursue ways of living that could enrich life, even though the chosen path might deviate from the norm. Generally speaking, this kind of struggle with liberty of expression characterized Chinese dynastic governments of the past and has even reached into the modern age (Jones 2004: 19–44). One concern among many regarding this trend is that difference in lifestyle may arguably not be immoral, even if Mozi's political theory seemed not to recognize this possibility. In some ways, this failure to appreciate the difference between divergence in individual lifestyle and morally destructive life choices has remained a challenge for Chinese political systems down to the present day.

Humane Government: Mencius (c. 372–289 BCE)

It is a pity that Mencius's political philosophy is often neglected in a study of Chinese thought. One reason this is so is that Mencius conceived of politics and rulership as a branch of morality. D. C. Lau observes that for Mencius, "the relationship between the ruler and the subject was looked upon as a special case of the moral relationship that holds between individuals" (Lau 2003: xxxviii). Mencius did not speculate about the beginning of government. Unlike Mozi, he did not offer a theory about what conditions produced the need for the invention of the state and law. Instead, he was interested in describing how an existing government should operate and what goals it ought to achieve.

Mencius set out a philosophical ideology that we may call "humane government" (*renzheng* 仁政). He offered this vision to rulers who would listen to him. Mencius was a *shi* (士). For our purposes, this means he was a scholar who traveled from state to state, seeking to be a ruler's political advisor. Such persons received compensation and housing from rulers for their service. These traveling advisors often had a significant influence on a ruler, and some of them even became powerful high-ranking officials themselves. Mencius seems to have had only moderate success influencing rulers and did not rise to any high position himself.

For Mencius, humane governance means governance that does not tolerate the suffering of the people (*Mengzi* 1A3). Speaking to King Hui, Mencius said,

> If you do not interfere with the timing of the farmers, there will be more grain than can be eaten. If you disallow finely meshed nets in the ponds and lakes, there will be more fish and turtles than you can eat. If loggers are restricted in their woodcutting, there will be more wood than can be used. When there is more grain, more fish and turtles than can be eaten, and more wood than can be used, the people will be able to nourish the living and mourn their dead without resentment ... But [in your kingdom], dogs and pigs eat the people's food, and you do not correct it. People are dying of starvation in the streets and you do not distribute grain from the storehouses. People die, and you say: "It's not my fault; it was a bad harvest this year." How is this different from stabbing a man to death and saying, "It wasn't me, it was the knife." If you would stop placing the blame on bad harvests, all of the people in the country would come to you. (*Mengzi* 1A3, my translation)

In order to avoid the conditions that might cause his people to suffer, a ruler who practices humane governance should do at least the following things according to the *Mengzi*:

- reduce punishment and taxation (1A5),
- take pleasure in making the lives of his people easier (1B1),
- make sure the masses are neither cold nor hungry (1A7),
- practice punishment and execution sparingly and with regret (1A6),
- allow no one to starve to death (1A4), and
- take care of "the four types of people" who are the most vulnerable (i.e., widows, widowers, old people without children, and young children without fathers) (1B5). (Xiao 2006: 266)

In the year 319 BCE, Mencius was in the city of Liang, capital city of the state of Wei. King Hui of Liang invited the wisest scholars from all of China to offer their advice on how to govern and Mencius was given a royal audience. The king asked him to provide guidance on how to make his state wealthy:

> If your Majesty asks, "How can I profit my state?" the chief counselors will say, "How can I profit my plan?" And the nobles and commoners will say, "How can I profit myself?" Superiors and subordinates will seize profit from each other and the state will be endangered. When the ruler in a state that can field 10,000 chariots is assassinated, it will invariably be by a [person from a] clan that can field [only] 1,000 chariots. When the ruler in a state that can field 1,000 chariots is assassinated, it will invariably be by a [a person from a] clan that can field [only] 100 chariots. 1,000 out of 10,000 or 100 out of 1000 is certainly not a large amount, but if one merely puts appropriateness last and profit first, no one will be satisfied without [trying to get more]. Never have the humane persons left their parents behind. Never have the righteous put the ruler last. So, let your Majesty speak only of humaneness (ren) and appropriateness (yi). (Mengzi 1A1, my changes)

The strategy Mencius employed in giving political counsel to King Hui was to argue that obsession with profit is itself unprofitable (Van Norden 2011: 85). Mencius took a position similar to that of Confucius: "To act with an eye to personal profit will incur a lot of resentment" (Analects 4.12). However, "A humane person (ren) is the most powerful" (Mengzi 1A5; also see 7B3 and 7B4). One who has the Way (Dao) will have many to support him; one who does not have the Way will have few to support him (Mengzi 2B1).

Yang Xiao argues that Mencius thought that a ruler pursuing humane government would do so only if he had cultivated the virtues of his inner nature and not because it was expedient to do so. This interpretation has merit because Mencius was no utilitarian in his political theory. He certainly did not recommend a political action based only on its favorable outcome economically or politically. He said, "Humans all have hearts that cannot bear the suffering of others. The Ancient Kings had such hearts, and that is why they established a government that did not allow the suffering of the people" (Mengzi 2A6, my translation). Here we see more clearly Mencius's argument for humane governance (renzheng). Practicing humane governance is not based on one's belief that it will profit the ruler to do so, or even because it will enrich the country in the long run; rather it is a natural expression of the meritorious ruler's heart-mind (xin). The virtuous ruler has cultivated compassion and this virtue will manifest itself in his actions (Xiao 2006: 267). Mencius claimed,

That which an exemplary person (*junzi*) follows in his nature, namely humaneness (*ren*), justice, propriety (*li*), and wisdom, is rooted in his heart-mind (*xin*), and expresses itself in his face, giving it a glowing appearance. It also shows in his back and extends to his limbs, rendering their message intelligible without words. (*Mengzi* 7A21, my translation; also see 4A15)

Mencius traveled from state to state seeking to find a ruler who he could convince to practice "humane government." He believed that a state ruled in such a manner would be free of crime because the people would have their needs met. If the people's needs were met, they would be free from the burden of fear of poverty and insecurity; therefore, the motivations for criminality would vanish. Whereas in a state that ignores justice, propriety, and humaneness, the people's needs would be neglected and lawlessness would be the result. Accordingly, Mencius insisted that the primary obligation of humane government is to ensure that the basic needs of the people are met. In contemporary political discourse, we call this "practicing social justice."

In contrast to his call for social justice, Mencius did not emphasize that the role of government is to maximize civil liberty. Freedom of expression, speech, and thought were not principal themes in Mencius's political theory. In fact, he advocated an educational system in the ideal state that would instruct people how to conform to acceptable cultural proprieties of conduct (*li* 禮) in their relationships as parent, child, ruler, minister, spouse, and friend (*Mengzi* 3A4). While it would certainly be too strong to call this indoctrination, he did advocate the transmission of a comprehensive and uniform system of value education and behavioral conformity.

Mencius provided specific advice about how the state could help secure the livelihood of the people, including recommendations about everything from tax rates, to farm management, to the compensation for government employees (*Mengzi* 3A3). In giving advice to King Xuan, Mencius made his views clear:

Now if you practice (humaneness) in the government of your state, then all those in the Empire who seek office will wish to find a place at your court, all tillers of land to till the land in outlying parts of your realm, all merchants to enjoy the refuge of your market-place, all travelers to go by way of your roads, and all those who hate their own rulers to lay their complaints before you. This being so, no one will fail to call you a true King. (*Mengzi* 1A7, my changes)

Mencius was not making the utilitarian argument that the king should rule humanely in order to enjoy the benefits of his kingdom. He was saying that he thought it was a simple fact that a ruler whose heart-mind leads him in this way will be recognized for his virtue and his kingdom will prosper because the bright, industrious, and ingenious will seek to live in the country he rules.

The analogy Mencius used for the relationship between the ruler and the people is that of parent–child. A ruler should be to his subjects as a father is to his children. No father wants to see his children starving or freezing. All fathers want to see their children have opportunities for success and a fulfilling life. A humane ruler, according to Mencius, should have the same heart-mind. If the ruler can extend his love for his own children to cover the people over whom he is sovereign, the people will love him just as they love their own parents.

Niccolò Machiavelli's *The Prince*

What Mencius thought about the role of a ruler is much different than Niccolò Machiavelli's teaching (Liu 2006: 83). Mencius believed that the use of political power was only appropriate if it was exercised by a ruler whose personal moral character was strictly virtuous and whose goals were to use government power to create a humane community. He thought that such rulers would behave in accordance with the standards of *ren* (humaneness) and *yi* (appropriate conduct). Rulers who behaved in this way would earn the right to be obeyed, just as a father secured obedience and loyalty from his children by unfailingly looking out for their interests and well-being. The Western political theorist Niccolò Machiavelli (1469–1527) wrote a work entitled *The Prince* (1513) that criticizes at length precisely a view of political authority similar to that of Mencius. His principal points include the following:

1. Whoever has power has the right to command and moral goodness cannot ensure power. The good person does not gain any additional authority by virtue of being good.
2. Neither the personal moral goodness of the ruler, nor the enactment of just and right policies is sufficient to gain and maintain political office.
3. It is power which is necessary for the enforcement of law; one can only choose not to obey if he possesses the power to resist the demands of the state, or if he is willing to accept the consequences of disobeying the law.

4. Morality has no necessary place in politics, although it may sometimes be used as an *instrument of politics*. The ruler must always be prepared to vary his conduct as needed in changing circumstances in order to retain his position and power.

"It would be best to be both loved and feared. But since the two rarely come together, any Prince compelled to choose will find greater security in being feared than in being loved" (Machiavelli 1988: 58–9).

Mencius was not the only thinker to occupy the role of an advisor to rulers. There were many others. One of these may have had a direct influence on Mencius's political philosophy. ShangYang (*c*. 390–338 BCE) lived in the middle period of what is known as the Warring States. While we have no record of Mencius and Shang encountering each other and there is no direct mention of Shang Yang in the *Mengzi*, nevertheless, their positions on political philosophy are opposing and given the specifics of Mencius's political arguments, it is hard to believe that he was unfamiliar with Shang's views (Xiao 2006: 262).

Shang was the primary theorist behind the empire building of his time, including the rise of the state of Qin to become the most powerful among the warring states. With respect to the ability of a humane ruler to survive in such a historical context, Shang preferred a strong military as the instrument for maintaining political authority, rather than the practice of social justice:

A country of a thousand chariots is able to preserve itself by defending itself, and a country of ten thousand chariots is able to round itself off by attacking others; even [a bad ruler like] Jie would not be able to twist words to subdue his enemies. If a country is incapable of attacking other countries, or defending itself, then [even a humane ruler like] Yao would have to surrender to stronger countries. Based on this observation, we know that whether a country is taken seriously and respected by other countries depends entirely on its [ability to project] force. Therefore, force is the basis on which a country gains both prestige and respect. (Xiao 2006: 263)

For Mencius, though, the question of government is not a strategic one about power, but a moral one, directed toward care for its people.

According to the *Mengzi* text, Mencius touched upon the removal of the ruler on several occasions. He said ministers should not hesitate to depose a ruler who repeatedly refuses to listen to admonitions against his serious mistakes (*Mengzi* 5B9). Speaking of historical instances in which rulers were removed, Mencius observed that a sovereign who mutilates humaneness (*ren*) or cripples appropriateness (*yi*) is an outcast from humanity, even if he is an emperor (*Mengzi* 1B8). By undertaking this line of reasoning, Mencius offered the first fully coherent defense of the replacement of government in the history of Chinese philosophy. The basis for such a disposition of the ruler is very simple from Mencius's point of view. If the king is not humane, if he abuses the people instead of taking care of their welfare, he can be legitimately removed. For Mencius, any time the ruler abuses his power in this manner, he ceases to be a genuine (*zhen* 真) ruler:

> Mencius said, "It was by humaneness (*ren*) that the three dynasties[5] gained the throne, and by not being humane that they lost it. It is by the same means that the decaying and flourishing, the preservation and perishing, of states are determined. If the sovereign be not humane, he cannot preserve the throne from passing from him. If the Head of a State be not humane, he cannot preserve his rule." (*Mengzi* 4A3, my translation)

> Mencius said, "Jie's and Zhou's" losing the throne, arose from their losing the people, and to lose the people means to lose their hearts. There is a way to get the kingdom: get the people, and the kingdom is got. There is a way to get the people: get their hearts, and the people are got. There is a way to get their hearts: it is simply to collect for them what they like, and not to lay on them what they dislike. The people turn to a humane ruler as water flows downwards, and as wild beasts fly to the wilderness … If among the present rulers of the kingdom, there were one who loved humaneness, all the other princes would aid him, by driving the people to him." (*Mengzi* 4A9, my translation)

However, although Mencius held that the validity of rulership rests on the people's judgment, he did not think that the task of replacing the ruler should be placed in the hands of the people. In such an extreme case as the removal of a leader, he was not a defender of popular revolution. Instead, the ruler should be removed by his own ministers in the ruling class, whom Mencius called "Heaven's Delegated Officials (*tianli* 天吏)" (*Mengzi* 2A5, 2B8).[6]

The reason Mencius took this position is that he believed the people lacked the political expertise, and certainly the military wherewithal, to succeed in removing a ruler. A populist uprising would bring the whole nation into chaos. But his justification for deposing an unjust ruler shows more clearly than any other feature of his thought that he reinterpreted the ancient explanation that the rise and fall of dynasties and centers of power was a result of the Mandate of Heaven (*tianming*) or Heaven's authorization of the ruler and his kingdom. He took the view that the right of a king to rule, or the legitimacy of the government bureaucracy as a whole, rests with the people. This is not to say that the people should choose their own rulers as in a democracy, but in Mencius's ranking, people are most valuable, land and grain are next, and the ruler is least valuable. Mencius thought the withdrawal of the Mandate of Heaven occurred when a ruler lost his legitimacy with the people.

Mencius lived in a time when the various neighboring dukes were constantly attacking one another and were all committed to increasing their own power and prestige. He believed that if the king is intent only on acquiring wealth or territory, his people will surely suffer. At the same time, Mencius recognized that not all warfare can be avoided. Sometimes war is necessary. Moreover, Mencius did not limit the war powers of a ruler merely to defensive ones, as Mozi did (*Mozi* 19.3).

We might call Mencius's view on warfare a "Just War Theory." For Mencius, a war should only be pursued if it is morally just and the justice of war-making activity has these characteristics:

- War should be a regrettable last resort (*Mengzi* 2B4). Mencius held that war should not be entered into lightly and neither should it preempt other means of restoring justice and the well-being of the people, whether internally or externally (Van Norden 2011: 86). Mencius believed war would inevitably bring great physical suffering and material waste upon the people, so it should only be pursued after other alternatives were exhausted.
- According to Mencius, a war must have a just purpose or end in mind. It should not be pursued for objectives such as expanding territory, gaining wealth, or simply increasing power (*Mengzi* 4A14). A just war restores the well-being of the people that has been threatened by external forces.
- Going to war with another kingdom or country can only be justified if it is corrective and not merely punitive. The analogy Mencius used is that war between states is what punishment is to a criminal within the state. The Chinese thinker Shang Yang also used this exact analogy, but he stressed the punitive force of the action, not its corrective one (*Mengzi* 7B4).[7] In contrast, Mencius argued that war with another country can be morally just only if it brings benefit to the people of the *other* country. This is an interesting shift in focus. Mencius directed our

philosophical attention beyond the consequences of war-making for one's own king and country. He held that one factor that makes a war just is when it is undertaken to deliver the people of another country from exploitation, abuse, or starvation. Mencius argued that when this is the motivation for war, then the people of the other country will welcome deliverance. In fact, he believed they would not put up resistance. Mencius believed they would actually bring food and drink to reward the incoming troops. Moreover, for Mencius, winning a war was more than victory on the battlefield. It was equivalent to winning the hearts of the people. In all just wars, one state must occupy the high moral ground and be rectifying the conditions of abuse being implemented by the other state. (*Mengzi* 1B11)

Just War Theory in Western Philosophy

There are many versions of a "Just War Theory" in Western philosophy, including the early versions found in Aristotle's *Politics* and Augustine of Hippo's *City of God*, but the philosophical characteristics typically include the following:

Justice in Going to War (jus ad bellum, *Justice before War*)

— War must be publicly declared by a proper authority (a state)— this separates the conduct of war from simple murder.
— War must have a just cause and be pursued with a right intention (e.g., self-defense, prevention of genocide, etc.).
— War must be prosecuted proportionally and avoid doing anything that prevents a reestablishment of peace at the conflict's conclusion.
— War must be a last resort, undertaken only after all other nonviolent means have been exhausted.

Justice in the Conduct of War (jus in bello, *Justice in War*)

The principle of distinction. The acts of war should be directed only toward enemy combatants, and not toward ordinary citizens who are not soldiers, or toward targets which are not supporting the war effort (e.g., hospitals, schools, and museums are not proper objects of war making). Moreover, enemy combatants who have surrendered, been captured, or who pose no threat because of their injuries are not to be attacked.

> *The principle of proportionality.* In a just war, combatants must make sure that the harm caused to civilians or civilian property is not excessive and be of only demonstrable concrete and direct military advantage. Combatants may not use weapons or other methods of warfare that are considered inherently evil or designed to create terror rather than proportional military advantage (e.g., mass rape, indiscriminate murder, torture, and using weapons whose effects cannot be controlled or which are indiscriminate in their damage).

Legalism's Two Handles of Government: Han Fei (c. 280–233 BCE)

The term "Legalist School" (*fa jia* 法家) first appeared in Sima Qian's historical work entitled *Records of the Historian* in about 90 BCE. The term refers to Chinese philosophers of the Classical period whose common conviction was that reward and punishment according to law rather than morality were the most reliable ordering mechanisms for society. A number of philosophers associated with this school were active in government and as imperial consultants from the mid-300s to about 200 BCE. For example, Shang Yang (d. 338 BCE) was a chancellor of the Qin state and Shen Buhai (d. 337 BCE) held a similar positon in the Han government. Master Han Fei (280–233 BCE) was a prince of the Han state just prior to its annexation by the Qin when China's first empire was created in 221 BCE (Wong 2003: 362). Han Fei's philosophical positions on government and politics may be found in the work entitled simply *Hanfeizi* (Q. Chen 2000). However, like virtually all of the collections of philosophical writings in early China, the *Hanfeizi* cannot be traced in its entirety to Han Fei himself. Nevertheless, recently, there has been a renewed interest in this work both in China and in the West (Goldin 2013).

Han Fei was a counselor to the rulers of the Han state during a very turbulent time when many sought to profit by the demise or even assassination of rulers and ministers. This specific historical context at least partially explains why he took the philosophical positions he did. He advised the rulers that no one could be trusted in politics. He claimed that relying on ministers in the complex and far-flung reaches of the state was unavoidable, but the wise ruler should always expect that ministers would characteristically seek their own advantage, conceal this from the emperor, and try to gain more power whenever possible. Moreover, Han Fei believed that the political proposals coming from even the most trusted officials would likewise always have behind them some private benefit that would redound to advantage of the minister recommending them.

Although it is generally agreed that Han Fei was influenced by Xunzi's views on human nature (see Chapter 3), he did not think that human nature is evil. He simply held that all humans act in their own self-interest, and yet, he held that self-interest in itself leads to the conflicts that require the establishment of government:

> The carriage maker ... hopes that men will grow rich and eminent; the carpenter fashioning coffins hopes that men will die prematurely. It is not that the carriage maker is kindhearted and the carpenter a knave. It is only that if men do not become rich and eminent, the carriages will never sell, and if men do not die, there will be no market for coffins. The carpenter has no feeling of hatred towards others; he merely stands to profit by their death. (*Han Fei Tzu*; Watson 1964: 86)

As Han Fei interpreted them, the human actions that provoke individuals to be humane and caring, or evil and miserly, are actually very much dependent on the *conditions* in which one lives and not on one's inherent human nature. Han Fei was not a complete economic determinist, of course, but he did hold that the relative abundance or scarcity of resources does play a role in the extent to which one will follow the laws and moral norms of society:

> In olden times, men did not need to till, for the seeds of grass and the fruits of trees were sufficient to feed them; nor did women have to weave, for the skins of birds and beasts were sufficient to clothe them. Thus, without working hard, they had an abundance of supply. As the people were few, their possessions were more than sufficient. Therefore the people never quarreled. As a result, neither large rewards were bestowed, nor were heavy punishments employed, but the people governed themselves. Nowadays, however, people do not regard five children as many. Each child may in his or her turn beget five offspring, so that before the death of the grandfather there may be twenty-five grand-children. As a result, people have become numerous and supplies scanty; toil has become hard and provisions meager. Therefore people quarrel so much that, though rewards are doubled and punishments repeated, disorder is inevitable. (*Hanfeizi* 49; Liao 1939)

By arguing in this manner, we see that far from maintaining that humans have a nature that is either good or evil, Han Fei insisted that human action is *a by-product of the socioeconomic environment in which persons find themselves.*

Accordingly, Han Fei held that creating a state in which the resources are sufficient for a wholesome life is one way to encourage a peaceful state and social order. Likewise, if a ruler wants his people to work diligently, he must motivate them by an appeal to their self-interests. Han Fei thought the ruler should set up policies and administrate the state so that whenever an individual is maximizing his own self-interest, the action will also enlarge the public interest of the state.

We can see, then, that Han Fei likewise did not claim that the appraisal of a ruler should be based on his expression of meritorious virtue as Confucius or Mencius might have had it. Neither is it based on following the Way of Heaven as Mozi insisted. In fact, for Han Fei, even a ruler who is morally deficient in his own personal life may nevertheless be a good ruler. The crucial test in evaluating the effectiveness of a ruler is whether he can use political instrumentation to manage the self-interests of the various power centers represented by landowners and farmers alongside the concerns of the common people. Instead of having as its end the creation of a community in which people are enabled to be humane persons and encouraged to cultivate themselves morally, Han Fei thought of politics as a form of social control, a set of tactics that must be balanced and rebalanced based on the people's preferences and the exigencies of the socioeconomic situation, for these are the keys to what they perceive to be in their self-interest.[8]

Han Fei largely separated politics from morality, taking an approach to rulership that Confucius would certainly not have condoned. To put it succinctly, Confucius insisted on rule by the virtuous (i.e., a meritocracy) and held that the ultimate goal of the state should be to employ government powers and structures to facilitate the self-cultivation of human persons. Such a view struck a harmony between morality and politics. In contrast, *Hanfei thought of both the ruler and politics as amoral.* In fact, he claimed that persons of virtue and morality might actually be detrimental to the state. In the chapter "Eight Fallacies," he offered these arguments:

The presence of kind-hearted men [leads to] the existence of culprits among the magistrates; the presence of humane persons, the losses of public funds; the presence of superior men, the difficulty in employing the people; the presence of virtuous men, the violation of laws and statutes; the appearance of chivalrous men, vacancies of official posts; the appearance of lofty men, the people's neglect of their proper duties; the emergence of unyielding heroes, the inefficacy of orders; and the appearance of popular idols, the isolation of the sovereign from the subjects. (*Hanfeizi* 47, ibid.)

How can the presence of kind-hearted persons lead to defilement among the magistrates or the ministers of the government? Han Fei said it works like this. If a person administers his office by kindness and not by justice and application of the law, he may be subject to emotions and thereby manipulation. A humane person, caring for the people's needs, might allow his compassion for the poor and needy to go too far and exhaust public funds, or he may be led to levy heavy taxes to pay for free riders benefiting from the state's generosity while contributing little to the state. Han Fei accused the Confucian humane rulers of saying, "Give the poor and the destitute land and thereby provide men of no property with enough." He offered this response:

> However, if there are men who were originally the same as others but have independently become able to be perfectly self-supporting, even without prosperous years or other income, it must be due to their diligence or to their frugality. Again, if there are men who were originally the same as others but have independently become poor and destitute without suffering from any misfortune of famine and drought, or illness and malignancy, or calamity and lawsuit, it must be due to their extravagance or to their laziness. Extravagant and lazy persons are poor; diligent and frugal persons are rich. Now, if the superior levies money from the rich in order to distribute alms among the poor, it means that he robs the diligent and frugal and rewards the extravagant and lazy. (*Hanfeizi* 50, ibid.)

So, we can see the very direct way in which Han Fei argued that the kinds of persons and conduct valued by Confucians could actually work to the counter-purposes of the state and the well-being of the people, and even undermine justice and order.

Han Fei put forward five political tactics necessary to a viable and effective government:

- the use of the power of position,
- the employment of administrative methods,
- the making of laws,
- taking hold of the two handles of government—reward and punishment, and
- the effortless action (*wu-wei*) of the ruler.[9]

The "power of position" (*shi* 勢) was a term used in Chinese military texts to refer to the strategic advantage that one army had over another by occupying the high ground. Han Fei recommended that rulers analogously employ their political power and authority to bring order to the society. Bryan Van Norden quotes this passage from the *Hanfeizi*:

> If Yao and Shun had relinquished the power of their positions as rulers and abandoned the law, and instead went from door to door persuading and debating with people, without any power to encourage them with veneration and rewards will correct them with punishments and penalties, they would not have been able to bring order to even a few households. (Van Norden 2011: 191)

One might think that since Han Fei emphasized the five tactics of government, then he must not have cared about the merits of the ruler. This is not true. However, he did have a different understanding of the ruler's merit than that of Confucius, Mozi, or Mencius. While he did not think that rulers should be uneducated or merely popular with the masses, he emphasized that they should be skilled in the employment of administrative methods (*shu* 術) of political management. In fact, Han Fei held that rising to a position of political leadership as a result of favoritism was a severe problem to be scrupulously avoided. The responsibility of the ruler, then, is to achieve his policies and tasks by appointing capable ministers, not cronies. Likewise, Han Fei believed that ministers should not perform the duties for someone else and they should not exceed their appointed assignments or overstep the boundaries of their office. Both of these laws for rulership were meant to guarantee that each minister was responsible for his proper sphere of activity and could be held accountable accordingly.

The creation of laws is the most important tactic of rulership necessary to the ideal state in Han Fei's view. For him, the power to determine what the laws permit and forbid is the sole right of the ruler:

> Government through law exists when the ruler's edicts and decrees are promulgated among the various departments and bureaus, when the certitude of punishments and penalties is understood in the hearts of the people, when rewards are given to those who respect the law, and when penalties are imposed on those who violate the rulers decrees. (*Han Fei Tzu*; Watson 1964: 336)

The importance of insuring adherence to the law is the most fundamental task of the ruler.

Han Fei held that other allegiances, whether to custom, tradition, or moral values, cannot be allowed to compete with the laws of the state. For example, the dutiful son (i.e., the Confucian filial son) must not be allowed to break the law even in order to be morally filial (*Hanfeizi*, ch. 49). Loyalty to the authority of the state, the law, and the ruler must come ahead of all other social and moral duties and obligations:

> Men of today who do not know the right way to political order all say, "Win the hearts of the people." But if they should think of winning the hearts of the people and thereby attaining political order, then even Yi Yin and Kuan Chung would find no use for their statesmanship and the superior would listen to the people only. The intelligence of the people, however, cannot be depended upon just like the mind of the baby ... if [the baby's] boil is not cut open, his trouble will turn from bad to worse ... Yet he keeps crying and yelling incessantly as he does not know that suffering the small pain will gain him a great benefit.
>
> ...
>
> Now, the superior urges the tillage of rice fields and the cultivation of grassy lands in order to increase the production of the people, but they think the superior is cruel. To perfect penalties and increase punishments is to suppress wickedness, but they think the superior is severe. Again, he levies taxes in cash and in grain to fill up the storehouses and treasures in order thereby to relieve famine and drought and provide for corps and battalions, but they think the superior is greedy. Finally, he traces out every culprit within the boundary, discriminates among men without personal favouritism ... and unites the forces for fierce struggle, in order thereby to take his enemies captive, but they think the superior is violent. These four measures are methods to attain order and maintain peace, but the people do not know that they ought to rejoice in them. (*Hanfeizi* 50, Liao 1939)

In short, the ruler should not take his directions from the common people, and moreover, Han Fei seemed not to think the general populace to be sufficiently intelligent or prudent to be taken seriously in the matters of rulership and lawmaking. According to Han Fei, the common people cannot rule themselves and must not be given the power to make or enforce law.

It is just such an understanding that led Han Fei to refer to the tactics of rewards and punishments as the "two handles" of government. He wrote, "When handing out rewards, it is best to make them substantial and dependable, so that people will prize them; when assigning penalties, it is best to make them heavy and inescapable, so that people will fear them" (*Han Fei Tzu*; Watson 1964: 343). Han Fei's position was that rulers must structure government in such a way that it is in the best interest of the citizens and the ministers alike to act for the common good and not merely for their private desires. "When a sage governs the state, he does not wait for people to be good in deference to him. Instead, he creates a situation in which people find it impossible to do wrong" (*Han Fei Tzu*; ibid., 357):

> For this reason, the intelligent ruler, in bestowing rewards, is as benign as the seasonable rain that the masses profit by his graces; in inflicting punishments, he is so terrific like the loud thunder that even divines and sages cannot atone for their crimes. Thus the intelligent ruler neglects no reward and remits no punishment. For, if reward is neglected, ministers of merit will relax their duties; if punishment is remitted, villainous ministers will become liable to misconduct. Therefore, men of real merit, however distant and humble, must be rewarded; those of real demerit, however near and dear, must be censured. (*Hanfeizi* 5, Liao 1939)

Just as we have seen in other classical Chinese political philosophies, the ruler is central in Han Fei's political theory. Even if all the other tactics of governing are followed, chaos can still be the result if one has an ineffectual ruler. Competency in political strategy, not inner virtue, was the most important factor for a ruler to possess. He thought of penal law as the expression of the ruler's power and control over society. However, he did not approve of the ruler using his power to legislate for the purpose of making arbitrary laws established at his whim, or designed only to aggrandize his power and luxury:

> If the lord of men institutes difficult requirements and convicts anybody whosoever falls short of the mark, then secret resentment will appear. If the minister disuses his merit and has to attend to a difficult work, then hidden resentment will grow. If toil and pain are not removed and worry and grief are not appeased; if the ruler, when glad, praises small men and rewards both the worthy and the unworthy, and, when angry, blames superior men and thereby makes Po-i and Robber Chê equally disgraced, then there will be ministers rebelling against the sovereign. (*Hanfeizi* 27, ibid.)

While Han Fei raised a number of cautions against the values and strategies of the Confucians, in chapter 5, "the Dao of the Ruler," he made use of a vocabulary taken from the *Daodejing*, but he gave it a quite unique meaning. For example, Han Fei instructed the ruler to be "empty" and "still." But these were not offered by Han Fei as disciplines designed to put the ruler in touch with the *Dao* and enable him to move in *wu-wei* as they are understood to do in the Lao-Zhuang tradition. This passage reveals Han Fei's distinctive use of these terms:

> Be empty and reposed and have nothing to do [i.e., *wu-wei*], then from the dark see defects in the light. See but never be seen. Hear but never be heard. Know but never be known. If you hear any word uttered, do not change it, nor move it, but compare it with the deed and see if word and deed coincide with each other. Place a censor over every official. Do not let them speak to each other. Then everything will be exerted to the utmost. Cover your tracks and conceal sources. Then the ministers cannot trace the origins of policies. Conceal your wisdom [i.e., do not state your views] and withhold your ability [i.e., do not recommend policies or acts yourself]. Then your subordinates cannot guess at your limitations. (*Hanfeizi* 5, ibid., my changes)

Han Fei was intentionally using Daoist concepts, but interpreting them in his own way. The ruler should be "empty" meant the ruler should not reveal his opinions or policy desires. He should "be still" by not handing down a policy or taking any action himself (i.e., he should let others do it). By not taking action,

> [the ruler] makes it so that the worthy refine their natural talents, while he makes use of those talents and employs them. Thus, he is never lacking in ability. He makes it so that when there are achievements he gets the credit for their worthiness, and when there are errors the ministers take the blame. Thus, he is never lacking in reputation ... The ministers perform the work, and the ruler enjoys the final achievement. (Van Norden 2011: 196)

Daoist-Influenced Political Theories

Government and Politics as an Obstruction to Human Flourishing: Lao-Zhuang Tradition (c. 350–139 BCE)

In introducing the Lao-Zhuang tradition, we have often noted the overlap between the teachings of the *Daodejing* (*DDJ*) and those sections of the *Zhuangzi* most reliably traced to the historical Zhuang Zhou and his disciples. This remains true with respect to the political philosophy characteristic of this tradition as well. Both of these texts took form in the turbulent period known as the Warring States (*c.* 475–221 BCE). During all this disruption, the *Daodejing* protested that rulers ignored the common people and their needs:

> The court is resplendent;
> Yet the fields are overgrown.
> The granaries are empty;
> Yet some wear elegant clothes;
> Fine swords hang at their sides;
> They are filled with food and drink;
> And possess wealth in exceeding abundance.
> This is known as taking pride in robbery.
> Far is this from the Way! (*DDJ*, 53)

In the *DDJ*, individuals are cautioned not to join the government and engage in its attempts to tamper with the conditions of human life and interactions between persons. The text advises those who would follow the *Dao* not to seek favor or position in the government. "To receive favor is to be in the position of a subordinate. When you get it be apprehensive; when you lose it be apprehensive" (*DDJ*, 13). However, the *DDJ* does say that if one is in a position of rulership, he should embody the *Dao* and thereby work for the good of all by simply letting the *Dao* take its course. Such rulers should keep their hands off of life's processes, rather than try to control them (*DDJ*, 16):

> The greatest of rulers is but a shadowy presence;
> (The next greatest) is the ruler who is loved and praised;
> (The next greatest) the ruler who is feared;
> (The next greatest) is the one who is reviled, those lacking in trust are not trusted. (*DDJ*, 17, my changes)

In this same connection, the *DDJ* text is famous for its aphorism that ruling a state is "like cooking a small fish," the point being that the least amount of tampering is best, as though the ruler should allow the *Dao* to process unaided and without obstruction or manipulation by government policies (*DDJ*, 60).

In the *DDJ*, rulers are told that they should not make a display of themselves and advised not to build up armament or wage war. While a cultivated person (i.e., a Confucian or Mencian), as a well-educated and trained ruler, may sometimes use weapons and fight wars, the one who has the *Dao* does not rely on such strategies and knows that sophisticated weapons are inauspicious instruments of social order and preservation (*DDJ*,

31). Even a military victory is never to be regarded as a thing of beauty, because it is built upon the destruction of human beings. One who delights in the slaughter of human beings will not realize the ambitions which drove him to undertake such action:

> Sage rulers say,
> I *wu-wei* and the people transform themselves.
> I choose stillness and the people regulate and correct themselves.
> I *wu-wei* and the people prosper on their own.
> I am without desires and the people simplify their own lives. (*DDJ*, 57, my changes)

It seems clear that the methods to rule a state properly according to the *DDJ* are quite distinctive when compared to other political traditions of China in the Classical period such as those of Confucius, Mozi, Mencius, and Han Fei:

> In ancient times, those good at practicing the Way (*Dao*) did not use it to enlighten the people, but rather to keep them in the dark.
> The people are hard to govern because they know too much.
> And so to rule a state [according to one's own wisdom] is to be a detriment to the state.
> Not to rule a state through [human] knowledge is to be a blessing to the state. (*DDJ*, 65, my changes)

Of course, the *DDJ* is not saying literally that a ruler is not to use his knowledge, and the text does not mean that there should be some conspiracy to keep the people uneducated and ignorant. It means that what is called "wisdom" by the Confucians and the Mohists is filled with conceptual moral and political discriminations and values of human construction and definition. Trying to rule by these concepts will actually tie the state into knots and create the circumstances for criminality and violence among the people. Once the ruler is empty of these moral and social distinctions, and governs without using such supposed knowledge, the state and the people will settle down and order themselves. According to the *DDJ*, government's role is to enable the people to order themselves, not to impose stability by external means of law or punishment as Han Fei and the Legalists thought.

In contrast to the rather consistent positions taken on rulership and government in the *DDJ*, no philosophical inquiry makes it more obvious that the *Zhuangzi* is a composite text resembling an anthology of teachings that sometimes differ in focus than does the subject of political philosophy. In the passages associated with the historical Zhuang Zhou (chapters 1–7) and his disciples (chapters 17–28), there is disapproval of government political intervention as a type of meddling with the *Dao* and also the follower of *Dao* is instructed not to be involved in statecraft, just as we have seen in the *DDJ*. However, in those passages of the *Zhuangzi* anthology connected with what is called Yellow Emperor Daoism, political activity and participation is not rejected, so long as the ruler undertakes it in *wu-wei*.

Chapters 1–7 of *Zhuangzi* teach that Daoist philosophical masters should not seek positions as officials or rulers. Instead, these texts recommend that the world should be left to the processes of the *Dao* that orders things itself, without man's help (*Zhuangzi* 1). Indeed, trying to force the world into a pattern by means of political activity is something the perfected person (*zhenren* 真人) must avoid. The justification underlying such a view is that political machinations run counter to what is natural. Of rulers who rely on political strategies, laws, and structures, Jie Yu said:

> [Political strategizing] is a bogus virtue! To try to govern the world like this is like trying to walk on the ocean, to drill through a river, or to make a mosquito shoulder a mountain! When the sage governs, does he govern what is on the outside? He makes sure of himself first, and then he acts. He makes absolutely certain that things can do what they are supposed to do, that is all. (*Zhuangzi* 7, Watson 1968: 93, my changes)

The teachers who were sources of this material create a story according to which even the great sage ruler of China's distant past Yao, when he visits the four philosophical masters of Gushe Mountain, realizes that there is no need for government and that the affairs of human politics can be forgotten by the one who follows the *Dao* (*Zhuangzi* 2).

The textual material having its source in Zhuangzi's disciples (chapters 17–28) also rejects rulership. For example, to explain why Zhuang Zhou himself was never a ruler, the disciples provide us with an account of the master fishing on the Pu River when two ministers from the King of Chu came to ask him to rule over all the territories of Chu (*Zhuangzi* 17). Zhuangzi refused their request, saying he would rather be like a turtle content to have his tail in the mud than be the long-dead sacred tortoise in the palace of the king. This distaste for official position is very clear throughout chapters 17–28 of the *Zhuangzi*. Another example of this approach is when Zhuangzi told his old debater (*bianshi*) friend Huizi that he had no desire to rule (*Zhuangzi* 17). Chapter 28 is also a part of the Zhuangzi Disciples material and contains a series of passages dealing with rulership. According to these texts, when several famous Daoist masters were approached with the offer of rulership, some simply refused it, others went into hiding, and one even committed suicide rather than rule (*Zhuangzi* 28; Watson 1968: 310, 312, 313–14, and 321–2). Consider this example:

> The men of Yue three times in succession assassinated their ruler. Prince Sou, fearful for his life, fled to the Cinnabar Cave and the state of Yue was left without a ruler. The men of Yue, searching for Prince Sou and failing to find him, trailed him to the Cinnabar Cave, but he refused to come forth. They smoked him out with mugwort and placed him in the royal carriage. As Prince Sou took hold of the strap and pulled himself up into the carriage, he turned his face to heaven and cried, "To be a ruler! A ruler! (Why couldn't I have been spared this?)" It was not that he hated to become their ruler; he hated the perils that go with being a ruler. Prince Sou, we may say, was the kind who would not allow the state to bring injury to his life. This, in fact, was precisely why the people of Yue wanted to obtain him for their ruler. (*Zhuangzi* 28, ibid., 311, my changes)

In sharp contrast to these sentiments about avoiding political involvement and government, we see the Yellow Emperor materials (Chs. 11–16) in the *Zhuangzi* take a very different view on rulership. In making its point about rulership, this section takes as its hero the legendary Yellow Emperor (i.e., the "Father" of the Chinese people) and says that in his early period of rule he applied the Confucian virtues of humaneness (*ren*) and appropriateness (*yi*) "to meddle with the minds of men." What followed was a history of consternation and confusion, all the way down to the Confucians and Mohists, who are mentioned by name (*Zhuangzi* 11). So, even the Yellow Emperor, relying only on his human wisdom and that of the great philosophers, was a failure as a ruler.

However, the *Zhuangzi* invents a story of the Yellow Emperor's visit to the Master Guangcheng (i.e., Master "Broadly Complete") on top of the Mountain of Emptiness and Identity (*Kongtong*). Clearly the symbolic names of the person and the mountain used in this passage reveal that the historicity of the tale is not as important as its philosophical message. Master Guangcheng guides the Yellow Emperor to experience the essence of the Perfect Dao, who then "withdrew, gave up his throne, built a solitary hut, spread a mat of white rushes, and lived for three months in retirement" (*Zhuangzi* 11). When the Yellow Emperor returned to rule thereafter, he followed *wu-wei* (effortless action). The point of this narrative is that the Yellow Emperor created disaster when he ruled as a Confucian or Mohist would, "meddling with persons' minds," but when he ruled in *wu-wei*, he was glorified and the world was well ordered. The argument is made that subsequent sage rulers followed the same path:

> Emptiness, stillness, limpidity, silence, *wu-wei* are the root of the ten thousand things. To understand them and face south is to become a ruler such as Yao was; to understand them and face north is to become a minister such as Shun was. To hold them in high station is the virtue (*de*) of emperors and kings, of the Son of Heaven; to hold them in lowly station is the way of the dark sage, the uncrowned king [i.e., Confucius]. Retire with them to a life of idle wandering and you will command first place among the recluses of the rivers and seas, the hills and forests. Come forward with them to succor the age and your success will be great, your name renowned, and the world will be united. In stillness you will be a sage, in action a king. Resting in *wu-wei*, you will be honored; of unwrought simplicity, your beauty will be such that no one in the world may vie with you. (*Zhuangzi* 13, ibid., 143, my changes)

In this passage, the much-honored Confucian sage-kings Yao and Shun are not blamed for the confusion and disorder of the world; rather, their success and greatness as rulers is attributed to the fact that they practiced *wu-wei*, emptiness, and stillness and not their skill in political machinations. Any true ruler should follow their example. To forsake this approach to rulership is to follow the way of the dark sage, known as the uncrowned king (Confucius).

A Plan for Effortless Rulership: *The Masters of Huainan* (*Huainanzi*) (c. 139 BCE)

As a synthetic work completed by a collection of editors at the Huainan Academy rather than a work by any single author, the *Masters of Huainan* (*c.* 139 BCE) strives to convey its sense of the truth about political theory in terms that recent scholarship has associated closely with the guiding intellectual influence of the Yellow Emperor Daoism tradition we notice also in the *Zhuangzi*. The original function of the *Masters of Huainan* was to educate the ruler regarding the tasks before him and how best to perform them. In the text, we find a theory of the fall of humanity from an original primitive harmony in the state of nature into human government and politics with its attendant disorder and violence. In this respect, the approach taken to the origination of government is similar to that found in *Zhuangzi* (e.g., chapters 10 and 12). Instead of being the result of an agreed-upon social contract between persons who find themselves in a "state of nature" where there is no law and the powerful can have their will over the weak, the text takes a completely reverse approach. In the *Masters of Huainan* the emergence of the political state is not a remedy to an original situation of disharmony and violence. Instead, the state of nature prior to the emergence of government is thought of as one of natural, spontaneous, peaceful coexistence. Thus, government is the *source* of humanity's problems, not the solution to them. As *Masters of Huainan* 8.3 says:

> The people of antiquity made their *qi* the same as that of heaven and earth; they wandered [free and easily] in an era of unity. At that time, there was no garnering advantage by praise and rewards, no intimidation by mutilations and punishments. Proprieties of conduct (*li*) and appropriateness (*yi*), purity and modesty, had not yet been established; slander and flattery, humaneness and contempt, had not yet been set up; and the myriad peoples had not yet begun to treat each other with fraud and oppression, cruelty and exploitation—it was as if they were still immersed in undefined innocence (*hun ming* 混冥). (*Huainanzi* 8.3, Major et al., 2010: 271 my changes)

> When the state of nature declined, in the reign of Fuxi, his way was obscure and indistinct. He possessed virtuous excellence (*de*) and embraced harmony, broadcasting them subtly and comprehensively. Even so, knowledge first stirred and sprouted. The people all wanted to part from their childlike and simple minds ... Coming to the age of Shennong and the Yellow Emperor ... the myriad things and hundred clans were each given structure and began to rule ... Thus there was order but not harmony. Coming down to the age of Kun Wu and the descendants of the Xia dynasty (*c.* 2070–1600 BCE), desires attached to things; hearing and sight were lured outward [and crime appeared] ...[10] Coming down to the house of Zhou (*c.* 1046–256 BCE), decadence dispersed simplicity; people deserted the *Dao* for their own artifices; they possessed only miserly *de* in conduct; and cleverness and oppression sprouted. When the Zhou house declined, the kingly way was abandoned. The Confucians and Mohists thus began spreading their way and debating, dividing up disciples, and campaigning [for their own points of view]. (*Huainanzi* 2.10, ibid., 99–100, my changes)

In the *Masters of Huainan* this theory of the fall from primitive harmony in the state of nature into the disorder of human government and political tampering with *Dao* is developed in great detail and used to make an assessment of the circumstances in effect at the time of the formation of this philosophical work:

The disciples of Confucius and Mozi all teach the techniques of humane persons (*ren*) and appropriateness (*yi*) to the age, yet they do not avoid destruction. If they personally cannot practice their own teachings, how much less may those they teach be able to do so? Why is this? Because their way is only external. (*Huainanzi* 2.12, ibid., 102 my changes)

Chapter 9 of the *Masters of Huainan* is entitled "The Ruler's Techniques" and is of particular interest to us as philosophers. The focus of this chapter is on the methods that a ruler should use to create a humane and orderly government. According to the text, the most important technique for a ruler is effortless action (*wu-wei*). This does not mean the ruler should do absolutely nothing; it is interpreted to mean that when the ruler acts he should be free of private personal motivations and desires (9.23), so his policies are neither biased by his private preferences (9.25) nor restricted by the limits of his own vision for the state (9.9–9.11). Instead, his actions implement the movement of the *Dao*. When this happens, the people find the policies suitable because they seem natural.

In order to move effortlessly in *wu-wei*, the ruler must undertake personal practices that refine his inner *qi*. In so doing he avails himself of the unlimited power of the *Dao* of Heaven (9.2):

[The Ruler's Techniques] consist of establishing effortless (*wu-wei*) management and carrying out "the wordless teachings" he knows as a result of his practices. Quiet and tranquil, he does not act [by his own intentions or deliberations]; by even one degree he does not waver; adaptive and compliant, he relies on his underlings; dutiful and accomplished, he does not labor.

…

Therefore, his considerations are without mistaken schemes; his undertakings are without erroneous content. His words are taken as scripture and verse; his conduct is taken as a model and gnomon for the world. (*Huainanzi* 9.1, ibid., 295, my changes)

…

The affairs of the world cannot be deliberately controlled. The ruler must draw them out by following their natural direction. The alterations of the myriad things cannot be fathomed. The ruler must grasp their essential tendencies and guide them to their resting place. (*Huainanzi* 1.5, ibid., 53, my changes)

Actually, although the *Masters of Huainan* offers instructions in the technique of ruling, the ultimate basis of these is the ruler's *qi*. If the ruler is one with the *Dao*, he can move in *wu-wei* and his action will be as efficacious as that of any of the sage rulers of the past.

When we read about the *wu-wei* of the ruler, we may think this means that the *Masters of Huainan* is recommending a state without established law. However, it is important to understand that Han Fei's version of Legalism was well established at the time of the formation of this book. Accordingly, the *Masters of Huainan* is not anti-law. Instead, the perfected person (*zhenren* 真人) as ruler is the *only proper source of the law*. He is able to make law because he knows "the wordless teaching" and carries out "the unalterable way" (*Dao*). Accordingly, the ruler's heart is one with the people. The comparison used to describe this relationship is that which obtains between a master chariot driver and the horses of his chariot:

> Now if the horses are matched to the chassis and the driver's heart is in harmony with the horses, a charioteer can travel perilous roads and go for long distances, advancing and retreating and turning circles, with nothing failing to accord with his will. But if even steeds as fine as Qiji and Lu'er were given to female bondservants to drive, they would revert to their own intractable ways, and the servants could not control them. Thus the ruler does not prize people being the way he wants them of their own accord but prizes there being no chance for them to go wrong. (*Huainanzi* 9.24, ibid., 322–3, my changes)

The point of the text is that although the ruler is the maker of laws, doing so depends on his effortless action (*wu-wei*). Thus, in the *Masters of Huainan*,

> law is not a gift of heaven, not a product of earth.
> It was devised by humankind but conversely is used by humans to rectify themselves …
> A country that can be said to be lost is not one without a ruler but one without laws. (*Huainanzi* 9.23, ibid., 321)

Since the *Masters of Huainan* holds that humans and the rest of nature are interconnected, this certainly has implications for its view of rulership:

> If there are cruel punishments, there will be whirlwinds.
> If there are wrongful ordinances, there will be plagues of devouring insects.
> If there are unjust executions, the land will redden with drought. (*Huainanzi* 3.3, ibid.: 117, my changes)

In order to get an answer to the question, "What is the best form of government?" we may look in the *Masters of Huainan* in several places. One description is as follows:

In ancient times, the Yellow Emperor ruled the world. Li Mu and Taishan Ji assisted him in regulating the movements of the sun and the moon, setting in order the *qi* of *yin* and *yang*, delimiting the measure of the four seasons, correcting the calculations of the pitch pipes and the calendar.

They separated men from women, differentiated female and male, clarified the high in the low, ranked the worthy and the mean; they took steps to ensure that the strong would not oppress the weak; the many would not oppress the few.

People lived out their allotted lifespans and did not suffer early death; crops ripened in season and were not subject to calamities.

All the officials were upright and not given to partiality.

High and low were in concord and did not find fault.

Laws and commandments were clear and there was no confusion. (*Huainanzi* 6.7, ibid., 223, my changes)

In contrast, the *Masters of Huainan* does not hesitate to criticize the methods of government practiced by those who were under the influence of the philosophy of Han Fei during the time of the formation of the text:

Now take, for example, the methods of government proposed by Shen Buhai, Han Fei, and Shang Yang. They proposed to pluck out the stems of disorder and weed out the roots of disobedience, without fully investigating where those undesirable qualities came from. How did things get to that point? They forcibly imposed the five punishments, employed slicing and amputations, and turned their backs on the fundamentals of the *Dao* and its virtuous power (*de*) while fighting over the point of an awl. They mowed the common people down like hay and exterminated more than half of them. Thus filled with self-admiration, they constantly took themselves as the model of government; but this was just like adding fuel to put out a fire or boring holes to stop water from leaking. (*Huainanzi* 6.9, ibid., 230, my changes)

In contrast, consider the description of the perfected person (*zhenren* 真人) as a ruler:

His mind is coextensive with his spirit; his physical form is in tune with his nature …

He follows his spontaneous nature and aligns himself with inevitable transformations.

He is profoundly effortless (*wu-wei*), and the world naturally becomes harmonious. (*Huainanzi* 8.5, ibid.: 274, my changes)

Government Enacting Social Justice: Wang Anshi (1021–1086)

Wang Anshi (1021–1086) was a political reformer in the period of what is known as the Song dynasty (Liu 1959). While it is true that not all political reformers are also philosophers, Wang's new policies for the organization of the Song imperial administration of state affairs were driven by his underlying philosophical beliefs. He was not interested in arguments about how government originated from the state of nature, or even what philosophical arguments could be developed for various alternatives for structuring the state. However, he was intensely interested in the proper tasks of government or what government is best. The best government according to Wang is one that creates an environment of social justice for the people. Accordingly, it is not surprising that he was deeply influenced by Mencius's understanding of "Humane Government," which, if we recall, included the following values:

- reduce punishment and taxation (*Mengzi* 1A5),
- make sure the masses are neither cold nor hungry (1A7),
- take no pleasure in executions (1A6),
- allow no one to starve to death (1A4), and
- take care of "the four types of people" who are the most vulnerable (i.e., widows, widowers, old people without children, and young children without fathers) (1B5). (Xiao 2006: 266)

Wang was a brilliant scholar and also a minister in the Song government. He finished fourth in the national exams which determined worthiness to rule at the imperial level. He was skilled in technical argument, as shown in his political treatise known simply as the "Ten Thousand Word Memorial" (*Wanyan Shu*). Nevertheless, he often expressed his political philosophy in the lines of his poems, demonstrating, as Zhuang Zhou had done, that literature and not merely discursive reasoning could be a medium for serious philosophical content. He experienced early success even in remote areas of the countryside, being well liked by the common people for his construction of infrastructure and attention to the financial plight of the ordinary citizens. Even in his first political appointment (1142–1150), he adopted the view that government's primary function was to provide for the economic and social stability and well-being of the working and farming classes of China. When an epidemic hit the region under his administration, the emperor offered medical aid to the district. Wang wrote to express his appreciation to the emperor and stated clearly what would become his lifelong commitment to the political theory of Mencius, according to which government's function was to monitor and constantly adjust the humane distribution of social goods throughout the state:

> We read in Mencius that the ancient rulers were compassionate and considerate in their government of the people. As I read this prescription for the emperor I mused: "This is an instance of compassionate government." (Wang 1959: XX, 7)

After Wang enjoyed a sabbatical of about two years from his early political appointments, he took a new post and upon his arrival he found a deeply unjust situation. He wrote about this calamity in his "Distribution of Grain" (*Fa Lin*):

> Free grants of grain were the regular rule
> Of the kings of the ancient day.
> But in recent times this has ceased to be
> For the rich over the poor hold sway.
> Not alone of the people does this hold true,
> The State revenues come from like sources,
> The ruler defers to the rich and the strong,
> Even ministers buy their posts.
> This is more than loyal ears can stand. (Wang 1959: XVII, 5)

In 1058, Wang was called to court and given a position in the imperial government. He took this occasion to write his most important philosophical work, a memorial (i.e., a kind of policy paper) to the emperor which he entitled "A Discussion of Current Affairs," but which we know by the title "The Ten Thousand Word Memorial" (Williamson 1937: 48). His arguments were regarded as so convincing that he was appointed as a special counselor to Emperor Shenzong (1048–1085) and charged with the responsibility to institute a series of reforms, which were called simply "new policies" (*xinfa*).

Wang used his memorial to offer a philosophical critique of the status of social justice in the realm. While he praised the emperor as benevolent and skillful, he lamented the poverty throughout the country and took the position that this was because the other ministers of government, while well-educated Confucian literati, nevertheless lacked the practical skills to administer the state's resources and lacked the practical abilities to actually get things done on behalf of the people. He wrote,

> My meaning, however, is not that we have no laws and regulations, but that the present system of administration is not in accordance with the principles and ideas of the ancient rulers ... I am not arguing that we should revive the ancient system of government in every detail. I suggest that we should just follow the main ideas and general principles of these ancient rulers. (ibid.: 49)

To administer the principles of the ancients, Wang called on the emperor to modify the education and selection system for government ministers. He wanted the educational system and examinations leading to authorized government service to include practical fields and not merely literati Confucian learning.

In 1069, Wang's greatest advancement occurred when he was appointed as the Vice-Grand Chancellor of the realm. His first major action was to undertake financial reform in the name of distributive justice.

Approaches to Distributive Justice

One end to which the laws, institutions, and policies of a state are directed is the regulation and sometimes the control of the ways in which social goods (e.g., food, shelter), benefits (e.g., health care, education), and burdens (e.g., taxation) are distributed across members of the society. Distributive justice is a philosophical concept with broad application. Its principles include the values by which a state implements fairness, equity, entitlement, and even benevolence in the distribution of goods, services, and burdens. Governments often differ fundamentally in the principles of distributive justice that they employ. There are many permutations and types of distributive justice models. Three of the most general principles under which various models appear are the following:

> Strict Egalitarian Distribution is a principle that says every person is entitled to an "equal" distribution of social goods, but how to define "equality" is always a concern. A strict egalitarian distribution is one of absolute equality in which everyone gets the same-size piece of the social goods pie. But hardly any philosopher advocates such a distribution model, nor the radical government intervention that its implementation would require.

So, the principle of strict egalitarianism is most often modified to the principle of equal treatment based on need. This principle says, "To each according to his/her need." Both strictly socialist and communist models can be derived from this principle.

Difference Principle Distribution is a principle advanced in the 1970s by the American philosopher John Rawls. According to this principle, differences in distribution, whether caused by effort, creativity, luck, or heredity, may yet be just, provided that the inequalities they represent are open to all and they redound to the benefit of the least advantaged of society. As with the Strict Egalitarian Principle, models of justice under the Difference Principle depend on substantial government intervention and manipulation of economic and social processes. In the United States of the 1970s, Rawls even recommended adding another branch to the American government, one responsible for distribution of social goods.

Distribution by Desert is a principle that says each person is entitled to such a distribution of social goods as they earn by their labor or acquire by just means and based on opportunities that are open to all. Models under this principle typically require less government intervention and exert less control than those distributing goods by need. Where government intervention occurs, the laws and regulations are most often aimed at controlling justice in acquisition of goods and in guaranteeing equality of opportunity to participate in institutions and processes that allow acquisition by what one deserves based on one's effort and work.

Principles of distributive justice are related to the moral guidance of political processes and structures that affect the distribution of goods, benefits, and burdens. Wang Anshi certainly understood this, and his reforms were largely based on his application of Mencius's understanding of humane government.

Wang set out his reforms in distributive justice in the essay "Current Extravagance" (*Feng Su*) (Wang 1959: XVII, 18). The principal claim of this essay was: "It should follow as a matter of course that every family should have enough for its needs, and every man sufficient for his maintenance" (Williamson 1937: 115). Wang believed that the state had a responsibility to provide for its people the essentials for a decent living standard. He held that undertaking this target meant that the government had to control, or at least regulate, what was produced, how much was produced, who was employed and for what, and which rules for lending and taxation were needed to fund the distribution of social goods by the principle: *to each according to his needs.* He held that the realization of distributive justice required that government have its fingerprints on virtually all aspects of the economy, whether these had to do with agriculture, manufacture, commerce, or trade. The basis of Wang's economics, in his own words, is the assumption that "the wealth of individual households depends on protection from the state; the state's wealth depends on taxes and tributes from the people; the people's wealth depends on extracting wealth from nature" (Zhao and Drechsler 2018: 1245). Or, to put it in another way: what is needed is "to prompt all resources in the country to generate wealth for the whole country and to collect and use that wealth to cover all expense in the country" (ibid.). As he said in "The Fourth Out of Nine Fables," the ancient great rulers' fiscal policies included the following aspects:

> Who can't afford wedding and funeral
>> Will be granted loan for relief.
> Who faced loss in bad harvest
>> Will be lent credit to continue undertakings.
> Surplus goods will be purchased;
> And sold out whenever there is shortage. (ibid.: 1246)

In order to empower the government to enact his theories of social justice, Wang sought and received approval from the Emperor in 1069 to create a new agency in the government called the Financial Reorganization Bureau. This bureau had among its responsibilities breaking up monopolies, enhancing state revenue, and distributing wealth back to the ordinary class through a system of loans at low interest, which helped ordinary citizens and farmers in times of drought, crisis, or oversupply:

> Of course, I quite see that it would be better if we could reduce the interest to one per cent, or even lend the money without interest at all. It would better still perhaps to give the people the grain outright, and not regard it as a loan. Why, then, is two percent necessary and regarded as the only alternative to free relief? Simply because the work is to be continued in the future, for failure to make such a good work permanent would show faulty thinking somewhere. (Wang 1959: XVII, 9–10)

This low-interest loan program was called the "Green Shoots Loan." It was designed to make it possible for poverty-stricken peasants or those farmers who had a bad harvest to avoid taking out high-interest ones from private lenders and loan sharks. Wang argued that the farmers could thus overcome temporary financial crises and focus on their crops; those who wanted to exploit them could not take advantage of the farmers should difficulty arise, and farmers would be motivated to reclaim more lands so that agricultural production would be improved. The program had the additional benefit of increasing government revenues by collecting interest on these loans. Unfortunately, the program backfired when drought set in and ruined the crops, which made the farmers unable to pay their debts and the taxes they owed the government.

In 1070, the Public Services Act (*Muyi fa*) authored by Wang was implemented, and it set up a procedure by which services that had been previously required of the people to benefit the officials in government as part of their civic obligations instead had to be compensated (Golas 2015: 167–70). This was an effort to stimulate the economy by actually paying persons for services performed for those of privileged status. These services included serving as watchmen, messengers, household servants, clerks, maintenance labors, road workers, and even tax collectors. The labor for such services was drawn largely from the farming class. So, from the point of view of these laborers such service interfered with the performance of activities necessary to be successful in agriculture. Wang's reform reduced the number of service positions and required that they become government-compensated appointments. Moreover, the actual responsibilities of these service positions were scaled down. Finally, the act provided that all households could pay a fee to avoid this compulsory service. All of this was standardized in great detail throughout the state and the program continued to evolve throughout the Ming and into the Qing dynasty.

Under Wang's political philosophy, the state also instituted public orphanages, hospitals, dispensaries, cemeteries, and reserve granaries. Wang also launched a public school system which aimed to educate the children of the poor, who could not join the established system of private tutorship that characterized education in China's past. In his poem entitled "On Exploitation" Wang wrote:

The Ancient Great Rulers treated the people as their own sons;
Controlled all wealth, public and private.
The states controlled all economic powers,
As the pole star centers the orbit of all stars.
The state controlled all wealth-granting and -collecting;
Exploitation was regarded as a crime. (Zhao and Drechsler 2018: 1247)

There is a great deal of controversy over whether Wang's reforms were deliberately sabotaged by his rivals in government who wanted to hold on to their privilege and wealth. Some critics claimed he destroyed the traditional social structure, while others did not like the forced uniformity of benefits. Still others who were part of the disaffected landholding class felt the reforms were being pushed too rapidly and were too costly. In "Remonstrance against the New Laws," Cheng Hao (1032–1085), a contemporary and former supporter of Wang, basically offered all of these arguments against Wang's reforms. Wang was compelled to resign in 1076 after a series of natural disasters left the peasants in extreme poverty and unable to repay the government loans his policies put into place. He spent the remaining years of his life writing poetry and scholarly literary works.

Critique of the Chinese Dynastic System: Huang Zongxi (1610–1695)

Huang Zongxi's *Waiting for the Dawn: A Plan for the Prince* (*Mingyi Daifang Lu*) was the product of Huang's philosophical reflection on politics in a specific historical period. It was an expansion of a set of essays he authored on statecraft in the 1650s (Delury 2013: 154). He lived in a time when the Ming dynasty (1368–1644) was led by autocratic rulers at all levels and by individuals who were self-absorbed opportunists who viewed government as a tool for their own benefit and privilege (Struve 1988: 475). It was a period of darkness which Huang had tried to correct for decades through various writings and political activism. So, the title of his important final treatise, *Waiting for the Dawn*, was chosen deliberately. Huang was waiting for a future time when the Ming would be reformed or replaced as he hoped by a version of political governance resembling his recommendations. Huang's book was finished in 1663 after all of his efforts to revive the Ming dynasty had failed. Indeed, it was only when he had no chance of implementing his political reforms that he chose to write a plan under the hope that future political leaders would act on his advice, bringing an end to political darkness and the dawn of a new era in government. Since Theodore de Bary's English translation (1993) and critical introduction of this work, Huang's ideas have attracted substantial attention from the field of political philosophy (e.g., Tan 2011; Madsen 2002).

Elton Chan argues that Huang called for a form of limited government that would be built upon laws and not the will of the ruler alone, offer political protection of academic freedom, and enact a separation of governmental powers. The question of whether Chinese rulers were above the law was a long-standing one in Chinese political philosophy and quite pressing in Huang's day (Fang and Des Forges 2006). Huang's approach to bring rulers under the law sounds a great deal like a constitutional government and has been called "constitutional Confucianism" (de Bary 1993: 63–5; Chan 2018: 206–7). John Delury calls Huang's approach to political philosophy a "mixed constitution approach" that both continues to have a strong central ruler (i.e., emperor) and limits his power though law (i.e., a constitution) (Delury 2013: 155).

Huang argued that the rise and fall of Chinese dynasties throughout history depended on how well the rulers provided for the people. He likewise stood firmly in the tradition of Confucian political theory because he accepted as axiomatic that the root of all social evils and hope for their improvement lay in the nature and moral virtue of the leaders of the state. He shared the classical belief that the government should be a meritocracy.

Huang offered an interpretation of the state of nature, describing it as a time without rulers. He held that in this state each person took care of himself and left others alone. To this extent, his view was similar to that of the Lao-Zhuang tradition. The state of nature was not one of conflict, but primitive stability, each one pursuing one's own interests, without treading on those of others. However, what was missing was that no one promoted the benefit and well-being of all. It was this deficiency, Huang believed, that led to the emergence of the first sage-king rulers: Yao and Shun. Accordingly, his opening objection to Ming dynasty rulership was that the ruler had come to regard the people as "guests" in his great estate, perpetuated only for the enjoyment of his progeny, rather than as fellow citizens whose interests were all worthy of attention (deBary 1993: 95–6):

> Without the least feeling of pity, the [Ming dynasty] prince says, "I'm just establishing an estate for my descendants." Yet, when he has established it, the prince still extracts the very marrow from people's bones, and takes away their sons and daughters to serve his own debauchery. It seems entirely proper to him. It is, he says, the interest on his estate. (de Bary 1993: 92)

Huang insisted that the intention of Heaven was that the needs of the common people would be met by a responsible ruler. Accordingly, he held both that the emperor and his advisors were not authorized by Heaven to decide on their own what laws to pursue without the input of public opinion (*gonglun*), and also that rule by law and not by man was the only just way to empower the social stability of the state (ibid.: 99). Huang wrote, "Should it be said that 'There is only governance by men, not governance by law,' my reply is that only if there is governance by law can there be governance by men" (ibid.).

Huang's elevation of rule by law, rather than by men, was not the historical Confucian line. Generally, following Confucius himself, the dynastic tradition of China had a distrust of law and its accompanying punishments as the proper means to create social order, and this was one major difference between that tradition and the Legalists. Confucius said,

> Lead the people with political policies (*zheng*) and keep them orderly with penal law (*xing* 刑), and they will only avoid punishments but will not possess a sense of shame. Lead them with moral excellence (*de* 德) and order society by cultural propriety (*li*) and they will develop a sense of shame and moreover character. (*Analects* 2.3, my translation)

While Huang continued to recommend a meritocracy, he held that the laws could function as guardrails for the ruler and thereby protect the people. He distinguished genuine laws, established for the good of the people, from "unlawful laws," which were arbitrarily decided on at the ruler's whim or for his selfish interests.

In his essay entitled "Selecting Good Men," Huang provided a reform program for the Chinese Civil Service Exam system of educating and testing new recruits for the vast Ming governmental bureaucracy. He held that candidates should not only exhibit a genuine command of the philosophical classics of China and the major histories but also be tested by actual performance in various minor bureaucratic capacities for three years before being assignment posts of responsibility (de Bary 1993: 117).

The Chinese Civil Service Exam System

This institution, also known as the Confucian Exam System or the Imperial Exam System, was essentially a test of knowledge of what were considered Confucian texts. The heart of the exam was the Four Great Books: *Analects*, the *Mencius*, the *Great Learning*, and the *Zhongyong*. The so-called Five Classics were also included in the core curriculum: *Classic of Poetry* (*Shijing*), *Classic of History*

(*Shujing*), *Classic of Rites* (*Liji*), *Classic of Changes* (*Yijing*), and *Spring and Autumn Annals* (*Chunqiu*). The theoretical underpinning of the exam system was the embrace of the philosophical doctrine that only the meritorious should rule, preventing the inordinate influences of rule by heredity alone, command of military power, and even domination of the state by wealthy landowners. One of the principal values of the exam system was that it ensured a literate and educated leadership. Over the history of the administration of the exams, the supply of persons holding the basic degree (*shengyuan*) eventually exceeded demand, so that only those holding the highest degree (*jinshi*) could hope to move into positions of any significant governmental authority.

The establishment of the exam system, and most specifically its Confucian foundations, is traditionally traced to Emperor Wu of the Han (born Liu Che, 157–87 BCE), the nephew of Liu An. Liu An was the principal person behind the collection of the *Masters of Huainan* anthology. It was Dong Zhongshu (179–104 BCE) who recommended creating an exam system which embraced the Confucian texts as its curriculum and this suggestion was approved by the emperor.

But this standard account of the founding of the exam system is somewhat of an exaggeration. While an exam system did exist in varying forms from the time of the Han, its role as the main gateway into bureaucratic political service actually dates more probably to the time of Yang Guang (569–618), the second emperor of the Sui dynasty. It was actually not until the Song dynasty (960–1279) that performance within the exam system began to play the most important role in the selection of scholar-officials. While the exam system was interrupted during the Yuan dynasty rule of the Mongols (1271–1368), the system was restored during the Ming (1368–1644) and continued through the Qing (1644–1912) until 1905. In the current People's Republic of China the ten to twelve million members of the civil service bureaucracy are also chosen by competitive civil service exams but these bear little resemblance to the exams given during the Song to Ming dynasties.

Although the intricacies of the examination system were labyrinthine, its basic process was rather straightforward. Throughout the period from about 589 to 1905, the central imperial government sponsored exams at the various capitals of China every three years. Those who performed best earned the right to receive government positions. The actual position one obtained was determined through a combination of exam scores, personal and family influence, and available openings in the state bureaucracy. In order to determine the thousands of young men (and men only) who could compete for these exams, lower level tests were administered annually at provincial and county levels. Typically, a candidate could expect to spend several years moving upward through the system, assuming that he was successful at the lower levels. After 1370, another tier of exams was added. This was the highest level and required candidates to come to Beijing for study and testing. The testing was offered every three years and successful students received the highest degree (*jinshi*) (Hays 2017).

Elton Chan observes that although loyalty to the emperor remained an important virtue, Huang rejected equating personal loyalty to the emperor with obedience to the state. Instead, he thought that proper functioning of all public offices was not defined by loyalty to a single person but only whether the officer facilitated good governance (Chan 2018: 206). Huang proposed a number of measures and institutions designed to limit the power exercised by the emperor. Institutionally, he argued for the reestablishment of a powerful Prime Minister, rather than having the emperor directly head the bureaucracy (de Bary1993: 101). Huang seems not to have anticipated the degree to which ruling elites could convince themselves not only that they knew what the people wanted or needed but also that they even knew better than the people themselves! In the China of the 1950s, Mao Zedong created the political doctrine of the "dictatorship of the people's democracy," according to which powerful leaders would decide what was best for the people. Huang argued for several means to safeguard against such a situation. He elevated the law above the ruler, designed the office of Prime Minister to stand as a buffer between the people and the emperor, and pressed hard on the importance of a ruling internship before one could take office. But as Theodore de Bary observes,

With no middle class to support him, with little of a popular press, without a consensus-making infrastructure other than the schools and academies of the scholar-official's (*shi*), and without a defined electoral process for expressing the wishes of the common people, the public service of the scholar-official, even when conscientiously rendered as a Confucian Noble Man (*junzi*), leaves him in a precarious, dubious, and insecure position between the ruler and the common people (*min*). (de Bary 2015: 205–6)

Huang proposed to impose restraints on the scope of governmental power in order to protect free intellectual pursuit apart from governmental censorship and control (at least for Confucian scholars). He had direct experience with a situation in which the state controlled the educational system. This made it possible for political officials to shape the opinion of students and scholars alike. The state could easily attack dissenting institutions and individuals, and Huang's political theory tried to control such abuse.

Re-envisioning Chinese Political Understanding of Government and Politics

On Liberty: Yan Fu (1854–1921)

According to the significant interpreter of Chinese philosophy Fung Yulan, Yan Fu (1854–1921) was not only the greatest authority on Western philosophy in China at the beginning of the twentieth century but also the first scholar to introduce Western philosophy to China by translating a significant number of works. As noted in Chapter 1, these translated texts included: Thomas Henry Huxley's *Evolution and Ethics* (1893), published in Chinese in 1898; Adam Smith's *The Wealth of Nations* (1776), published in Chinese in 1902; Herbert Spencer's *The Study of Sociology* (1872). In addition to these works, Yan also translated Western texts with relevance to political philosophy, including John Stuart Mill's *On Liberty* (1859), published in Chinese in 1904; Charles de la Secondat de Montesquieu's *The Spirit of the Laws* (1748), published in Chinese in 1909; and William Stanley Jevons's *The Theory of Political Economy* (1878), also published in Chinese in 1909 (Fung 1948: 326).[11]

Yan followed the lead of Herbert Spencer in applying Darwinism to society generally in the manner known as "Social Darwinism." Although he translated both Huxley and Spencer, Yan was well aware of the conflict between these two thinkers over the applicability of the concepts of "survival of the fittest" and "natural selection" not only to the evolution of the natural world but also to society and culture. Huxley thought that society and culture were products of human decision and rational intelligence, whereas Darwin studied nonhuman evolution in nature. So, Huxley did not think that Darwin's findings could transfer to human social and political constructs.

Accordingly, he did not apply the concepts of survival of the fittest and natural selection to human society but emphasized conscious decision-making as determinative for human development. However, Yan Fu agreed with Spencer in thinking that human social organization is nevertheless a product of evolution and subject to the same natural laws and processes as those which hold for nature.

In Yan's commentary on Huxley's *Evolution and Ethics*, he wrote, "In natural evolution, the higher level a society has evolved to, the more liberty the society has" (Yan 1986: I, 133). He declared that both the Western powers and Japan were scientifically and socially more advanced than China because they were also freer societies. In his view, China's position of inferiority revealed itself in the nation's inability to excel in the international competition of worldviews, technology, science and sociopolitical structure. He warned that if China did not fight for its own existence, it would succumb to Western domination, because the West was more fitted for survival than was the China of his day. As can be imagined, the translation itself, and especially Yan's position on China's weakness, set off a heated debate among intellectuals largely focused on Yan's applications of the concept of "survival of the fittest" in general and the way he used it to underscore the importance of liberty and freedom as a mechanism of societal survival.

Yan insisted that China fared badly in the competition of states compared with the powers of the West and Japan because Chinese society was not structured to maximize science through freedom of thought and expression. He argued that for China to fare well in the global competition with other nations it must alter its societal structure in ways that would allow greater scientific and political progress (ibid.: I, 12). Yan located the principal cause of China's retarded development at the specific point of its lack of liberty for its people. He held that this deficiency represented China's greatest weakness and displayed its backwardness (ibid.: I, 2).

Since he accepted the evolutionary connection between the rise of greater liberty and the success of a society, Yan wanted to understand how liberty worked in the advanced Western nations. Accordingly, he examined John Stuart Mill's (1806–1873) arguments in his famous treatise entitled *On Liberty* (1859). According to Mill, the strength of a body politic lies in its commitment to the discovery of truth, liberty of thought and expression, and the freedom to choose one's own life plan. Yan held that the intersection of these values in the West made possible the novelty and progress present in Western countries but absent in China. He argued that liberty is essential in order to produce a strong nation. When people lack liberty, they are not motivated to fight for the state or work hard in order to create a productive, inventive society. He wrote:

> People in the West are respected and appreciated, even more than their kings or dukes, but the people in China are regarded as so low that they are all the property of their ruler. When the state needs people to fight for it, in the West people will naturally go to fight for their common interests and property, while in China slaves have to fight for their masters. When slaves fight against those who have been given human dignity, how can they not be defeated? (ibid.: I, 36)

In this way, Yan made use of Mill's line of argument in *On Liberty* that a state will not prevail if its members are not invested in their own development by virtue of being free to choose their own life ends (Mill 1956: 143).

Some Central Theses of John Stuart Mill's *On Liberty* (1859)

From the "Introduction":

> *The object of this Essay is to assert one very simple principle, as entitled to govern absolutely the dealings of society with the individual in the way of compulsion and control. ... That principle is, that the sole end for which mankind are warranted, individually or collectively, in interfering with the liberty of action of any of their number, is self-protection. That the only purpose for which power can be rightfully exercised over any member of a civilized community, against his will, is to prevent harm to others.*
>
> ...
>
> *This, then, is the appropriate region of human liberty. It comprises, first, the inward domain of consciousness; demanding liberty of conscience ... liberty of thought and feeling; absolute freedom of opinion and sentiment on all subjects ... liberty of tastes and pursuits; of framing the plan of our life to suit our own character; of doing as we like, subject to such consequences as may follow: ... so long as what we do does not harm others, even though they should think our conduct foolish, perverse or wrong ... No society in which these liberties are not, on the whole, respected, is free, whatever may be its form of government.*

From "On the Liberty of Thought and Discussion":

First, if any opinion is compelled to silence, that opinion may, for aught we can certainly know, be true. To deny this is to assume our own infallibility.

...

Secondly, though the silenced opinion be an error, it may, and very commonly does, contain a portion of truth; and since the general or prevailing opinion on any object is rarely or never the whole truth, it is only by the collision of adverse opinions that the remainder of the truth has any chance of being supplied.

...

Thirdly, even if the received opinion be not only true, but the whole truth; unless it is suffered to be, and actually is, vigorously and earnestly contested, it will, by most of those who receive it, be held in the manner of a prejudice, with little comprehension or feeling of its rational grounds. And not only this, but, fourthly, the meaning of the doctrine itself will be in danger of being lost, or enfeebled, and deprived of its vital effect on the character and conduct: the dogma becoming a mere formal profession, inefficacious for good, but cumbering the ground, and preventing the growth of any real and heartfelt conviction, from reason or personal experience.

Because of his close defense of Western libertarian ideas, Yan was forced to defend himself against conservative critics in China who thought his call for greater liberty of thought and expression would lead to social instability. The strategy he employed in defense of his views was to claim that although society should not interfere with individual liberty, neither should the individual do anything to harm society by his free expression. Yan appropriated Mill's "harm principle," according to which one's freedom of expression is limited only at the point in which pursing it causes harm to another. He extended this principle beyond its use as a limitation on an individual's action and claimed that it is legitimate to restrict freedom in the name of the protection of societal and communal stability and values. For Yan, the concept of liberty did not mean unlimited freedom to do whatever one wants. He held that society has genuine interests that might be harmed by indiscriminate liberty of action.

Yan believed that a society has not only a right but also a duty to transmit a set of values and cultural practices throughout its population. Law and government policy could and should be used to these ends. He certainly understood that such a proactive advocacy for a set of values could limit freedom of expression and speech for the individual. In fact, it is significant that Yan's translation of Mill's *On Liberty* was published in China with this full subtitle: *On the Borderline between Society's and Individuals' Power* (*Qunji quanjie lun* 群己權界論).

Nevertheless, Yan Fu was concerned that China's highly structured moral beliefs and social rituals could overwhelm liberty if not properly monitored. He wrote,

> In Western countries, there is nothing that prohibits free speech more than religion. ... In China, cultural proprieties (*li*) for human relationships function in the same way. As far as those moral norms are concerned, no free discussion is allowed. Chinese cultural proprieties even do more than Western religions in prohibiting free discussion. (Yan 1986: I, 134)

We should not undervalue the importance of Yan Fu's engagement with Mill's ideas and the concept of liberty. Xinyan Jiang reminds us that there had never before been a full philosophical analysis of the nature and place of liberty in Chinese political philosophy (X. Jiang 2009: 477). While we can find some defenses of remonstrating with rulers over matters of policy in a kind of mild-mannered political dissent in the history of Chinese philosophy, that kind of activity bore little resemblance to the radicality of what Mill meant by liberty of expression.[12] In Chinese remonstrance, a minister, or even a citizen, might sometimes protest that an action or policy of the ruler was unjust or unproductive and, in this way, influence a change. Examples of this practice which we have discussed earlier include the engagement with political rulers by Mencius, Wang Anshi, and Huang Zongxi. However, the actual manner in which political dissent was expressed historically in China required one to be indirect and even attribute one's own ideas to those in power in such a manner that they did not challenge a ruler, or leave the impression that he was wrong or had made a mistake. Yan's advocacy of Mill's more direct freedom of expression was quite different than the traditional remonstrance known in China previously.

Yan demonstrated that the life of the common person in China was often more restricted in its free expression by the norms of custom and moral expectation (i.e., the Confucian *li*) than by law.[13] Likewise, although we might find examples of nonconformity to social and moral norms in Chinese history, these were relatively few and far between. Accordingly, when Chinese intellectuals began to read Mill and study Yan's commentaries on his translation of *On Liberty*, a new way of looking at society and a person's place within it came into view. Yan even went so far as to argue that the beliefs and practices that hold a society together and make it stable cannot be placed outside of the realm of examination and critical scrutiny. And, in fact, this is the ultimate value of liberty of thought and discussion that Mill stressed and Yan Fu defended. Yan's advocacy for liberty became an impetus for the New Cultural Movement that began in 1915.

The New Cultural Movement in China

The New Cultural Movement (*Xin wenhua yundong*) was a trend among Chinese intellectuals to criticize traditional ideas and norms by making use of Western values such as empirical scientific inquiry and democratic libertarian political structure (Spence 1999b: 290–313). Among the many goals of these thinkers was their desire to view China as one nation among others, not a distinctively unique (and superior) Confucian culture. They also sought to overturn patriarchal structures that promoted male dominance, and instead emphasized the right of women to pursue their own life goals, obtain education, and be treated with equal opportunity and compensation for their work. They wanted to shift China's orientation toward what they considered to be "a forward-looking vision," rather than an emphasis on the past and the requirements it placed on where China could go in the future. They promoted democratic participatory expression in political policy and choice of leadership (Kuo 2017). The movement adopted the practice of calling persons who actively pursued its goals "Mr. Science" (*Sai xiansheng*) or "Mr. Democracy" (*De xiansheng*), and those out of step with its objectives were the traditional and reactionary minded "Mr. Confucius" (*Kong xiansheng*). Although largely empowered by the universities and intellectuals, the movement also modernized China's journalism through its newspapers and magazines, opening them up to publish more objective and critical content.

Oddly enough, although the New Cultural Movement derived much of its impetus from Western philosophical arguments and values, it became the ground from which grew the May Fourth Movement (1919), which flourished in Beijing at its major universities, Peking University and Tsinghua University, as well as in Shanghai. The May Fourth Movement pushed back against Western imperialism, particularly as this was expressed in international treaties which effectively ceded

Chinese provinces to Japan and Germany. The movement produced an upsurge in Chinese nationalism. But it also retained the basic libertarian emphases of the New Cultural Movement and grouped them under the concept of "anti-feudalism." Two of the May Fourth Movement's leaders, Li Dazhao (1889–1927) and Chen Duxiu (1879–1942), would later be co-founders of the Chinese Communist Party and mobilize the peasants and workers of China to overturn the traditional social and political structures of the country and establish a New China.

Yan understood that the task of implementing liberty varies under different political systems. The challenges faced in Mill's England around 1860 were not the same as those facing China coming out of a long history of imperial and despotic political systems. Still, Yan claimed that governmental protection of the people's liberty is more fundamental than any other single political doctrine humans had previously devised. He thought liberty was even more basic than democracy. Accordingly, Yan argued that liberty could exist in systems that were not themselves democracies. In fact, he recommended that China move toward a constitutional monarchy, such as that found in the Britain of his day. He did not think that China was ready for democracy, but that other models could still establish the liberties he sought to defend.

Yan did not support China's 1911 revolution to create a Republic and disestablish the Qing dynasty. He called instead for gradual reform and political change. He thought that the Chinese populous needed to establish slowly a new reality where liberty could take root and the Chinese people might pursue their own life projects. As a philosopher, Yan believed the Chinese people at the turn of the twentieth century were not yet ready or capable of participatory government and responsible use of free expression. Li Zhehou argues that Yan thought that the imitation of Western democratic practice in the China of his own day would lead to disaster (Li 2003: 259).

A Great One-World Government: Kang Youwei (1858–1927)

Kang Youwei (1858–1927) was a committed Chinese nationalist whose reformist ideas in political philosophy were despised by Empress Dowager Cixi (1835–1908) in the last years of the Qing dynasty. He wanted to reform the Chinese government and establish a constitutional monarchy, which, we recall, was also the model Yan Fu advocated. However, the actual function of Kang's one-world utopian government was very different in conception than that anticipated by Yan Fu. Kang called for an entirely new social order in China during the period when the Qing dynasty was withering away and revolution was in the wind.

According to Kang, the government should establish socialist institutions to provide for the needs of the people. In this sense, he shared Wang Anshi's views on the responsibility of government to insure social justice and even recalled Mencius's understanding of a humane government. Kang was a strong critic of capitalism. He argued that capitalism was an economic system that feeds on the greed and selfishness of persons and leads inevitably to an evil and unjust distribution of the goods of the society. So, he advocated for a utopian government that he believed would begin in China but spread throughout the world regardless of established national boundaries (Hao 1987).

Kang's work *Book of Great Unity* (*Da Tong* 大同) was developed in a first draft between 1884 and 1885, when he was only twenty-seven years of age. It was not published in its entirety until 1935, eight years after his death.[14] This philosophical work may be compared to Plato's *Republic* and other theoretical models for utopian governments. A major difference between Plato's work and Kang's is that in 1898, Kang's program for political structure and reform was adapted by the ruler of China for a brief period. The Guangxu Emperor (i.e., Aisin Gioro Zaitian, 1871–1908) began the "Hundred Days' Reform" from June to September 1898, directing China to follow the course laid out by Kang. Although the reforms Kang supported at this time were not as far-reaching as the program that he defended in the final version of the *Book of Great Unity* completed in 1902; nevertheless, opposition to the reforms was intense among the conservative ruling elites, who considered them too radical. The result was that the Empress Dowager Cixi organized the removal of the emperor and the execution of the reform's major advocates. Kang himself fled to Japan to escape arrest and probable execution.

According to Kang, the only reason for government to exist is to increase human happiness and decrease human suffering (Thompson 1958: 271). He began by arguing that the ideal government must first abolish the "nine boundaries" of human suffering, giving one chapter in the *Book of Great Unity* (chapters 2–10) to each boundary that produces human suffering. He identified these as: the very concept of the nation-state itself (national identities over which peoples go to war), class, race, sex, family, occupation (as a differentiation in wealth or status), disorderly or unjust laws, distinguishing kinds (i.e., the separation of humans from animals and the abuse of the natural world), and suffering itself. Speaking of Kang's theory, Kuo-cheng Wu wrote,

> When the great principle prevails, the whole world is bent upon the common good. The virtuous and able are honoured, sincerity is praised, and harmony is cultivated. Hence, the people not only treat their own parents and children as they should be treated, but [they so treat children of] others' as well. They provide that all the old are given comfort, all the adults are given work, all the young are given development, all the widowed, orphaned, helpless, disabled and defective people are given nourishment ... The people dislike to have wealth wasted; but they do not like to hoard it up for themselves ... Hence, all cunning designs become useless, and theft and banditry do not exist [in the world of great unity]. (Wu 1928: 299–300)

Kang held that there was no way to create a harmonious existence for human beings as long as nation-states existed. "Coming now to the matter of the existence of state. Having states, then there is quarrelling over land, quarrelling over cities, and the people are trained to be soldiers. In a single war those who die will number in the thousands and tens of thousands" (Thompson 1958: 81). Kang also argued that in order to abolish the evils of nation-states disarmament had to be universal as the first step. Following disarmament, the next essential step would be the founding of a one-world, public parliament (ibid.: 91).

Kang detested inequality of treatment based on class, gender, and race in a society. He said there were three kinds of false concepts about boundaries between persons that were created by humans and these bred injustice in all forms of government. These three erroneous concepts are: there are inferior/superior races, some people are fitted to be slaves, and women are expendable and inferior to men (ibid.: 134). He argued for the abolition of slavery by means of a universal law forbidding it. He believed the only way to eradicate racism was by amalgamating the races through intermarriage, migration, and assimilation. He thought that erasing injustice toward women required a sequence of political and social corrections:

1 Women should be freed from imprisonment and slavery (i.e., from being regarded as possessions of their father or husband).
2 Women should be freed from restriction in dress and social movement.
3 Women should have access to education, holding office, and voting as full citizens. (Thompson 1958: 159)

Kang called for the radical alteration of the traditional Chinese family structure, replacing the birth family model with state-run institutions, such as womb-teaching institutions, nurseries and schools, and retirement homes for the elderly. He recommended that permanent monogamous marriage be replaced by temporary but renewable contracts between a woman and a man (ibid.: 183–98).

In his chapter "Abolishing Boundaries of Suffering and Attaining Utmost Happiness," Kang offered some of his most controversial views. His One World included features such as everyone living in publicly owned housing, maintained and equipped by governmental authorities and resources. Since there would be no private homes in Kang's utopia, everyone likewise would dine together, imbibing only liquid food containing the complete nutritional essences of food and lacking unhealthy foods such as meat. Although there would be public hospitals available in Kang's one-world government, he thought they would be almost empty, because everyone would receive a daily medical checkup administered by health authorities in their living areas. Stating several objections to the exclusivity and violence associated with religions such as Christianity and Islam, Kang argued that only two spiritual practices would remain in the new One World: pursuing the goal of becoming a spirit immortal through Daoism and becoming enlightened as a Buddha (ibid.: 275):

> Therefore after One World [is formed] there will first be the study of immortality. After that, there will be the study of Buddhahood. The inferior knowledge is the study of immortality; the superior knowledge is the study of Buddhahood. After the studies of immortality and Budhahood will come the study of roaming through the heavens [a belief in Daoism]. I have another book on that subject. (ibid.: 276)

A Philosophical Defense of National Civic Virtues: Liang Qichao (1873–1929)

Xiao Yang calls Liang Qichao (1873–1929) "the most widely read public intellectual during the transitional period from the late Qing dynasty (1644–1912) to the early Republican era (1912–1919)" (Xiao 2002: 17).[15] The beginning of Liang's philosophical career can be traced to his studies with Kang Youwei. Liang was only twenty-two years old when he and Kang organized what became known as "the Scholars' Protest" in Beijing in 1895, and he worked alongside Kang in bringing about the "One Hundred Days' Reform" in 1898. After the suppression of this movement by the Empress

Dowager Cixi, Liang fled to Japan and his political philosophy developed in a direction different to that of Kang. Liang supported the New Cultural Movement, but he was not an advocate for revolution. While he was away from China in 1899, he met and collaborated with Sun Yatsen, who became the first president of the Chinese Republic in 1912 (Chou 2003).

For Liang Qichao, the central task of philosophy is to perfect the principles and rules necessary for social affairs within a political system. He thought an authentic philosopher is not so much an ontologist or epistemologist as he is a *jingshi* (i.e., statesman or scholar who practices statesmanship). Liang's analysis of the relevance of new Western philosophical texts showing up in China led him to put aside the distinction between Chinese learning and Western learning commonly made by the scholars of his day. He preferred to speak of the entirety of philosophy as *political learning* (*zheng xue*) that included *both* Chinese and Western thought.

Liang built his early political philosophy (from about 1898 to 1903) based on his reading of Huxley's work *Evolution and Ethics* through the translation made by Yan Fu. He interpreted Huxley's views to mean that higher evolutionary development always takes place when solidarity and group harmony become overriding intentions, replacing mere individualism. In his "A Treatise on Reform," Liang advocated constitutional forms of political organization to create one united government for China with shared values. In this work, we can hear the echoes of Kang's voice calling for one-world order, but Liang's work lacks the radical reformulation of China's social structure advocated by Kang.

Liang distinguished between the moral virtues that relate to personal conduct (*side*) in which there should be great freedom of expression and the civic or public virtues (*gongde*) that are necessary for the creation of a healthy and ideal society. He took the position that Chinese philosophical reflection on the moral virtues had been substantial and stretched over centuries of reflective analysis; however, China's history of political philosophy or public virtue was anemic and impotent.

Accordingly, Liang proposed a modern Chinese political philosophy designed to produce what he called a "new citizenry" (*xinmin*) for China (Liang 1999: I, 389). The new citizenry would be centered on a set of public virtues. In this model, he elevated the nation above the individual and argued for the development of a type of civic virtue for the people resting on a national consciousness and one toward which the people should be ever ready to express loyalty and service to the state. So, it is rather easy to see why Liang was one of the central philosophical figures in China's shift away from privileging only the veneration of the country's cultural heritage to the creation of a strong nationalism. In fact, Liang held that competitive nationalism was the most important reason for the rise of the West, and that joining in this struggle would benefit China and its people (Xiao 2002: 21). Accordingly, he separated himself from Kang Youwei, who recommended the total abolition of distinctive nation-states in order to eliminate the competition that created war and imperialistic oppression.

Struggle between states, like that among individuals, is not something Liang wanted to erase. In fact, he claimed that the competition between nation-states was a basic source of human development and evolution. With respect to internal reform and reconstitution of a political system for China, Liang was not shy in putting forward his positions. He held that China's historical valorization of harmony and cooperation had led to political authoritarianism and drained the people of their energy for innovation and diversity (Lee 1992: 243). He blamed both Daoism and Confucianism for this cultural anemia. He criticized the Daoists for praising simplicity and failing to recommend active change and reshaping of society. The Confucians, on the other hand, were well known for their stress on harmony (*he*), which Liang believed all too easily turned into stagnation and lack of novelty and creativity for fear of ideological or social conflict.

Liang focused on three cultural assumptions to be found among the Chinese that were the main causes of their civic weakness and inferior place among other nation-states:

> First, there has been no awareness of the distinction between *guojia* [nation] and *tianxia* [the world]. The Chinese have not been aware that their *guo* was one nation or state [among many]. For China has remained united since ancient time; it has been surrounded by "little barbarians," who do not have civilization or government and thus could not be called a nation or state. We Chinese people do not see them as equals. Therefore, for thousands of years, China has been isolated. We call China the world, not a nation. ...
>
> Second, there has been no awareness of the distinction between a nation [or state] and a dynasty [bureaucracy]. The biggest problem of the Chinese people is that we do not know what kind of thing a nation is and thus confuse the nation and the [bureaucracy], mistakenly believing that the nation is the property of the [government]. ...
>
> Third, there is no awareness of the relationship between the nation or state [*guo*] and the citizens [*guomin*]. A nation consists of the people. Who is the master of the nation? The people of the nation. ... The Western people regard the nation as being shared by the king and the people ... This is not the case

in China. One family owns the nation and all the rest of the people are slaves of the family. This is why, although there are forty million people in China, there are actually only dozens of human persons (*ren*). When such a nation of dozens of human beings encounters the [Western] nations of millions of human beings, how can it not be defeated? (Liang 1999: 1, 413–14)

Liang thought that the competition of ideas and lifestyles brought about by engagement with the West would bring the blood back into what he called China's "pale" society. Accordingly, he was both an activist and an intellectual father of reform in China in the late Qing dynasty. He was involved in the new Republican government of China after 1911, holding several political positions. He freely appropriated many Western political ideas, regarding them as answers to universal political quandaries all societies faced.

Liang eventually turned the philosophical focus away from competing with Western nations individually and moved toward a theory of "the universal laws of all nations" (*wanguo gongfa*) (Xiao 2002: 21). He held that the preeminent place given to freedom of thought in the West had exposed the universal laws of political and social organization that all humans recognize as necessary to the pursuit of meaning and satisfaction in life. Nonetheless, while Liang was an advocate for the state protection of freedom among its citizens, he also insisted that freedom does not mean license, and it must find its expression within a system of laws that foster the integration of the people and the group (*qun*). In these respects, he shared Yan Fu's philosophical views on the need for limitations on liberty of expression and thought.

Liang did not think of the body politic as the result of a "social contract." While we might expect him to say that individuals group themselves into a body politic by agreeing to laws that govern their relationships, he actually intentionally moved nearer to Jeremy Bentham's (1748–1832) utilitarian ideal that the public interest is equivalent to what brings the greatest happiness to the greatest number. He held that it was on this utilitarian ground that the new civic values of Chinese nationalism should rest. Accordingly, he thought that political systems rest not on a contract to avoid harm and injury among the citizens but on the more constructivist principle that government exists to enhance the lives of the maximum number of its people. In a kind of inversion of Western utilitarianism, Liang claimed that what benefits the greatest number is what the individual should submit to. In this way, Liang made a clear difference between liberty and freedom as political principles and the maximization of human freedom on a personal level, which he thought should be restricted:

> Outside politics, one should not appeal to these [i.e., liberty and equality] as one's reasons for action. When they are applied to politics, they mean no more than that everyone has liberty protected by the law and that everyone is equal before the law. They should not be interpreted as going beyond this domain. (Liang 1999: V, 284; Xiao 2002: 27)

While this may sound like a formula for a repressive or censorist state in which the group might run roughshod over the individual, Liang's position must be understood in the context of his construction of the principle he called "popular sovereignty" (*minquan*). As John Locke (1632–1704) had done in his *Two Treatises on Civil Government* (1689), Liang used the explanation of his political philosophy to offer a critique of the government then in power (the Qing imperial rule in Liang's case). He protested against arbitrary taxation that denied citizens their property, complained that the government spied on the free speech of the people, and exposed the government's fabrication of evidence in order to deprive the citizens of their liberty and take away their freedom of conscience (ibid.). Liang argued that the people should express their right to self-mastery by creating a constitutional government. He even participated in the drafting of the Chinese constitution for the short-lived Republican government in 1912.

One of Liang's more noteworthy moves philosophically was taking the Chinese term *min* (people), which was used to mark the people who made up a population, and replacing it with the concept *guomin* (citizens) in an intentional effort to tie identity and nationalism together. He believed a philosophically viable political body is not made up merely of a population of isolated individuals. Instead, the people must be brought into being as citizens who express their powers over against the state and assert their right to self-government; otherwise, the nation itself ceases to exist and becomes something ultimately destructive to human flourishing (Liang 1999: 1, 273).

In his essay "On the Progress China has made in the Last Fifty Years" (1922), Liang developed two principles of political philosophy. The first was "Anyone who is not Chinese has no right to govern Chinese affairs." The second was "Anyone who is Chinese has the right to govern Chinese affairs." Liang called the first of these "the spirit of nation building" and the second he dubbed "the spirit of democracy" (Liang 1999: 7, 4031). By 1922, his understanding of political philosophy had moved gradually toward support for a strong government because he felt the Chinese people were not yet ready for self-governance in the form of democracy. His work *Travels in the New World* explained how he came to see the differences between the American citizenry and that of China. He advocated the concept of "Enlightened Despotism" as a gradualist program of liberty and change for a China led by a strong central ruler.[16] As it turned out, by 1949, China had just such a ruler.

The Sinification of Marxism in China: Mao Zedong (1893–1976)

Karl Marx's (1818–1883) socialist writings were part of the movement called "Western Learning" (*Xi xue*)[17] in China, and no thinker is as important to the Sinification of Marxism in China during the twentieth century as Mao Zedong (1893–1976) (Dirlik 1997; Martinich and Tsoi 2015). Mao became the first Chairman of the Central Committee of the Communist Party of China, the founder of the "New China" (October 1, 1949), and the "Father of the Nation."[18] For Mao, the adoption of Marxist political philosophy was equivalent to (1) rejecting China's traditional past with its social and economic oppression of women, workers, and peasants by the privileged class and the landowners and (2) making a commitment that China will stand up to imperialist powers of the West and chart its own national destiny with a new pride (Zhou 2013).

While some question Mao's credentials as a philosopher, actually he did educate himself extensively on the history of Chinese philosophy. To be sure, Mao's true concerns were directed into a relatively narrow range of philosophical inquiry: social, political, and economic thought. Nevertheless, few philosophers have had their writings distributed as widely and used in so many different ways as the book *Quotations from Chairman Mao* (aka the *Little Red Book*).[19]

"Table of Contents," *Quotations from Chairman Mao Zedong* (aka the *Little Red Book*)

Ch. 4 The Correct Handling of Contradictions among the People
Ch. 5 War and Peace
Ch. 6 Imperialism and All Reactionaries Are Paper Tigers
Ch. 7 Dare to Struggle and Win
Ch. 8 People's War
Ch. 9 The People's Army
Ch. 10 Leadership of Party Committees
Ch. 11 The Mass Line
Ch. 12 Political Work
Ch. 13 Relations between Officers and Men
Ch. 14 Relations between the Army and the People
Ch. 15 Democracy in the Three Main Fields
Ch. 16 Education and the Training of Troops
Ch. 17 Serving the People
Ch. 18 Patriotism and Internationalism
Ch. 19 Revolutionary Heroism
Ch. 20 Building Our Country through Diligence and Frugality
Ch. 21 Self-Reliance and Arduous Struggle
Ch.22 Thinking and Methods of Work
Ch. 23 Investigation and Study
Ch. 24 Correcting Mistaken Ideas
Ch. 25 Unity
Ch. 26 Discipline
Ch. 27 Criticism and Self-criticism
Ch. 28 Communists
Ch. 29 Cadres
Ch. 30 Youth
Ch. 31 Women
Ch. 32 Culture and Art
Ch. 33 Study

Of the early philosophers who engaged Western philosophy and Marxism in particular, Mao sent out a particular challenge when he encouraged Chinese to learn how to apply the theories of Marxism–Leninism to concrete situations in China. In order to make Marxism particularized, he thought the Chinese must let Communism possess a nature that was necessarily and uniquely Chinese in all circumstances, making Marxism fit in accord with Chinese distinctiveness. Mao rejected a slavish allegiance to ideological doctrine that ignored Chinese styles of life and their historical endowments (Tian 2002).

His call in October 1938 for the "Sinification of Marxism" resulted in a social construction built around Chinese culture but applying several fundamental concepts of Marxist political philosophy with Chinese characteristics and is often called, simply, *Mao Zedong Thought* (*Mao Zedong Sixiang*). This philosophical system has several basic features.

Politics as Dialectics

Mao recreated the Marxist understanding of the concept of dialectical materialism, or the notion that human history is moved by material economic forces, not by philosophy, religion, geography, or even technology. In fact, when it seems that one of these factors is moving history, we should look deeper and will find that it is really economics or the material conditions of the people's lives that drive the matter. The term *dialectical* was rendered into Chinese as *tongbian* or, literally, "continuity through change." This concept had been used before in Chinese tradition but Mao gave it a new meaning. He used the terms *mao* (矛 spear) and *dun* (盾 shield) to express his understanding of the dialectic exchange of economic and class forces, as well as views and proposals in political and social contexts. He appropriated the ancient Chinese story "His Spear against His Shield" (*zi xiang mao dun* 自相矛盾):

> Once upon a time in the Chu state there was a man who made a living by selling both *mao* (spear) and *dun* (shield). He hawked in turn his spear and shield. Holding his shield, he bragged that it was so solid and hard that no spear could damage it. Then, picking up his spear, he resumed, boasting that it was so sharp and powerful that no shield could withstand it. He was not able to make any response, however, when someone from the crowd asked: "What would happen if you jabbed your shield with your spear?"

As this story was used over time in Chinese intellectual history, the compound of *mao* and *dun* (*maodun*) came to indicate any statement or position that involved a contradiction, but as used by Mao in his appropriation of Marxism, it refers to the inevitability of the dynamic clash of divergent views, classes, or social processes. Mao observed:

> Changes in society are due chiefly to the development of the internal contradictions in society, that is, the contradiction between the productive forces and the relations of production, the contradiction between classes and the contradiction between the old and the new; it is the development of these contradictions [i.e., *mao* and *dun*] that pushes society forward and gives the

impetus for the suppression of the old society by the new. (Mao 1937: "On Contradiction")

In Mao's appropriation of the philosophical theory of dialectics (*tongbian*) he did not argue that the oppositions of viewpoints or policies could be lifted up intellectually and reconciled into a type of synthesis, nor did he think that one point of view simply triumphs over the other. Progress is revealed in actual practice as a dynamic interaction of views and voices, ideologies and philosophies. Mao's understanding of dialectics as contradiction refers both to the process of engagement of difference and to the creative, even revolutionary, expression of novelty in actual practice that results from the clash of ideas and classes. Mao thought that the outcome of dialectics cannot be explicated philosophically. It can only be embodied in political action.

Mao held that several basic contradictions in his political world required dialectical engagement. These included the contradiction between imperialist and oppressed nations, between the working class and the capitalists/landowners, and, more broadly, between socialism and capitalism as overarching systems:

> Consider the contradiction between the exploiting and the exploited classes. Such contradictory classes coexist for a long time in the same society, be it a slave society, feudal society or capitalist society, and they struggle with each other; but it is not until the contradiction between the two classes develops to a certain stage that it assumes the form of open antagonism and develops into revolution. (ibid.)

According to Mao, the emergence of political order is not as smooth as either the Chinese philosophers of his own era or the Western advocates of representative government believed. The process of the coming of a new political structure is messy, transient, and conflicted. It occurs only as a result of disorder and revolution:

> A revolution is not a dinner party, or writing an essay, or painting a picture, or doing embroidery; it cannot be so refined, so leisurely and gentle, so temperate, kind, courteous, restrained and magnanimous. A revolution is an insurrection, an act of violence by which one class overthrows another. (Mao 1966: "Class and Class Struggle")

Political change in a revolutionary form is an expression of the dialectical understanding of history that Mao adapted from Marx. In his "Report on an Investigation of the Peasant Movement in Hunan" (March 1927), Mao wrote:

The present upsurge of the peasant movement is a colossal event. In a very short time, in China's central, southern and northern provinces, several hundred million peasants will rise like a mighty storm, like a hurricane, a force so swift and violent that no power, however great, will be able to hold it back. They will smash all the trammels that bind them and rush forward along the road to liberation. They will sweep all the imperialists, warlords, corrupt officials, local tyrants and evil gentry into their graves. Every revolutionary party and every revolutionary comrade will be put to the test, to be accepted or rejected as they decide. There are three alternatives: to march at their head and lead them; to trail behind them, gesticulating and criticizing; or, to stand in their way and oppose them. Every Chinese is free to choose, but events will force you to make the choice quickly. (Mao 1954: "Report on an Investigation of the Peasant Movement in Hunan")

New Democracy

Like Liang Qichao, Mao argued that China could only establish a New Culture if there were a New Nationalism as the point of departure. Although it was not delivered until 1940, Mao's essay "On New Democracy" reflected his passion for creating a new nation in China. About his vision of New Democracy Mao stated:

The historical characteristic of the Chinese revolution lies in its division into the two stages, democracy and socialism, the first being no longer democracy in general, but democracy of the Chinese type, a new and special type, namely, New Democracy … Clearly, it follows from the colonial, semi-colonial and semi-feudal character of present-day Chinese society that the Chinese revolution must be divided into two stages. The first step is to change the colonial, semi-colonial and semi-feudal form of society into an independent, democratic society. The second is to carry the revolution forward and build a socialist society. At present the Chinese revolution is taking the first step. (Mao 1940: "On New Democracy")

Mao's understanding of democracy was quite different from that articulated in Western philosophy. This is why he was careful to speak of "New" Democracy in order to underscore the unique philosophical constructions he advocated and the way such a new political rule should be established:

There is in China an imperialist culture which is a reflection of imperialist rule, or partial rule, in the political and economic fields. This culture is fostered not only by the cultural organizations run directly by the imperialists in

> China but by a number of Chinese who have lost all sense of shame. Into this category falls all culture embodying a slave ideology. China also has a semi-feudal culture which reflects her semi-feudal politics[20] and economy, and whose exponents include all those who advocate the worship of Confucius, the study of the Confucian canon, the old ethical code and the old ideas in opposition to the New Culture and new ideas … This kind of reactionary culture serves the imperialists and the feudal class and must be swept away. Unless it is swept away, no New Culture of any kind can be built up. There is no construction without destruction, no flowing without damming and no motion without rest; the two are locked in a life-and-death struggle. (ibid.)

According to Mao, the political leaders of the New Democracy would make themselves known by their actions on behalf of the Chinese people. He wrote:

> In China, it is perfectly clear that whoever can lead the people in overthrowing imperialism and the forces of feudalism can win the people's confidence, because these two, and especially imperialism, are the mortal enemies of the people. Today, whoever can lead the people in driving out Japanese imperialism and introducing democratic government will be the saviours of the people. History has proved that the Chinese bourgeoisie cannot fulfil this responsibility, which inevitably falls upon the shoulders of the proletariat … The Chinese democratic republic which we desire to establish now must be a democratic republic under the joint dictatorship of all anti-imperialist and anti-feudal people led by the proletariat, that is, a new-democratic republic. (ibid.)

Mao also advocated a powerful centralized governmental structure for the New Democracy. Following the Anti-Japanese War (aka the Second World War) and the triumph of the Chinese communists in China's civil war (1945–9), Mao wrote an essay addressed to questions coming within the Communist Party itself. In "On the People's Democratic Dictatorship" (June 30, 1949), he took the following position:

> [You ask], "Don't you want to abolish state power?" Yes, we do, but not right now. We cannot do it yet. Why? Because imperialism still exists, because domestic reaction still exists, because classes still exist in our country. Our present task is to strengthen the people's state apparatus—mainly the people's army, the people's police and the people's courts—in order to consolidate national defence and protect the people's interests. (Mao 1949: "Democratic Dictatorship")

Mao called on this new state system to represent a joint dictatorship of all the revolutionary classes expressed in a democratic centralism. He defined the full scope of the power of this dictatorship in "On the Correct Handling of Contradictions among the People" (February 27, 1957):

> Our state is a people's democratic dictatorship led by the working class and based on the worker–peasant alliance. What is this dictatorship for? Its first function is to suppress the reactionary classes and elements and those exploiters in our country who resist the socialist revolution, to suppress those who try to wreck our socialist construction, or in other words, to resolve the internal contradictions between ourselves and the enemy. For instance, to arrest, try and sentence certain counterrevolutionaries, and to deprive landlords and bureaucrat—capitalists of their right to vote and their freedom of speech for a specified period of time—all this comes within the scope of our dictatorship. To maintain public order and safeguard the interests of the people, it is likewise necessary to exercise dictatorship over embezzlers, swindlers, arsonists, murderers, criminal gangs and other scoundrels who seriously disrupt public order. The second function of this dictatorship is to protect our country from subversion and possible aggression by external enemies. (Mao 1957: "Correct Handling")

New Economy

Mao understood that if such a republic were to be established in China, it had to be erected on what he called the New Economy. Philosophical ideology was insufficient of itself to bring about the New China:

> It [the new government] will own the big banks and the big industrial and commercial enterprises. Enterprises, such as banks, railways and airlines, whether Chinese-owned or foreign-owned, which are either monopolistic in character or too big for private management, shall be operated and administered by the state, so that private capital cannot dominate the livelihood of the people: this is the main principle of the regulation of capital. (Mao 1940: "New Democracy")

Mao insisted that the new state should take the steps necessary to confiscate the land of the landlords and distribute it to those peasants who possessed little or no land. He thought of this as an example of dialectical activity undertaken to abolish the "feudal relations" between the peasants and the landowners in the rural areas. He held that this redistribution of land would result in a rich peasant economy and he coined the activity of "equalization of landownership" as a principle of political philosophy (ibid.). Offering a defense of this process, Mao recalled the traditional Chinese saying, "If there is food, let everyone share it." He observed:

> This old Chinese saying contains much truth. Since we all share in fighting the enemy, we should all share in eating, we should all share in the work to be done, and we should all share access to education. Such attitudes as "I and I alone will take everything" and "No one dare harm me" are nothing but the old tricks of feudal lords which simply will not work in the Nineteen Forties. (ibid.)

Equalization of landownership eventually found practical expression in agricultural collectives and even communal kitchens set up during the period from 1949 to 1958.

Also developing from 1949 was a program designed to implement other economic aspects of the new state. These included what was known as the "work unit" (*danwei*) employment model. In Mao's day, the work units were typically based within state-owned enterprises (SOEs) designed to offer large-scale, universal employment. SOEs included economic sectors such as rail transportation and heavy manufacturing. They were protected from failure by government funding and arrangement of contracts and loans.

The "iron rice bowl" (*tie fanwan*) was another economic program of the New China. This program guaranteed a steady income and provided a set of universal socioeconomic benefits for all the people. After Mao's death, the iron rice bowl collapsed under its own weight, as the number of recognized "essential social goods" continued to expand beyond the ability of the state to provide them.

New Culture

Mao argued that the emerging new state required not only a new definition of democracy and a new economics but also a New Culture. "As for the New Culture, it is the ideological reflection of the new politics and the New Economy which it sets out to serve" (ibid.). Mao held that the culture of the new Chinese state must belong to the broad masses and not merely to an educated elite. The revolutionary leaders in the towns and villages known as *cadres* were charged with the responsibility of raising the cultural standards and educational level of the peasants. Mao took the position that one role of government is to recognize the importance of language, reading, and writing to the cultural task of the education of the people. Accordingly, he called for a complete revision of Chinese language, providing a widespread standardization of speech (i.e., Beijing dialect, Mandarin) and a modification of the way in which the language was actually written in order to make it more accessible to the people. *Pinyin* simplified Romanization of Chinese characters had its genesis in this philosophical commitment to the place of education in culture.

New Science

Mao held that the new state required a new science. This philosophical commitment to seek truth from facts in both the social and natural sciences included a call for the unity of theory and practice, and it had significant implications for the everyday lives of the Chinese people from the 1950s through the 1970s. Along with an emphasis on the new science, there were several campaigns designed to suppress and destroy what was known as "feudalistic cultural ideas and superstitious beliefs." One area in which the consequences of the New Science had impact was religion. Buddhism and Daoism, as well as popular religious practices of the common people, were considered full of superstition. Religious belief was already under assault in the New China as an "opiate" for the masses that kept them content in their deprived state economically and socially by promising miracles or futures in heavenly realms. The stress on the New Science ratcheted up the attack on religion by offering empirical explanations for social and material conditions.

New Nationalism

According to Mao, this New Democracy, Economics, Culture and Science would give rise to a new Chinese Nationalism:

> It [New Nationalism] opposes imperialist oppression and upholds the dignity and independence of the Chinese nation. It belongs to our own nation and bears our own national characteristics. It links up with the socialist and new-democratic cultures of all other nations and they are related in such a way that they can absorb something from each other and help each other to develop, together forming a new world culture; but as a revolutionary national culture it can never link up with any reactionary imperialist culture of whatever nation. To nourish her own culture China needs to assimilate a good deal of foreign progressive culture, not enough of which was done in the past. We should assimilate whatever is useful to us today not only from the present-day socialist and new-democratic cultures but also from the earlier cultures of other nations, for example, from the culture of the various capitalist countries in the Age of Enlightenment. However, we should not gulp any of this foreign material down uncritically, but must treat it as we do our food—first chewing it, then submitting it to the working of the

stomach and intestines with their juices and secretions, and separating it into nutriment to be absorbed and waste matter to be discarded—before it can nourish us. To advocate "wholesale Westernization" is wrong. (ibid.)

Forms of Current Confucian Political Theory

New Confucianism: Tu Weiming (1940–)

Western academic political philosophy has begun to pay some minor attention to non-Western models, as is suggested by the inclusion of a section entitled "Political Theory in the World" in the 2006 *Oxford Handbook of Political Theory* (Dryzek, Honig, and Phillips 2006). Indeed, in that same work, Daniel Bell's contribution is entitled "East Asia and the West: the Impact of Confucianism on Anglo-American Political Theory" (Bell 2006). In his later work *The China Model: Political Meritocracy and the Limits of Democracy* (2015), Bell argues for meritocratic governance, and holds that popular democracy has shown itself incapable of resolving the most important human problems facing a government. But all this notwithstanding, we must admit that Confucianism itself as a political theory has received relatively little attention by Western philosophers because of its antiquity and remoteness, as well as the several decades of suppression it underwent during the period of the rise of the New China (1950s–1980). What interest it has received has almost exclusively been directed at the recent movement known as New Confucianism (*xin rujia*). This movement is a braided string of thought generated by scholars from mainland China to the United States. According to John Makeham (2003) three generations of the movement can be identified. The first generation of New Confucians included scholars all based in mainland China after the May Fourth Movement (1919), the second included those in either Hong Kong or Taiwan, and the third includes thinkers who principally base their work on engagement with the West.

One thinker who is contributing to New Confucianism is Tu Weiming (1940–), chair professor of humanities and founding director of the Institute for Advanced Humanistic Studies at Peking University and professor emeritus and senior fellow of Asia Center at Harvard University.[21] In his *Reinventing Confucianism*, Umberto Bresciani names Tu as the leader of the "third generation" of New Confucians (2001: 29).[22] Commenting in his "Response" to a special issue of *Dao: A Journal of Comparative Philosophy* devoted to his thought, Tu stated his purpose and sense of philosophical self-identity clearly:

> Frankly, my intention is to show in both practical and normative terms what a modern society with Confucian characteristics might look like. I assume that if it is modern, it is inevitably under the influence of the modern West and, by implication, the Enlightenment mentality. Yet, as my edited collection of essays, *Confucian Traditions in East Asian Modernity* shows, the East Asian cultural forms—Chinese, Vietnamese, Korean, and Japanese—all share notably Confucian features that are significantly different from European and American cultural forms (Tu 1996). My explanation is predicated on two assumptions: (1) the continuous presence of traditions in modernity, and (2) the likelihood that the modernizing process may assume different cultural forms. (Tu 2008: 441)

A distinctive mark of Tu's writings and presentations on Confucianism is his understanding of politics as the "rectification" of social order undertaken to make possible the self-cultivation of the citizens. In taking this position, he appeals to Confucius's remark, "politics is rectifying" (*Analects* 12.17). He takes this to mean that the work of government should extend beyond making laws and maintaining security. Instead, the purpose of politics is to monitor and constantly adjust social processes of communal life, including the distribution of economic goods, in order to bring about what he calls a "fiduciary community." This sort of community is one in which the citizenry can be said to "trust" the government to set up policies and structures that enable self-cultivation of each person. We may compare the government able to gain and retain the trust of the people to Mencius's notion of a humane government, placing Tu within the stream of Confucian political philosophy.

The idea of a fiduciary community was first introduced by Tu in his writings from the late 1970s, but it is perhaps most clearly described in his work *Centrality and Commonality: An Essay on Confucian Religiousness* (1989a). In this book, Tu uses the English term "fiduciary," which is associated with the responsibility of a trustee in financial and legal interchanges to demonstrate trustworthiness (i.e., *xinlai*) (Tu 1989a: 60). For Tu, while the body politic may assume the form of family, clan, school, village, local government, or central bureaucracy, if it fails to put into place and monitor the processes and structures required for the self-cultivation and creation of humane persons (*ren*) among its members, it will inevitably lose the trust and loyalty of the people. To keep that trust, the government must continuously be a self-correcting political system, changing policies to fit the ever-altering needs and circumstances of its people.

Rectification of public policy is clearly a value-laden concept. It means correction, implying that policies are constantly monitored and righted as needed.[23] To better understand what Tu is driving at, consider that the overarching purpose of civil libertarian politics in the West is preventing harm, while creating the greatest space for liberty of expression and freedom of lifestyle choice, generally in the pursuit of happiness as an end. In contrast, Tu holds that the goal in Confucian politics is creating the confidence within the citizenry that the government is pursuing policies designed for their development and flourishing as persons. In such circumstances, government may sometimes reduce the liberty to pursue certain actions if these would retard or be a detriment to the citizens becoming more humane persons.

While the new application of Confucian politics being recommended by Tu does not rest on the idea of a community as an aggregate of autonomous individuals, neither does it deny individuality. In fact, the fiduciary community's guiding purpose is the betterment of each individual, not the homogenization of selves and loss of one's identity in the group (ibid.: 56). Neither are self-cultivation and humanization built on a monolithic conception of the good. In the Confucian community Tu advocates, divergent interests and plural desires are dealt with differently than in social contract and civil libertarian systems. He sees these models as adversarial by nature and fears the tyranny of the majority may be expressed in the democratic ballot. In the fiduciary community, no political decision can be legitimate and just if it destroys the ethos of trustworthiness among the people or between the people and the government. So, political action is not so much based on what the majority desires but on the teleological goal of what increases the likelihood that persons can and will become better human beings. The ultimate test of whether a new law or policy is appropriate is simply, "Does it increase the relationship of trust between citizen and government?" Trustworthiness, confidence that the government cares for that which is life furthering for its citizens, is the sort of delimitation on political power that creates in the community what Tu calls a "convergence of orientations" (Tu 1984: 10). Indeed, it is not too much to say that this is the acid test of any governmental action.

Tu insists that the concept of a self-rectifying government always depends on having responsible leaders who are themselves engaged in enriching their own character as persons and avoiding corruption and pride of power. Accordingly, the requirement for leader self-cultivation is expressed by Tu through the classical Confucian ideal "internally a sage, externally a ruler" (*nei sheng wai wang*) (Tu 1989b: 19). Tu argues that engaged concern for the people, born of the ruler's personal self-cultivation, makes a leader into the sort of politically relevant person who is able to create and sustain a community of trust. He claims that in the ideal Confucian community, leaders will have cultivated themselves to the point that their self-consciousness is able to represent the greater interests (*da li*) of the entire community and their hearts will be in tune with the hearts of the people (*min xin*). The resulting benefit will be a fiduciary community of trust in which the citizens "exhort one another to do good" (*bai xing quan*).

Tu says that well-cultivated leaders demonstrate their knowledge by never relying exclusively on themselves, but always on the institutionalized authority of an interlocking system of other self-cultivating officials. Bureaucracy is not a bad thing in Tu's version of New Confucian political theory, just as it was not so in classical Confucianism either. In fact, Tu imagines that the requirement of rectification and a monitoring government will require a large bureaucracy in the New Confucian reality. Moreover, the government will need to be multilayered and complex in order to insure the provision of social goods for the needs of the people in order to create trust between the people and the state. As for the qualifications of the ministers who make up this bureaucracy, Tu sums up his views on rulers by quoting Confucius, who says simply that they should be "good (*shan*) and competent (*xian neng*)" (*Analects* 2.20).

Speaking of the people's role in the process of the government of the new Confucian community, Tu holds that they should engage in an activity he calls "communal critical self-consciousness" (*qunji de pipan de ziwo yishi*). Communal critical self-consciousness goes beyond the personal individual and yet the individual is not absorbed into an amorphous collective interest (i.e., "the people"). This is why Tu speaks of a fiduciary community as a "learning culture" (Tu 2002: 129). The learning represented by the activity of communal critical self-consciousness is not as simple as winning an election or succeeding in implementing a policy over conscientious objections of others. Its result is not the victory of an individual or a party, but the emergence of policies that both enhance the ongoing development of each individual and reinforce trust among all. Accordingly, many political machinations and practices commonly employed in Western representative governments would run counter to a critical communal self-consciousness.

For Tu, this approach contrasts with those expressions of democracy that are not built on trust, but on a calculus of weighing interests and tradeoffs, or simply tallying votes to decide which policy prevails.

Tu also distinguishes his notion of a "learning culture" from what he calls, "Politicized Confucianism" (*zhengzhihua de ruxue*). Politicized Confucianism is the lineage of rule and politics displayed in Chinese history and associated with authoritarianism and repression, closely related to what the mid-twentieth-century Chinese Communist Party objected to as "Confucian Feudalism." Tu recognizes that Politicized Confucianism is an undeniable part of the historic tradition, but he considers it a perversion of an appropriate expression of Confucianism for the modern era (Tu 1984: 105). He is particularly critical of the use of coerced and superimposed values and practices in order to create uniformity and inhibit the development of individual persons (ibid.: 105, 106). For Tu, whenever forced conformity occurs in a state, it is evidence of the sort of Politicized Confucianism that destroys the trust that is essential to a community of self-cultivating persons.

A difficult task for Tu is to explain just how the communal critical self-consciousness can achieve trust and preserve individual self-cultivation apart from authoritarianism or imposed prescriptions and laws. To account for how this can occur, he turns to the classical Chinese notion of the proprieties of conduct (*li* 禮). He radicalizes this idea by claiming that *li* consists of nothing more or less than a record of how generations of humans have become humane persons (*ren*) (Tu 1979: 28). For Tu, it is not the moral rules or laws of a community that create trust in one another in a society, but *the process* of creating and recreating patterns of humanization that does so. When each person looks to another and sees that person also striving to be more humane, then evils like suspicion, prejudice, and inequality recede and ultimately vanish. The communal critical self-consciousness is nothing more or less than every person helping to identify the policies and structures necessary to the self-cultivation of themselves and others.

Tu argues that the Confucian concept of *li* can represent an alternative to the Western social contractual understanding of the function of law. *Li* is not an authoritarian imposition of a morality or set of laws believed to enhance humaneness and moral worthiness on a community but neither is it merely a calculus of the minimal agreed-upon rules designed to prevent one person from harming another. *Li* is a set of norms in a culture that bubble up from the dynamism of a nation of people committed to their own humanization. He argues that when coercion through law is used by a government on its people this practice runs the danger of becoming an overzealous attempt to force conformity and destroys the environment of trustworthiness. On the other hand, he holds that when *li* arises from persons who are engaged in the processes of self-transcending humanization, imposition and coercion become unnecessary.

Since the goal of politics is the rectification of all the processes that advance humanization and self-cultivation, Tu thinks the government's reach must extend to care for the economic and material life of its people. He accepts the Confucian principle of distributive justice as "graded love" and interprets it to mean that government policies should consider equality in the consideration of need, rather than employ an abstract principle of universal equality of benefits. In this sense, Tu's position has historical analogues in the work of Wang Anshi, with the added emphasis that the distribution of social goods is administrated in such a way as to reinforce the ethos of trustworthiness between the people and the government. This approach to distributive justice differs starkly from the overriding Western justice value of "impartiality as equality." While we may think primarily of justice as fairness in a Western political system, Tu argues that the Confucian model for social justice is not marked by impartiality, but by grading or ranking the distribution of social goods in such a way as to reach to the diverse needs of the people and thereby create trust between citizens themselves, as well as between citizens and their government.

We can see that Tu's New Confucian construction of political theory surfaces numerous strategic and important differences from Western understandings of the nature and task of politics. For one thing, the webbing of the fiduciary community is mutual trust in each other and in one's governmental leadership. Such a view stands in contrast to the kind of adversarial system that characterizes not only American but also many other Western democratic societies. To put this contrast starkly, two points may be made. First, while democratic systems may ensure each person a vote, they do not necessarily have as their principal aim the creation of an ethos of trust. Indeed, decision according to majority vote by itself may undermine trust in government and in one's fellow citizens. In Tu's version of Confucianism, the creation of a trustworthy community is paramount in the hierarchy of political values. Second, we also cannot really claim that Western civil libertarian systems have as their overarching goal the creation of an environment that makes possible the self-cultivation of each individual. Liberty and freedom, while dominant and important values in Western political theory, may be preserved quite apart from both the realization of individual self-cultivation and the concomitant humanization of the citizens. Strange as it may sound, one implication of civil libertarian political systems is that the citizens are free to decide not merely what might contribute to their self-cultivation, but whether to hold this goal as prominent at all in their individual decisions.

Political Confucianism: Jiang Qing (1953–)

Certainly one of the most controversial recent voices enriching philosophical debates about the political structure of China outside of the official Chinese Communist Party is that of Jiang Qing (b. 1953). Jiang's father was a high-ranking Communist official. Jiang went to high school during the Cultural Revolution (1966–76) and served in the Red Army. He made himself into a scholar of Mao's "Socialism with Chinese Characteristics" ideology. Early on, during the period of Deng Xiaoping's reforms (1980–97), Jiang resigned the army and attended the Southwest University of Politics and Law in Chongqing. His studies there introduced him for the first time to a serious encounter with Western political philosophy, especially the writings of John Locke (1632–1704) and Jean Jacques Rousseau (1712–1778). He wrote several student essays which rather uncritically accepted Western approaches to political philosophy and were condemned and suppressed by collegiate and provincial authorities, but he continued to insist that individual rights were central to Marxism, bringing into dialogue Western political philosophy and the Chinese appropriations of Marxism with which he was familiar. After his appointment to a rural court upon graduation from law school, he continued his intellectual search for a guiding philosophy for social order and individual fulfillment. He studied Buddhism and Christianity, but soon returned to the Confucianism he knew from the education he received under the example of his grandmother.

In 1985, Jiang came under the influence of Liang Shuming (1893–1988), a notable Confucian scholar. When the political challenges of the late 1980s reached a fever pitch at Tiananmen Square on June 4, 1989, he realized that the legitimacy of the government was deeply undermined, but he also objected to the superficial view held by some of the student democracy-advocates that Western ideology and political structure should be embraced uncritically in China. He came to the conclusion that China must draw on its past cultural resources in Confucianism to establish a new order.

Jiang Qing's *Political Confucianism: The Reorientation, Characteristics, and Development of Contemporary Confucianism* (2003) is an effort to engage Western schools of political thought, while showing how Confucianism may provide correctives and improvements that recommend it as a sound political model. The framework for which Jiang argues is what he called "Political Confucianism." In his writings, Jiang makes a stark contrast between his approach and that of Tu Weiming's "Self-cultivation Confucianism." Jiang holds that "Self-cultivation Confucianism" is too abstract to be a political philosophy substantial enough to implement in actual policy. According to Jiang, "New Confucians" such as Tu assume that individual self-cultivation of virtue will solve external social and political problems when, in fact, it lacks such power. He thinks "Political Confucianism" is practicable and preferable as a model when compared to the three options of (1) the present political system of China, (2) "New Confucianism," and (3) Western-style democracy. He wants to restore Confucianism to its traditional position of a guiding political ideology and set aside Marxism by establishing a Confucian state (Q. Jiang 2013a), an approach that has brought him a great deal of criticism within China, including from Fang Keli, Director of the Studies on Modern New Confucian Thought research project (Lee 2017: 103).

Criticism of Democratic Rule by Popular Sovereignty

Daniel Bell notes that Jiang has a very clear and compelling philosophical objection to democracy and it may be put quite succinctly. "In a democracy, political choices are always down to the desires and interests of the electorate" (Bell 2013: 6). This is all the more significant because Bell has himself explored the idea of democracy with Chinese characteristics (Bell 1999). But Jiang argues that a democratic political system overlooks two major problems:

1. One of these is that the will of the people expressed as the electorate may not be morally driven. It might endorse unjust and destructive beliefs such as racism, classism, sexism, and so forth.
2. Another difficulty with basing political decisions on popular suffrage as is done in democracy is that the people almost universally put current short-term interests above long-term interests of the present body-politic and future generations. Jiang thinks the most obvious example of this failing is the inability for electorates in democratic countries to muster the political will to confront the environmental crisis of global warming and scarcity of resources.

Jiang holds that the solution, then, is obvious. A political system must be value centered. It should possess an ability to project its policies over the welfare of humanity as a whole, across classes, races, and generations. Such a system cannot hand over the most significant political decisions of the survival and well-being of its citizens and the world to rule by a majority of the voting public. Jiang's critics see this approach as a formula for authoritarianism.

Jiang defines the philosophical foundation of his Political Confucianism as "the Confucian Way of Humane Authority" traceable to Mencius (Q. Jiang 2013d: 27–43). In this theory, political authority does not lie solely in the hands of the people. Their voice is not suppressed, but it is only one of a threefold equilibrium of powers by which government should act. Jiang employs traditional Confucian language, speaking of the legitimacy of *heaven* (a transcendent morality binding on all), *earth* (the history and culture of the nation/people), and *humanity* (the will of the people). Jiang holds that creating a humane government requires bringing these three foci of authority into equilibrium (Q. Jiang 2013d: 29).

Jiang's choice of the Chinese concept "equilibrium" (*zhong* 中) is significant and he derives it from Zhu Xi's discussion of *zhonghe* (see Chapter 3). Equilibrium is not always build on the exact equality of the sources of authority in each instance of deciding about policy. To render this theory into practice Jiang calls for a tricameral legislature, with each "House" corresponding to one of the three forms of legitimacy designed to create equilibrium. He goes into great detail describing the House of *Ru* (Scholars), representing transcendent morality binding on all persons everywhere; the House of the Nation, representing the history and culture of the Chinese nation; and the House of the People, representing the voice of the people in voting. He argues that members of the House of *Ru* should be selected by a competitive system of examinations and work their way up in government through a period of service at various levels of the bureaucracy, much as is done in China now, but based on merit rather than party affiliation. His suggestions for such education and on-the-job preparation follow the reforms suggested by Huang Zongxi, as covered earlier in this chapter. Members of the House of the Nation ought to be selected by a direct descendant of Confucius from among the descendants of famous patriots, officials, judges, and diplomats. That is, the members are descendants of what Confucianism would call exemplary persons (*junzi*). Members of the House of the People should be elected by the people. The interrelations between these houses are guided by a constitution, thus leading Jiang to speak of his political philosophy as "Confucian Constitutionalism" (Q. Jiang 2013c: 47–70).

The Chinese political system should have a symbolic monarch, according to Jiang. In his theory, the monarch is head of the House of the Nation. The power of the monarch is largely symbolic. However, the monarch mediates conflicts between the three Houses, concludes international treaties, distributes honors, and proclaims pardons when appropriate (Q. Jiang 2013a: 79–94). Belief in the practicality of such sweeping changes in contemporary China has never gained any momentum. Binfan Wang calls Jiang's political structure and ideology a "meaningful fantasy," worthy of discussion but hopelessly unrealizable in China (2015).

The Translatability of Jiang Qing's Political System

Jiang's political theory may be summarized in this passage:

> Political Confucianism proposes the Way of the Humane Authority as a response to the difficulties of modernity that affect not only China but also the whole of humanity. Political Confucianism is not only intended for China. It is also of significance for all humanity … Political modernity uses an extreme form of Western Enlightenment reason to disenchant and remove the sacred from politics, so that politics is freed from the transcendent values and completely secularized and humanized, leading to many difficulties and problems for politics. Hence, the struggle is also one of the sacred against the secular, or, in Confucian language, the principle of Heaven against human desires. In my language it is one of disenchantment opposed by re-enchantment. It is precisely here that we come up against an ultimate and basic value of all humanity in the struggle of the times. Confucian constitutionalism seeks to reenchant politics so as to overcome the extreme secularism of the enlightenment. Under the restraint of sacred values, it seeks to realize a political order in which human desires have a justifiable place, where they are harmonized and humanity is elevated. That order is Confucian constitutionalism. (Q. Jiang 2013a,b: 207–8)

If we take Jiang to mean that his elevation of Confucianism will result in a state enacting a legally established morality, we should note that such a move would surely require more censorship and suppression than is even now apparent in the People's Republic of China and we may certainly doubt its translatability as an overarching political philosophy for human governments outside of China. China, for all its strands of enforced conformity, is nevertheless somewhat pluralistic in terms of its value system. Joseph Chan has criticized Jiang on this very point. Chan holds that it is unrealistic and perhaps even immoral to suggest promoting Confucian values and practices as Jiang recommends. Chan holds that such an approach could not avoid social conflict and unrest on a massive scale:

> Promoting Confucianism as a comprehensive doctrine is undesirable in the main because it damages civility. In modern society, citizens live according to various ways of life and beliefs, including different religions. For a pluralistic society, civility is of crucial importance. Civility is a certain kind of attitude toward fellow citizens of a society. It is marked by a concern for the *common bond* among citizens despite their differing opinions or conflicts of interest … Civility is against "ideological politics" based on comprehensive doctrines. (Chan 2013b: 102–3)

Jiang Qing has pushed back rather strongly against the criticisms of Chan:

> Confucian values are not like other values, such as those that stress individual freedom, rights, or class struggle. The central values of Confucianism are the practical values of overcoming the self, acting morally, and keeping to the mean. Moreover, these practical values were established by the sages in preference to all other values as the high values. They embody the way of the sages and the values of the sages. When everyone in society universally accepts these values of the sages, social harmony—Chan's civility—will be realized. This social harmony requires, therefore, that from the top downward there be a promotion of Confucian values as a comprehensive doctrine … These universal values of Confucianism are not like the values promoted by salvation religions [e.g., Christianity and Islam], which are special values and that not everyone can be expected to accept, such as believing in some particular god, religious doctrine, or rite. (Q. Jiang 2013b: 179, 180)

An often overlooked issue that Jiang must face based on his advocacy for Confucianism as the root morality of his political system is that Confucian tradition has itself never been monolithic. Quite a diverse group of philosophers historically have offered Confucian political theories, as we have seen. Jiang faces the challenge of which version of Confucianism to fund as the tradition of moral authority (Bai 2013: 121–3).

Daniel Bell, who has made one of the most detailed critical studies of the model of government employed in China (Bell 2015), offers another challenge to Jiang Qing's political philosophy. Bell notes that while establishing the membership of the House of *Ru* (Scholars) according to Jiang is done by merit and not popular vote, one would still have to anticipate debate and pluralism of views within that section of government. However, if this difference in interpretations is resolved by voting internal to the House of *Ru*, then Jiang's principal concern about voting within political systems is not erased but comes back at a different level. The desires of the persons casting the votes may deviate sharply from the transcendent morality of Confucianism, if there is such a monolithic system. Succeeding in votes within the House of *Ru* could still be a result of the pursuit of narrow interests, fawning, hypocrisy, and pandering to the populace (Bell 2013: 13).

Easily the most public criticism of Jiang's political Confucianism is directed at his views on gender, first expressed directly in an interview entitled "Only Confucianism Can Settle Modern Women" in the Chinese work *The Paper* (Q. Jiang 2015; Qian 2016). Jiang makes no secret of his view that gender relations, marriage, and family are in dire straits and in need of reform, not only in China but worldwide. His interview started out well enough by calling attention to the fact that the oppression of women in traditional Chinese society had little at all to do with Confucianism. But Jiang went on to extol the merits of polygamy and suggested that as a social practice it paired with arranged marriage to avoid the kinds of family breakdown that he associates with the contemporary crisis. Jiang also compared Chinese footbinding to plastic surgery and other "beauty fashions" of the time, although he stressed that Confucianism opposed the custom. When asked about the way to teach women in the future under a Confucian government, he recommended the *Classic for Girls* (*Nuerjing*) and *Lives of Exemplary Women* (*Lienu zhuan*), both representing classical conduct manuals for women that have been highly criticized for their oppressive and restrictive requirements and expectations. Jiang insisted that the preeminent accomplishment of women is to be a good daughter, a good mother, and a good wife, and that these roles express a female's inborn natural abilities from which she draws her highest sense of accomplishment and belonging, and has her ultimate value (Q. Jiang 2015). Almost two thousand internet comments have been posted on Jiang's "Interview," the vast majority of which consistently label him as a "feudal moralist." More than the issue of the practicality of his recommended political structure, Jiang's remarks on women resulted in a great loss of interest in his philosophical writings among Chinese academicians (Qian 2016). An example of such concerns can be seen in the writings of Zhang Hongping (2015), who claimed that in spite of his cautions to the contrary, Jiang consistently confused traditional practices with Confucian teachings.

One of the most important critics of Jiang's entire project is Wang Shoguang (b. 1954). In many ways, Wang's criticisms are the most significant of all because he disagrees with Jiang's fundamental view that China has a legitimacy crisis in politics. He holds instead that the Chinese people have a well-documented confidence in their present government and that recent changes made under Xi Jinping have only increased this trust. However, Jiang thinks that Wang has confused the subjective endorsement of the actual current political reality in China with the normative philosophical construction of which government is best. For example, Jiang calls specifically for replacing the financial elite of the current government with scholar-officials (House of *Ru*), who will represent the interests of the common people because of their moral virtues and political abilities (Q. Jiang 2013b: 201).

Other Contemporary Confucian-Based Political Philosophies: Kang Xiaoguang and Fan Ruiping

It seems clear that there is a renaissance of Confucianism in current China, but what form it will take in any political iteration is still yet to be determined (Tan 2007; Fan 2011, and Kim 2012). Kang Xiaoguang (1963–) has taken up the challenge to offer a political philosophy for China's post-Mao years in several works (2003a, 2003b, 2005, and 2006). A good overview of his views in English is that of David Ownby (2009). Kang holds that the Chinese Communist Party must be Confucianized. He thinks Marxism should be replaced with a reconstituted and adapted philosophy of Confucius and Mencius. While the educational system will keep the party schools, their syllabi should be changed, listing the Confucian Four Books and Five Classics as required courses. There should be a return to the examination system for all political promotions, and Confucian philosophical teachings should be added to each examination. Moreover, he also maintains that Chinese society must also be Confucianized. Here the key is to introduce Confucianism into the national education system, adding courses in Chinese culture that Kang claims will impart a value system, a faith, and soul for the culture. In the long term, Kang holds that this can be achieved only if Confucianism becomes the state's civil value system.

Fan Ruiping's (1962–) project differs from Kang's. It is set out most clearly in his *Reconstructionist Confucianism* (Fan 2010). In this work, he calls for reclaiming and articulating resources from the Confucian tradition to address contemporary moral and public policy challenges. He sets his effort over against both Western civil libertarian democracies that conceive of morality by agreement and the New Confucianism of Tu Weiming and others. He holds that, while Western social philosophy is founded on abstract and general principles, Confucianism is defined by specific rules that identify particular practices leading to a virtuous mode of life developed in the forge of a properly harmonious Confucian family. Fan argues that in such families persons learn how to treat others as unequals and gain mastery of the push and pull of graded love, creating a sort of *virtuous familism* that is transferable to the society at large. Instead of Western language about rights, Fan holds that the goal in political policy is to set up arrangements that effectively allow one to *treat all persons as relatives* and the nation and global community *as a household* drawing on the archetype of a traditional Chinese family that brought many persons into its circle of influence. Instead of norms such as "justice as fairness," Fan characterizes the Confucian model as "justice as harmony."

The current political philosophy most definitely expressed in China now is not any of these versions of Confucianism, but "Xi Jinping Thought."

"Xi Jinping Thought"

Xi Jinping (1953–) was born in Beijing and he has served as president of the People's Republic of China since 2013. He holds the title *lingxiu* (领袖), a term of reverent respect for a leader. In 2018, the National People's Congress removed the term limits for the positions of president and vice president of China, enabling Xi to continue in office for the indefinite future. Xi was trained as a chemical engineer at Tsinghua University but accepted various offices in the Chinese provincial and national bureaucracy, having previously held political positions in several provinces, most prominently Fujian and Zhejiang. During those years, and now in the period of his presidency, he has formulated a political philosophy embodied in his essays and speeches published in nine languages and three volumes as *The Governance of China* (Xi 2014, 2017, 2020). The philosophical condensation of these ideas is currently known very simply as *Xi Jinping Sixiang* His policy and philosophical positions have been incorporated into the Constitution of the Chinese Communist Party (C. Li 2016).

Xi's political thought objects to several Western values such as multiparty governance by popular suffrage; the notion that there is a set of universal human rights and goods, transferable across nationalities and cultures; the Western elevation of individualism as the central way to define one's identity and conduct one's life in the world; and the globalization of economic values and processes based on capitalist market economics.

In terms of the practical pursuit of "Xi Jinping Thought" in China, several internal social processes have been adjusted to conform to Xi's political philosophy. These include control of access to global media outlets by social monitoring and censorship of all forms of internal media and information, as well as the identification and prosecution of corruption at all levels of the bureaucracy.

Several emphases of Xi Jinping Thought as philosophical notions from which political policies may be derived are worthy of note.

The China Dream. This concept is meant to hold up the ideal of a revival and ascendancy of the Chinese nation which will bring the Chinese people along with it (Garrick and Bennett 2018).

Trust in Cultural Values. Xi Jinping Thought looks to the resources of Chinese philosophical history as substitutes for any pure ideology, even Communism. Xi has identified both with Confucius and, especially, with the Legalist philosophical traditions, having often cited Han Fei's ideas in his speeches and writings.

People-centered Governance. Although not specifically referring to the concept of Humane Governance such as one might find in Mencius, Xi Jinping Thought does call for the elevation of the public interest and well-being as the proper goal for all policy decisions and specific policies are directed at the alleviation of poverty and raising the living standard and life prospects of rural Chinese.

Socialism with Chinese Characteristics for a New Era. This ideal is more than a socioeconomic theory. It builds on the original emphasis of Mao Zedong that socialism in China would not be reducible to Marxism or Leninism, but it goes further. Xi's version now represents ideas "for a New Era" (Zhao 2016). The twelve central values of this political philosophy are as follows:

National values: Prosperity throughout society (*fuqiang* 富强); democracy (*minzhu* 民主); civility (*wenming* 文明); harmony (*hexie* 和谐).

Social values: Freedom (*ziyou* 自由); equality (*pingdeng* 平等); justice (*gongzheng* 公正); rule of law (*fazhi* 法治).

Individual values: Patriotism (*aiguo* 爱国); dedication (*jingye* 敬业); integrity (*chengxin* 诚信); friendship (*youshan* 友善).

Chapter Reflections

Throughout the period of Chinese political philosophy several themes have recurred over and over. To the question of what form of government is best, Chinese thinkers from all periods answer that meritocracy is the most effective approach to the equipping and selection of rulers and the one most likely to enact a humane government. Chinese philosophers defended neither divine right to rule theories, nor ruler selection by vote of the people. Confucius insisted that an exemplary person should rule because he thought the ruler would follow his inner virtue (*de*) and be like the pole star, providing a center of value for the entire community. Mozi advanced a number of arguments arranged in the *Mozi* under the title "Exalting the Worthy," in which he held that in order to have an orderly government, all the people should conform to the ruler's morality come down from Heaven. The people were admonished to "Exalt Unity" in the state by identifying upward. On the other hand, Han Fei thought that even an immoral person could still be a proper and fine ruler. The crucial test in evaluating the effectiveness of a ruler is whether he can use political instrumentation to manage the self-interests of the various power centers represented by landowners and farmers alongside the concerns of the common people. Huang Zongxi recognized that dynastic rulers of weak virtue could treat the people as mere "guests" rather than citizens or "children." In his essay "Selecting Good Men," he advocated for a revision of the Confucian Exam System in order to insure both a virtuous and a competent ruler.

Most philosophers were concerned to provide a theory of the natural state of humans prior to government and law, and thereby explain how governments arose and why. Mozi thought this period was one in which the people had different understandings of right and wrong and this created tension and conflict. This situation continued until Heaven sent a wise ruler, the Son of Heaven, who could enact the will of Heaven in law and morality. Han Fei also held that there was conflict and violence in the state of nature before government. But he did not consider this to be traceable to an evil human nature, but only to every person's drive to pursue his self-interest. The Daoists and the Daoist-influenced *Huainanzi* thought the state of nature was one of innocence and simple naturalness, it was not until the people drifted away from the *Dao* that the distinctions of morality and law came into existence, and they actually brought about conflict and consternation, rather than resolving it. Daoists thought law and morality were enemies to the free wandering with the *Dao* and so government service should be avoided, and if one were unfortunate enough to be involved in politics, only the path of *wu-wei* held any hope, because political strategizing is a bogus virtue that leads to failure.

Another fundamental philosophical question asks what government is best. In this case, a sweeping generalization may be made about Chinese political philosophy from the time of Confucius to Mao Zedong, and including Jiang Qing and Xi Jinping. Humane government (*renzheng*) is the ideal form of political structure for humans. Government has the responsibility to identify and anticipate the needs of the people for social justice and enact policies that would meet them. There is a robust advocacy for government intervention in matters of the distribution of social goods by most of the philosophers we have introduced, the Daoists being the principal exception. Early traces of this position can be found in Mozi's doctrine of "inclusive concern" (*jian ai*), Mencius's explicit call for humane government, and major thinkers thereafter. Wang Anshi's "Ten Thousand Word Memorial" was a call for the implementation of a humane government and eventuated in a number of Song dynasty policy changes, including a "Financial Reorganization Bureau," to redistribute social goods throughout the society. Mao Zedong shared this same commitment, and indeed the drive toward social justice may be regarded as the single most significant philosophical concept of the Communist revolution and a passion that motivated millions of peasants to take up arms. Confucius and Mozi shared the belief in the ideal of a Grand Unity (*Book of Rites*, "Li Yun"), that a society of harmony was one in which men of talent, virtue, and ability create what Tu Weiming calls a state of trustworthiness (*xinlai*) between the government and the people, with the former exercising its fiduciary responsibility to care for the people.

What are human laws and from where do they come (e.g., do we arrive at them by participatory exchange of views, or are they part of the nature of reality, or are they codifications of the lives of exemplary persons, or are they decrees of virtuous rulers or a divine being)? There is no uniform position on the origin and nature of law among Chinese philosophers. The Legalists like Han Fei value the forces of law and punishment as essential, and Mozi called "the five punishments" the controlling rope of government, expressing the moral will of Heaven through the ruler. Generally speaking, Chinese thinkers tended to equate morality with law and did not distinguish them in establishing a humane state. What is moral should be legal, and what is immoral should be illegal. And yet, Wang Anshi held that law was a way to limit overreach by government, and he issued a plan for government called "Constitutional Confucianism." On the other hand, Confucius thought that if a government or state had to depend on law and punishment to order and control the society, it had already failed. He preferred to substitute cultural proprieties (*li*) derived from the great exemplary persons of the past, and he insisted that the function of government is to create a community in which persons can self-regulate their behavior.

What is the proper balance between governmental authority and individual liberty of expression and thought? Since the time of Confucius, government was understood as a process of rectification. Chinese philosophers recognized that government required frequent "rectification" and correction in order to respond to the needs of the people (*Analects* 12.17) and continue to be seen as trustworthy (*xinlai*), as Tu Weiming puts it. Yan Fu held that the dual forces of cultural propriety and law in China worked like a stranglehold on individual expression throughout Chinese history and created social problems like those caused by religious sectarianism in the West.

Although there were some limited realms of freedom prior to the nineteenth century, a formal philosophical discussion of the role of liberty and freedom in the Chinese state was delayed until Yan Fu's translation and commentary on John Stuart Mill's *On Liberty*. One of the most significant challenges of Xi Jinping's governance of China is how to find an equilibrium between the preservation of the value system of "Socialism with Chinese Characteristics" and the right measure of freedom of expression and self-determination for the Chinese people.

Confucius and Mencius were itinerate scholar-advisors (*shi*) seeking to influence rulers in the process of rectifying policies, as did Han Fei, and Huang Zongxi and Wang Anshi. Beginning with Kang Youwei and Liang Qichao several philosophers turned their attention to rectifying the last Chinese dynasty political system and this culminated with the collapse of the Qing and the establishment of the People's Republic of China in 1949, built on the philosophical arguments and revolutionary activism of Mao Zedong. By the turn of the twenty-first century, New Confucian thinkers like Tu Weiming and Political Confucians like Jiang Qing began boldly calling for revisions in China's central government and the reorientation of politics in China along the lines of reconstructionist Confucianism. China is, indeed, experiencing a reorientation, but it is specifically aligned with "Xi Jinping Thought," rather than any of the intentional versions of New Confucianism we have discussed. While Xi values the cultural history of China's social and political theory, including many aspects of Confucianism, he does not set himself or his policies up as a type of New Confucianism.

Additional Readings and Resources

Angle, S. (2012), *Contemporary Confucian Political Philosophy*, Oxford: Polity Press.

Bai, T. (2013), "An Old Mandate for a New State: On Jiang Qing's Political Confucianism," in D. Bell and R. Fan (eds.), *A Confucian Constitutional Order: How China's Ancient Past Can Shape Its Political Future*, 113–28, Princeton, NJ: Princeton University Press.

Bell, D. (2015), *The China Model: Political Meritocracy and the Limits of Democracy*, Princeton, NJ: Princeton University Press.

Bloom, I. (2004), "The Moral Autonomy of the Individual in Confucian Tradition," in W. Kirby (ed.), *Realms of Freedom in Modern China*, 19–44, Stanford, CA: Stanford University Press.

Chan, E. (2018), "HUANG Zongxi as a Republican: A Theory of Governance for Confucian Democracy," *Dao: A Journal of Comparative Philosophy*, 17 (3): 203–18.

De Bary, W., trans. (1993), *Waiting for the Dawn: A Plan for the Prince*, New York: Columbia University Press.

Dirlik, A. (1997), "Mao Zedong and 'Chinese Marxism,'" in B. Carr and I. Mahalingam (eds.), *Companion Encyclopedia of Asian Philosophy*, 75–104, New York: Routledge.

Fan, R., ed. (2011), *The Renaissance of Confucianism in Contemporary China*, Heidelberg: Springer.

Garrick, J. and Bennett, Y. (2018), "'Xi Jinping Thought': Realisation of the Chinese Dream of National Rejuvenation?" *China Perspectives*, 1 (1–2): 99–105.

Jiang, Q. (2013d), "The Way of the Humane Authority," in D. Bell and
R. Fan (eds.), *A Confucian Constitutional Order: How China's Ancient
Past Can Shape Its Political Future*, 27–43, Princeton, NJ: Princeton
University Press.

Jiang, Q. (2015). "专访 | 大陆新儒家领袖蒋庆：只有儒家能安顿现代女性
(Interview: Jiang Qing, the Leader of New Confucianism in Mainland
China: Only Confucianism Can Settle Modern Women)," *The Paper*, https://
www.thepaper.cn/newsDetail_forward_1362813. Accessed July 7, 2020.

Jones, W. (2004), "Chinese Law and Liberty in Comparative Historical
Perspective," in W. Kirby (ed.), *Realms of Freedom in Modern China*, 19–44,
Stanford, CA: Stanford University Press.

Kang X. (2006), "Confucianization: A Future in the Tradition," *Social Research*,
73 (1): 77–121.

Kim, S. (2012), "A Pluralist Reconstruction of Confucian Democracy," *Dao: A
Journal of Comparative Philosophy*, 11 (3): 315–36.

Knight, N. (2007), *Rethinking Mao: Explorations in Mao Zedong's Thought*,
Lanham, MD: Lexington Books.

Li, C. (2016). *Chinese Politics in the Xi Jinping Era: Reassessing Collective
Leadership*, Washington, DC: Brookings Institution Press.

Liao, W. trans. (1939), *Complete Works of Hanfeizi*,
London: Arthur Probsthain, http://www2.iath.virginia.edu/saxon/servlet/
SaxonServlet?source=xwomen/texts/hanfei.xml&style=xwomen/xsl/
dynaxml.xsl&chunk.id=d1.1&toc.depth=1&toc.id=0&doc.lang=bilingual.
Accessed January 23, 2020.

Major, J., S. Queen, A. Meyer, and H. Roth, trans. (2010), *The Huainanzi: A
Guide to the Theory and Practice of Government in Early Han China*,
New York: Columbia University Press.

Makeham, J., ed. (2003), *New Confucianism: A Critical Examination*,
New York: Palgrave Macmillan.

Mao, Z. (1917–71), *Collected Works of Mao Zedong*, U.S. Government's Joint
Publications Research Service, https://www.marxists.org/reference/archive/
mao/index.htm. Accessed March 12, 2020.

Peerenboom, R. (1993), *Law and Morality in Ancient China: The Silk
Manuscripts of Huang-Lao*, Albany: State University of New York Press.

Struve, L. (1988), "Huang Zongxi in Context: A Reappraisal of His Major
Writings," *Journal of Asian Studies*, 47 (3): 474–502.

Tan, S. (2011), "The Dao of Politics: Li (Rituals/Rites) and Laws as Pragmatic
Tools of Government," *Philosophy East and West* 61 (3): 468–91.

Tao, L. (2010), "Political Thought in Early Confucianism," *Frontiers of
Philosophy in China*, 5 (2): 212–36.

Tiwald, J. (2008), "A Right of Rebellion in the *Mengzi*?" *Dao: A Journal of
Comparative Philosophy*, 7 (3): 269–82.

Tu, W. (1989a), *Centrality and Commonality: An Essay on Confucian Religiousness*, Albany: State University of New York Press.

Williamson, H. (1937), *Wang An Shih: A Chinese Statesman and Educationalist of the Sung Dynasty*, 2 vols. London: Arthur Probsthain, https://archive.org/details/11411623. Accessed November 11, 2020.

Xiao, Y. (2002), "Liang Qichao's Political and Social Philosophy," in C. Cheng and N. Bunnin (eds.), *Contemporary Chinese Philosophy*, 17–36, Oxford: Blackwell.

Xiong, M., and L. Yan (2019), "Mencius's Strategies of Political Argumentation," *Argumentation*, 33 (3): 365–89.

A Quick Guide to Pronunciation

Taken from Terry Kleeman and Tracy Barrett, *The Ancient Chinese World* (New York: Oxford University Press).

ai	the y in fry
an	the on in on
ang	the ong in gong
ao	the ow in cow
c	the ts in fits
cao	is pronounced tsaow
chiang	is pronounced cheeahng
e	the oo in foot
ei	the ay in bay
en	the un in fun
eng	the ung in fungus
er	the are in are
fan	is pronounced fahn
fang	is pronounced fahng
fei	is pronounced fay
g	the g in girl
gao	is pronounced gaow
hao	is pronounced haow

gu	is pronounced goo
guo	is pronounced gwoh
hai	is pronounced hi
hua	is pronounced hwah
huan	is pronounced hwahn
huang	is pronounced hwahng
i	the ee in glee
ia	the ca in caveat
iang	ee, plus the yang in yang
ie	ee, plus the yeah in yeah
in	the ee in been
iu	ee, plus the ow in blow
jiu	is pronounced jeeoh
men	is pronounced muhn
meng	is pronounced muhng
mo	is pronounced mwho
mu'er	is pronounced moo-er
o	the aw in awful
ou	oh
q	the ch in child
qi	is pronounced chee
qie	is pronounced cheeyeh
qin	is pronounced cheen
quan	is pronounced chooen
que	is pronounced chooeh
se	is pronounced suh

shi	is pronounced shur
sun	is pronounced swun
u	the ew in few
u	the oo in boo
ua	the wa in water
uan	the wan in wander
uan	oo, plus the en in men
uang	the wan in wander, plus ng
ue	oo, plus the e in went
un	the won in won
uo	the awe in awful
x	the sh in should
xia	is pronounced sheeah
xin	is pronounced sheen
xing	is pronounced shing
yu	is pronounced yew
yuan	oo, plus the en in went
yuan	is pronounced yuwen
z	the ds in yards
zeng	is pronounced dzeng
zh	the j in juice
zhou	is pronounced jo

哲学

Comparative Chronology of Philosophers

Chinese Philosophy	Western Philosophy
2200 BCE	
Xia dynasty (2070–1600 BCE)	
2000 BCE	
Shang dynasty (1600–1046 BCE)	
Zhou dynasty (1046–256 BCE)	
800 BCE	
Spring and Autumn period (722–481 BCE)	Thales (c. 640–546 BCE)
Confucius (Kong Qiu/Kongzi, 551–479 BCE)	Founding of Rome (508 BCE)
Laozi? (?500 BCE)	Heraclitus of Ephesus (c. 535–475 BCE)
500 BCE	
Warring States period (480–222 BCE)	Parmenides of Elea (c. 515–450 BCE)
Mozi (Mo Di, c. 470–391 BCE)	Anaxagoras (c. 500–428 BCE)
Yangzi (fifth century BCE)	Empedocles (c. 495–435 BCE)

Chinese Philosophy	Western Philosophy
	Protagoras (485–415 BCE)
	Zeno of Elea (*c.* 470 BCE)
	Socrates (*c.* 470–399 BCE)
400 BCE	Democritus (*c.* 460–370 BCE)
	Plato (*c.* 427–347 BCE)
Zhuangzi (Zhuang Zhou, 375–300 BCE)	Aristotle (*c.* 384–322 BCE)
Mencius (Mengzi, *c.* 372–289 BCE)	Pyrrho of Elis (*c.* 360–279 BCE)
Hui Shi (350–280 BCE)	
Gongsun Long (320–250 BCE)	
300 BCE	
Xunzi (Xun Kuang, *c.* 310–220 BCE)	
Han Fei (*c.* 280–233 BCE)	Archimedes (*c.* 287–*c.* 212 BCE)
Qin dynasty (221–206 BCE)	Chrysippus (*c.* 280–207 BCE)
Han dynasty (206 BCE–220 CE)	
200–100 BCE	
Dong Zhongshu (179–104 BCE)	
Masters of Huainan (*Huainanzi*, 139 BCE)	Cicero (*c.* 106–43 BCE)
	Lucretius (*c.* 99–55 BCE)
ce	
Wang Chong (*c.* 25–100)	Philo (*c.* 20 BCE–50 CE)
100	Epictetus (*c.* 55–135)

Chinese Philosophy	Western Philosophy
	Marcus Aurelius (121–180)
200	
The Three Kingdoms period (220–280)	Sextus Empiricus (early third century)
He Yan (*ca.* 204–249)	Plotinus (*c.* 205–270)
Wang Bi (226–249)	
Jin dynasty (265–420)	
300	
Guo Xiang (d. 312)	Augustine (*c.* 354–430)
Dao An (312–385)	
Hui Yan (336–416)	
400	
Northern and Southern dynasties (420–589)	
Seng Zhao (384–414)	Fall of Roman Empire (476)
Bodhidharma (f. 460–534)	Boethius (*c.* 480–*c.* 524)
500	
Sui dynasty (581–618)	
Zhiyi (538–597)	
600	
Xuanzang (596–664)	
Shen Xiu (ca. 605–706)	
Tang dynasty (618–907)	
Hui Neng (638–713)	

Chinese Philosophy	Western Philosophy
Fa Zang (643–712)	
700–800	John of Damascus (*c.* 680–750)
	Al-Kindi (*c.* 801–874)
900	
The Five Dynasty period (907–960)	Al-Razi (*c.* 865–925)
Song dynasty (960–1279)	Al-Farabi (*c.* 870–950)
1000	Ibn Sina (Avicenna) (*c.* 980–1037)
Shao Yong (1011–1077)	
Zhou Dunyi (1017–1073)	
Zhang Zai (1020–1077)	Anselm of Canterbury (1033–1109)
Wang Anshi (1021–1086)	
Cheng Hao (1032–1085)	
Cheng Yi (1033–1107)	Al-Ghazali (*c.* 1058–1111)
1100	Peter Abelard (*c.* 1079–1142)
Zhu Xi (1130–1200)	Averroes (Ibn Rushd) (*c.* 1126–1198)
Lu Jiuyuan (1139–1193)	Maimonides (*c.* 1135–1204)
1200	
Yuan dynasty (1206–1368)	Roger Bacon (*c.* 1214–1294)
	Thomas Aquinas (1224–1274)
1300	William of Ockham (1285–1347)
Ming dynasty (1368–1644)	

Chinese Philosophy	Western Philosophy
1400	
Wang Yangming (1472–1529)	Niccolo Machiavelli (1469–1527)
	Copernicus (1473–1543)
1500	Francis Bacon (1561–1626)
	Galileo Galilei (1564–1642)
	Thomas Hobbes (1588–1679)
1600	Rene Descartes (1596–1650)
Huang Zongxi (1610–1695)	Baruch Spinoza (1632–1677)
Wang Fuzhi (1619–1692)	John Locke (1632–1704)
	Issac Newton (1643–1727)
	Gottried Leibniz (1646–1716)
	George Berkeley (1685–1753)
1700	Voltaire (1694–1778)
	David Hume (1711–1776)
Dai Zhen (1723–1777)	Jean-Jacques Rousseau (1712–1778)
	Immanuel Kant (1724–1804)
	French Revolution (1789–1791)
	G. W. F. Hegel (1770–1831)
	Arthur Schopenhauer (1788–1860)
1800	John Stuart Mill (1806–1873)
Opium Wars (1839–1843)	Charles Darwin (1809–1882)

Chinese Philosophy	Western Philosophy
Taiping Revolution Civil War (1851–1864)	Karl Marx (1818–1883)
Yan Fu (1854–1920)	Friedrich Engels (1820–1895)
Kang Youwei (1858–1927)	William James (1842–1910)
Liang Qichao (1873–1929)	Friedrich Nietzsche (1844–1900)
Wang Guowei (1877–1927)	Edmund Husserl (1859–1938)
Xiong Shili (1885–1968)	Alfred North Whitehead (1861–1947)
Zhang Dongsun (1886–1973)	Bertrand Russell (1872–1970)
Hu Shi (1891–1962)	Ludwig Wittgenstein (1889–1951)
Mao Zedong (1893–1976)	Martin Heidegger (1889–1976)
Liang Shuming (1893–1988)	John Dewey (1895–1952)
1900	
The Boxer Movement (1900)	Gilbert Ryle (1900–1976)
He Lin (1902–1992)	Hans Georg Gadamer (1900–2002)
Xu Fuguan (1903–1982)	Jean Paul Sartre (1905–1980)
Hong Qian (1909–1992)	Willard V. Quine (1908–2000)
Tang Junyi (1909–1978)	The First World War (1914–1917)
Republic of China (1912–)	Russian Revolution (1917)
Mou Zongsan (1909–1995)	Donald Davidson (1917–2003)
May Fourth Movement (1919)	John Rawls (1921–2002)
Tu Weiming (1940–)	Jacques Derrida (1930–2004)

Chinese Philosophy	Western Philosophy
Jiang Qing (1953–)	Richard Rorty (1931–2007)
Xi Jinping (1953–)	
Fan Ruiping (1962–)	
Kang Xiaoguang (1963–)	
Great Proletarian Cultural Revolution (1966–76)	

Notes

1 Ontology—Questions about the Nature of Reality

1   Cheng sets out his view in several places. The essays he contributed to *Philosophy of the Yi: Unity and Dialectics* (2010) are good examples of the way he works with this concept.

2   Tradition says that King Wen of the Zhou dynasty (*c.* 1150 BCE) created the hexagrams. Actually, each of these heuristics is also in continual transition as well. In the divination process using milfoil sticks, there was a mechanism for what was known as the "moving line," which meant that the *yin* and *yang* aspects of a situation were changing even as the divination was being done. While it is not in the scope of our present introduction to go into the layers of how a hexagram itself reflects change, we may say that the practitioners had an elaborate numerology for making this point and a vocabulary of "old" and "new" *yin* or *yang* in addition to the idea of "moving line." In this respect, the purpose of the *Zhouyi* is not simply a text taking the position that reality is in process, but it means to help its readers reflect on how the world changes and how things change the world, thereby enabling its reader to engage in penetrating self-introspection, considering the outer world, and creatively engaging in the processes of the future.

3   John Major (1993) provides evidence that *yin/yang* categories can be documented as explanatory mechanisms as far back as the Shang dynasty (*c.* 1600–1046 BCE).

4   The classic exposition and description of what it is to make a "category mistake" is in Gilbert Ryle (1949).

5   See chapters 1, 4, 8, 9, 14, 16, 18, 21, 23–5, 30–32, 34–5, 37, 38, 40–2, 46–8, 51, 53–6, 59, 60, 62, 65, 67, 77, 79, and 81.

6   This is the only instance in the *DDJ* of the character *di* (帝), a name for the high god of ancient Shang dynasty Chinese religion.

7   The term *ao* (奥) is used in Chinese religion for the southwest corner of one's home where the household altar is located and offerings are made to spirits, whose presence is associated with that sacred space lodged and worshipped; a sacred space where they are present, even if they are not visible.

8   Although it is impossible to say for sure whether he is correct, nevertheless, in the "Preface" to his commentary on the *Masters of Huainan* (written *c.* 212 CE), Han dynasty scholar Gao You wrote,

> Many of the empire's masters of esoteric techniques journeyed [to Huainan] and made their home [at Liu An's court]. Subsequently [Liu An], with the following eight men, Su Fei, Li Shang, Zuo Wu, Tian You, Lei Bei, Mao Beig, Wu Bei and Jin Chang, and various Confucians who were disciples of the Greater and Lesser Mountain [traditions], together discoursed upon the Way and its Potency [*Dao de*] and synthesized and unified Humaneness [*ren*] and Appropriateness [*yi*] to compose this work. (Zhang 1997: 1, 1–2)

9   See John Major et al. (2010: 27–32). Harold Roth (1991, 1992) argues that the Yellow Emperor-Laozi (*Huang-Lao* 黄老) version of Daoism that first shows up in the *Zhuangzi* was the primary influence on the arguments and positions of the book *Masters of Huainan*.

10   The "four binding cords" (*si wei* 四维) are the "corners" of the compass-circle: Northeast, Southeast, Southwest, and Northwest.

11   These are long life, riches, soundness of body and serenity of mind, love of virtue, and fulfilling the will of Heaven ("Great Plan," 11).

12   These are misfortune, early death, sickness, distress and confusion of mind, corrupt character, and weakness ("Great Plan," 11).

13   This is not to say that there were no attempts to make predictions based on the Five Phase physics. There is in chapter five ("Seasonal Rules") of the *Masters of Huainan* a kind of almanac that tells rulers and the people generally what would most likely happen each month and what they should do accordingly in order to obtain harmony with Heaven and *Dao*. What is interesting is that as applied in various ways the recommendations actually yield a kind of rudimentary ecology and environmental balance by protecting natural resources and balancing supply and demand.

14   Introductions to the nature of Buddhism and the challenges it faced in the Chinese context include the following: Karyn Lai (2008: 235–68), JeeLoo Liu (2006: 209–20), Wing-Tsit Chan (1957), Leon Hurvitz (1999), Kenneth Ch'en (1964), John Kieschnick (2003), and Arthur Wright (1959).

15   We can compare this argument to George Berkeley's approach to proving the incoherence of the notion of matter as a substratum or the stuff from which objects are made in the third dialogue of his *Three Dialogues between Hylas and Philonous* (1713) (Berkeley 1979).

16   Shu-shien Liu tries to make a case that the most prominent of these new philosophers, Zhu Xi, did not borrow concepts or vocabulary from Daoism or Buddhism (Liu 1998: ch. 10).

17 Some basic studies of Neo-Confucian thought include Percy Bruce (1923), Carsun Chang (1962), Theodore De Bary (1975), and Shu-shien Liu (2009a and 2009b).

18 The primary source of information on the life of Zhu Xi was written by his pupil and son-in-law, Huang Kan (1152–1221). It was written in consultation with a number of Zhu Xi's students and published twenty-one years after Zhu's death.

19 An important historical study on the various uses of Principles (*li*) in Neo-Confucianism is Wing-tsit Chan (1964). The centrality of the concept of li (理, pattern, principle) to Zhu Xi's thought is confirmed by the fact that his thought is still sometimes referred to as "the School of Li" (*Lixue*) (Ivanhoe 1998).

20 Kirill Thompson (1998) offers a different point of view.

21 Tu Wei-ming (1976) has written a spiritual biography of Wang Yang-ming's early life.

22 For an extended discussion of the characteristics of Dai Zhen's naturalism see David Nivison (1996).

23 These included missionaries of the following nationalities: Italian (Matteo Ricci; Nicolo Longobardi; Sabbatino De Urbsis, Giulio Aleni, and Giacomo Rho); Portuguese (Francisco Furtado); Swiss (Jean Terrenz); Polish (Jean Nicolas Smogolenshi); and French (Ferdinand Verbiest and Nicolas Trigaut).

24 Xu Guangqi and Li Zhizao were two of the "Three Pillars of Chinese Catholicism," along with Yang Tingyun, who was the third.

2 Epistemology—Questions about the Nature and Scope of Knowledge

1 There has been considerable discussion whether *ming* is anything like an equivalent to the Western notion of "fate," if by that we mean that events are fixed and destined unalterably to occur as they do. For two essays addressing this topic in the context of Mencius's thought, see Chen Ning (1997) and Ronnie Littlejohn (2001).

2 The modern Chinese philosopher Hu Shi classified the *mingjia* and *bianshi* thinkers together in the category of Later Mohists (Hu 1928). A. C. Graham (1978) provides an important study of the Later Mohist texts.

3 This particular *bian* (辨) includes in the Chinese character a component (called a radical) for "knife" (刀). The character is also used for "investigate" and "resolve," and is used in the idiom "This person *cannot distinguish* beans

from wheat *bubian shu mai* (不辨菽麦)," meaning that such a person is of no use in practical matters.

4   Ian Johnston (2010: 372–4) has an overview of these problems and how various scholars have dealt with them.

5   My reconstructions here depend, of course, on my own interpretations of the text and A1 is one of the most badly mutilated of the entire canons of Later Mohism in the *Mozi*.

6   In my view, it was actually this kind of epistemological insight that led to what some scholars take to be the logic chopping of the *mingjia* and *bianshi* and of course to the famous discussion of what is known as the White Horse Debate (i.e., "a white horse is not a horse") in the text *Gongsun Longzi* attributed to Gongsun Long (b. 380 BCE). For an English translation see Yi-Pao Mei (1953). On the nature of this text see Jianguo Liu (2004), Karyn Lai (2008: 118–23), and A. C. Graham (1989).

7   I do not include in this group the philosopher or the text of *Deng Xi* (546–501 BCE), which is almost certainly a forgery.

8   In Burton Watson's (1968) translation of the *Zhuangzi*, these five passages are pages 132–3, 149–50, 161–2, 162–3, and 165–6. See also Ronnie Littlejohn (2010: 35–6).

9   In Western philosophy, the example of Edmund Husserl's (1931) procedure of bracketing may be offered as a point of comparison.

10   For a discussion of Xunzi's philosophy of religion see Edward Machle (1976 and 1993).

11   Some recent studies of Wang Chong's *Lunheng* include Guidian Zhou (1994), Michael Puett (2005), and Alexus McLeod (2011).

12   Studies of Wang's method of pursuing truth which are specifically directed at a chapter from the *Lunheng* that is concerned with Confucius include those of Alexus McLeod (2007 and 2018).

13   Huan Tan (43 BCE–28 CE) was admired by Wang Chong. His major work was the "New Discussions" (*Xinlun*). Huan is reported to have said that the Chinese fascination with belief in the Daoist immortals (*xian* 仙) was owing to nothing more than fabricated stories told by the lovers of the strange.

14   Antonio Cua specifically suggests the affinities between Wang Yangming's views of *liangzhi* (pure knowledge) and Francis Hutcheson's theory of a moral sense (2003: 771). For an interpretation of Hutcheson's position, see D. D. Raphael (1969: I, 269–71).

15   I refer to the question of what an object is itself as distinguished from its attributes. Many examples could be given of how Russell and Wittgenstein wrested with this problem; I mention only these: Russell's *The Problems of Philosophy* (1912), esp. Chapters 1–5, and *Our Knowledge of the External World* (1914), esp. Chapters 3 and 4, and Wittgenstein's *Tractatus*

Logico-Philosphicus (1922), esp. 2.02, 2.021, 2.0272, 2.04, 2.05, 3.203, 3.221, and 3.26.

3 Moral Theory—Questions about the Nature and Application of Morality

1   Consider that Yan Lingfeng (1966) edited hundreds of versions of commentaries on the *Analects* that filled a 408-volume edition.
2   A place to begin with a study of the approaches to virtue taken in Confucius and Aristotle is Jiyuan Yu (1998). For an extended discussion of the relationship between Aristotle and Confucius on a number of philosophically significant issues related to morality, see May Sim (2007).
3   Some Western philosophers have also questioned the appropriateness of the concept of moral saint as an ethical ideal for optimization of human life and its richness. Susan Wolf (1982) argues that persons also must not neglect important nonmoral values which enrich life.
4   An exception to this statement is the work of Chris Fraser (2014).
5   As a test case, consider the famous exchange between Confucius and the Governor of She about whether a son should report his father for stealing a sheep. Confucius insisted he should not. He should cover for his father (*Analects* 13.18). I recommend Tim Murphy and Ralph Weber (2010) for further discussion of this intriguing incident.
6   I am following A. C. Graham's translation of *jian ai* as "inclusive concern" and I recommend reading his defense of this translation (1989: 41–2).
7   Karyn Lai discusses this matter of extension (*tui*) (2008: 60–3).
8   The *Masters of Huainan* (see ch. 4) also stresses the importance of one's inborn nature. That text calls on its readers to "return to their nature" (*fan xing*). In both of these sets of materials, becoming a "perfected person" (*zhenren* 真人) means not straying from one's inborn nature.
9   There is a wide divergence in the claims of moral ethologists. As a place to begin, I recommend Frans De Waal (1996) and Steven Pinker (2006). Works that generally lack De Waal's empirical rigor, but build upon his research and that of other ethologists include Marc Hauser (2007).
10 A good bit of what I say here and in what follows draws its inspiration from the really fine analysis of Mencius on self-cultivation in Ivanhoe (2000).
11 I wish to acknowledge the work of Peter Gregory that has influenced my assessment of these comparisons between Confucianism and Buddhism.

12 We may think here of Kant's *Critique of Practical Reason* and also *Metaphysics of Morals* as the classic examples.

13 Zhu Xi objected to Buddhism because he believed it undervalued the Five Relationships and actually encouraged persons to abandon them in order to extinguish their attachments to others. In other words, it sought equilibrium only, but not harmony (Adler 2008: 60).

14 A thorough discussion of "harmony" in Confucian thought is Chenyang Li (2014).

15 Julia Ching (1976) provides a full-scale study of Wang's thought.

16 See Kwong-loi Shun (2002) and Justin Tiwald (2009) for extended discussions of Dai Zhen's moral philosophy.

17 The formulation I use here is only one of three different versions Kant employs. It is basically the universality test, and a good place to find it discussed in isolation is "Kant and the German Enlightenment" (Paul Edwards 1972).

4 Political Philosophy—Questions about the Nature and Purpose of Government

1 A substantial and thorough overview of classical Chinese political thought is Roger Ames (1993) and an ambitious effort at a survey of the entire scope of Chinese political philosophy is Gongquan Xiao's two-volume work (Xiao 1945).

2 See Stephen Angle (2012) and Sor-hoon Tan (2011) for discussions of the relationship of morality and government in Confucianism.

3 See Liang Tao (2010) for a general overview of early Confucian political thought related to the adjustment of social conditions to enhance self-cultivation.

4 For a much fuller discussion of Confucian political philosophy with suggestions for its application in current times see Joseph Chan (2013a) and the quite different alternatives held up by Jiang Qing (2013b) and Ruiping Fan (2010).

5 That is, Yao, Shun, and Yu, the three great dynasties of Chinese antiquity.

6 See Justin Tiwald (2008) for a discussion of the issue of revolution in Mencius.

7 Shang Yang actually called his political model "governing by punishment."

8 JeeLoo Liu (2006: 187–94) has a very clear discussion of the profound difference between Han Fei and Confucius on the relation of morality and politics.

9   I am indebted to Bryan Van Norden (2011: 190–6) for this categorization of Han Fei's techniques of government.

10 *Masters of Huainan* provides us a horrifying picture of the excesses and violence of the Xia period, including trying to govern by tortuous punishments such as cooking people alive, forcing persons to walk across fire on hot metal beams and laughing when they fell in, removing hearts from living persons, and grinding persons into meat jam between massive stones (*Huainanzi* 2.14).

11 For key thinkers in the development of Chinese political thought in the twentieth century who worked from these translations, see Chester Tan (1971).

12 For political dissent in China, one can begin with Irene Bloom (2004) and William Jones (2004).

13 See Alan T. Wood (1995) for an argument defending this claim.

14 Laurence Thompson (1958), Richard Howard (1962), and Kung-Chuan Hsiao (1975) offer important studies of Kang Youwei in English.

15 Some helpful studies of Liang Qichao's thought in English include Hao Chang (1971) and Joseph Levenson (1970).

16 The periodization of Liang Qichao's thought which I am following is informed by Alison Adcock Kaufman (2007).

17 The first reference to Western socialism seems to be in an essay by Yan Fu (Li Yuning 1971). Ma Zuyi holds that Zhao Bizhen's translation of Fukui Junzo's *Modern Socialism* in 1903 was the first comprehensive introduction of Marxism into China (Ma 1984: 277). The monumental work *Das Kapital* (1859), the fundamental text of Marxist economics, was translated by Chen Qixiu in 1931. For an overview of Marxism in China, 1922–45, see Nick Knight (2010).

18 There are many studies of Mao's thought. Readers may find helpful Nick Knight (2007). Among the great number of biographies of Chairman Mao, Jonathan Spence's work (1999a) is both reliable and readable. For English readers, the complete collected works of Mao from 1917 to 1945 are at the US government's Joint Publications Research Service, where every article signed by Chairman Mao individually or jointly, as well as those unsigned but verified as his, is available: https://www.marxists.org/reference/archive/mao/works/collected-works-pdf/index.htm.

19 A delightfully interesting study of the uses and forms of Mao's *Quotations* (i.e., *The Little Red Book*), ranging from its use as the handbook of the Red Guards of the Cultural Revolution (1966–76) to its appearance in literature, art, and song, is Alexander Cook (2014).

20 "Semi-feudalism" is an expression used by Mao for the kind of social structure that evolved over several hundred years and co-opted Confucian texts and thinkers into its intellectual justification of class and gender repression.

21   Eske Mollgaard (2007) explores the argument surrounding whether Tu may be considered a "Confucian."

22   A blog site with considerable information about the publications and activities of Tu Weiming is http://tuweiming.net/.

23   John Berthrong (1994) interprets Tu's fiduciary society on the analogy of the Christian concept of "the beloved community" and compares both of these to the model of Alfred North Whitehead's "vision of a civilized society."

Glossary

aiguo 爱国

ao 奥

ba zheng 八政

bagong 八公

bagua 八卦

baijia 百家

beidou 北斗

bian 辨, discriminate

bian 辯, debate, argue

biandong 變動

bianshi 辯士

buke 不可

buran 不然

cheng de zhi jiao 成德之教

Cheng Hao 程顥

Cheng Yi 程頤

chengxin 诚信

Confucius, Kong zi, 孔子

da li 大利

da qingming 大清明

Da Tong 大同

dadao 大道

Dai Zhen 戴震

dao 道

Daodejing 道德經

Daojia 道家

Daoxue 道学

Dazhuan 大傳

De xiansheng 德先生

de 德

di 帝

duan 端

dun 盾

fa jia 法家, Legalist School

fa 法 law, standard

Fan Ruiping 范瑞平

fangshi 方士

Fazang 法藏

fazhi 法治

fei 非

Fu Xi 伏羲

fuqiang 富强

Gaozi 告子

gewu 格物

gong 公

gongde 公德

gongzheng 公正

guo 国

guomin 国民

Han Fei 韩非

Hanfeizi 韩非子

hanwen 寒溫

haoran zhi qi 浩然之氣

he 和

hexie 和谐

Huainanzi 淮南子

Huang Zongxi 黃宗羲

Huangdi 黃帝

Hua-yan 華嚴

Hui Shi 惠施

hun ming 混冥

jia 家

jian ai 兼爱

Jiang Qing 蔣慶

Jie Zang 節葬

jing 精

jingshen 精神

jingye 敬业

junzi 君子

Kang Xiaoguang 康曉光

Kang Youwei 康有為

ke 可

Kong xiansheng 孔先生

Kunlun 崑崙

Lao Dan 老聃

Lao-zhuang 老庄

Laozi 老子

li 理 Principles of reality

li 禮 cultural proprieties

Liang Qichao 梁啓超

Liang Shuming 梁漱溟

liangzhi 良知

Liji 禮記

lingxiu 领袖

Lunheng 論衡

Ma Junwu 馬君武

Mao Zedong Sixiang 毛澤东思想

Mao Zedong 毛澤東

mao 矛

maodun 矛盾

Mengzi 孟子

Miaofa Lianhua Jing 妙法蓮華經

min 民

ming 名, name

ming 命, fate, destiny, decree

mingjia 名家

minquan 民權

minzhu 民主

Mou Zongsan 牟宗三

Mozi 墨子

Mo Di 墨翟

Muyi fa 募役法

Nu lunyu 女論語

Nuerjing 女兒經

pingdeng 平等

qi qing 七情

qi 器, concrete object

qi 氣

qiangao 譴告

ran 然

ren 人, human being

ren 仁, humaneness

renzheng 仁政

ru 儒

Sai xiansheng 賽先生

sanjiao 三教

Sanzijing 三字經

shan 善

shang tong 尚同

shang xian 尚賢

Shang Yang 商鞅

shen 神

sheng 生

shengren 聖人

shi 勢, power of position

shi 士, teacher, advisor

shi 實, true

Shiji 史记

shiyi 十翼

shu 恕, reciprocity

shu 術, administrative techniques

Shujing 書經

shuogua 說卦

side 私德

Sima Qian 司馬遷

siyu 私慾

Taiji tu 太極圖

Taishang Ganying Pian 太上感應篇

taishi 太始

tian 天

tian zhi 天智, heaven's intention

tiandao 天道, heaven's way

tiandi 天地, heaven and earth

tianli 天吏, heaven's delegated officials

tianli 天理, heaven's Principles

tianming, 天命, heaven's will

Tiantai 天台

Tiantai zong 天台宗

tianwen 天文

tong 同, same

tongbian 通变

Tu Weiming 杜維明

Wang Anshi 王安石

Wang Chong 王充

Wang Yangming 王陽明

wanwu 萬物

Wanyan Shu 萬言書

Wei-shi 唯識

wenming 文明

wu-wei 無為

wuxing 五行

Xi Jinping 習近平

Xi Jinping Sixiang 習近平思想

xiang ai 相愛

xiangke 相剋

xiangsheng 相勝

xiao 孝

xin rujia 新儒家

Xin wenhua yundong 新文化运动

xin 信 trustworthy

xin 心 heart-mind

xinfa 新法 new policies

xing 刑, penal law

xing 性, nature of something

xingming 性命

xinlai 信赖

xinmin 新民

Xinru jia 新儒家, New Confucianism

Xiwangmu 西王母

xu 虛

xuande 玄德

Xuanzang 玄奘

Xun Kuang 荀況

Xunzi 荀子

Yan Fu 嚴復

yan 言

yang 陽

Yangzi 楊子

Yasheng Mengzi 亞聖孟子

yi 異 different

yi 意, intentional action

yi 義, appropriate(ness)

Yijing 易經

yin 陰

yiti 一體

you fa 有法

you shi 有師

youshan 友善

yu 欲

yu zhou 宇宙

zaohua 造化

Zhang Dongsun 張東蓀

zhaozhi 招致

zhen 真

Zhengzhihua de ruxue 政治化的儒學

zhenren 真人

zhi 智, know

zhi 質, substance

zhixing heyi

Zhiyi 智顗

zhong 中

zhonghe 中和

Zhongni 仲尼

Zhongyong 中庸

Zhouyi 周易

Zhu Xi 朱熹

Zhuang Zhou 莊周

Zhuangzi 庄子

zi xiang mao dun 自相矛盾

ziyou 自由

哲学
References

Abe, M. (1990), "Kenotic God and Dynamic Sunyata," in J. Cobb and C. Ives (eds.), *The Emptying God: A Buddhist-Jewish-Christian Conversation*, 3–68, Eugene, OR: Wipf and Stock Publishers.

Adler, J. (2008), "Zhu Xi's Spiritual Practice as the Basis of His Central Philosophical Concepts," *Dao: A Journal of Comparative Philosophy*, 7 (1): 57–79.

Adler, J. (2012), "Epistemological Problems of Testimony," in E. Zalta (ed.), *The Stanford Encyclopedia of Philosophy*, https://plato.stanford.edu/archives/win2017/entries/testimony-episprob/. Accessed February 12, 2020.

Ames, R. (1986), "Taoism and the Nature of Nature," *Environmental Ethics*, 8 (4): 317–50.

Ames, R. (1993), *The Art of Rulership: A Study of Ancient Chinese Political Thought*, Albany: State University of New York Press.

Ames, R. (2011), *Confucian Role Ethics*, Honolulu: University of Hawaii Press.

Ames, R., and H. Rosemont, trans. (1998), *The Analects of Confucius: A Philosophical Translation*, New York: Ballantine Books.

Angle, S. (2009), *Sagehood: The Contemporary Significance of Neo-Confucian Philosophy*, New York: Oxford University Press.

Angle, S. (2012), *Contemporary Confucian Political Philosophy*, Oxford: Polity Press.

Arjo, D. (2011), "*Ren Xing* and What It Is to Be Truly Human," *Journal of Chinese Philosophy*, 38 (3): 455–73.

Bai, T. (2013), "An Old Mandate for a New State: On Jiang Qing's Political Confucianism," in D. Bell and R. Fan (eds.), *A Confucian Constitutional Order: How China's Ancient Past Can Shape Its Political Future*, 113–28, Princeton, NJ: Princeton University Press.

Barrett, W., ed. (1956), *Zen Buddhism: Selected Writings of D. T. Suzuki*, New York: Doubleday.

Batchelor, S., trans. (1979), *A Guide to the Bodhisattva's Way of Life*, Dharamsala: Library of Tibetan Works and Archives, https://www.tibethouse.jp/about/buddhism/text/pdfs/Bodhisattvas_way_English.pdf. Accessed November 16, 2020.

Batchelor, S. (1997), *Buddhism without Beliefs*, New York: Riverhead Books.

Bell, D. (1999), "Democracy with Chinese Characteristics: A Political Proposal for the Post-Communist Era," *Philosophy East and West*, 49 (4): 451–93.

Bell, D. (2006), "East Asia and the West: The Impact of Confucianism on AngloAmerican Political Theory," in J. Dryzek, B. Honig, and A. Phillips (eds.), *The Oxford Handbook of Political Theory*, 262–81, Oxford: Oxford University Press.

Bell, D. (2013), "Introduction," in D. Bell and R. Fan (eds.), *A Confucian Constitutional Order: How China's Ancient Past Can Shape Its Political Future*, 1–24, Princeton, NJ: Princeton University Press.

Bell, D. (2015), *The China Model: Political Meritocracy and the Limits of Democracy*, Princeton, NJ: Princeton University Press.

Berkeley, G. (1979), *Three Dialogues between Hylas and Philonous 1713*, R. Adams (ed.), Indianapolis: Hackett.

Berthrong, J. (1994), *All under Heaven: Transforming Paradigms in Confucian Christian Dialogue*, Albany: State University of New York Press.

Bishop, D., ed. (1985), *Chinese Thought: An Introduction*, Delhi: Motilal Banarsidass.

Blakeley, D. (2004), "The Lure of the Transcendent in Zhu Xi," *History of Philosophy Quarterly*, 21 (3): 223–40.

Bloom, I. (2004), "The Moral Autonomy of the Individual in Confucian Tradition," in W. Kirby (ed.), *Realms of Freedom in Modern China*, 19–44, Stanford, CA: Stanford University Press.

Bresciani, U. (2001), *Reinventing Confucianism/Xian dai xin rujia: The New Confucian Movement*, Taipei: Taipei Ricci Institute for Chinese Studies.

Brokaw, C. (1987), "Yuan Huang (1533–1606) and the Ledgers of Merit and Demerit," *Harvard Journal of Asiatic Studies*, 47 (1): 137–95.

Brokaw, C. (1991), *The Ledgers of Merit and Demerit: Social Change and Moral Order in Late Imperial China*, Princeton, NJ: Princeton University Press.

Brooks, E., and A. Brooks (1998), *The Original Analects: Sayings of Confucius and His Successors*, New York: Columbia University Press.

Bruce, P. (1923), *Chu Hsi and His Masters: An Introduction to Chu Hsi and the Sung School of Chinese Philosophy*, London: Probsthain.

Carr, K., and P. Ivanhoe (2000), *The Sense of Antirationalism: The Religious Thought of Zhuangzi and Kierkegaard*, New York: Seven Bridges Press.

Carter, R. (2001), "The 'Do-Nothing' and the Pilgrim: Two Approaches to Ethics," in R. Carter and Y. Yuasa (eds.), *Encounter with Enlightenment: A Study of Japanese Ethics*, 11–34, Albany: State University of New York Press.

Chan, E. (2018), "HUANG Zongxi as a Republican: A Theory of Governance for Confucian Democracy," *Dao: A Journal of Comparative Philosophy*, 17 (3): 203–18.

Chan, J. (2013a), *Confucian Perfectionism: A Political Philosophy for Modern Times*, Princeton, NJ: Princeton University Press.

Chan, J. (2013b), "On the Legitimacy of Confucian Constitutionalism," in D. Bell and R. Fan (eds.), *A Confucian Constitutional Order: How China's Ancient Past Can Shape Its Political Future*, 99–112, Princeton, NJ: Princeton University Press.

Chan, W. (1957), "Transformation of Buddhism in China," *Philosophy East and West*, 7 (3/4): 107–16.

Chan, W., trans. (1963a), *Instructions for Practical Living and Other Neo-Confucian Writings by Wang Yang-Ming*, New York: Columbia University Press. https://archive.org/details/instructionsforp00wang. Accessed April 4, 2020.

Chan, W., trans. (1963b), *A Sourcebook in Chinese Philosophy*, 4th ed., Princeton, NJ: Princeton University Press.

Chan, W. (1964), "The Evolution of the Neo-Confucian Concept Li 理 as Principle," *Tsing Hua Journal of Chinese Studies*, New Series 4 (2): 121–48.

Chang, C. (1962), *The Development of Neo-Confucian Thought*, 2 vols., New York: Bookman Associates.

Chang, H. (1971), *Liang Ch'i-Ch'ao and Intellectual Transition in China*, London: Oxford University Press.

Chang, R. (2000), "Understanding *Di* and *Tian*: Deity and Heaven from Shang to Tang," *Sino-Platonic Papers*, 108: 1–54.

Ch'en, K. (1964), *Buddhism in China: A Historical Survey*, Princeton, NJ: Princeton University Press.

Chen, J., ed. (2000), 《朱子文集》 (*Zhuxi Wenji, The Collected Writings of Zhu Xi*), Taibei: 德富文教基金會: 允晨文化總經銷De fu wen jiao ji jin hui: Yun chen wen hua zong jing xiao.

Chen, Q. (2000), *Han Feizi, with New Collations and Commentary*, Shanghai: Guji chubanshe.

Chen, Y. (2021), "The Core of Pragmatism and Its Echo in Chinese Philosophy," in R. Ames, Y. Chen, and P. Hershock (eds.), *Confucianism and Deweyan Pragmatism: Resources for a New Geopolitics of Interdependence*, 27–39, Honolulu: University of Hawaii Press.

Cheng, C. (2009a), "Philosophical Development in Late Ming and Early Qing," in Bo Mou (ed.), *History of Chinese Philosophy*, 429–69, New York: Routledge.

Cheng, C. (2009b), "The *Yi-jing* and Yin-Yang Way of Thinking," in B. Mou (ed.), *History of Chinese Philosophy*, 71–106, New York: Routledge.

Cheng, C., and N. Bunnin, eds. (2002), *Contemporary Chinese Philosophy*, Oxford: Blackwell.

Cheng, C., and O. Ng, eds. (2010), *Philosophy of the Yi: Unity and Dialectics*, Oxford: Wiley-Blackwell.

Chin, A., and M. Freeman (1990), *Tai Cheng on Mencius: Explorations in Words and Meaning*, New Haven, CT: Yale University Press.

Ching, J. (1976), *To Acquire Wisdom: The Way of Wang Yang-ming*, New York: Columbia University Press.

Chou, C., ed. (1995), *Collection of Hu Shih's English Writings*, 3 vols., Heidelberg: Foreign Language Teaching and Research Publishing.

Chou, M. (2003), "Liang Qichao (Liang Chi'i-ch'ao)," in A. S. Cua (ed.), *Encyclopedia of Chinese Philosophy*, 388–94, New York: Routledge.

Clark, M. (1990), *Nietzsche on Truth and Philosophy*, Cambridge: Cambridge University Press.

Cline, E. (2013), *Confucius, Rawls and the Sense of Justice*, New York: Fordham University Press.

Connolly, T. (2015), *Doing Philosophy Comparatively*, London: Bloomsbury.

Cook, A. (2014), *Mao's Little Red Book: A Global History*, Cambridge: Cambridge University Press.

Cook, D., and H. Rosemont, trans. and eds. (1994), *Gottfried Wilhelm Leibniz, Writings on China*, Chicago: Open Court.

Cook, S., trans. (2013), *The Bamboo Texts of Guodian: A Study and Complete Translation*, Ithaca, NY: Cornell East Asia Series.

Cua, A. S. (1982), *The Unity of Knowledge and Action: A Study in Wang Yangming's Moral Psychology*, Honolulu: University of Hawaii Press.

Cua, A. S. (2003), "Wang Yangming," in A. Cua (ed.), *Encyclopedia of Chinese Philosophy*, 760–81, New York: Routledge.

D'Arcy, E. (1963), *Human Acts: An Essay in Their Moral Evaluation*, Oxford: Oxford University Press.

Dai, Z. (1980), 《戴震文集》 (*Dai Zhen Wenji, Works of Dai Zhen*), Beijing: Zhonghua.

Darwall, S., A. Gibbard, and P. Railton (1992), "Toward Fin de siècle Ethics: Some Trends," *Philosophical Review*, 101 (1): 115–89.

Davidson, D. (1974), "On the Very Idea of a Conceptual Scheme," *Proceedings and Addresses of the American Philosophical Association*, 47: 5–20.

Davidson, D. (2001), *Essays on Actions and Events*, Oxford: Clarendon Press.

Dawkins, R. (1986), *The Blind Watchmaker: Why the Evidence of Evolution Reveals a Universe without Design*, New York: W. W. Norton.

De Bary, W., ed. (1975), *The Unfolding of Neo-Confucianism*, New York: Columbia University Press.

De Bary, W., trans. (1993), *Waiting for the Dawn: A Plan for the Prince*, New York: Columbia University Press.

De Bary, W. (2015), "Waiting for the Dawn: Huang Zongxi"s Critique of the Chinese Dynastic System," in W. De Bary (ed.), *Finding Wisdom in East Asian Classics*, 199–208, New York: Columbia University Press.

De Bary, W., and I. Bloom, trans. and eds. (1999), *Sources of the Chinese Tradition*, vol. 1, New York: Columbia University Press.

De Waal, F. (1996), *Good Natured: The Origins of Right and Wrong in Humans and Other Animals*, Cambridge, MA: Harvard University Press.

Delury, J. (2013), "The Constitutional Debate in Early Qing China," *Sungkyun Journal of East Asian Studies*, 13 (2): 149–68.

Dennett, D. (1976), "The Conditions of Personhood," in A. Rorty (ed.), *Identities of Persons*, 175–96, Berkeley: University of California Press.

Devlin, P. (1965), *The Enforcement of Morals*, Oxford: Oxford University Press.

Dirlik, A. (1997), "Mao Zedong and 'Chinese Marxism,'" in B. Carr and I. Mahalingam (eds.), *Companion Encyclopedia of Asian Philosophy*, 75–104, New York: Routledge.

Donner, N., and D. Stevenson (1993), *The Great Calming and Contemplation: A Study and Annotated Translation of the First Chapter of Chih-I's Mo-ho chih-kuan*, Honolulu: University of Hawaii Press.

Dryzek, J. S., B. Honig, and A. Phillips, eds. (2006), *The Oxford Handbook of Political Theory*, Oxford: Oxford University Press.

Edwards, P., ed. (1972), "History of Ethics," *Encyclopedia of Philosophy*, vol. 4, New York: Macmillan.

Fan, R. (2010), *Reconstructionist Confucianism: Rethinking Morality after the West*, Heidelberg: Springer.

Fan, R., ed. (2011), *The Renaissance of Confucianism in Contemporary China*, Heidelberg: Springer.

Fang, Q., and R. Des Forges (2006), "Were Chinese Rulers above the Law: Toward a Theory of the Rule of Law in China from Early Times to 1949 CE," *Stanford Journal of International Law*, 44, http://www.thefreelibrary.com/Were+Chinese+rulers+above+the+law%3f+Toward+a+theory+of+the+rule+of+law...-a0182200366. Accessed April 14, 2020.

Fingarette, H. (1972), *Confucius – The Secular as Sacred*, New York: Harper & Row.

Flanagan, O. (2011), *The Bodhisattva's Brain: Buddhism Naturalized*, Cambridge: MIT Press.

Forke, A., trans. (1907), *Philosophical Essays of Wang Ch'ung*, London: Luzac, https://ia800907.us.archive.org/35/items/lunheng01wang/lunheng01wang.pdf. Accessed January 18, 2020.

Fraser, C. (2011), "Knowledge and Error in Early Chinese Thought," *Dao: A Journal of Comparative Philosophy*, 10 (2): 127–48.

Fraser, C. (2013), "Distinctions, Judgment, and Reasoning in Classical Chinese Thought," *History and Philosophy of Logic*, 34 (1): 1–24.

Fraser, C. (2014), "The Mohist Conception of Reality," http://cjfraser.net/2013/02/21/chinese-metaphysics-conference/. Accessed February 21, 2020.

Fraser, C. (2016), "Language and Logic in the *Xunzi*," in E. Hutton (ed.), *Dao Companion to the Philosophy of Xunzi*, 291–321, Dordrecht: Springer.

Frohlich, T. (2017), *Tang Junyi: Confucian Philosophy and the Challenge of Modernity*, Leiden: Brill.

Fung, Y. (1948), *A Short History of Chinese Philosophy*, New York: Macmillan.

Fung, Y. (1953), *A History of Chinese Philosophy*, 2 vols., Princeton, NJ: Princeton University Press.

Gardner, D. (1990), *Learning to Be a Sage: Selections from the Conversations of Master Chu, Arranged Topically*, Berkeley: University of California Press.

Garfield, J., and B. Van Norden (2016), "If Philosophy Won't Diversify, Let's Call It What It Really Is," *New York Times*, https://www.nytimes.com/2016/05/11/opinion/if-philosophy-wont-diversify-lets-call-it-what-it-really-is.html. Accessed November 2, 2020.

Garrick, J., and Y. Bennett (2018), " 'Xi Jinping Thought:' Realisation of the Chinese Dream of National Rejuvenation?," *China Perspectives*, 1 (1–2): 99–105.

Ginet, C. (1990), *On Action*, Cambridge: Cambridge University Press.

Golas, P. (2015), "The Sung Fiscal Administration," in J. Chaffee and D. Twitchett (eds.), *The Cambridge History of China*, 139–213, New York: Cambridge University Press.

Goldin, P., trans. (2005), "Xunzi and the Confucian Way," in V. Mair, N. Steinhardt, and P. Goldin (eds.), *Hawai'i Reader in Traditional Chinese Culture*, 121–30, Honolulu: University of Hawaii Press.

Goldin, P. (ed.) (2013), *Dao Companion to the Philosophy of Han Fei*, Dordrecht: Springer.

Govier, T. (1985), "Logical Analogies," *Informal Logic*, 7 (1): 27–33.

Graham, A. C. (1978), *Later Mohist Logic: Ethics and Science*, Hong Kong: Chinese University Press.

Graham, A. C. (1989), *Disputers of the Tao: Philosophical Argument in Ancient China*, Chicago: Open Court.

Hansen, C. (1985), "Chinese Language, Chinese Philosophy, and 'Truth,' " *Journal of Asian Studies*, 44 (3): 491–519.

Hao, C. (1987), *Chinese Intellectuals in Crisis: Search for Order and Meaning (1890–1911)*, Berkeley: University of California Press.

Hardy, J. (1998), "Influential Western Interpretations of the Tao-te-ching," in L. Kohn and M. LaFargue (eds.), *Lao-tzu and the Tao-te-ching*, 165–88, Albany: State University of New York Press.

Harris, S. (2018), "Promising across Lives to Save Non-existent Beings: Identity, Rebirth, and the Bodhisattva's Vow," *Philosophy East and West*, 68 (2): 386–407.

Hauser, M. (2007), *Moral Minds: The Nature of Right and Wrong*, New York: Harper.

Hays, J. (2017), "Chinese Imperial Examination System," *Facts and Details*, http://factsanddetails.com/china/cat2/4sub9/entry-5385.html. Accessed October 4, 2020.

Hobbes, T. (2018), *Leviathan, or, the Matter, Form, and Power of a Commonwealth Ecclesiastical and Civill*, 1651 ed., Minneapolis, MN: Lerner.

Holloway, K. (2009), *Guodian: The Newly Discovered Seeds of Chinese Religion and Political Philosophy*, Oxford: Oxford University Press.

Horgan, T., and M. Timmons (2000), "Nondescriptivist Cognitivism: Framework for a New Metaethic," *Philosophical Papers*, 29: 121–53.

Howard, R. (1962), "K'ang Yu-wei: His Intellectual Background and Early Thought," in A. F. Wright and D. Twitchett (eds.), *Confucian Personalities*, 294–316, Stanford, CA: Stanford University Press.

Hsiao, K. (1975), *A Modern China and a New World—K'ang Yu-Wei, Reformer and Utopian, 1858-1927*, Seattle: University of Washington Press.

Hsu, S. (1995), "Hu Shih," in D. Bishop (ed.), *Chinese Thought: An Introduction*, 364–91, Delhi: Motilal Banarsidass.

Hu, S. (1921), "Mr. Dewey and China," in S. Hu (ed.), *The Complete Works of Hu Shih: Collected Essays of Hu Shih*, vol. 2, 533–7, Taipei: Far East Book.

Hu, S. (1928), *The Development of the Logical Method in Ancient China*, Shanghai: Oriental Book.

Hu, S. (1931), "My Credo and Its Evolution," in H. G. Leach (ed.), *Living Philosophies: A Series of Intimate Credos*, 235–63, New York: Simon and Schuster.

Hu, X. (2002), "Hu Shi's Enlightenment Philosophy," in C. Cheng and N. Bunnin (eds.), *Contemporary Chinese Philosophy*, 82–102, Oxford: Blackwell.

Hurvitz, L. (1999), "Schools of Buddhist Doctrine," in W. De Bary and I. Bloom (eds.), *Sources of Chinese Tradition: From Earliest Times to 1600*, vol. 1, 433–80, New York: Columbia University Press.

Husserl, E. (1931), *Cartesian Meditations*, D. Cairns (trans.), Dordrecht: Kluwer.

Hutton, E., trans. and ed. (2014), *Xunzi: The Complete Text*, Princeton, NJ: Princeton University Press.

Irwin, T., trans. (1999), *Nicomachean Ethics*, Indianapolis: Hackett.

Ivanhoe, P. (1998), "*Li*," in Edward Craig (ed.), *Routledge Encyclopedia of Philosophy*, New York: Routledge.

Ivanhoe, P. (2000), *Confucian Moral Self-Cultivation*, Indianapolis: Hackett.

Ivanhoe, P., trans. (2002), *The Daodejing of Laozi*, New York: Seven Bridges.

Ivanhoe, P. (2007), "Heaven as a Source for Ethical Warrant in Early Confucianism," *Dao: A Journal of Comparative Philosophy*, 6 (3): 211–20.

Ivanhoe, P., trans. and ed. (2009), *Readings from the Lu-Wang School of Neo-Confucianism*, Indianapolis: Hackett.

Ivanhoe, P. (2011), "McDowell, Wang Yangming, and Mengzi's Contributions to Moral Perception," *Dao: A Journal of Comparative Philosophy*, 10 (3): 273–90.

James, W. (1907), *Pragmatism: A New Name for Some Old Ways of Thinking*, Cambridge, MA: Harvard University Press.

James, W. (2000), *Pragmatism and Other Writings*, New York: Penguin.

Janik, A., and S. Toulmin (1996), *Wittgenstein's Vienna*, New York: Simon and Schuster.

Jiang, Q. (2003), 《政治儒學》 (*Zhengzhi Ruxue, Political Confucianism: The Reorientation, Characteristics, and Development of Contemporary Confucianism*), Taipei: Yangzhengtang wenhua shiye gongsi.

Jiang, Q. (2013a), "A Confucian Constitutionalist State," in D. Bell and R. Fan (eds.), *A Confucian Constitutional Order: How China's Ancient Past Can Shape Its Political Future*, 71–95, Princeton, NJ: Princeton University Press.

Jiang, Q. (2013b), "Debating with My Critics," in D. Bell and R. Fan (eds.), *A Confucian Constitutional Order: How China's Ancient Past Can Shape Its Political Future*, 161–208, Princeton, NJ: Princeton University Press.

Jiang, Q. (2013c), "The Supervisory System," in D. Bell and R. Fan (eds.), *A Confucian Constitutional Order: How China's Ancient Past Can Shape Its Political Future*, 44–70, Princeton, NJ: Princeton University Press.

Jiang, Q. (2013d), "The Way of the Humane Authority," in D. Bell and R. Fan (eds.), *A Confucian Constitutional Order: How China's Ancient Past Can Shape Its Political Future*, 27–43, Princeton, NJ: Princeton University Press.

Jiang, Q. (2015), "专访 | 大陆新儒家领袖蒋庆：只有儒家能安顿现代女性 (Interview: Jiang Qing, the Leader of New Confucianism in Mainland China: Only Confucianism Can Settle Modern Women)," *The Paper*, https://www.thepaper.cn/newsDetail_forward_1362813. Accessed July 7, 2020.

Jiang, X. (2002), "Zhang Dongsun: Pluralist Epistemology and Chinese Philosophy," in C. Cheng and N. Bunnin (eds.), *Contemporary Chinese Philosophy*, 57–81, Oxford: Blackwell.

Jiang, X. (2009), "Enlightenment Movement," in B. Mou (ed.), *History of Chinese Philosophy*, 473–511, New York: Routledge.

Johnston, I., trans. (2010), *The Mozi: A Complete Translation*, New York: Columbia University Press.

Jones, W. (2004), "Chinese Law and Liberty in Comparative Historical Perspective," in W. Kirby (ed.), *Realms of Freedom in Modern China*, 19–44, Stanford, CA: Stanford University Press.

Kalupahana, D. (1976), *Buddhist Philosophy: A Historical Analysis*, Honolulu: University of Hawaii Press.

Kang, X. (2003a), "A Theoretical Outline of Cultural Nationalism (*Wenhua minzu zhuyi lungang*)," *Strategy and Management* (*Zhanlue yu guanli*), 2: 9–27.

Kang, X. (2003b), "Searching for a Political Development Strategy for China's New Decade (*Weilai shinian Zhongguo zhengzhi fazhan celüe tansuo*)," *Strategy and Management* (*Zhanlue yu guanli*), 1: 75–81.

Kang, X. (2005), *Benevolent Government: The Third Path for China's Political Development* (*Renzheng: Zhongguo zhengzhi fazhan de disan tiao daolu*), Singapore: Shijie Keji Chubanshe.

Kang X. (2006), "Confucianization: A Future in the Tradition," *Social Research*, 73 (1): 77–121.

Kant, I. (1956), *Groundwork of the Metaphysic of Morals (1785)*, H. Paton (trans.), New York: Harper & Row.

Kant, I. (2002), *The Critique of Practical Reason (1788)*, T. Abbot (trans.), Project Gutenberg, http://www.gutenberg.org/files/5683/5683-h/5683-h. htm#link2H_4_0037. Accessed April 13, 2020.

Kaufman, A. (2007), "One Nation among Many: Foreign Models in the Constitutional Thought of Liang Qichao," PhD diss., University of California, Berkeley. UMI: 3306191.

Kawamura, L., ed. (1981), *The Bodhisattva Doctrine in Buddhism*, Waterloo, ON: Wilfrid Laurier University Press.

Kieschnick, J. (2003), *The Impact of Buddhism on Chinese Material Culture*, Princeton, NJ: Princeton University Press.

Kim, S. (2012), "A Pluralist Reconstruction of Confucian Democracy," *Dao: A Journal of Comparative Philosophy*, 11 (3): 315–36.

Kleeman, T., and T. Barrett (2005), *The Ancient Chinese World*, New York: Oxford University Press.

Knight, N. (2007), *Rethinking Mao: Explorations in Mao Zedong's Thought*, Lanham, MD: Lexington Books.

Knight, N. (2010), *Marxist Philosophy in China: From Qu Qiubai to Mao Zedong*, Heidelberg: Springer.

Kuo, Y. (2017), "The Making of the New Cultural Movement: A Discursive History," *Twentieth-Century China*, 42 (1): 52–71. https://doi.org/10.1353/ tcc.2017.0007. Accessed April 4, 2020.

Lai, K. (2008), *An Introduction to Chinese Philosophy*, Cambridge: Cambridge University Press.

Lau, D., trans. (2003), *Mencius*, New York: Penguin.

Lee, H. (2006), "Dai Zhen's Ethical Philosophy of the Human Being," PhD diss., School of Oriental and African Studies, University of London.

Lee, M. (2017), *Confucianism: Its Roots and Global Significance*, D. Jones (ed.), Honolulu: University of Hawaii Press.

Lee, S. (1992), "Was There a Concept of Rights in Confucian-Based Morality?," *Journal of Chinese Philosophy*, 19 (3): 241–61.

Legge, J., trans. (1885), *The Li Ki: A Collection of Treatises on the Rules of Propriety or Ceremonial Usages*, Chinese Text Project, https://ctext.org/liji.

Legge, J., trans. (1891), *The Texts of Taoism*, in Max Muller (ed.), *Sacred Books of the East*, vol. 40, Oxford: Clarendon Press.

Leibniz, G. (1994), *Leibniz: Writings on China*, D. Cook and H. Rosemont (trans.), Chicago: Open Court.

Levenson, J. (1970), *Liang Ch'i-Ch'ao and the Mind of Modern China*, Los Angeles: University of California Press.

Li, C. (2014), *The Confucian Philosophy of Harmony*, New York: Routledge.

Li, C. (2016), *Chinese Politics in the Xi Jinping Era: Reassessing Collective Leadership*, Washington, DC: Brookings Institution Press.

Li, Y. (1971), *The Introduction of Socialism into China*, New York: Columbia University Press.

Li, Z. (2003), 《中国近代思想史論》 (*Zhongguo Jindai Sixiang Shilun, A Study of the Modern History of Chinese Thought*), Tianjing: Tianjing Academy of Social Science Press.

Liang, Q. (1999), 《梁啟超全集》 (*Liang Qichao Quanji, The Collected Works of Liang Qichao*), 10 vols., Beijing: Beijing Publishing House.

Liao, W., trans. (1939), *Complete Works of Hanfeizi*, London: Arthur Probsthain, http://www2.iath.virginia.edu/saxon/servlet/SaxonServlet?source=xwomen/texts/hanfei.xml&style=xwomen/xsl/dynaxml.xsl&chunk.id=d1.1&toc.depth=1&toc.id=0&doc.lang=bilingual. Accessed January 23, 2020.

Littlejohn, R. (2001), "The Received Tradition on Ming 命 in the Mencius 孟子," *Southeast Review of Asian Studies*, 23: 33–45.

Littlejohn, R. (2005), "Comparative Philosophy," *Internet Encyclopedia of Philosophy*, J. Fieser (ed.), https://iep.utm.edu/comparat/.

Littlejohn, R. (2008), "Did Kongzi Teach Us How to Become Gods?" in M. Chandler and R. Littlejohn (eds.), *Polishing the Chinese Mirror: Essays in Honor of Henry Rosemont, Jr.*, 188–212, New York: Global Scholarly.

Littlejohn, R. (2010), "Kongzi in the *Zhuangzi*," in V. Mair (ed.), *Experimental Essays on Zhuangzi*, 175–95, Dunedin, FL: Three Pines.

Littlejohn, R. (2011), *Confucianism: An Introduction*, London: I.B. Tauris.

Littlejohn, R. (2017), "Kongzi on Religious Experience," in K. Clark (ed.), *Readings in the Philosophy of Religion*, 456–63, Peterborough, ON: Broadview.

Littlejohn, R. (2021), "Which Button Do I Push? More Thoughts on Resetting Moral Philosophy in the Western Tradition," *Dao: A Journal of Comparative Philosophy*, 20 (1): 49–67, https://doi.org/10.1007/s11712-020-09761-w. Accessed January 12, 2021.

Littlejohn, R., and Q. Li (2019), "Chinese and Western Philosophy in Dialogue," *Educational Philosophy and Theory*, https://doi.org/10.1080/0013 1857.2019.1701386.

Liu, C. (2017), "On the Analogical Rhetoric in *Mencius*," *Journal of Tsinghua University (Philosophy and Social Sciences)*, 32 (1): 67–73.

Liu, J. (1959), *Reform in Sung China: Wang An-shih (1021–1086) and His New Policies*, Cambridge, MA: Harvard University Press.

Liu, J. (2004), *Distinguishing and Correcting the Pre-Qin Forged Classics*, Xi'an: Shaanxi People's Press.

Liu, J. (2006), *An Introduction to Chinese Philosophy: From Ancient Philosophy to Chinese Buddhism*, Oxford: Blackwell.

Liu, S. (1998), "Background for the Emergence of Confucian Philosophy," in S. Liu (ed.), *Understanding Confucian Philosophy: Classical and SungMing*, 3–15, Westport, CT: Praeger.

Liu, S. (2009a), "Neo-Confucianism (I): from Cheng Yi to Zhu Xi," in B. Mou (ed.), *History of Chinese Philosophy*, 365–95, New York: Routledge.

Liu, S. (2009b), "Neo-Confucianism (II): from Lu Jiu-Yuan to Wang Yang-Ming," in B. Mou (ed.), *History of Chinese Philosophy*, 396–428, New York: Routledge.

Locke, J. (1959), *An Essay Concerning Human Understanding*, 2 vols., A. C. Fraser (ed.), New York: Dover.

Loy, H. (2010), "Mozi," in *Internet Encyclopedia of Philosophy*, J. Fieser (ed.), http://www.iep.utm.edu/mozi/. Accessed August 14, 2020.

Ma, Zuyi (1984), 《中国翻懿簡史》 (*Zhongguo Fanyi Jianshi, An Outline History of Chinese Translation of Foreign Literature*), Beijing: China Foreign Translation Publishing Co.

Machiavelli, N. (1988), *The Prince*, Q. Skinner and R. Price (trans. and eds.), Cambridge: Cambridge University Press.

Machle, E. (1976), "Hsun Tzu as a Religious Philosopher," *Philosophy East and West*, 26 (4): 443–61.

Machle, E. (1993), *Nature and Heaven in the Xunzi*, Albany: State University of New York Press.

Mackinnon, B., and A. Fiala (2018), *Ethics: Theory and Contemporary Issues*, Boston, MA: Cengage Learning.

Madsen, R. (2002), "Confucian Concept of Civil Society," in S. Chambers and W. Kymlicka (eds.), *Alternative Conceptions of Civil Society*, 190–206, Princeton, NJ: Princeton University Press.

Major, J. (1993), *Heaven and Earth in Early Han Thought*, Albany: State University of New York Press.

Major, J., S. Queen, A. Meyer, and H. Roth, trans. (2010), *The Huainanzi: A Guide to the Theory and Practice of Government in Early Han China*, New York: Columbia University Press.

Makeham, J., ed. (2003), *New Confucianism: A Critical Examination*, New York: Palgrave Macmillan.

Mao, Z. (1917–45), *Collected Works of Mao Zedong*, US Government's Joint Publications Research Service, https://www.marxists.org/reference/archive/mao/works/collected-works-pdf/index.htm. Accessed March 12, 2020.

Mao, Z. (1937), "On Contradiction," in 《毛泽东選集》 (*Mao Zedong Xuanji, Selected Works of Mao Zedong*), Beijing: Renmin, https://www.marxists.org/reference/archive/mao/selected-works/date-index.htm. Accessed March 2, 2020.

Mao, Z. (1940), "On New Democracy," in 《毛泽东選集》 (*Mao Zedong Xuanji, Selected Works of Mao Zedong*), Beijing: Renmin, https://www.marxists.org/reference/archive/mao/selected-works/volume-2/mswv2_26.htm.Accessed March 12, 2020.

Mao, Z. (1949), "On the People's Democratic Dictatorship," in 《毛泽东選集》 (*Mao Zedong Xuanji, Selected Works of Mao Zedong*), Beijing: Renmin, https://www.marxists.org/reference/archive/mao/selected-works/volume-4/mswv4_65.htm. Accessed March 12, 2020.

Mao, Z. (1954), "Report on an Investigation of the Peasant Movement in Hunan," in *Selected Works of Mao Tse Tung, Vol. 1, 1926–1937*, London: Lawrence and Wishart, https://www.marxists.org/reference/archive/mao/selected-works/sw-from-lw/mao-sw-lw-v1.pdf. Accessed March 12, 2020.

Mao, Z. (1957), "On the Correct Handling of Contradictions among the People," in 《毛泽东選集》 (*Mao Zedong Xuanji, Selected Works of Mao Zedong*), Beijing: Renmin, https://www.marxists.org/reference/archive/mao/selected-works/volume-5/mswv5_58.htm. Accessed March 12, 2020.

Mao, Z. (1966), "Class and Class Struggle," *Quotations from Mao Tse Tung*, Beijing: Peking Foreign Languages Press. *Mao Tse Tung Internet Archive*, 2000, https://www.marxists.org/reference/archive/mao/works/red-book/index.htm. Accessed March 12, 2020.

Martinich, A. P., and S. Tsoi (2015), "Mozi's Ideal Political Philosophy," *Asian Philosophy*, 25 (3): 253–74.

McKeon, R., trans. and ed. (1973), *Introduction to Aristotle*, Chicago: University of Chicago Press.

McLeod, A. (2007), "A Reappraisal of Wang Chong's Critical Method through the Wenkong Chapter," *Journal of Chinese Philosophy*, 34 (4): 581–96.

McLeod, A. (2011), "Pluralism about Truth in Early Chinese Philosophy: A Reflection on Wang Chong's Approach," *Comparative Philosophy*, 2 (1): 38–60.

McLeod, A. (2018), *The Philosophical Thought of Wang Chong*, New York: Palgrave Macmillan.

McNaughton, D. (1991), *Moral Vision: An Introduction to Ethics*, Oxford: Wiley-Blackwell.

Mei, Y. (1953), "The Kung-sun Lung Tzu with a Translation into English," *Harvard Journal of Asiatic Studies*, 16 (3/4): 404–37.

Metzger, T. (1977), *Escape from Predicament: Neo-Confucianism and China's Evolving Political Culture*, New York: Columbia University Press.

Mill, J. (1882), *A System of Logic: Ratiocinative and Inductive*, New York: Harper and Brothers.

Mill, J. S. (1956), *On Liberty*, Englewood Cliffs, NJ: Prentice Hall.

Miller, A. V., trans. (1977), *Hegel's Phenomenology of Spirit*, Oxford: Oxford University Press.

Mollgaard, E. (2007), "Is Tu Wei-ming Confucian?," *Dao: A Journal of Comparative Philosophy*, 6 (4): 397–411.

Monk, R. (1991), *Ludwig Wittgenstein: The Duty of Genius*, New York: Penguin.

Mou, B. (ed.) (2008), *History of Chinese Philosophy*, New York: Routledge.

Mou, Z. (1968), "Metaphysical Mind and Metaphysical Nature (*Xinti yu xingti*)," in *Mou Zongsan's Complete Works*, vol. 5, Taipei: Lianjing.

Mou, Z. (1971), "Intellectual Intuition and Chinese Philosophy (*Zhide zhijue yu zhongguo zhexue*)," in *Mou Zongsan's Complete Works*, vol. 20, Taipei: Lianjing.

Mou, Z. (1985), "On the Perfect Good (*Yuan shan lun*)," in *Mou Zongsan's Complete Works*, vol. 22, Taipei: Lianjing.

Murphy, T., and R. Weber (2010), "Confucianizing Socrates and Socratizing Confucius—on Comparing *Analects* 13:18 and the *Euthyphro*," *Philosophy East and West*, 60 (2): 187–206.

Muzumdar, H. (1956), "A Chinese Philosopher's Theory of Knowledge," *Midwest Sociologist*, 19 (1): 12–17.

Nagel, T. (1986), *The View from Nowhere*, New York: Oxford University Press.

Ng, Y. (1993), *T'ien-t'ai Buddhism and Early Madhyamika*, Honolulu: University of Hawaii Press.

Ni, P. (2010), *Confucius: Making the Way Great*, Shanghai: Shanghai Translation Publishing House.

Nietzsche, F. (1968), *The Will to Power*, W. Kaufmann and R. Hollingdale (trans.), New York: Random House.

Ning, C. (1997), "The Concept of Fate in Mencius," *Philosophy East and West*, 47 (4): 495–520.

Nivison, D. S. (1996), "Two Kinds of 'Naturalism': Dai Zhen and Zhang Xuecheng," in B. Van Norden (ed.), *The Ways of Confucianism: Investigations in Chinese Philosophy*, 261–82, Chicago: Open Court.

Nussbaum, M. (1998), *Cultivating Humanity: A Classical Defense of Reform in Liberal Education*, Cambridge, MA: Harvard University Press.

Nylan, M. (2003), "Wang Chong," in A. Cua (ed.), *Encyclopedia of Chinese Philosophy*, 745–8, New York: Routledge.

Ownby, D. (2009), "Kang Xiaoguang: Social Science, Civil Society, and Confucian Religion," *China Perspectives*, 4, http://chinaperspectives.revues.org/4928. Accessed November 8, 2020.

Peirce, C. S. (1992), *The Essential Peirce*, vol. 1, Bloomington: Indiana University Press.

Penn, J. (1972), *Linguistic Relativity versus Innate Ideas: The Origins of the Sapir-Whorf Hypothesis in German Thought*, The Hague: Mouton Press.

Pinker, S. (1994), *The Language Instinct: How the Mind Creates Language*, New York: William Morrow.

Pinker, S. (2003), *The Blank Slate: The Modern Denial of Human Nature*, New York: Penguin.

Pinker, S., ed. (2006), *Primates and Philosophers: How Morality Evolved*, Princeton, NJ: Princeton University Press.

Puett, M. (2005), "Listening to Sages: Divinations, Omens, and the Rhetoric of Antiquity in Wang Chong's *Lunheng*," *Oriens Extremis*, 45: 271–81, https://doi.org/10.2307/24047651. Accessed January 21, 2020.

Qian, J. (2016), "Return Home and 'Settle,' Confucians Tell Women," *Sixth Tone*, https://www.sixthtone.com/news/745/return-home-and-settle%2C-confucians-tell-women. Accessed October 11, 2020

Rahula, W. (1974), *What the Buddha Taught: Revised and Expanded Edition with Texts from Suttas and Dhammapada*, New York: Grove.

Raphael, D., ed. (1969), *British Moralists: 1650–1800*, vol. 1, Oxford: Clarendon Press.

Rawls, J. (1971), *A Theory of Justice*, Cambridge, MA: Harvard University Press.

Reginster, B. (2006), *The Affirmation of Life: Nietzsche on the Overcoming of Nihilism*, Cambridge, MA: Harvard University Press.

Robins, D. (2007), "Xunzi," in E. Zalta (ed.), *The Stanford Encyclopedia of Philosophy*, http://plato.stanford.edu/entries/xunzi/. Accessed March 9, 2020.

Rosemont, H. (2002), "Is There a Universal Path of Spiritual Progress in the Texts of Early Confucianism?," in T. Weiming and M. Tucker (eds.), *Confucian Spirituality*, vol. 1, 183–96, New York: New Crossroads.

Rosker, J. (2008), *Searching for the Way: Theory of Knowledge in Premodern and Modern China*, Hong Kong: Chinese University Press.

Rosker, J. (2010), "The Concept of Structure as a Basic Epistemological Paradigm of Traditional Chinese Thought," *Asian Philosophy*, 20 (1): 79–96.

Roth, H. (1991), "Who Compiled the Chuang-tzu?," in H. Rosemont (ed.), *Chinese Texts and Philosophical Contexts*, 79–128, LaSalle: Open Court.

Roth, H. (1992), *The Textual History of the Huai-nan Tzu*, Ann Arbor, MI: Association for Asian Studies Monograph Series, No. 46.

Russell, B. (1912), *The Problems of Philosophy*, London: Williams and Norgate.

Russell, B. (1914), *Our Knowledge of the External World as a Field for Scientific Method in Philosophy*, London: George Allen and Unwin.

Rutt, R., trans. (2002), *Zhouyi: The Book of Changes*, New York: Routledge/Curzon.

Ryle, G. (1949), *The Concept of Mind*, London: Hutchinson.

Ryle, G. (1951), "Systematically Misleading Expressions," in G. Ryle and A. Flew (eds.), *Logic and Language (First Series) Essays*, 11–37, Oxford: Basil Blackwell.

Shaughnessy, E., trans. (1997), *The I Ching: The Classic of Changes*, New York: Ballatine.

Shen, V. (2015), "Evolutionism through Chinese Eyes: Yan Fu, Ma Junwu and Their Translations of Darwinian Evolutionism," *ASIANetwork Exchange*, 22: 49–60.

Shi, Z. (2007), *The Making of a Savior Bodhisattva: Dizang in Medieval China*, Honolulu: University of Hawaii Press.

Shun, K. (2002), "Mencius, Xunzi, and Dai Zhen: a Study of the *Mengzi ziyi shuzheng*," in A. Chan (ed.), *Mencius: Contexts and Interpretations*, 216–41, Honolulu: University of Hawaii Press.

Shun, K. (2005), "Zhu Xi on *Gong* (Impartial) and *Si* (Partial)," *Dao: A Journal of Comparative Philosophy*, 5 (1): 1–9.

Sim, M. (2007), *Remastering Morals with Aristotle and Confucius*, Cambridge: Cambridge University Press.

Slote, M. (2015), "The Philosophical Reset Button: A Manifesto," *Dao: A Journal of Comparative Philosophy*, 14 (1): 1–11.

Smith, N., trans. (1965), *Critique of Pure Reason*, New York: St. Martin's.

Spence, J. (1999a), *Mao Zedong: A Life*, New York: Penguin.

Spence, J. (1999b), *The Search for Modern China*, New York: W. W. Norton.

Sprague, E. (1962), *What Is Philosophy?*, New York: Oxford University Press.

Sterckx, R. (2013), "*Mozi* 31: Explaining Ghosts, Again," in C. Defoort and N. Standaert (eds.), *The Mozi as an Evolving Text: Different Voices in Early Chinese Thought*, 95–142, Leiden: Brill.

Stitzlein, S. (2004), "Replacing the 'View from Nowhere': A Pragmatist-Feminist Science Classroom," *Electronic Journal of Science Education*, 9 (2): 1–24.

Struve, L. (1988), "Huang Zongxi in Context: A Reappraisal of His Major Writings," *Journal of Asian Studies*, 47 (3): 474–502.

Sturgeon, D., ed. (2019), "Great Plan," in *Classic of History, The Chinese Text Project*, http://ctext.org/shang-shu/great-plan. Accessed February 3, 2020.

Sturgeon, N. (1986), "Harman on Moral Explanations of Natural Facts," *Southern Journal of Philosophy*, 24 (Supplement): 69–78.

Suzuki, D., and P. Carus, trans. (1906), *Treatise of the Exalted One on Response and Retribution (T'ai-Shang kan-ying P'ien)*, Chicago: Open Court.

Swanson, P. (1989), *Foundations of T'ien-t'ai Buddhism: The Flowering of the Two Truths Theory in Chinese Buddhism*, Berkeley: Asian Humanities Press.

Tan, C. (1971), *Chinese Political Thought in the Twentieth Century*, Garden City, NY: Anchor Books.

Tan, S. (2007), "Confucian Democracy as Pragmatic Experiment: Uniting Love of Learning and Love of Antiquity," *Asian Philosophy*, 17 (2): 141–66.

Tan, S. (2009), "Contemporary Neo-Confucian Philosophy," in B. Mou (ed.), *History of Chinese Philosophy*, 539–70, New York: Routledge.

Tan, S. (2011), "The Dao of Politics: Li (Rituals/Rites) and Laws as Pragmatic Tools of Government," *Philosophy East and West*, 61 (3): 468–91.

Tan, S., ed. (2016), *The Bloomsbury Research Handbook of Chinese Philosophy Methodologies*, London: Bloomsbury.

Tao, L. (2010), "Political Thought in Early Confucianism," *Frontiers of Philosophy in China*, 5 (2): 212–36.

Thompson, K. (1998), "*Li* and *Yi* as Immanent: Chu Hsi's Thought in Practical Perspective," *Philosophy East and West*, 28 (1): 30–46.

Thompson, L., trans. (1958), *Ta tung shu: The One-world Philosophy of K'ang Yu-wei*, London: George Allen and Unwin.

Thomson, J. (1977), *Acts and Other Events*, Ithaca, NY: Cornell University Press.

Tian, C. (2002), "Development of Dialectical Materialism in China," in B. Mou (ed.), *History of Chinese Philosophy*, 516–38, New York: Routledge.

Tiwald, J. (2008), "A Right of Rebellion in the *Mengzi*?," *Dao: A Journal of Comparative Philosophy*, 7 (3): 269–82.

Tiwald, J. (2009), "Dai Zhen on Human Nature and Moral Cultivation," in J. Makeham (ed.), *The Dao Companion to Neo-Confucian Philosophy*, 399–422, Heidelberg: Springer.

Tiwald, J. (2010a), "Dai Zhen," in *Internet Encyclopedia of Philosophy*, J. Fieser (ed.), http://www.iep.utm.edu/dai-zhen. Accessed January 23, 2020.

Tiwald, J. (2010b), "Dai Zhen on Sympathetic Concern," *Journal of Chinese Philosophy*, 37 (1): 76–89.

Tiwald, J. (2012), "Xunzi on Moral Expertise," *Dao: A Journal of Comparative Philosophy*, 11 (3): 275–93.

Tu, W. (1976), *Neo-Confucian Thought in Action: Wang Yang-ming's Youth (1472–1509)*, Berkeley: University of California Press.

Tu, W. (1979), *Humanity and Self-Cultivation: Essays in Confucian Thought*, Berkeley: Asian Humanities Press.

Tu, W. (1984), *Confucian Ethics Today: The Singapore Challenge*, Singapore: Federal.

Tu, W. (1989a), *Centrality and Commonality: An Essay on Confucian Religiousness*, Albany: State University of New York Press.

Tu, W. (1989b), *Way, Learning and Politics: Essays on the Confucian Intellectual*, Singapore: Institute of East Asian Philosophies.

Tu, W. (1996), *Confucian Tradition in East Asian Modernity*, Cambridge, MA: Harvard University Press.

Tu, W. (2002), "Mutual Learning as an Agenda for Social Development," in D. Sachsenmaier (ed.), *Reflections on Multiple Modernities: European, Chinese and Other Interpretations*, 129–36, Leiden: Brill.

Tu, W. (2008), "Response," *Dao: A Journal of Comparative Philosophy—Special Issue, Tu Weiming and Confucian Humanism*, 7 (4): 437–47.

Van Norden, B. (1996a), "An Open Letter to the APA," *Proceedings and Addresses of the American Philosophical Association*, 70 (2): 161–3.

Van Norden, B. (1996b), "What Should Western Philosophy Learn from Chinese Philosophy," in P. Ivanhoe (ed.), *Chinese Language, Thought, and Culture: Nivison and His Critics*, 224–50, Chicago: Open Court.

Van Norden, B. (2011), *Introduction to Classical Chinese Philosophy*, Indianapolis: Hackett.

Van Norden, B. (2017), *Taking Back Philosophy: A Multicultural Manifesto*, New York: Columbia University Press.

Von Glasenapp, H. (1954), *Kant und die Religionendes Osten*, Kitzingen-Main: Holzner Verlag.

Wang, A. (1959), *Linchuan Xiansheng Wenji* [临川先生文集, *Mr. Linchuan's (i.e., Wang Anshi's) Collected Works*], Beijing: Zhonghua.

Wang, B. (2015), "蒋庆的儒家宪政：一个意义重大的狂想 (Jiang Qing's Confucian Constitutionalism: A Meaningful Fantasy)," China Open Research Network. Asian Institute at the Munk School of Global Affairs, University of Toronto, https://corn.groups.politics.utoronto.ca/?p=478. Accessed December 4, 2020.

Wang, R. (2012), *Yinyang: The Way of Heaven and Earth in Chinese Thought and Culture*, Cambridge: Cambridge University Press.

Watson, B., trans. (1964), *Han Fei Tzu: Basic Writings*, New York: Columbia University Press.

Watson, B., trans. (1968), *The Complete Works of Chuang-Tzu*, New York: Columbia University Press.

Watson, B., trans. (2002), *The Essential Lotus: Selections from the Lotus Sutra*, New York: Columbia University Press.

Wei, T., trans. (1973), *Ch'eng Wei-shi lun Doctrine of Mere-Consciousness by Husan Tsang*, Hong Kong: Ch'eng Wei-shi lun Publication Committee.

Whitehead, A. (1979), *Process and Reality*, New York: Free Press.

Willaschek, M. (2010), "The Primacy of Practical Reason and the Idea of a Practical Postulate," in A. Reath and J. Timmermann (eds.), *Kant's Critique of Practical Reason: A Critical Guide*, 168–96, Cambridge: Cambridge University Press.

Williams, P. (2005), "Bodhisattva Path," in *Encyclopedia of Religion*, vol. 2, 996–1000, Gale Books, http://www.sacred-magick.com/PDF.php?cid=32.147.

Williams, P. (2009), *Mahayana Buddhism: The Doctrinal Foundations*, London: Routledge.

Williamson, H. (1937), *Wang An Shih: A Chinese Statesman and Educationalist of the Sung Dynasty*, 2 vols., London: Arthur Probsthain, https://archive.org/details/11411623wanganshihachinesestatesmanandeducationalistofthesuangdynastywilliamsonh/page/n7/mode/2up. Accessed November 11, 2020.

Winkler, K., ed. (1988), *A Treatise Concerning the Principles of Human Knowledge*, Indianapolis: Hackett.

Wittgenstein, L. (1922), *Tractatus Logico-Philosophicus*, F. Ramsey and C. K. Ogden (trans.), London: Kegan Paul.

Wittgenstein, L. (1969), *On Certainty*, G. E. M. Anscombe and G. H. VonWright (trans. and eds.), Oxford: Basil Blackwell.

Wolf, S. (1982), "Moral Saints," *Journal of Philosophy*, 79 (8): 419–39.

Wong, D. (1989), "Three Kinds of Incommensurability," in M. Krausz (ed.), *Relativism, Interpretation, and Confrontation*, 140–59, Notre Dame, IN: Notre Dame University Press.

Wong, Y. (2003), "Legalism," in A. Cua (ed.), *Encyclopedia of Chinese Philosophy*, 361–3, New York: Routledge.

Wood, A. T. (1995), *Limits to Autocracy: From Sung Neo-Confucianism to a Doctrine of Political Rights*, Honolulu: University of Hawaii Press.

Wright, A. (1959), *Buddhism in Chinese History*, Stanford, CA: Stanford University Press.

Wu, K. (1928), *Ancient Chinese Political Theories*, Shanghai: Commercial Press.

Xi, J. (2014, 2017, 2020), 《谈治国理政》 (*Tan zhiguo li zheng, The Governance of China*), 3 vols., Beijing: Foreign Languages Press, https://www.xuexi.cn/d6399cd070074625b24eb5952a5ea64c/b7dd5b56969a59022b5a12ff049cc2eb.html. Accessed November 8, 2020. Available in nine languages, including English.

Xiao, G. (1945), 《中國政治思想史》 (*Zhongguo Zhengzhi Sixiang Shi, A History of Chinese Political Thought*), 2 vols., Chongqing: Shangwu yinshuguan. Vol. 1 trans. into English by Frederick W. Mote as *A History of Chinese Political Thought: From the Beginning to the Sixth Century AD*, Princeton, NJ: Princeton University Press, 1979.

Xiao, Y. (2002), "Liang Qichao's Political and Social Philosophy," in C. Cheng and N. Bunnin (eds.), *Contemporary Chinese Philosophy*, 17–36, Oxford: Blackwell.

Xiao, Y. (2006), "When Political Philosophy Meets Moral Psychology: Expressivism in the *Mencius*," *Dao: A Journal of Comparative Philosophy*, 5 (2): 257–71.

Xie, Y. (2019), "Argument by Analogy in Ancient China," *Argumentation*, 33 (3): 323–47.

Xiong, M., and L. Yan (2019), "Mencius's Strategies of Political Argumentation," *Argumentation*, 33 (3): 365–89.

Yan, F. (1986), *Yan Fu Ji (Collected Works of Yan Fu)*, 5 vols., Beijing: Zhonghua Shju.

Yan, L., ed. (1966), 《無求備齋論語集 成》 (*Wuqiu beizhai Lunyu jicheng, Compilation of the Analects*), Taibei: Yiwen yinshuguan.

Yan, L., and M. Xiong (2019), "Refutational Strategies in Mencius's Argumentative Discourse on Human Nature," *Argumentation*, 33 (3): 541–78.

Yu, J. (1998), "Virtue: Confucius and Aristotle," *Philosophy East and West*, 48 (2): 323–47.

Zhang, D. (1939), "Thought, Language and Culture," *Sociological World*, 5 (10), trans. A. Li as "A Chinese Philosopher's Theory of Knowledge" (Summer 2011): 1–23, http://www.vordenker.de/downloads/chang-tung-sun_thought-language-culture.pdf. Accessed March 4, 2020.

Zhou, G. (1994), *Xu shi zhi bian: Wang Chong Zhexue de zong zhi (The Distinction between Truth and Falsity: The Purpose of Wang Chong's Philosophy)*, Beijing: Renmin Chubanshe.

Zhang, S. (1997), 《淮南子教釋》 (*Huainanzi jiaoshi*, Interpreting the Huainanzi's Teachings), Beijing: Beijing University Press.

Zhang, H. (2015), "我为什么批驳蒋庆的性别言论 (Why Do I Criticize Jiang Qing's Gender Remarks)," *Confucianism Network*儒家網. First published in *China's Legal Weekly*, https://www.rujiazg.com/article/6228. Accessed September 19, 2020.

Zhao, S. (2016), "Xi Jinping"s Maoist Revival," *Journal of Democracy*, 27 (3): 83–97.

Zhao, X., and W. Drechsler (2018), "Wang Anshi's Economic Reforms: Proto-Keynesian Economic Policy in Song Dynasty China," *Cambridge Journal of Economics*, 42 (5): 1239–54.

Zhou, G. (1994), *Xu shi zhi bian: Wang Chong Zhexue de zong zhi (The Distinction between Truth and Falsity: The Purpose of Wang Chong's Philosophy)*, Beijing: Renmin Chubanshe.

Zhou, X. (2013), "The Studies of Western Philosophy in China: Historical Review, Present Status and Prospects," paper presented at the Chinese Academy of Social Sciences (July 2007), http://www.cnki.com.cn/Article/CJFDTOTAL-ZXYJ200707008.htm. Accessed March 7, 2020.

Index

www.ingramcontent.com/pod-product-compliance
Ingram Content Group UK Ltd.
Pitfield, Milton Keynes, MK11 3LW, UK
UKHW020653280225
455688UK00004B/106